word and world

word and world

A CRITICAL THINKING READER

KENT LEWIS
Capilano College

THOMSON
NELSON

Australia   Canada   Mexico   Singapore   Spain   United Kingdom   United States

THOMSON

NELSON

Word and World: A Critical Thinking Reader
by Kent Lewis

Associate Vice President,
Editorial Director:
Evelyn Veitch

Executive Editor:
Anne Williams

Marketing Manager:
Sandra Green

Developmental Editor:
Colleen Shea

Permissions Coordinator:
Nicola Winstanley

Senior Production Editor:
Natalia Denesiuk

Copy Editor:
Erin Moore

Proofreader:
Rodney Rawlings

Indexer:
Christopher Blackburn

Production Coordinator:
Ferial Suleman

Design Director:
Ken Phipps

Interior-Design
Modifications:
Katherine Strain

Cover Design:
Faith

Compositor:
Integra

Printer:
Transcontinental

Library and Archives Canada Cataloguing in Publication Data

Lewis, Kent Richard Arthur, 1964–
    Word and world : a critical thinking reader / Kent Lewis.

Includes bibliographical references and index.
ISBN 0-17-641496-7

1. College readers. 2. English language—Rhetoric—Problems, exercises, etc.   3. Critical thinking—Problems, exercises, etc.   I. Title.

PE1417.L485 2006
808'.0427   C2005-907295-4

PREFACE

A Word to Instructors

This text offers a different approach to an academic writing course. Although it contains many familiar subjects, they've been arranged to tell a slightly different story: the power of language to affect perception. English instructors can use these lessons to help students sharpen essay writing, clarify thought, and receive better grades. More importantly however, these lessons help students become aware of how words create meaning—on the printed page, in the courtroom, on the job, in the video screen, in the bedroom, across the nation—and how sometimes meaning is created for them.

Taking its cue from the social thinker Neil Postman, the story starts with the power of the single word to influence perception, and slowly works up to larger units of meaning (the definition, metaphor, simple word, question, genre, media, and finally argument). The rationale behind the order of chapters is to begin with simple elements of language and build in cumulative fashion towards more complex, holistic models. However, as with any order, this one is largely arbitrary. Instructors can easily arrange materials in patterns to their liking.

This book assumes all writing is inherently persuasive, and so contains little discussion of exposition as a traditional form of writing. In my experience, "expository" texts usually contain as many opinions, agendas, and dubious propositions as their argumentative kin, although expository texts tend to conceal them better. When cross-examined, expository texts tend to unveil themselves as persuasion guised in the style of fact and consensus.

This text presents contentious and disturbing topic material to show that *language is always political*. Some topics touch nerves—sexuality, race, consumption, abuse, globalism—but with educational

purpose. Such "hot" subjects show how language is actively constructing our perception of the world. Rhetoric intensifies precisely at
the places of social conflict, and so its lessons are clearest at the
extremes. The controversial topics also have the advantage of
nudging students out of their comfort zones, encouraging them to
analyze their own assumptions.

Of course, if language is always political and ideological, then
that makes writing a textbook a challenge. How can one adopt the
impartial style of a textbook while teaching that all writing is relative? Well, I can't. So, I have given up the usual pretense to
authority and neutrality that comes along with a course manual. The
chapters tend to be driven by my own anarchist, liberal, and
humanist views. Of course, I have striven to make them fair and
accurate, but the result is that this textbook tends to be more
polemical than the average university reader. This "attack" strategy
often shows my personal beliefs. Instructors may need to point out
the bias of this anthology itself, reminding them that the author is
but another voice in the fray.

Once again, there is a plan here. The pedagogy is to provoke,
but also to teach students to question any source, especially the
ones that claim to be neutral and disinterested. If we teach students
to question authority in all forms, then that includes the professor
and his or her textbook as well.

ACKNOWLEDGEMENTS

I would like to thank the many people whose feedback shaped and
guided the writing of this book, including Jillian Garrett, University of
Alberta; Marcia Goldberg, Vanier College; Ryan Knighton, Capilano
College; David McCarthy, Centennial College; Anthony Murphy,
University of Saskatchewan; Jennifer Read, Capilano College; Kate
Sutherland, University College of the Caribo; Lynn Szabo, Trinity
Western University; John Le Blanc, Okanagan University College;
Hasan Malik, Sheridan Institute of Technology; Karen Manarin,
Mount Royal College; Bruce Raskob, Kwantlen University College;
and Anne Taylor, Yukon College. Special thanks go to my patient
and attentive editors, Colleen Shea, Mike Thompson, and Anne
Williams. The help, encouragement, critical eye, and good cheer of
Roger Clark and Wilhelm Emilsson from Douglas College have
been invaluable, as has the support from my wife, Pamela
Schofield, and children, Kai and Shayden.

CONTENTS

CHAPTER 8: ARGUMENT

APPENDIX A: COMMON GRAMMATICAL MISTAKES

APPENDIX B: PARAGRAPHS

APPENDIX C: SUMMARY

APPENDIX D: DOCUMENTATION

COPYRIGHT ACKNOWLEDGEMENTS

INDEX

INTRODUCTION

In the Thrall of Language

"Let me say a few words about Gluppity-Glup."

—Dr. Seuss, *The Lorax*

"A different language is a different vision of life."

—Federico Fellini

This book works with a very old, yet hotly debated thought: language affects perception. The idea is very simple, almost obvious—words give shape and meaning to our experience, influence our thoughts, alter our perception of reality, and ultimately affect our behaviour and fortunes. And the idea has an ancient pedigree, dating back at least as far back as Plato in the 6th century, and probably further. Even the Bible begins with a similar notion: "In the beginning was the word." In linguistic circles today, the theory goes by the unwieldy name of the Sapir-Whorf Hypothesis, in honour of Edward Sapir and his student Benjamin Whorf who studied the Hopi language of the American Southwest. Whorf believed that the unique structure of their language makes a Hopi native see the universe differently than a European does. Hopi verbs do not have a tense, for example, and so a Hopi Indian does not differentiate between the "now" and "then" as simply as a German or a Finn does. Given their verbal blending of yesterday and today, it is not surprising that the Hopi value tradition so highly—their language literally sees the past as a seamless con-tinuation of the present.

The Hopi example suggests that language isn't a neutral window, but a force that shapes minds and nations. To use a more technological analogy, if the brain resembles a computer, then language works like the operating system or computer program that processes data in the CPU. Language is hard at work inside the nervous system, turning electric signals and neural impulses into meaningful patterns, transforming sense and sensation into names, ideas, classifications, relationships, and propositions.

Just as a computer can't read a disk if it does not have the proper program, so too does a newborn baby struggle to make sense of its environment, for it does not have the language skills to differentiate between subject and object, inside and outside, black and white, before and behind, and so on. Of course these objective differences really exist, and we will bang our shins against a table whether we have the word for it or not. However, without language, the infant sees the world as more chaotic and undefined than the linguistically skilled adult, perceiving sensation without form, figure, or meaning. A word like "mommy" gives this sensory maelstrom a recognizable face—literally. And so language begins to name familiar patterns (such as "nose" or "dinner"), set boundaries ("me" vs. "you"), build relationships ("family"), classify and divide ("cats" and "dogs"), see similarity ("a teacher is like a parent"), and ascribe value throughout the child's life ("Stop that! That's wrong! That's a sin!"). By the time we reach adulthood, language is deeply entrenched in our consciousness and its task is executed almost invisibly. So accustomed do we become to our operating system, we may not even know that it is there, shaping our thoughts, ordering the world into familiar patterns, influencing our decisions.

Because language is etched into our consciousness, we have difficulty seeing it for what it is: a program that exists in the virtual space of our minds, not a thing in the physical world. Take a simple matter such as colour. Imagine for a moment the spread of colours seen when a prism breaks white light into the familiar band of a spectrum, or when rain clouds make a rainbow in the sky. How many colours do you count there? If you think in English, you break the visible spectrum into six basic colours—purple, blue, green, yellow, orange, and red. In contrast, if you speak Shona (a Rhodesian language), you divide the spectrum into only three basic colours; and if you use the Bassa language (from Liberia), you use only two words for all the variation in the spectrum (Thomson 85). Although we may all see the same raw data, the languages organize the wavelengths in different groups, assigning different meanings to each. Language and speech habits literally make you see the world differently. Obviously, English has an advantage over Bassa because it provides more tools for colour discrimination. Yet the Hanunóo language (from the Philippines) has an advantage over English, for it has 92 different names for rice, while we have only two or three (Thomson 85). The precise German language has words for emotions, such as "Angst" or "Weltschmerz," that have no equivalent in English. Greek has different terms for affection, ranging from male friendship, to romance, to lust, to spiritual devotion, all translated by the clumsy English word "love." And Thai has over 500 words for "heart" that gives it a spiritual precision that English can only envy. As a computer geek might say, your hardware is only as good as your software.

If we really want to know the world and our place in it, we have to understand this lens through which we comprehend almost everything: language. As students, parents, professionals, or citizens, we have an obligation to become aware of our linguistic programming, its arbitrary divisions, biases, quirks, gaps, and sensitivities. As the German philosopher Ludwig Wittgenstein reminds us, the word is not the thing named. Without the knowledge of this difference, we run an enormous risk: language ceases to be our tool, and begins to program us.

And this subtle programming happens all the time, deliberately and accidentally. If you have ever bought an expensive designer shampoo, for example, you have been swayed by beautiful, treacherous words. Most premium brands are chemically indistinguishable from their cheaper, generic competition (as are most cold medicines, car oils, pet foods, and a host of other merchandise). Indeed, manufacturers often put the same product into two separate containers that differ in one way alone: the name. We spend more money for the same product based entirely upon the power of the label affixed on it. Advertisers earn a sizeable salary exploiting language, making a dud of a product seem like a blast. As William Burroughs says in a famous aphorism, "Language is a virus from outer space" that has the power to put our brains in a fever.

And the problem is more widespread than just a few annoying commercials. All around us corporations, army generals, politicians, spin doctors, professors, and lobbyists on the left and right, manipulate words to try to trick us into believing that the good is the bad, and the bad, good. When the murder of protesters is referred to as a "clean-up action" that is the power of language to mislead. When the revered Canadian author Margaret Laurence has her classic novel *The Diviners* defined as "pornography," that is the power of language to distort. When free speech is presented as "subversion" or "treason" that is the power of language to hoodwink.

In these cases, words have become intensely political, and even worse, deceptive. Plato was so worried about the power of language to mislead, he banished all poets, rhetoricians, and linguistic manipulators from his ideal Republic. In a free society such as ours, Plato's suggestion strikes us as draconian, yet his concern is real: language can deceive, distort, and trick. Perhaps a more practical and beneficial plan lies in the route of education: teach people how to use language effectively, and to recognize the ways language can deceive as well as inform. Modestly, these are the aims of the book held in your hands.

If it is true that language affects our perception of reality, then a course such as University Writing takes on a special significance. English composition is the only post-secondary course that looks explicitly at writing, the manipulation of language, and its effects on perception. At the core of this book, I have taken up a challenge set by Neil Postman in his essay "Defending Against the Indefensible," and set the curriculum around seven key linguistic principles suggested by the late thinker: *Names*, *Definition*, *Metaphors*, *Simple Words*, *Questions*, *Genres*, and *Media*. Each of these topics details a feature of language that has a profound impact on the way we understand the universe and construct meaning in our society. The topics have been arranged in order from the smallest in scope (the single word) to the largest (sprawling media conglomerates spewing out news across the globe), so that students can quickly gain mastery over simple ideas and work towards bigger concepts. Of course the arrangement is somewhat arbitrary, as these principles tend to work simultaneously and resist being mapped out in the linear sequence dictated by a book. For our purposes, language is a seven-part chorus that must be heard all at once, or the harmony and counterpoint is lost. When taken all together, these seven concepts can help students become better critical thinkers and more rounded citizens.

Names looks at the power of the individual word or name to attract or repulse; *Definition* examines the social institutions that decide the meaning of words, and considers the arbitrary and purposeful nature of some definitions; *Metaphors* looks at the power of figurative language to both explain and distort; *Simple Words* provides a list of powerful terms that ground and energize our culture, yet are little understood and often abused; *Questions* suggests that the ability to ask pointed questions is vital to freedom and democracy, but is a power that can be easily misused; for the sixth concept, I have altered Postman's terminology by changing his original phrase "Language Games" to

Genres, for the notion of genre is not only familiar, but accurately describes the conventions, rules, reading communities, and invisible contracts that Postman felt were critical to writing and interpretation; *Media* looks at the way a physical medium of expression can influence information—a vital idea given our increasing reliance on television and the Internet.

To the seven chapters set by Postman, I have added one more, *Argument*. The purpose behind this addition is to provide a forum where the seven linguistic forces come together in a more complex and sustained form. Yet, in some ways, this supplement is unnecessary, for this book assumes that all language is argument, a contest of wills that begins at the smallest level of meaning, the word. When somebody refers to toxic waste as "effluvium," they are most probably trying to manipulate you, just as pro-lifers do when they use the term "pre-born human," or pro-choice people do with the terms "fetus" or "pregnancy." Names brand every subject, giving it a character and political force that can be subtle, if not invisible, a sly form of propaganda. If all words are prejudiced to a degree, then the higher forms of communication such as journalism, essay writing, science, and law are also somewhat partisan. The seven key principles that start this book look at the various ways that pride and prejudice (to steal a line from Jane Austen) sneak themselves into all our talk, even the discourses that strive to be neutral, balanced, and expository.

This book has deliberately tried to make the traditional university writing course more political and relevant by showing that language use has tangible consequences for society. Most students take an academic writing course in order to learn how to write a university-level essay. This anthology tries to achieve this traditional goal, but it also has a more ambitious purpose: to show where the language issues studied in a composition class literally apply to real social situations. Where possible, I have provided case histories in which a specific word choice has translated into concrete social problems, real instances where the government, corporations, advertisers, and unscrupulous groups have used the power of language to lead us into inhumanity, recklessness, and brutality. The more I researched for this book, the more I found that events in history often pivot upon the use and abuse of language: as goes the word, so goes the world. The debates that rage today are no less tilts of language.

I wrote this book with the conviction that English Composition has the potential to be the most important course that a student may take in his or her academic career. The goals are ambitious, but worthy: to help students understand themselves and their society better; to question assumptions; to become informed citizens, to exert more control over subjects that matter to them. An English class can't be apolitical, nor should it try to be; on the contrary, an English class should teach students precisely how we create *meaning* in society.

I also wrote this book with the famous experiments of psychologist Stanley Milgram in the back of my mind. Milgram showed that the majority of average, decent people would torture another person, even until the point of death, if ordered to do so by a voice of "authority." In this case, Milgram himself provided the intimidation—a Harvard professor dressed in a white lab coat insisting the electrocutions continue despite the agonizing screams of the patient (in reality, an actor playing the part of the tortured victim). Sixty percent of Milgram's test subjects trusted the lab coat more than their own ears or moral objections (later studies achieved 85 percent compliance). Milgram's experiments testify to the horrifying extent of our modern conditioning, our tepid willingness to commit atrocities based on illusions and phantoms. This is nothing new. Throughout history, people have clamoured to kill and be killed for little more than a few rousing words. Who knows how many people died in the name of gods such as Zeus or Quetzalcoatl? Nobody fears or exhorts these deities or their names anymore, and we tend to mock these primitives so beguiled by their words that they butchered captives by the thousands and volunteered their own bodies for the slaughter on an Aztec pyramid or Macedonian battlefield. Yet I wonder, are we so very different? The words may have changed since then, it seems to me, but little else. Nobody dies for Zeus, but plenty of hale and happy youth risk their lives (or take others) for the empty bubbles of duty, nation, freedom, law, honour, and reputation. We poison the seas in the name of "growth." We pay slave wages in the name of "fiscal responsibility." We scorch the sky in the name of "progress." We stock plutonium, anthrax, and bubonic plague in the name of "security."

Language, it seems, still has us in its thrall.

Works Cited

Burroughs, William S. *Wikiquote*. January 21, 2005. <http://en.wikiquote.org/wiki/William_S._Burroughs>.

Thomson, David S. "The Sapir-Whorf Hypothesis: Worlds Shaped by Words." *Conformity and Conflict: Readings in Cultural Anthropology*. 9th ed. Ed. James Spradley and David McCurdy. New York: Longman, 1997. 80–92.

Politics and the English Language (1946)

GEORGE ORWELL

A major 20th-century prose writer, George Orwell is best known for his novels *1984* and *Animal Farm*, two parables of totalitarian government. These novels introduced now commonplace phrases such as "Big Brother," "newspeak," "thought control," "doublethink," and "thought police." The term "Orwellian" has since become an adjective for authoritarian government and the abuse of power. Also known for his journalism, Orwell documented the brutality of British colonial rule. In this classic essay, Orwell shows how common language errors can have distressing political consequences.

Most people who bother with the matter at all would admit that the English language is in a bad way, but it is generally assumed that we cannot by conscious action do anything about it. Our civilization is decadent and our language—so the argument runs—must inevitably share in the general collapse. It follows that any struggle against the abuse of language is a sentimental archaism, like preferring candles to electric light or hansom cabs to aeroplanes. Underneath this lies the half-conscious belief that language is a natural growth and not an instrument which we shape for our own purposes.

Now, it is clear that the decline of a language must ultimately have political and economic causes: it is not due simply to the bad influence of this or that individual writer. But an effect can become a cause, reinforcing the original cause and producing the same effect in an intensified form, and so on indefinitely. A man may take to drink because he feels himself to be a failure, and then fail all the more completely because he drinks. It is rather the same thing that is happening to the English language. It becomes ugly and inaccurate because our thoughts are foolish, but the slovenliness of our language makes it easier for us to have foolish thoughts. The point is that the process is reversible. Modern English, especially written English, is full of bad habits which spread by imitation and which can be avoided if one is willing to take the necessary trouble. If one gets rid of these habits one can think more clearly, and to think clearly is a necessary first step toward political regeneration: so that the fight against bad English is not frivolous and is not the exclusive concern of professional writers. I will come back to this presently, and I hope that by that time the meaning of what I have said here will have become clearer. Meanwhile, here are five specimens of the English language as it is now habitually written.

These five passages have not been picked out because they are especially bad—I could have quoted far worse if I had chosen—but because they illustrate various of the mental vices from which we now suffer. They are a little below the average, but are fairly representative examples. I number them so that I can refer back to them when necessary:

1. I am not, indeed, sure whether it is not true to say that the Milton who once seemed not unlike a seventeenth-century Shelley had not become, out of an experience ever more bitter in each year, more alien [sic] to the founder of that Jesuit sect which nothing could induce him to tolerate.

   —Professor Harold Laski (Essay in *Freedom of Expression*)

2. Above all, we cannot play ducks and drakes with a native battery of idioms which prescribes egregious collocations of vocables as the Basic *put up with* for *tolerate*, or *put at a loss* for *bewilder*.

   —Professor Lancelot Hogben (*Interglossia*)

3. On the one side we have the free personality: by definition it is not neurotic, for it has neither conflict nor dream. Its desires, such as they are, are transparent, for they are just what institutional approval keeps in the forefront of consciousness; another institutional pattern would alter their number and intensity; there is little in them that is natural, irreducible, or culturally dangerous. But *on the other side*, the social bond itself is nothing but the mutual reflection of these self-secure integrities. Recall the definition of love. Is not this the very picture of a small academic? Where is there a place in this hall of mirrors for either personality or fraternity?

   —Essay on psychology in *Politics* (New York)

4. All the "best people" from the gentlemen's clubs, and all the frantic fascist captains, united in common hatred of Socialism and bestial horror at the rising tide of the mass revolutionary movement, have turned to acts of provocation, to foul incendiarism, to medieval legends of poisoned wells, to legalize their own destruction of proletarian organizations, and rouse the agitated petty-bourgeoise to chauvinistic fervor on behalf of the fight against the revolutionary way out of the crisis.

   —Communist pamphlet

5. If a new spirit is to be infused into this old country, there is one thorny and contentious reform which must be tackled, and that is the humanization and galvanization of the B.B.C. Timidity here will bespeak canker and atrophy of the soul. The heart of Britain may be sound and of strong beat, for instance, but the British lion's roar at present is like that of Bottom in Shakespeare's *A Midsummer Night's Dream*—as gentle as any sucking dove. A virile new Britain cannot continue indefinitely to be traduced in the eyes or rather ears, of the world by the effete languors of Langham Place, brazenly masquerading as "standard English." When the Voice of Britain is heard at nine o'clock, better far and infinitely less ludicrous to hear aitches honestly dropped than the present priggish, inflated, inhibited, school-ma'amish arch braying of blameless bashful mewing maidens!

—Letter in *Tribune*

Each of these passages has faults of its own, but, quite apart from avoidable ugliness, two qualities are common to all of them. The first is staleness of imagery; the other is lack of precision. The writer either has a meaning and cannot express it, or he inadvertently says something else, or he is almost indifferent as to whether his words mean anything or not. This mixture of vagueness and sheer incompetence is the most marked characteristic of modern English prose, and especially of any kind of political writing. As soon as certain topics are raised, the concrete melts into the abstract and no one seems able to think of turns of speech that are not hackneyed: prose consists less and less of *words* chosen for the sake of their meaning, and more and more of *phrases* tacked together like the sections of a prefabricated henhouse. I list below, with notes and examples, various of the tricks by means of which the work of prose construction is habitually dodged:

Dying metaphors. A newly invented metaphor assists thought by evoking a visual image, while on the other hand a metaphor which is technically "dead" (e.g. *iron resolution)* has in effect reverted to being an ordinary word and can generally be used without loss of vividness. But in between these two classes there is a huge dump of worn-out metaphors which have lost all evocative power and are merely used because they save people the trouble of inventing phrases for themselves. Examples are: *Ring the changes on, take up the cudgel for, toe the line, ride roughshod over, stand shoulder to shoulder with, play into the hands of, no axe to grind, grist to the mill, fishing in troubled waters, on the order of the day, Achilles' heel, swan song, hotbed.*

Many of these are used without knowledge of their meaning (what is a "rift," for instance?), and incompatible metaphors are frequently mixed, a sure sign that the writer is not interested in what he is saying. Some metaphors now current have been twisted out of their original meaning without those who use them even being aware of the fact. For example, *toe the line* is sometimes written as *tow the line*. Another example is *the hammer and the anvil*, now always used with the implication that the anvil gets the worst of it. In real life it is always the anvil that breaks the hammer, never the other way about: a writer who stopped to think what he was saying would avoid perverting the original phrase.

Operators or verbal false limbs. These save the trouble of picking out appropriate verbs and nouns, and at the same time pad each sentence with extra syllables which give it an appearance of symmetry. Characteristic phrases are *render inoperative, militate against, make contact with, be subjected to, give rise to, give grounds for, have the effect of, play a leading part (role) in, make itself felt, take effect, exhibit a tendency to, serve the purpose of, etc., etc*. The keynote is the elimination of simple verbs. Instead of being a single word, such as *break, stop, spoil, mend, kill*, a verb becomes a *phrase*, made up of a noun or adjective tacked on to some general-purpose verb such as *prove, serve, form, play, render*. In addition, the passive voice is wherever possible used in preference to the active, and noun constructions are used instead of gerunds (*by examination of* instead of *by examining*). The range of verbs is further cut down by means of the *-ize* and *de-* formations, and the banal statements are given an appearance of profundity by means of the *not un-* formation. Simple conjunctions and prepositions are replaced by such phrases as *with respect to, having regard to, the fact that, by dint of, in view of, in the interests of, on the hypothesis that*; and the ends of sentences are saved by anticlimax by such resounding commonplaces as *greatly to be desired, cannot be left out of account, a development to be expected in the near future, deserving of serious consideration, brought to a satisfactory conclusion*, and so on and so forth.

Pretentious diction. Words like *phenomenon, element, individual* (as noun), *objective, categorical, effective, virtual, basic, primary, promote, constitute, exhibit, exploit, utilize, eliminate, liquidate*, are used to dress up a simple statement and give an aire of scientific impartiality to biased judgements. Adjectives like *epoch-making, epic, historic, unforgettable, triumphant, age-old, inevitable, inexorable, veritable*, are used to dignify the sordid process of international politics, while writing that aims at glorifying war usually takes on an archaic color, its characteristic words being: *realm, throne, chariot, mailed fist, trident, sword, shield, buckler, banner, jackboot, clarion*. Foreign words and expressions such as *cul de sac, ancien régime, deus ex machina, mutatis mutandis, status quo, gleichschaltung, weltanschauung*, are used to give an air of culture and elegance. Except for the useful abbreviations *i.e., e.g.*, and *etc.*, there is no real need for any of the hundreds of foreign phrases now current in the English language. Bad writers, and especially scientific, political, and sociological writers, are nearly always haunted by the notion that Latin or Greek words are grander than Saxon ones, and unnecessary words like *expedite, ameliorate, predict, extraneous, deracinated, clandestine, subaqueous*, and hundreds of others constantly gain ground from their Anglo-Saxon numbers. The jargon peculiar to Marxist writing (*hyena, hangman, cannibal, petty bourgeois, these gentry, lackey, flunkey, mad dog, White Guard*, etc.) consists largely of words translated from Russian, German, or French; but the normal way of coining a new word is to use Latin or Greek root with the appropriate affix and, where necessary, the *-ize* formation. It is often easier to make up words of this kind (*deregionalize, impermissible, extramarital, non-fragmentary* and so forth) than to think up the English words that will cover one's meaning. The result, in general, is an increase in slovenliness and vagueness.

Meaningless words. In certain kinds of writing, particularly in art criticism and literary criticism, it is normal to come across long passages which are almost completely lacking in meaning. Words like *romantic, plastic, values, human, dead, sentimental, natural, vitality*, as used in art criticism, are strictly meaningless, in the sense that they not only do not point to any discoverable object, but are hardly ever expected to do so by the reader. When one critic writes, "The outstanding feature of Mr. X's work is its living quality," while another writes, "The immediately striking thing about Mr. X's work is its peculiar deadness," the reader accepts this as a simple difference of opinion. If words like *black* and *white* were involved, instead of the jargon words *dead* and *living*, he would see at once that language was being used in an improper way. Many political words are similarly abused. The word *Fascism* has now no meaning except in so far as it signifies "something not desirable." The words *democracy, socialism, freedom, patriotic, realistic, justice* have each of them several different meanings which cannot be reconciled with one another. In the case of a word like *democracy*, not only is there no agreed definition, but the attempt to make one is resisted from all sides. It is almost universally felt that when we call a country democratic we are praising it: consequently the defenders of every kind of regime claim that it is a democracy, and fear that they might have to stop using that word if it were tied down to any one meaning. Words of this kind are often used in a consciously dishonest way. That is, the person who uses them has his own private definition, but allows his hearer to think he means something quite different. Statements like *Marshal Petain was a true patriot, The Soviet press is the freest in the world, The Catholic Church is opposed to persecution*, are almost always made with intent to deceive. Other words used in variable meanings, in most cases more or less dishonestly, are: *class, totalitarian, science, progressive, reactionary, bourgeois, equality*.

Now that I have made this catalogue of swindles and perversions, let me give another example of the kind of writing that they lead to. This time it must of its nature be an imaginary one. I am going to translate a passage of good English into modern English of the worst sort. Here is a well-known verse from *Ecclesiastes*:

> I returned and saw under the sun, that the race is not to the swift, nor the battle to the strong, neither yet bread to the wise, nor yet riches to men of understanding, nor yet favour to men of skill; but time and chance happeneth to them all.

Here it is in modern English:

> Objective considerations of contemporary phenomena compel the conclusion that success or failure in competitive activities exhibits no tendency to be commensurate with innate capacity, but that a considerable element of the unpredictable must invariably be taken into account.

This is a parody, but not a very gross one. Exhibit (3) above, for instance, contains several patches of the same kind of English. It will be seen that I have not made a full translation. The beginning and ending of the sentence follow the original meaning fairly closely, but in the middle the concrete illustrations—race, battle, bread—dissolve into the vague phrases "success or failure in competitive activities." This had to be so, because no modern writer of the kind I am discussing—no one capable of using phrases like "objective considerations of contemporary phenomena"—would ever tabulate his thoughts in that precise and detailed way. The whole tendency of modern prose is away from concreteness. Now analyze these two sentences a little more closely. The first contains forty-nine words but only sixty syllables, and all its words are those of everyday life. The second contains thirty-eight words of ninety syllables: eighteen of those words are from Latin roots, and one from Greek. The first sentence contains six vivid images, and only one phrase ("time and chance") that could be called vague. The second contains not a single fresh, arresting phrase, and in spite of its ninety syllables it gives only a shortened version of the meaning contained in the first. Yet without a doubt it is the second kind of sentence that is gaining ground in modern English. I do not want to exaggerate. This kind of writing is not yet universal, and outcrops of simplicity will occur here and there in the worst-written page. Still, if you or I were told to write a few lines on the uncertainty of human fortunes, we should probably come much nearer to my imaginary sentence than to the one from *Ecclesiastes*. As I have tried to show, modern writing at its worst does not consist in picking out words for the sake of their meaning and inventing images in order to make the meaning clearer. It consists in gumming together long strips of words which have already been set in order by someone else, and making the results presentable by sheer humbug. The attraction of this way of writing is that it is easy. It is easier—even quicker, once you have the habit— to say *In my opinion it is not an unjustifiable assumption that* than to say *I think*. If you use ready-made phrases, you not only don't have to hunt about for the words; you also don't have to bother with the rhythms of your sentences since these phrases are generally so arranged as to be more or less euphonious. When you are composing in a hurry—when you are dictating to a stenographer, for instance, or making a public speech—it is natural to fall into a pretentious, Latinized style. Tags like *a consideration which we should do well to bear in mind* or *a conclusion to which all of us would readily assent* will save many a sentence from coming down with a bump. By using stale metaphors, similes, and idioms, you save much mental effort, at the cost of leaving your meaning vague, not only for your reader but for yourself. This is the significance of mixed metaphors. The sole aim of a metaphor is to call up a visual image. When these images clash—as in *The Fascist octopus has sung its swan song, the jackboot is thrown into the melting pot*—it can be taken as certain that the writer is not seeing a mental image of the objects he is naming; in other words he is not really thinking. Look again at the examples I gave at the beginning of this essay. Professor Laski (1) uses five negatives in fifty three words. One of these is superfluous, making nonsense of the whole passage, and in addition there is the slip—*alien* for akin—making further nonsense, and several avoidable pieces of clumsiness which increase the general vagueness. Professor Hogben (2) plays ducks and drakes with a battery which is able to write prescriptions, and, while disapproving of the everyday phrase *put up with*, is unwilling to look *egregious* up in the dictionary and see what it means; (3), if one takes an uncharitable attitude towards it, is simply meaningless: probably one could work out its intended meaning by reading the whole of the article in which it occurs. In (4), the writer knows more or less what he wants to say, but an accumulation of stale phrases chokes him like tea leaves blocking a sink. In (5), words and meaning have almost parted company. People who write in this manner usually have a general emotional meaning—they dislike one thing and want to express solidarity with another—but they are not interested in the detail of what they are saying. A scrupulous writer, in every sentence that he writes, will ask himself at least four questions, thus:

1. What am I trying to say?
2. What words will express it?
3. What image or idiom will make it clearer?
4. Is this image fresh enough to have an effect?

And he will probably ask himself two more:

1. Could I put it more shortly?
2. Have I said anything that is avoidably ugly?

But you are not obliged to go to all this trouble. You can shirk it by simply throwing your mind open and letting the ready-made phrases come crowding in. They will construct your sentences for you—even think your thoughts for you, to a certain extent—and at need they will perform the important service of partially concealing your meaning even from yourself. It is at this point that the special connection between politics and the debasement of language becomes clear.

In our time it is broadly true that political writing is bad writing. Where it is not true, it will generally be found that the writer is some kind of rebel, expressing his private opinions and not a "party line." Orthodoxy, of whatever color, seems to demand a lifeless, imitative style. The political dialects to be found in pamphlets, leading articles, manifestoes, White papers and the speeches of undersecretaries do, of course, vary from party to party, but they are all alike in that one almost never finds in them a fresh, vivid, homemade turn of speech. When one watches some tired hack on the platform mechanically repeating the familiar phrases—*bestial, atrocities, iron heel, bloodstained tyranny, free peoples of the world, stand shoulder to shoulder*—one often has a curious feeling that one is not watching a live human being but some kind of dummy: a feeling which suddenly becomes stronger at moments when the light catches the speaker's spectacles and turns them into blank discs which seem to have no eyes behind them. And this is not altogether fanciful. A speaker who uses that kind of phraseology has gone some distance toward turning himself into a machine. The appropriate noises are coming out of his larynx, but his brain is not involved as it would be if he were choosing his words for himself. If the speech he is making is one that he is accustomed to make over and over again, he may be almost unconscious of what he is saying, as one is when one utters the responses in church. And this reduced state of consciousness, if not indispensable, is at any rate favorable to political conformity.

In our time, political speech and writing are largely the defense of the indefensible. Things like the continuance of British rule in India, the Russian purges and deportations, the dropping of the atom bombs on Japan, can indeed be defended, but only by arguments which are too brutal for most people to face, and which do not square with the professed aims of the political parties. Thus political language has to consist largely of euphemism, question-begging and sheer cloudy vagueness. Defenseless villages are bombarded from the air, the inhabitants driven out into the countryside, the cattle machine-gunned, the huts set on fire with incendiary bullets: this is called *pacification*. Millions of peasants are robbed of their farms and sent trudging along the roads with no more than they can carry: this is called *transfer of population* or *rectification of frontiers*. People are imprisoned for years without trial, or shot in the back of the neck or sent to die of scurvy in Arctic lumber camps: this is called *elimination of unreliable elements*. Such phraseology is needed if one wants to name things without calling up mental pictures of them. Consider for instance some comfortable English professor defending Russian totalitarianism. He cannot say outright, "I believe in killing off your opponents when you can get good results by doing so." Probably, therefore, he will say something like this:

> While freely conceding that the Soviet regime exhibits certain features which the humanitarian may be inclined to deplore, we must, I think, agree that a certain curtailment of the right to political opposition is an unavoidable concomitant of transitional periods, and that the rigors which the Russian people have been called upon to undergo have been amply justified in the sphere of concrete achievement.

The inflated style itself is a kind of euphemism. A mass of Latin words falls upon the facts like soft snow, blurring the outline and covering up all the details. The great enemy of clear language is insincerity. When there is a gap between one's real and one's declared aims, one turns as it were instinctively to long words and exhausted idioms, like a cuttlefish spurting out ink. In our age there is no such thing as "keeping out of politics." All issues are political issues, and politics itself is a mass of lies, evasions, folly, hatred, and schizophrenia. When the general atmosphere is bad, language must suffer. I should expect to find—this is a guess which I have not sufficient knowledge to verify—that the German, Russian and Italian languages have all deteriorated in the last ten or fifteen years, as a result of dictatorship.

But if thought corrupts language, language can also corrupt thought. A bad usage can spread by tradition and imitation even among people who should and do know better. The debased language that I have been discussing is in some ways very convenient. Phrases like *a not unjustifiable assumption, leaves much to be desired, would serve no good purpose, a consideration which we should do well to bear in mind*, are a continuous temptation, a packet of aspirins always at one's elbow. Look back through this essay, and for certain you will find that I have again and again committed the very faults I am protesting against. By this morning's post I have received a pamphlet dealing with conditions in Germany. The author tells me that he "felt impelled" to write it. I open it at random, and here is almost the first sentence I see: "[The Allies] have an opportunity not only of achieving a radical transformation of Germany's social and political structure in such a way as to avoid a nationalistic reaction in Germany itself, but at the same time of laying the foundations of a co-operative and unified Europe." You see, he "feels impelled" to write—feels, presumably, that he has something new to say—and yet his words, like cavalry horses answering the bugle, group themselves automatically into the familiar dreary pattern. This invasion of one's mind by ready-made phrases (*lay the foundations, achieve a radical transformation*) can only be prevented if one is constantly on guard against them, and every such phrase anaesthetizes a portion of one's brain.

I said earlier that the decadence of our language is probably curable. Those who deny this would argue, if they produced an argument at all, that language merely reflects existing social conditions, and that we cannot influence its development by any direct tinkering with words and constructions. So far as the general tone or spirit of a language goes, this may be true, but it is not true in detail. Silly words and expressions have often disappeared, not through any evolutionary process but owing to the conscious action of a minority. Two recent examples were *explore every avenue* and *leave no stone unturned*, which were killed by the jeers of a few journalists. There is a long list of flyblown metaphors which could similarly be got rid of if enough people would interest themselves in the job; and it should also be possible to laugh the *not un-* formation out of existence, to reduce the amount of Latin and Greek in the average sentence, to drive out foreign phrases and strayed scientific words, and, in general, to make pretentiousness unfashionable. But all these are minor points. The defense of the English language implies more than this, and perhaps it is best to start by saying what it does *not* imply.

To begin with it has nothing to do with archaism, with the salvaging of obsolete words and turns of speech, or with the setting up of a "standard English" which must never be departed from. On the contrary, it is especially concerned with the scrapping of every word or idiom which has outworn its usefulness. It has nothing to do with correct grammar and syntax, which are of no importance so long as one makes one's meaning clear, or with the avoidance of Americanisms, or with having what is called a "good prose style." On the other hand, it is not concerned with fake simplicity and the attempt to make written English colloquial. Nor does it even imply in every case preferring the Saxon word to the Latin one, though it does imply using the fewest and shortest words that will cover one's meaning. What is above all needed is to let the meaning choose the word, and not the other way around. In prose, the worst thing one can do with words is surrender to them. When you think of a concrete object, you think wordlessly, and then, if you want to describe the thing you have been visualizing you probably hunt about until you find the exact words that seem to fit it. When you think of something abstract you are more inclined to use words from the start, and unless you make a conscious effort to prevent it, the existing dialect will come rushing in and do the job for you, at the expense of blurring or even changing your meaning. Probably it is better to put off using words as long as possible and get one's meaning as clear as one can through pictures and sensations. Afterward one can choose—not simply *accept*—the phrases that will best cover the meaning, and then switch round and decide what impressions one's words are likely to make on another person. This last effort of the mind cuts out all stale or mixed images, all prefabricated phrases, needless repetitions, and humbug and vagueness generally. But one can often be in doubt about the effect of a word or a phrase, and one needs rules that one can rely on when instinct fails. I think the following rules will cover most cases:

1. Never use a metaphor, simile, or other figure of speech which you are used to seeing in print.
2. Never use a long word where a short one will do.
3. If it is possible to cut a word out, always cut it out.
4. Never use the passive where you can use the active.
5. Never use a foreign phrase, a scientific word, or a jargon word if you can think of an everyday English equivalent.
6. Break any of these rules sooner than say anything outright barbarous.

These rules sound elementary, and so they are, but they demand a deep change of attitude in anyone who has grown used to writing in the style now fashionable. One could keep all of them and still write bad English, but one could not write the kind of stuff that I quoted in those five specimens at the beginning of this article.

I have not here been considering the literary use of language, but merely language as an instrument for expressing and not for concealing or preventing thought. Stuart Chase and others have come near to claiming that all abstract words are meaningless, and have used this as a pretext for advocating a kind of political quietism. Since you don't know what Fascism is, how can you struggle against Fascism? One need not swallow such absurdities as this, but one ought to recognize that the present political chaos is connected with the decay of language, and that one can probably bring about some improvement by starting at the verbal end. If you simplify your English, you are freed from the worst follies of orthodoxy. You cannot speak any of the necessary dialects, and when you make a stupid remark its stupidity will be obvious, even to yourself. Political language—and with variations this is true of all political parties, from Conservatives to Anarchists—is designed to make lies sound truthful and murder respectable, and to give an appearance of solidity to pure wind. One cannot change this all in a moment, but one can at least change one's own habits, and from time to time one can even, if one jeers loudly enough, send some worn-out and useless phrase—some *jackboot, Achilles' heel, hotbed, melting pot, acid test, veritable inferno,* or other lump of verbal refuse—into the dustbin, where it belongs.

Defending Against the Indefensible

NEIL POSTMAN

Neil Postman is a professor, cultural critic, and author of *Teaching as a Subversive Activity*, *Amusing Ourselves to Death*, *The Disappearance of Childhood*, *Conscientious Objections*, *Building a Bridge to the 18th Century*, *The End of Education*, and *Technopoly*. A humanist, Postman views progress skeptically, seeing new media and technology as potentially harmful, especially for children and educational institutions. In "Defending Against the Indefensible," he outlines seven critical ideas that help people identify and reject bad ideas.

This essay originated as a lecture I gave in The Hague, Holland, to an audience of people who teach in English-language independent schools throughout Europe. I should stress that they were not primarily teachers of English, whom I have for the most part stopped addressing, since I came to the conclusion several years ago that they are the educators least likely to depart in any significant way from their pedagogical traditions. I do not know why this is so, but it is a serious deficiency, since English teachers are better positioned than any others to cultivate intelligence.

I am sure many of you will recognize that my title derives from a phrase in George Orwell's famous essay "Politics and the English Language." In that essay, Orwell speaks of the dangerously degraded condition of modern political thought, and proceeds to characterize its language as mainly committed to "defending the indefensible."

In the thirty-five years or so since Orwell wrote his essay, it has become even more obvious that the principal purpose of most political language is to justify or, if possible, to make glorious the malignant ambitions of nation states. Perhaps it has always been so—at least since the seventeenth century—and I don't suppose many of us expect it to be different in the future. With the exception of the much misunderstood Machiavelli, no one ever said politics is a pretty profession, and if Orwell thought it could be otherwise, he was an optimist.

I, too, am an optimist. But not because I look for any improvement in the purposes of political discourse. I am an optimist because I think it might just be possible for people to learn how to recognize empty, false, self-serving, or inhumane language, and therefore to protect themselves from at least some of its spiritually debasing consequences. My optimism places me in the camp of H. G. Wells, who said that civilization is in a race between education and disaster, and that although education is far behind, it is not yet out of the running. In other words, while I do not think we can count on any relaxation in the defense of the indefensible, I believe we may mount a practical counteroffensive by better preparing the minds of those for whom such language is intended.

Thus our attention inevitably turns to the subject of schools and to the possibility of their actually doing something that would help our youth acquire the semantic sophistication that we associate with minds unburdened by prejudice and provinciality. Of course, I am well aware that in most of the world, school is the last place you would expect such an education to be seriously conducted; in most places, school is conceived of as a form of indoctrination, the continuation of politics by gentle means.

The idea that schooling should make the young compliant and easily accessible to the prejudices of their society is an old and venerable tradition. This function of education was clearly advocated by our two earliest and greatest curriculum specialists, Confucius and Plato. Their writings created the tradition that requires educators to condition the young to believe what they are told, in the way they are told it.

But the matter does not rest there. We are fortunate to have available an alternative tradition that gives us the authority to educate our students to *disbelieve* or at least to be skeptical of the prejudices of their elders. We can locate the origins of this tradition in some fragments from Cicero, who remarked that the purpose of education is to free the student from the tyranny of the present. We find elaborations of this point of view in Descartes, Bacon, Vico, Goethe, and Jefferson. And we find its modern resonances in John Dewey, Freud, and Bertrand Russell.

It is in the spirit of this tradition—that is, education as a defense *against* culture—that I wish to speak. I will not address the important issue of how such an education in disbelief can be made palatable to those who pay for our schools. I know next to nothing about that, and what I know seems to be wrong. Rather, my remarks are aimed at those who would be interested to know how one might proceed if one had the authority and the desire to do so.

The method I have chosen for this purpose is to provide you with seven concepts, all of which have to do with language. I will not presume to call these concepts the Seven Pillars of Wisdom, but I believe that, if taken seriously, they have the potential to clear away some of the obtuseness that makes minds vulnerable to indefensible discourse. Before setting them out, I must stress that the education I speak of is *not* confined to helping students immunize themselves against the *politically* indefensible. Such an education would be in itself indefensible, and, fortunately, there is no need for it. We can assume that if we find a way to promote critical intelligence through language education, such intelligence can defend itself against almost anything that is indefensible—from Newspeak to commercial huckstering to bureaucratese to that most debilitating of all forms of nonsense that afflict the young, school textbooks. The assumption that critical intelligence has wide applicability is, I believe, what the medieval Schoolmen had in mind in creating the Trivium, which in their version consisted of grammar, logic, and rhetoric. These arts of language were assumed to be what may be called "meta-subjects," subjects about subjects. Their rules, guidelines, principles, and insights were thought to be useful in thinking about *anything*. Our ancestors understood well something we seem to have forgotten, namely, that all subjects are forms of discourse—indeed, forms of literature—and therefore that almost all education is language education. Knowledge of a subject mostly means knowledge of the language of that subject. Biology, after all, is not plants and animals; it is language about plants and animals. History is not events that once occurred; it is language describing and interpreting events. And astronomy is not planets and stars but a special way of talking about planets and stars.

And so a student must know the language of a subject, but that is only the beginning. For it is not sufficient to know the definition of a noun, or a gene, or a molecule. One must also know what a definition is. It is not sufficient to know the right answers. One must also know the questions that produced them. Indeed, one must know what a question is, for not every sentence that ends with a rising intonation or begins with an interrogative is necessarily a question. There are sentences that look like questions but cannot generate any meaningful answers, and if they linger in our minds, they become obstructions to clear thinking. One must also know what a metaphor is and what is the relationship between words and the things they describe. In short, one must have some knowledge of a meta-language—a language about language. Without such knowledge, a student can be as easily tyrannized by a subject as by a politician. That is to say, the enemy here is not, in the end, indefensible discourse but our ignorance of how to proceed against it.

Now, what I want to recommend to you is not so systematic or profound as the Trivium. I do not even propose a new subject—only seven ideas or insights or principles (call them what you will) that are essential to the workings of the critical intelligence and that are in the jurisdiction of every teacher at every level of school.

My first principle is about the process of definition. Most people are overcome by a sort of intellectual paralysis when confronted by a definition, whether offered by a politician or by a teacher. They fail to grasp that a definition is not a manifestation of nature but merely and always an instrument for helping us to achieve our purposes. I. A. Richards once remarked, "We want to do something, and a definition is a means of doing it. If we want certain results, then we must use certain definitions. But no definition has any authority apart from a purpose, or any authority to bar us from other purposes." This is one of the most liberating statements I know. But I have, myself, never heard a student ask of a teacher, "Whose definition is that and what purposes are served by it?" It is more than likely that a teacher would be puzzled by such a question, for most of us have been as tyrannized by definitions as have our students. But I do know of one instance where a student refused to accept a definition provided by an entire school. The student applied to Columbia University for admission and was rejected. In response, he sent the following letter to the admissions officer:

Dear Sir:

I am in receipt of your rejection of my application. As much as I would like to accommodate you, I find I cannot. I have already received four rejections from other colleges, which is, in fact, my limit. Your rejection puts me over this limit. Therefore, I must reject your rejection, and as much as this might inconvenience you, I expect to appear for classes on September 18 . . . .

Columbia would have been well advised to reconsider this student's application, not because it doesn't have a right to define for its own purposes what it means by an adequate student, but because here is a student who understands what some of Columbia's professors probably do not—that there is a measure of arbitrariness in every definition and that in any case an intelligent person is not required to accept another's definition, even if he can't do much about it.

What students need to be taught, then, is that definitions are not given to us by God; that we may depart from them without risking our immortal souls; that the authority of a definition rests entirely on its usefulness, not on its correctness (whatever that means); and that it is a form of stupidity to accept without reflection someone else's definition of a word, a problem, or a situation. All of this applies as much to a definition of a verb or a molecule as it does to a definition of art, God, freedom, or democracy. I can think of no better method of helping students to defend themselves than to provide them with alternative definitions for every important concept and term they must deal with in school. It is essential that they understand that definitions are hypotheses and that embedded in each is a particular philosophical or political or epistemological point of view. It is certainly true that he who holds the power to define is our master, but it is also true that he who holds in mind an alternative definition can never quite be his slave.

My second concept is best introduced by a story attributed to the American psychologist Gordon Allport. He tells of two priests who were engaged in a dispute on whether or not it is permissible to pray and smoke at the same time. One believed that it is, the other that it is not, and so each decided to write to the Pope for a definitive answer. After doing so, they met again to share their results and were astonished to discover that the Pope had agreed with both of them. "How did you pose the question?" the first asked. The other replied, "I asked if it is permissible to smoke while praying. His Holiness said that it is not, since praying is a very serious business. And how did you phrase the question?" The first replied, "I asked if it is permissible to pray while smoking, and His Holiness said that it is, since it is always appropriate to pray."

The point of this story, of course, is that the form in which we ask our questions will determine the answers we get. To put it more broadly: all the knowledge we ever have is a result of questions. Indeed, it is a commonplace among scientists that they do not see nature as it is, but only through the questions they put to it. I should go further: we do not see *anything* as it is except through the questions we put to it. And there is a larger point even than this: since questions are the most important intellectual tool we have, is it not incredible that the art and science of question-asking is not systematically taught? I would suggest that we correct this deficiency and not only put question-asking on our teaching agenda but place it near the top of the list. After all, in a profound sense, it is meaningless to have answers if we do not know the questions that produced them—whether in biology, grammar, politics, or history. To have an answer without knowing the question, without understanding that you might have been given a different answer if the question had been posed differently, may be more than meaningless; it may be exceedingly dangerous. There are many Americans who carry in their heads such answers as "America should proceed at once with our Star Wars project," or, "We should send Marines to Nicaragua." But if they do not know the questions to which these are the answers, their opinions are quite literally thoughtless. And so I suggest two things. First, we should teach our students something about question-asking in general. For example, that a vaguely formed question produces a vaguely formed answer; that every question has a point of view embedded in it; that for any question that is posed, there is almost always an alternative question that will generate an alternative answer; that every action we take is an answer to a question, even if we are not aware of it; that ineffective actions may be the result of badly formed questions; and most of all, that a question is language, and therefore susceptible to all the errors to which an unsophisticated understanding of language can lead. As Francis Bacon put it more than 350 years ago: "There arises from a bad and unapt formation of words a wonderful obstruction to the mind." This is as good a definition of stupidity as I know: a bad and unapt formation of words. Let us, then, go "back to Bacon," and study the art of question-asking. But we must also focus on the specific details of asking questions in different subjects. What, for example, are the sorts of questions that obstruct the mind, or free it, in the study of history? How are these questions different from those one might ask of a mathematical proof, or a literary work, or a biological theory? The principles and rules of asking questions obviously differ as we move from one system of knowledge to another, and this ought not to be ignored.

Which leads me to my third principle: namely, that the most difficult words in any form of discourse are rarely the polysyllabic ones that are hard to spell and which send students to their dictionaries. The troublesome words are those whose meanings appear to be simple, like "true," "false," "fact," "law," "good," and "bad." A word like "participle" or "mutation" or "centrifugal," or, for that matter, "apartheid" or "proletariat," rarely raises serious problems in understanding. The range of situations in which such a word might appear is limited and does not tangle us in ambiguity. But a word like "law" is used in almost every universe of discourse, and with different meanings in each. "The law of supply and demand" is a different "law" from "Grimm's Law" in linguistics or "Newton's Law" in physics or "the law of the survival of the fittest" in biology. What is a "true" statement in mathematics is different from a "true" statement in economics, and when we speak of the "truth" of a literary work, we mean something else again. Moreover, when President Reagan says it is "right" to place cruise missiles in Europe, he does not appeal to the same authority or even logic as when he says it is "right" to reduce the national deficit. And when Karl Marx said it was "right" for the working class to overthrow the bourgeoisie, he meant something different altogether, as does a teacher who proclaims it is "right" to say "he doesn't" instead of "he don't."

If we insist on giving our students vocabulary tests, then for God's sake let us find out if they know something about the truly difficult words in the language. I think it would be entirely practical to design a curriculum based on an inquiry into, let us say, fifty hard words, beginning with "good" and "bad" and ending with "true" and "false." Show me a student who knows something about what these words imply, what sources of authority they appeal to, and in what circumstances they are used, and I will show you a student who is an epistemologist—which is to say, a student who knows what textbooks try to conceal. And a student who knows what textbooks try to conceal will know what advertisers try to conceal, and politicians and preachers, as well.

Fourth, I think it would also be practical to design a curriculum based on an inquiry into the use of metaphor. Unless I am sorely mistaken, metaphor is at present rarely approached in school except by English teachers during lessons in poetry. This strikes me as absurd, since I do not see how it is possible for a subject to be understood in the absence of any insight into the metaphors on which it is constructed. All subjects are based on powerful metaphors that direct and organize the way we will do our thinking. In history, economics, physics, biology, and linguistics, metaphors, like questions, are organs of perception. Through our metaphors, we see the world as one thing or another. Is light a wave or a particle? An astrophysicist I know tells me that she and her colleagues don't know, and so at the moment they settle for the word "wavicle." Are molecules like billiard balls or force fields? Is language like a tree (some say it has roots) or a river (some say it has tributaries) or a building (some say it has foundations)? Is history unfolding according to some instructions of nature or according to a divine plan? Are our genes like information codes? Is a literary work like an architect's blueprint or is it a mystery the reader must solve? Questions like these preoccupy scholars in every field because they are what is basic to the field itself. Nowhere is this more so than in education. Rousseau begins his great treatise on education, *Emile*, with the following words: "Plants are improved by cultivation, and men by education." And his entire philosophy is made to rest upon this comparison of plants and children.

There is no test, textbook, syllabus, or lesson plan that any of us creates that does not reflect our preference for some metaphor of the mind, or of knowledge, or of the process of learning. Do you believe a student's mind to be a muscle that must be exercised? Or a garden that must be cultivated? Or a dark cavern that must be illuminated? Or an empty vessel that must be filled to overflowing? Whichever you favor, your metaphor will control—often without your being aware of it—how you will proceed as a teacher. This is as true of politicians as it is of academics. No political practitioner has ever spoken three consecutive sentences without invoking some metaphorical authority for his actions. And this is especially true of powerful political theorists. Rousseau begins *The Social Contract* with a powerful metaphor that Marx was to use later, and many times: "Man is born free but is everywhere in chains." Marx himself begins *The Communist Manifesto* with an ominous and ghostly metaphor—the famous "A specter haunts Europe . . ." Abraham Lincoln, in his celebrated Gettysburg Address, compares America's forefathers to God when he says they "brought forth a new nation," just as God brought forth the heavens and the earth. And Adolf Hitler concludes *Mein Kampf* with this: "A state which in this age of racial poisoning dedicates itself to the care of its best racial elements must someday become the lord of the earth." All forms of discourse are metaphor-laden, and unless our students are aware of how metaphors shape arguments, organize perceptions, and control feelings, their understanding is severely limited.

Which gets me to my fifth concept, what is called reification. Reification means confusing words with things. It is a thinking error with multiple manifestations, some merely amusing, others extremely dangerous. This past summer in the sweltering New York heat, a student of mine looked at a thermometer in our classroom. "It's ninety-six degrees," he said. "No wonder it's so hot!" He had it the wrong way around, of course, as many people do who have never learned or cannot remember these three simple notions: that there are things in the world and then there are our names for them; that there is no such thing as a real name; and that a name may or may not suggest the nature of the thing named—as, for example, when the United States government called its South Pacific hydrogen-bomb experiments Operation Sunshine. What I am trying to say here is what Shakespeare said more eloquently in his line "A rose by any other name would smell as sweet." But Shakespeare was only half right, in that for many people a rose would *not* smell as sweet if it were called a "stinkweed." And because this is so, because people confuse names with things, advertising is among the most consistently successful enterprises in the world today. Advertisers know that no matter how excellent an automobile may be, it will not sell if it is called the "Lumbering Elephant." More important, they know that no matter how rotten a car may be, you *can* sell it if it is called a "Vista Cruiser" or a "Phoenix" or a "Grand Prix." Politicians know this as well, and, sad to say, so do scholars, who far too often obscure the emptiness of what they are talking and writing about by affixing alluring names to what is not there. I suggest, therefore, that reification be given a prominent place in our studies, so that our students will know how it both works and works them over.

Sixth, some attention must be given to the style and tone of language. Each universe of discourse has its own special way of addressing its subject matter and its audience. Each subject in a curriculum is a special manner of speaking and writing, with its own rhetoric of knowledge, a characteristic way in which arguments, proofs, speculations, experiments, polemics, even humor, are expressed. Speaking and writing are, after all, performing arts, and each subject requires a somewhat different kind of performance. Historians, for example, do not speak or write history in the same way biologists speak or write biology. The differences have to do with the degree of precision their generalizations permit, the types of facts they marshal, the traditions of their subject, and the nature of their training. It is worth remembering that many scholars have exerted influence as much through their manner as their matter— one thinks of Veblen in sociology, Freud in psychology, Galbraith in economics. The point is that knowledge is a form of literature, and the various styles of knowledge ought to be studied and discussed, all the more because the language found in typical school textbooks tends to obscure this. Textbook language, which is apt to be the same from subject to subject, creates the false impression that systematic knowledge is always expressed in a dull, uninspired monotone. I have read recipes on the back of cereal boxes that were written with more style and conviction than textbook descriptions of the causes of the American Revolution. Of the language of grammar books I will not even speak, for, to borrow from Shakespeare, it is unfit for a Christian ear to endure. But the problem is not insurmountable. Teachers who are willing to take the time can find materials that convey ideas in a form characteristic of their discipline. And while they are at it, they can help their students to see that what we call a prayer, a political speech, and an advertisement differ from each other not only in their content but in their style and tone; one might say *mostly* in their style and tone and manner of address.

Which brings me to the seventh and final concept—what I shall call the principle of the non-neutrality of media. I mean by this what Marshall McLuhan meant to suggest when he said, "The medium is the message": that the form in which information is coded has, itself, an inescapable bias. In a certain sense, this is an entirely familiar idea. We recognize, for example, that the world is somewhat different when we speak about it in English and when we speak about it in German. We might even say that the grammar of a language is an organ of perception and accounts for the variances in world view that we find among different peoples. But we have been slow to acknowledge that every extension of speech—from painting to hieroglyphics to the alphabet to the printing press to television—also generates unique ways of apprehending the world, amplifying or obscuring different features of reality. Each medium, like language itself, classifies the world for us, sequences it, frames it, enlarges it, reduces it, argues a case for what the world is like. In the United States, for example, it is no longer possible for a fat person to be elected to high political office—not because our Constitution forbids it but because television forbids it, since television exalts the attractive visual image and has little patience with or love for the subtle or logical word.

Our students must understand two essential points about all this. Just as language itself creates culture in its own image, each new medium of communication re-creates or modifies culture in *its* image; and it is extreme naïveté to believe that a medium of communication or, indeed, any technology is merely a tool, a way of doing. Each is also a way of *seeing*. To a man with a hammer, everything looks like a nail. To a man with a pencil, everything looks like a sentence; to a man with a television camera, everything looks like a picture; and to a man with a computer, the whole world looks like data. To put it another way, and to paraphrase the philosopher Wittgenstein, a medium of communication may be a vehicle of thought but we must not forget that it is also the driver. A consideration of how the printing press or the telegraph or television or the computer does its driving and where it takes us must be included in our students' education or else they will be disarmed and extremely vulnerable.

There is one more principle about language that is probably occurring to many of you right about now: namely, that one ought not to put up with any lecturer who takes more of your time than he has been allotted. And so I will conclude with three points. First, I trust you understand that the suggestions I have made are not directed exclusively or even primarily at language teachers, English or otherwise. This is a task for everyone. Second, I want to reiterate that to provide our students with a defense against the indefensible, it is neither necessary nor desirable to focus exclusively on political language. Whenever this is attempted, it is apt to be shallow and limited. The best defense is one with a wider reach, which has implications for all language transactions. And finally, I do not claim that my proposals will solve all our problems, or even provide full protection from indefensible discourse. They are only a reasonable beginning, and there is much more to be done. But we have to start somewhere and, as Ray Bradbury once wrote, somewhere lies between the right ear and the left.

Politics and the English Language (1991)

BRIAN FAWCETT

Born in Prince George, B.C., Brian Fawcett is a journalist and fiction writer whose work dramatizes the ills of globalization, especially for local communities. His works include *The Secret Journals of Alexander Mackenzie*, *Capital Tales*, *My Career with the Leafs*, *Cambodia: A Book for People Who Find Television Too Slow*, *Public Eye*, *Gender Wars*, *Virtual Clearcut*, and *Local Matters*. In his update of George Orwell's classic essay, Fawcett encourages students to develop the skills of clear thinking and expression.

Almost a half century has passed since George Orwell wrote "Politics and the English Language." For most English-speaking writers who have had a strong desire to discover and tell the truth, the essay has been a basic text. In it, Orwell argued that clear thinking and good writing are integral to the health of democracy, and that bad language can and does corrupt thought. Those ideas are almost self-evident truths today, and the detailed arguments Orwell made in the essay remain remarkably current. My renovation of the essay's contents will therefore be—as my title suggests—a bracketed and respectful addendum.

Since 1946, when Orwell published his essay, there have been profound changes in the way human beings speak, write, and use knowledge. Radio, television and a number of less public but powerful cybernetic technologies now occupy our days, often filling our heads with information we either haven't asked for or don't have the right equipment or the wealth to make use of. We "communicate" or "process information" through immensely powerful and fast electronic systems, but we write less, and, I suspect, think less. Certainly the critical thought going on these days concerning the crucial subjects of politics and culture is in a state of conceptual disarray. Contemporary electronic communications are a matter of fewer and fewer people speaking to (and for) more and more people.

Despite this, the English language itself has taken only one major turn Orwell didn't foresee. In 1946, he feared that the undefeated totalitarianisms of World War II would breed Newspeak, the official language of his novel *1984*. Newspeak made understanding impossible by truncating or outlawing all the textures and nuances of language. But instead of Newspeak, the 1990s are filled with technogibberish dialects that glamourize the obvious and the trivial, and obscure (or sever) connections to other fields of meaning. The intent of these dialects is to make it difficult for anyone to communicate beyond their "lifestyle" enclave. The dialects serve the same purpose as Newspeak—creating political silence—by conning us into thinking that we're somehow more fashionable and smarter than the next enclave, and by getting us to fiddle endlessly with an assortment of disposable commodities, fake threats to our well-being, and obsessive notions of correct behaviour that border on fanaticism.

What that means is that politics—or maybe it is just authority—has changed. Some changes have been for the better, and some haven't. Within the industrialized nations, violent authority can no longer successfully operate indefinitely, and police states have demonstrated that they simply aren't efficient enough to compete with cybernetic economies—as witnessed by the recent economic and political collapse of the Soviet bloc. Violent authority is still the rule outside the industrialized part of the world, where, if anything, life has become more violent and arbitrary. In the privileged societies like ours, authority has merely gotten itself out of our faces and into our lowest appetites. Universal social justice, it should be noted, is as distant as it has ever been.

For an individual trying to think and write accurately in the intellectual and informational environments of the 1990s, politics are no longer a matter of complaining about the stupidity or corruption of the government. Politics—and they are a plural now—are the things we do to one another, or allow to be done to us by others through indifference or lust or whatever we've decided is self-interest. As the millennium nears, and as the referent ideologies that have guided and/or deluded us through the century collapse around us, politics have more to do with how we allow ourselves to be lied to and deceived than how we are imprisoned or liberated. In the industrialized democracies, most of us are free as the birds. We just happen to be turkeys and chickens, with a few aggressive but deluded raptors tossed into the mix to make the peaceful cower and to give the brainlessly ambitious something to aspire to.

Communists, capitalists, fascists and all the permutations in between have become meaningless epithets. Orwell himself saw that coming. Everything he wrote from *Homage to Catalonia* to his death argues against the structuring of politics by ideological claim. For us, his essay "Second Thoughts on James Burnham" (1946) ought to be read as the companion piece to "Politics and the English Language" because it reveals his characteristic skill at eluding the seductive ideological nets of his time. In that essay he summarizes Burnham's future scenario in *The Managerial Revolution* (1940) in terms that will be chillingly familiar to us: "Capitalism is disappearing, but socialism is not replacing it. What is now arising is a new kind of planned, centralized society which will be neither capitalist nor, in any accepted sense of the word, democratic. The rulers of this new society will be the people who effectively control the means of production: that is, business executives, technicians, bureaucrats and soldiers, lumped together by Burnham under the name of 'managers.'" That's a fair description of the corporate oligarchy that controls the world today—an oligarchy that operates on eighteen-month financial horizons and proudly promises an end to the excesses of ideological politics. That Orwell was able to foresee and critique the weaknesses of a vast political change that contemporary analysts are just now learning to bend their minds around is typical of just how brilliant his intellectual method was.

Understanding how the new politics work will require a few conceptual simplifications. One of them is recognizing that there are only three kinds of political beings in the world First, there are people who will try to see and tell the truth, and try to act on it in the interests of everyone. Second, there are—let me put this as suc- briefly cinctly as possible—assholes. Third, there are people who are too weakened by poverty, disease and violence to care about being either of the first two. Good politics consists of behaviours that enlarge the numbers of type A and reduce, without violence or arrogance, the numbers of types B and C. I'm pretty sure that George Orwell would agree with this simplification.

In the new environment, clear political writing and thinking is perhaps more urgently needed than ever. It remains an essential component of democracy—which is, after all, not a political state but a social, intellectual and moral activity. For that activity to regain the alertness it requires to be effective, the toolbox a political writer needs to deal with the 1990s needs some additions.

I'm going to suggest a few tools. For the sake of convenience, I'll divide them into two categories, practical and conceptual. Most of the practical ones have to do with keeping writing direct and simple and personal, which is the only antidote I know for the poison of technogibberish. The conceptual tools I use are generally attitudinal tactics aimed at inducing and nourishing the habitual skepticism Orwell taught me. What follows isn't meant to be either an exclusive or exhaustive toolbox on its own, merely an addition to Orwell's. Intellectual tools don't work the same way for everyone, but I can at least testify that the ones I offer help me to keep my eyes open in the cyclone of lies daily life has become. And sometimes, they help me to close them with laughter.

Practical Writing Tools

1. George Orwell's "Politics and the English Language" ought to be reread about every six months. Nearly everything he said remains relevant. His examples should be periodically updated with your own.
2. Write simple sentences whenever you can, and let your musicianship take care of the need for melody. If you've got a tin ear, get into another line of work.
3. Fill your writing with nouns and verbs. Naming things accurately makes them palpable, and making them move in specific ways enables them to be tested. Beware of adjectives and adverbs because they are linguistic grease. Using more than two successive adjectives in a single sentence is a reliable signal that a Mazola party is going on in the writer's head.
4. Never use a semicolon. I know I'm repeating Orwell, but this is so important it bears repeating. Semicolons are absolutely reliable signals that a sentence should be rewritten, generally to make it more direct. And incidentally, you should only use a colon if you're wearing a tuxedo or sitting on white porcelain.
5. Contemporary writers should learn how to use a word processor, and how to manipulate data systems. If you're a working writer, it is more important to own a word processor than a car. Word processors are necessary to keep up to the current speeds of information transmission and production, and because having other people decipher your lousy hand-writing is vile and exploitive political behaviour.

Conceptual Tools

1. Beware of sacred cattle. They are stupid, filled with inflated ideas about their importance and the unimportance of everything in their projected path, and if you let them run around inside your head they will eat or trample everything, including your intelligence. On the other hand, do not attempt to run anyone else's sacred cattle over a cliff unless you're certain you can succeed. Today's sacred cattle are a new and much more dangerous breed than the ones that emerged in the 1950s and are now dying out. The new breed are very aggressive, they're used to living in information-overloaded cities, and if you wave a red flag at them they'll pin you to the nearest concrete abutment without a qualm.

2. Good political writing always recognizes when it is running in a stampede and attempts to get out of it as quickly as possible, preferably without trying to work the herd. This is a fancy way of saying that the job of a political writer is to ask the questions that aren't being addressed by the visible agendas of authority or exclusive interest. Generally speaking, figuring out—or making up—answers is someone else's job—someone you probably won't trust or like. Never trust anyone with an answer to a question you haven't asked.

3. Recognize that everyone is sincere and that sincerity has no relationship to anything but righteousness, which is an enemy of good political writing, and usually, death to clear thinking. Accusing anyone of insincerity precludes the possibility of further political debate, and you're supposed to be writing in order to start and keep people talking to one another.

4. The language of political speeches and official communiques is never meaningless. Most of the time, speeches, press releases and official communiques are cybernetic devices meant to occupy a vital political moment or space without committing the originating speaker, institution or agency to action. They require full translation, which involves an analysis of what they both say and don't say. This is also true of commercial language, which is becoming indistinguishable from political language.

5. If you don't believe in God, don't quote Her. By this I mean that writers must try to be personal, and should not make their voices out to be more than they are—the words and gestures of a single person who has thought through and researched a subject matter. Practising this successfully involves a number of mental habits, some of which are as follows:

   a) never using the word "we" unless you know who you're collectivizing and are willing to kiss them all on the mouth—and mean it.

b) never using the word "reality" without putting quotes around it.

c) recognizing that there is no such thing as a rhetorical question.

d) never dismissing a dead or older writer for not knowing what is currently fashionable around the office or inside your dopey head.

e) remembering that the surface of any important truth will more resemble the skin of a toad than an alabaster statue or brochure materials that promise to make you into a human bullet. Warts are not something that will disappear from writing and thinking just because we don't approve of bumps and lesions. They're what used to be called texture, and without texture there is no such thing as meaning. Bullets, whatever form they come in, are the opposite of meaning, and they are signals of the collapse of human intelligence.

6. Try not to contribute to the cacophony of disinformation and nonsense. In a democracy the only opinion anyone is entitled to is an informed and preferably detailed one. If all you're hearing is the sound of your own voice, silence is the right option.

7. Finally, make people laugh with your writing. Laughter disrupts narrow logic, which is the operating system for authority, cattle stampedes, and ill-conceived judgments of all sorts. People who are laughing find it hard to start wars, molest children, and are unlikely to discover that the person or persons in their immediate vicinity are in league with the devil. Orthodoxy most easily breeds where laughter is absent.

Names

"Every word is a prejudice."

—Friedrich Nietzsche

"What's in a name?" wonders Juliet on her balcony, as she pines for Romeo. "A rose by any other name would smell as sweet." Words, after all, are mere conveniences; they do not alter the reality of the things they name.

Or do they?

As memorable as Juliet's line is, it doesn't tell the whole story about language, for words have tremendous power. They can modify our perceptions, change our desires, alter our actions, bring us to the altar, or to war. From a linguistic point of view, words can influence us along two different channels of meaning: denotation and connotation.

Denotation refers to the dictionary meaning of a word, the physical object, action, or idea. For example, the denotation of the word "green" refers to a colour that falls between blue and yellow on the spectrum, or to get more scientifically precise, a colour whose wavelengths lie between 490 and 570 nanometres. Denotation is the literal meaning of a word, the person, place, act, concept, or thing explicitly named.

However, language also contains another level of significance, a level both exciting and troublesome. Connotation refers to the implied meaning, the associations, feelings, overtones, and semantic baggage carried by a word, in addition to the thing explicitly named. In our previous example, the word "green" carries a number of connotations—including jealousy, inexperience, greed, nature, and decay—none having anything to do with wavelength of light. Profanity and racial slurs give a stinging illustration of connotative language. The denotation of a word like "nigger" is simple and declarative: a person of African-American heritage. However, the connotation of that word is charged with centuries of racial antagonism, injustice, slavery, discrimination, and pain, making the term unusable except as a verbal weapon. In swearing and racial epithets, the connotative level of meaning—the feelings attached to a word—becomes more important than the literal meaning, so important that we ignore connotation at great risk.

Dictionaries, encyclopedias, professions, and courts of law all work to clarify the denotative meanings of words. Such attempts at definition are not without problems (as we shall see in Chapter 2), but they help standardize a word's denotative meaning, making it easier for us to communicate precisely and unambiguously. The same can't be said for connotation, which is unregulated and erratic.

A writer ignorant of the connotative register of language can make serious gaffes, such as referring to a group of adult women with the diminutive "girls," or a group of black men as "boys." A poorly chosen word can even create international problems. When U.S. President George Bush Jr. described his pursuit of the 9/11 terrorists as a *crusade*, he probably meant it as a passionate and zealous endeavour, a heartfelt battle. However, the president overlooked the fact that the historic Crusades were an unprovoked Christian assault against Muslims. In short, the president missed the connotations of hypocrisy and violence that the word Crusade suggests, especially to a Muslim audience. The choice of the word "crusade" alienated Bush's Arab audience, and constituted a major public relations blunder. In this case, the emotional impact of the word eclipsed the president's intended literal meaning.

In contrast, an author wary of connotative subtleties can have an enormous influence on the way a reader perceives the world. Depending on the choice of words, a writer can inflame or soothe, win friends or create enemies. Imagine you're a reporter at a glitzy New York fashion show, and the evening's first barely-robed model saunters down the catwalk. What words do you use to describe her? Here are but a few choices:

> Skinny, Scrawny, Thin, Emaciated, Ectomorphic, Slender, and Svelte

All these words refer to a similar, if not identical body shapes, yet each carries a distinct emotional charge. The term "scrawny" or "emaciated" suggests a malnourished body; "skinny" evokes an undeveloped but healthy one; "thin" lacks strong positive or negative feelings; "ectomorphic" sounds bizarre and clinical; "slender" carries an erotic flavour; and "svelte" becomes distinctly glamorous. What impression will you create for your readers? A critical feminist one? A chic one? In part, the world you build depends on the words chosen.

A good writer manipulates connotation in order to manage the perceptions of the audience. Like a magician creating an illusion, the writer selects terms to influence the thoughts and feelings of the audience, provoking disgust or enthusiasm through diction alone. With an enormous list of English synonyms, the writer-illusionist can *spin* a story, slipping a bias into the text that subtly affects our understanding of events. Consider the list of words below. Each line contains terms that have the same denotation, but strongly different connotations.

> stingy, cheap, thrifty, frugal, parsimonious, fiscally-restrained
> corpulent, fat, husky, Rubenesque
> abattoir, meatpacking plant, rendering facility, slaughterhouse
> pig-headed, stubborn, resolute, determined
> narcotic, drug, medication, treatment, remedy
> torture, interrogation, physical coercion, information recovery
> cultist, disciple, devotee, follower, adherent, faithful
> handicapped, physically challenged, disabled, differently-abled
> masturbation, manual gratification, self-abuse
> whore, hooker, prostitute, escort, sex trade worker
> pregnant, with child, expectant, knocked up
> partly cloudy, partly sunny
> muckraker, hack, reporter, investigative journalist

These synonyms present identical topics, yet the minor changes in diction mark profound changes in our attitude towards the subject. What's in a name, Juliet? As it turns out, a great amount.

An effective writer manipulates the connotative register of language in order to influence an audience, often with political purpose. Both sides of the abortion debate have made strategic use of emotionally rich language to win sympathy for their causes, starting with the names used by each. Those in favour of maintaining access to abortion refer to themselves with the affirming and uplifting name *pro-choice*, which focuses attention on the woman's control of her body; in contrast, their opponents refer to them with the unpleasant title *pro-abortion*. Those in favour of banning abortion call themselves with the heartening phrase *pro-life*, while their opponents besmirch them with the name *anti-choice*. Just as contentious are the terms used to describe the occupant of the pregnant woman's womb. The pro-choice camp downplays any romance, relying on scientific jargon such as zygote, fetus, or fertilized egg. Pro-life advocates, in contrast, intensify the human dimension, employing lingo such as the unborn, pre-born person, or child. Each side uses emotional terms to lull listeners into accepting their agenda.

Although language is central to the abortion dispute, we find similar polarization in the debate around euthanasia, known as "deliverance" or "aid-in-dying" to its proponents, and as "mercy-killing" or "doctor-assisted suicide" to detractors. More examples come from the "historical revision" controversy, which Jews strip down to "Holocaust denial." Or look at government-run heroin injection centres, slandered by opponents as "shooting galleries," yet trumpeted by advocates as "harm reduction centres." Connotative language flourishes wherever we find political disagreement.

For this reason, connotative language tips us off to a writer's prejudices and allegiances. If an author refers to strip-mining and clear-cut logging as "sustainable utilization," we can be pretty sure he or she is sympathetic to business interests. If someone speaks of "transfer tubes" instead of the common "body bags," that person probably sympathizes with the military. Loaded terms subtly declare a writer's attitude, and alert us to his or her agenda. Thus, a good ear for connotative language can act as a distant early warning system, letting us know when we're being influenced, misinformed, or fed propaganda.

Connotative language has two distinct rhetorical forms: euphemisms and name-calling. Name-calling attaches an unpleasant label onto an attractive, agreeable thing. When a writer refers to the public with the terms "the masses" or "rabble," that's name-calling. When we refer to a spokesperson as a "shill," that term denigrates the profession.

The reverse of name-calling, a euphemism, gives a pleasant, attractive name to something embarrassing, ugly, disagreeable, or worse. A euphemism speaks nicely about an objectionable subject. We frequently use euphemisms to describe bodily functions, such as saying, "powder my nose" instead of urinate/defecate. Even common phrases like "restroom," "washroom," and bathroom" are euphemisms, unless we go there to rest, wash, or bathe.

Although at times funny, euphemisms can lead to misunderstanding, and even harm. At their worst, euphemisms deceive people about horrible realities. In his classic book *1984*, George Orwell showed how a totalitarian society makes use of euphemisms; in his dystopia, the government body responsible for circulating lies and disinformation is known as the Ministry of Truth; the legislative arm that enforces obedience and order as the Ministry of Love; the army and war machine as the Ministry of Peace. Euphemisms run the risk of making language meaningless and untrustworthy, and its speakers powerless. Although Orwell's vision hasn't yet come true, we seem surrounded by lovely sounding phrases and slogans that hide grisly, sordid truths.

Let's take a close look at three of the most troublesome discourses: advertising, military, and government, corporate, and economic speech.

ADVERTISING

"Advertising is the modern substitute for argument; its function is to make the worse appear the better."

—George Santayana

Advertising takes advantage of the confusion between a literal message (denotation) and an implied message (connotation). That's to say, a typical ad ranks high on emotion, innuendo, and suggestion, but low on facts. Advertisers count on the audience paying heed to the connotative signal, not the denotative one. And here begins the consumer's troubles. Ads make unbridled hints and insinuations, for companies are legally responsible for only literal claims, not connotative messages. They consequently make gross, misleading, and exaggerated implications, knowing that the reader or viewer will infer a meaning that they don't have to satisfy.

Consider Starbucks' translation of the words "small," "medium," and "large" into their in-house lingo, "tall," "grande," and "venti." The company wishes to avoid the negative feelings associated with "small" or "medium," and hopes the new terms create a positive image for all coffee sizes. In the process, however, coffee-drinkers face a ridiculous situation where "tall" refers to "small," "high" means "low." Ad-speak robs words of their meaning.

If we can distinguish between connotation and denotation, if we winnow the connotative chaff down to the denotative seed, few ads will mislead us.

In the article "With These Words I Can Sell You Anything," William Lutz provides a summary of dishonest advertising techniques that numb us into senseless acts of purchasing. In a euphemism of his own, he refers to these deceptions as "weasel words," based on the weasel's ability to suck all nutrition from an egg, leaving only the shell. Lutz blasts advertisers use of imprecise language, misleading comparisons, relative terms, subjective claims, and statements of potential—all of which rely on the consumer to free-associate, while the ad makes no legally binding claim. To Lutz's list we can add a few more techniques of deception.

Names and Titles: Every manufacturer knows the value in a good brand name, but calling a car a "Reliant" does not necessarily make it any more or less reliable. A food line called "Healthy Meals" may still be fattening and dangerous. "Ducks Unlimited" ironically names a coalition of hunters, whose goal is to shoot ducks.

Invented Words: Companies create neologisms (new words), such as "aspartame" or "lite." They feel fair, but may be foul.

Fragments: An ad may have the words "fat free," but unless it places them in a sentence, it makes no statement at all. Words without grammatical context are empty, meaningless shells.

Commands: Ads that make commands don't literally make claims. Nike may exhort us to "Just do it," but such orders have zero information. Their psychological appeal rests in the pleasure of following orders, of becoming obedient.

Luckily, we tend to be skeptical about advertising, at least some of the time. Our level of doubt is not as high, unfortunately, in the next two examples.

MILITARY EUPHEMISMS

"War is peace. Freedom is slavery. Ignorance is strength."

—George Orwell, *1984*

Because war is nasty and violent, the discourse that justifies it tends to be highly misleading and opaque. Rather than speak the plain truth about their bloody business, generals choose words to soften, confuse, and foster popular consent for military campaigns. Again, names provide telling examples. In a more honest past, the American military called itself the Department of War; it has since been renamed the Department of Defense. In World War I, soldiers suffered from the fairly descriptive condition of "shell shock"; the language gradually morphed into the more pleasant-sounding "combat fatigue" before finally settling on "post-traumatic stress disorder"—a bit of bafflegab that completely removes any hint of battle. In 2003, the Americans launched "Operation: Iraqi Freedom," a military offensive that placed Iraq under American control. No other discourse has more euphemisms than army talk. In the business of death, military jingoists concoct neologisms—new words whose connotations contrast with the physical reality named. As Orwell predicted, white becomes black, freedom becomes slavery, and peace becomes "pre-hostilities." And the "war on terror" commits atrocities as inhumane as any by the "axis of evil."

Consider the phrase "coalition of the willing," used by the U.S. to describe the nations supporting the second invasion of Iraq in 2003. This turn of phrase described the commitment and popular support of more than 40 participating countries. However, the slogan tends to gloss over the uncomfortable reality that far more nations opposed the military action, as did the vast majority of citizens. In the context of these inconvenient truths, a phrase like "coalition of the willing" seems at best distorted, at worst, dishonest.

Point of view is critical for deciphering military rhetoric. With a gentle tweak of language, a good soldier can shape the appearance of reality, making his conduct shine, while slandering his opponent for the exact same action. The difference between "us" and "them" can be little more than a carefully chosen word. An adversary engages in espionage or spying; we conduct intelligence gathering. The enemy funds terrorists and mercenaries; we support freedom fighters and libertarians. They are ultra-nationals, partisans, and zealots; we are patriots and loyalists. They have weapons of mass destruction; we have nuclear deterrents (one of which is called—without a hint of irony—the "Peacekeeper"). They practise "censorship," while we enforce "reporting guidelines."

Below is a list of some sneaky military words. Alas, it's incomplete, and unlikely to ever be finished. As citizens grow wise to phrases like "collateral damage," the military invents new terms to "shock and awe" us into a cooperative stupor. In the end, the list is not as important as the skill of deciphering biased and deceptive language.

Military Term	Literal Meaning
Acceptable losses, Attrition	Death.
Aerial ordnance	Bombs and missiles.
Carpet bombing	Indiscriminate bombing that devastates an area.
Containment	Combat that leaves the enemy undefeated.
Decapitation strike	The assassination of a national leader. The decapitation strike against Saddam Hussein exposed this linguistic fraud when it described bombing of civilian targets.

(Continued)

Military Term	Literal Meaning
Degrading the enemy's capabilities for war	Destruction of enemy forces and civilian infrastructure: roads, sewage and water treatment plants, television and radio stations, etc. The term blurs differences between military and civilian targets, making it easier to attack the former.
Embedded reporters	A journalist assigned to a military unit, controlled and censored by the Armed Forces.
Ethnic cleansing	Genocide, the murder of people based on race or religion.
Friendly fire	Soldiers accidentally killed by their own troops.
Incursion	Invasion.
Liquidate	Killing, a depersonalization of murder.
Low intensity warfare	Combat that kills many enemy soldiers but few of your own.
Pacification/Peace-keeping forces	The use of military force.
Pre-emptive detention	Jail without a trial, legal representation or rights.
Pre-emptive strike/ Pre-emptive defence/ Anticipatory self defence	A first strike designed to cripple enemy forces before they can attack. The term transforms the aggressor into a defender.
Pre-hostility	Peace.
Protective reaction strike	Bombing.
Radiance of concussion	Bomb blast area, the term removes the human dimension of injury, and uses the glowing connotation of "radiance."
Security zone	Disputed territory occupied and policed by a military force.
Service the target	Kill, bomb, destroy, eviscerate.
Soft target	A target lacking heavy armour, making it easy to penetrate with weapons. The term may apply to anything from a truck, to a building, to a human being.

Military Term	Literal Meaning
Sorties	Bombing missions.
Spillover	Unintentional death and destruction, usually to civilians.
Transfer of population	The removal of indigenous people from their homelands.
Vertically deployed antipersonnel devices	Bombs.
Wet work	Assassination.

Can you guess the grim meanings behind the civilized veneer of the following military jargon?

Blowback
Collateral damage
Cointel
Counterinsurgency
Covert operations
Critical regions
Daisycutter
Detain
Disinformation
Divergent truths
Enhancing
democracy

Final solution
Forward deterrence
Free fire zone
Homicide bomber
Host-nation support
Insurgency
Military solution
New life hamlet
Paramilitary units
Pockets of
resistance
Police action

Precision bombing
Proactive
Preemptive
Operation group
Racial purification
Regime change
Smart bombs
Softening
Surgical strikes
Terminate

GOVERNMENT, CORPORATE, AND ECONOMIC EUPHEMISMS

"Smug, greedy well-fed white people have invented a language to conceal their sins. It's as simple as that."

—George Carlin

Like generals, politicians and CEOs often conceal nasty things in pleasant-sounding packages. Because politics and business interests don't always coincide with the public good, leaders resort to loaded language to foster support for their endeavours. At its extreme, such sloganeering conceals greed, crime, human rights violation, pollution, and misconduct. It's a perversion of language that leads to phrases such as the Clean Air Act to describe the amount of allowable pollution a factory can spew; or the Healthy Forest Initiative to describe the number of trees a lumber company can cut; or the Family Development Initiative Act to hide reduced funding for poor families; or "Green Lawn Strategies" to conceal the heavy use of pesticides; or "flexibility" and "choice" to direct our attention from cuts to public education.

Consider the sizeable vocabulary that CEOs have to describe the firing of workers. The public quickly figured out that "downsizing" meant more than lean corporations with muscular profits; it also meant unemployed workers, hungry families, and devastated neighbourhoods. "Right-sizing" removed the negative connotation of downsizing, just as "inplacement" improved upon "outplacement." From the PR flaks soon flowed a stream of baffling neologisms and misnomers to describe the same scenario: externalization, involuntary force reductions, managing down staff resources, rationalizing, re-engineering, restructuring, streamlining. The terms started to show refinement for special purposes. If a company needed to trim middle management, for example, it may "delayer." Perhaps the most euphemistic of the bunch, the word "empowered" describes a newly fired employee, who then may spend leisurely afternoons at the Career Placement Centre (previously the Unemployment Office).

The following examples of corporate and governmental doublespeak help us recognize the times when a politician or CEO is hawking shoddy wares.

Corporate Term	Literal Meaning
Biosolids	Sewage.
Constructive engagement/ Quiet diplomacy	Trade with a nation that violates human rights.
Decadent lumber/Over-mature forest	Old growth forests. The term presents uncut trees as sickly and wasteful, and ignores environmental, aesthetic, spiritual, and tourist values.
Economically disadvantaged	The poor.
Economic production zone (EPZ)	A walled slum of sweatshops, where workers sacrifice rights, health, and safety, in exchange for slave wages.
High net worth individuals	The rich.
Industrial effluvium/ Environmental contaminant	Pollution.
Labour flexibility	Lower pay, fewer benefits, and greater instability for workers.
Managed care	"Run-for-profit" health care.

Market correction	A sudden crash in stock prices.
Market forces	The power of money, millionaires, and monopolies to steer society. In the media, used almost always as a positive term.
Merger/Synergy	The creation of mega-corporations and monopolies that decrease consumer choice.
Negative gain/Negative cash flow	Loss.
Non-performing asset	Business failure.
Outsourcing	Closing manufacturing plants in North America in favour of cheaper plants in the third world to avoid high salaries as well as environmental and labour laws.
Perception or crisis management	The manipulation of public opinion: advertising, lobbying, propaganda, and lies.
Revenue enhancement	Tax increase.
Trickle-down economics	Massive tax breaks for the rich.
Wise use	The usual process of resource extraction that pays lip service to environmental concerns.
Working forest	A logging area.

What do you think government or industry means when using these loaded words?

Coherence	Free trade	Restatement of
Competition	Intellectual property	earnings
Demographic	Theft	Risk management
profiling	Plateauing	Solution
Deregulation	Privatization	Structural reform
Externalization	Public relations	

HOW TO COPE WITH BIASED LANGUAGE

When you spot emotionally charged language, ask a few vital questions.

- What does the word literally mean?
- Can the word be rephrased in more neutral fashion?

- Does my emotional response to the word differ from its literal meaning?
- Do my feelings interfere with understanding the idea?
- Why does the author spin the language? What purpose does it have? What does the connotative language tell us about the author's attitude?
- Is a harmful idea presented in an attractive fashion?
- Is a beneficial idea presented in a repellent manner?

By decoding connotative language, by restating it in denotative form, you better understand a subject, and free yourself from the tyranny of the author's perspective.

Exercises

1. Decide whether the words below carry a positive, negative, or neutral connotation. Try to find a neutral equivalent, an opposite meaning, or a less biased phrase.

    Anarchist
    Assimilation
    Beautician
    Comfort women
    Conservative
    Conspiracy theory
    Credibility gap
    Emissions
    Group home
    Gun control
    Harm reduction society
    Home-worker
    Housewife
    Invader species
    Landscaping engineer
    Liberal
    Male genital mutilation
    Monster home
    Mortician
    Negative patient care outcome
    New World
    Occupied territories/Disputed
        territories
    Organic
    Performance enhancers
    Prairie oysters
    Proletariat

Propaganda
Public relations officer
Queer
Radical feminist
Rake
Rape seed
Reactionary
Residential school
Sodomy
Spin doctor
Spinster
Tree hugger
Tree surgeon
Veal, Spotted Dick, Escargot

2. Identify the loaded terms in the following sentences, and then describe the actions or ideas that lurk behind the connotative language.

   a) A major relocation effort was implemented today, encouraging migrant Inuit to move to permanent reservations where the jobless could receive social amenities.

   b) In a volatile market, a successful corporation must remain flexible.

   c) Because the UN is soft on terror, it's in danger of losing relevance.

   d) Israeli defence forces entered the security zone and re-established the rule of law.

   e) Biopirates like Monsanto spread genetic and knowledge pollution.

   f) Creating a healthy climate for investment is the surest way to attack the causes of global poverty.

   g) "I was provided with additional input that was radically different from the truth. I assisted in furthering that version" (from Oliver North's Iran-Contra testimony).

   h) The livestock were dispatched and rendered into con-gestibles and meat by-products.

   i) Our intelligence confirms the presence of weapons-of-mass-destruction-related program activities, as well as an arsenal of tactics.

   j) Strays unsuccessful in the adoption process are euthanized.

   k) Market forces are at work making structural reforms and bureaucratic adjustments to enhance democracy and build the nation.

   l) Janet Jackson experienced a wardrobe malfunction during her half-time show.

3. Write a promotion for the following programs, all of which have measurable harm. Choose words carefully to create a positive impression, but don't lie.

a) Persuade a school board to install soft drink machines and fast-food franchises in elementary schools.
b) Legalize a device that sterilizes the mentally handicapped without their consent or knowledge.
c) Restart the seal hunt for the fur industry.
d) Advertise cigarettes directly and indirectly by sponsoring arts and sporting events.
e) Sell a new weapon that kills people efficiently.

4. Write a public statement for *both* sides of the following controversies, using strongly connotative language to smear your opponent, and glamourize your own position.

Pro-life/Pro-choice
Euthanasia
Censorship/Free speech
Protection of old growth forests
Genetic engineering
Cloning
Privatization of water/health/education
Whaling
Work for welfare
Gay adoption
Affirmative action
Mega-box stores

5. Discuss the connotations and meanings of the following:

Indian, Aboriginals, Primitives, Natives, Indigenous People, First Nations, Tribal People

What's the best term? Why?

With These Words I Can Sell You Anything

WILLIAM LUTZ

William Lutz is a fierce and funny critic of "Doublespeak," inflated and misleading language. For years, he edited the *Quarterly Review of Doublespeak*, and has authored several books that expose Orwellian language, including *Doublespeak*, *Doublespeak Defined*, and *The New*

Doublespeak. This excerpt looks at the ways advertisers manipulate language to deceive consumers.

One problem advertisers have when they try to convince you that the product they are pushing is really different from other, similar products is that their claims are subject to some laws. Not a lot of laws, but there are some designed to prevent fraudulent or untruthful claims in advertising. Even during the happy years of non-regulation under President Ronald Reagan, the FTC did crack down on the more blatant abuses in advertising claims. Generally speaking, advertisers have to be careful in what they say in their ads, in the claims they make for the products they advertise. Parity claims are safe because they are legal and supported by a number of court decisions. But beyond parity claims there are weasel words.

Advertisers use weasel words to appear to be making a claim for a product when in fact they are making no claim at all. Weasel words get their name from the way weasels eat the eggs they find in the nests of other animals. A weasel will make a small hole in the egg, suck out the insides, then place the egg back in the nest. Only when the egg is examined closely is it found to be hollow. That's the way it is with weasel words in advertising: Examine weasel words closely and you'll find that they're as hollow as any egg sucked by a weasel. Weasel words appear to say one thing when in fact they say the opposite, or nothing at all.

"HELP"—THE NUMBER ONE WEASEL WORD

The biggest weasel word used in advertising doublespeak is "help." Now "help" only means to aid or assist, nothing more. It does not mean to conquer, stop, eliminate, solve, heal, cure, or anything else. But once the ad says "help," it can say just about anything after that because "help" qualifies everything coming after it. The trick is that the claim that comes after the weasel word is usually so strong and so dramatic that you forget the word "help" and concentrate only on the dramatic claim. You read into the ad a message that the ad does not contain. More importantly, the advertiser is not responsible for the claim that you read into the ad, even though the advertiser wrote the ad so you would read that claim into it.

The next time you see an ad for a cold medicine that promises that it "helps relieve cold symptoms fast," don't rush out to buy it. Ask yourself what this claim is really saying. Remember, "helps" means only that the medicine will aid or assist. What will it aid or assist in doing? Why, "relieve" your cold "symptoms." "Relieve" only means to ease, alleviate, or mitigate, not to stop, end, or cure.

Nor does the claim say how much relieving this medicine will do. Nowhere does this ad claim it will cure anything. In fact, the ad doesn't even claim it will *do* anything at all. The ad only claims that it will aid in relieving (not curing) your cold symptoms, which are probably a runny nose, watery eyes, and a headache. In other words, this medicine probably contains a standard decongestant and some aspirin. By the way, what does "fast" mean? Ten minutes, one hour, one day? What is fast to one person can be very slow to another. Fast is another weasel word.

Ad claims using "help" are among the most popular ads. One says, "Helps keep you young looking," but then a lot of things will help keep you young looking, including exercise, rest, good nutrition, and a facelift. More importantly, this ad doesn't say the product will keep you young, only "young *looking."* Someone may look young to one person and old to another.

A toothpaste ad says, "Helps prevent cavities," but it doesn't say it will actually prevent cavities. Brushing your teeth regularly, avoiding sugars in foods, and flossing daily will also help prevent cavities. A liquid cleaner ad says, "Helps keep your home germ free," but it doesn't say it actually kills germs, nor does it even specify which germs it might kill.

"Help" is such a useful weasel word that it is often combined with other action-verb weasel words such as "fight" and "control." Consider the claim, "Helps control dandruff symptoms with regular use." What does it really say? It will assist in controlling (not eliminating, stopping, ending, or curing) the *symptoms* of dandruff, not the cause of dandruff nor the dandruff itself. What are the symptoms of dandruff? The ad deliberately leaves that undefined, but assume that the symptoms referred to in the ad are the flaking and itching commonly associated with dandruff. But just shampooing with *any* shampoo will temporarily eliminate these symptoms, so this shampoo isn't any different from any other. Finally, in order to benefit from this product, you must use it regularly. What is "regular use"—daily, weekly, hourly? Using another shampoo "regularly" will have the same effect. Nowhere does this advertising claim say this particular shampoo stops, eliminates, or cures dandruff. In fact, this claim says nothing at all, thanks to all the weasel words.

Look at ads in magazines and newspapers, listen to ads on radio and television, and you'll find the word "help" in ads for all kinds of products. How often do you read or hear such phrases as "helps stop . . . ," "helps overcome . . . ," "helps eliminate . . . ," "helps you feel . . . ," or "helps you look . . ."? If you start looking for this weasel word in advertising, you'll be amazed at how often it occurs. Analyze the claims in the ads using "help," and you will discover that these ads are really saying nothing.

There are plenty of other weasel words used in advertising. In fact, there are so many that to list them all would fill the rest of this book. But, in order to identify the doublespeak of advertising and understand the real meaning of an ad, you have to be aware of the most popular weasel words in advertising today.

VIRTUALLY SPOTLESS

One of the most powerful weasel words is "virtually," a word so innocent that most people don't pay any attention to it when it is used in an advertising claim. But watch out. "Virtually" is used in advertising claims that appear to make specific, definite promises when there is no promise. After all, what does "virtually" mean? It means "in essence of effect, although not in fact." Look at that definition again. "Virtually" means *not in fact*. It does *not* mean "almost" or "just about the same as," or anything else. And before you dismiss all this concern over such a small word, remember that small words can have big consequences.

In 1971 a federal court rendered its decision on a case brought by a woman who became pregnant while taking birth control pills. She sued the manufacturer, Eli Lilly and Company, for breach of warranty. The woman lost her case. Basing its ruling on a statement in the pamphlet accompanying the pills, which stated that, "When taken as directed, the tables offer virtually 100 percent protection," the court ruled that there was no warranty, expressed or implied, that the pills were absolutely effective. In its ruling, the court pointed out that, according to the *Webster's Third New International Dictionary*, "virtually" means "almost entirely" and clearly does not mean "absolute" (*Whittington v. Eli Lilly and Company*, 333 F. Supp. 98). In other words, the Eli Lilly company was really saying that its birth control pill, even when taken as directed, *did not in fact* provide 100 percent protection against pregnancy. But Eli Lilly didn't want to put it that way because then many women might not have bought Lilly's birth control pills.

The next time you see the ad that says that this dishwasher detergent "leaves dishes virtually spotless," just remember how advertisers twist the meaning of the weasel word "virtually." You can have lots of spots on your dishes after using this detergent and the ad claim will still be true, because what this claim really means is that this detergent does not *in fact* leave your dishes spotless. Whenever you see or hear an ad claim that uses the word "virtually," just translate that claim into its real meaning. So the television set that is "virtually trouble free" becomes the television set that is not in fact trouble free, the "virtually foolproof operation" of any appliance becomes an operation that is in fact not foolproof, and the product that "virtually never needs service" becomes the product that is not in fact service free.

NEW AND IMPROVED

If "new" is the most frequently used word on a product package, "improved" is the second most frequent. In fact, the two words are almost always used together. It seems just about everything sold these days is "new and improved." The next time you're in the supermarket, try counting the number of times you see these words on products. But you'd better do it while you're walking down just one aisle, otherwise you'll need a calculator to keep track of your counting.

Just what do these words mean? The use of the word "new" is restricted by regulations, so an advertiser can't just use the word on a product or in an ad without meeting certain requirements. For example, a product is considered new for about six months during a national advertising campaign. If the product is being advertised only in a limited test market area, the word can be used longer, and in some instances has been used for as long as two years.

What makes a product "new"? Some products have been around for a long time, yet every once in a while you discover that they are being advertised as "new." Well, an advertiser can call a product new if there has been "a material functional change" in the product. What is "a material functional change," you ask? Good question. In fact it's such a good question it's being asked all the time. It's up to the manufacturer to prove that the product has undergone such a change. And if the manufacturer isn't challenged on the claim, then there's no one to stop it. Moreover, the change does not have to be an improvement in the product. One manufacturer added an artificial lemon scent to a cleaning product and called it "new and improved," even though the product did not clean any better than without the lemon scent. The manufacturer defended the use of the word "new" on the grounds that the artificial scent changed the chemical formula of the product and therefore constituted "a material functional change."

Which brings up the word "improved." When used in advertising, "improved" does not mean "made better." It only means "changed" or "different from before." So, if the detergent maker puts a plastic pour spout on the box of detergent, the product has been "improved," and away we go with a whole new advertising campaign. Or, if the cereal maker adds more fruit or a different kind of fruit to the cereal, there's an improved product. Now you know why manufacturers are constantly making little changes in their products. Whole new advertising campaigns, designed to convince you that the product has been changed for the better, are based on small changes in superficial aspects of a product. The next time you see an ad for an "improved" product, ask yourself what was wrong with the old one. Ask yourself just how "improved" the product is. Finally, you might check to see whether the "improved" version costs more than the unimproved one. After all, someone has to pay for the millions of dollars spent advertising the improved product.

Of course, advertisers really like to run ads that claim a product is "new and improved." While what constitutes a "new" product may be subject to some regulation, "improved" is a subjective judgment. A manufacturer changes the shape of its stick deodorant, but the shape doesn't improve the function of the deodorant. That is, changing the shape doesn't affect the deodorizing ability of the deodorant, so the manufacturer calls it "improved." Another manufacturer adds ammonia to its liquid cleaner and calls it "new and improved." Since adding ammonia does affect the cleaning ability of the product, there has been a "material functional change" in the product, and the manufacturer can now call its cleaner "new," and "improved" as well. Now the weasel words "new and improved" are plastered all over the package and are the basis for a multimillion-dollar ad campaign. But after six months the word "new" will have to go, until someone can dream up another change in the product. Perhaps it will be adding color to the liquid, or changing the shape of the package, or maybe adding a new dripless pour spout, or perhaps a ———. The "improvements" are endless, and so are the new advertising claims and campaigns.

"New" is just too useful and powerful a word in advertising for advertisers to pass it up easily. So they use weasel words that say "new" without really saying it. One of their favorites is "introducing," as in, "Introducing improved Tide," or "Introducing the stain remover." The first is simply saying, here's our improved soap; the second, here's our new advertising campaign for our detergent. Another favorite is "now," as in, "Now there's Sinex," which simply means that Sinex is available. Then there are phrases like "Today's Chevrolet," "Presenting Dristan," and "A fresh way to start the day." The list is really endless because advertisers are always finding new ways to say "new" without really saying it. If there is a second edition of this book, I'll just call it the "new and improved" edition. Wouldn't you really rather have a "new and improved" edition of this book rather than a "second" edition?

ACTS FAST

"Acts" and "works" are two popular weasel words in advertising because they bring action to the product and to the advertising claim. When you see the ad for the cough syrup that "Acts on the cough control center," ask yourself what this cough syrup is claiming to do. Well, it's just claiming to "act," to do something, to perform an action. What is it that the cough syrup does? The ad doesn't say. It only claims to perform an action or do something on your "cough control center." By the way, what and where is your "cough control center"? I don't remember learning about that part of the body in human biology class.

Ads that use such phrases as "acts fast," "acts against," "acts to prevent," and the like are saying essentially nothing, because "act" is a word empty of any specific meaning. The ads are always careful not to specify exactly what "act" the product performs. Just because a brand of aspirin claims to "act fast" for headache relief doesn't mean this aspirin is any better than any other aspirin. What is the "act" that this aspirin performs? You're never told. Maybe it just dissolves quickly. Since aspirin is a parity product, all aspirin is the same and therefore functions the same.

WORKS LIKE ANYTHING ELSE

If you don't find the word "acts" in an ad, you will probably find the weasel word "works." In fact, the two words are almost interchangeable in advertising. Watch out for ads that say a product "works against," "works like," "works for," or "works longer." As with "acts," "works" is the same meaningless verb used to make you think that this product really does something, and maybe even something special or unique. But "works," like "acts," is basically a word empty of any specific meaning.

LIKE MAGIC

Whenever advertisers want you to stop thinking about the product and to start thinking about something bigger, better, or more attractive than the product, they use that very popular weasel word, "like." The word "like" is the advertiser's equivalent of a magician's use of misdirection. "Like" gets you to ignore the product and concentrate on the claim the advertiser is making about it. "For skin like peaches and cream" claims the ad for a skin cream. What is this ad really claiming? It doesn't say this cream will give you peaches-and-cream skin. There is no verb in this claim, so it doesn't even mention using the product. How is skin ever like "peaches and cream"? Remember, ads must be read literally and exactly, according to the dictionary definition of words. (Remember "virtually" in the Eli Lilly case.) The ad is making absolutely no promise or claim whatsoever for this skin cream. If you think this cream will give you soft, smooth, youthful-looking skin, you are the one who has read that meaning into the ad.

The wine that claims "It's like taking a trip to France" wants you to think about a romantic evening in Paris as you walk along the boulevard after a wonderful meal in an intimate little bistro. Of course, you don't really believe that a wine can take you to France, but the goal of the ad is to get you to think pleasant, romantic thoughts about France and not about how the wine tastes or how expensive it may be. That little word "like" has taken you away from crushed grapes into a world of your own imaginative making. Who knows, maybe the next time you buy wine, you'll think those pleasant thoughts when you see this brand of wine, and you'll buy it. Or, maybe you weren't even thinking about buying wine at all, but now you just might pick up a bottle the next time you're shopping. Ah, the power of "like" in advertising.

How about the most famous "like" claim of all, "Winston tastes good like a cigarette should"? Ignoring the grammatical error here, you might want to know what this claim is saying. Whether a cigarette tastes good or bad is a subjective judgment because what tastes good to one person may well taste horrible to another. Not everyone likes fried snails, even if they are called escargots. (*De gustibus non est disputandum*, which was probably the Roman rule for advertising as well as for defending the games in the Colosseum.) There are many people who say all cigarettes taste terrible, other people who say only some cigarettes taste all right, and still others who say all cigarettes taste good. Who's right? Everyone, because taste is a matter of personal judgment.

Moreover, note the use of the conditional, "should." The complete claim is, "Winston tastes good like a cigarette should taste." But should cigarettes taste good? Again, this is a matter of personal judgment and probably depends most on one's experiences with smoking. So, the Winston ad is simply saying that Winston cigarettes are just like any other cigarette: Some people like them and some people don't. On that statement, R. J. Reynolds conducted a very successful multimillion-dollar advertising campaign that helped keep Winston the number-two-selling cigarette in the United States, close behind number one, Marlboro.

CAN'T IT BE UP TO THE CLAIM?

Analyzing ads for doublespeak requires that you pay attention to every word in the ad and determine what each word really means. Advertisers try to wrap their claims in language that sounds concrete, specific, and objective, when in fact the language of advertising is anything but. Your job is to read carefully and listen critically so that when the announcer says that "Crest can be of significant value . . .," you know immediately that this claim says absolutely nothing. Where is the doublespeak in this ad? Start with the second word.

Once again, you have to look at what words really mean, not what you think they mean or what the advertiser wants you to think they mean. The ad for Crest only says that using Crest "can be" of "significant value." What really throws you off in this ad is the brilliant use of "significant." It draws your attention to the word "value" and makes you forget that the ad only claims that Crest "can be." The ad doesn't say that Crest *is* of value, only that it is "able" or "possible" to be of value, because that's all that "can" means.

It's so easy to miss the importance of those little words, "can be." Almost as easy as missing the importance of the words "up to" in an ad. These words are very popular in sales ads. You know, the ones that say, "Up to 50 percent Off!" Now, what does that claim mean? Not much, because the store or manufacturer has to reduce the price of only a few items by 50 percent. Everything else can be reduced a lot less, or not even reduced. Moreover, don't you want to know 50 percent off of what? Is it 50 percent off the "manufacturer's suggested list price," which is the highest possible price? Was the price artificially inflated and then reduced? In other ads, "up to" expresses an ideal situation. The medicine that works "up to ten times faster," the battery that lasts "up to twice as long," and the soap that gets you "up to twice as clean" all are based on ideal situations for using those products, situations in which you can be sure you will never find yourself.

UNFINISHED WORDS

Unfinished words are a kind of "up to" claim in advertising. The claim that a battery lasts "up to twice as long" usually doesn't finish the comparison—twice as long as what? A birthday candle? A tank of gas? A cheap battery made in a country not noted for its technological achievements? The implication is that the battery last twice as long as batteries made by other battery makers, or twice as long as earlier model batteries made by the advertiser, but the ad doesn't really make these claims. You read these claims into the ad, aided by the visual images the advertiser so carefully provides.

Unfinished words depend on you to finish them, to provide the words the advertisers so thoughtfully left out of the ad. Pall Mall cigarettes were once advertised as "A longer finer and milder smoke." The question is, longer, finer, and milder than what? The aspirin that claims it contains "Twice as much of the pain reliever doctors recommend most" doesn't tell you what pain reliever it contains twice as much of. (By the way, it's aspirin. That's right; it just contains twice the amount of aspirin. And how much is twice the amount? Twice of what amount?) Panadol boasts that "nobody reduces fever faster," but, since Panadol is a parity product, this claim simply means that Panadol isn't any better than any other product in its parity class. "You can be sure if it's Westinghouse," you're told, but just exactly what it is you can be sure of is never mentioned. "Magnavox gives you more" doesn't tell you what you get more of. More value? More television? More than they gave you before? It sounds nice, but it means nothing, until you fill in the claim with your own words, the words the advertisers didn't use. Since each of us fills in the claim differently, the ad and the product can become all things to all people, and not promise a single thing.

Unfinished words abound in advertising because they appear to promise so much. More importantly, they can be joined with powerful visual images on television to appear to be making significant promises about a product's effectiveness without really making any promises. In a television ad, the aspirin product that claims fast relief can show a person with a headache taking the product and then, in what appears to be a matter of minutes, claiming complete relief. This visual image is far more powerful than any claim made in unfinished words. Indeed, the visual image completes the unfinished words for you, filling in with pictures what the words leave out. And you thought that ads didn't affect you. What brand of aspirin do you use?

Some years ago, Ford's advertisements proclaimed "Ford LTD—700 percent quieter." Now, what do you think Ford was claiming with these unfinished words? What was the Ford LTD quieter than? A Cadillac? A Mercedes Benz? A BMW? Well, when the FTC asked Ford to substantiate this unfinished claim, Ford replied that it meant that the inside of the LTD was 700 percent quieter than the outside. How did you finish those unfinished words when you first read them? Did you even come close to Ford's meaning?

COMBINING WEASEL WORDS

A lot of ads don't fall neatly into one category or another because they use a variety of different devices and words. Different weasel words are often combined to make an ad claim. The claim, "Coffee-Mate gives coffee more body, more flavor," uses Unfinished Words ("more" than what?) and also uses words that have no specific meaning ("body" and "flavor"). Along with "taste" (remember the Winston ad and its claim to taste good), "body" and "flavor" mean nothing because their meaning is entirely subjective. To you, "body" in coffee might mean thick, black, almost bitter coffee, while I might take it to mean a light brown, delicate coffee. Now, if you think you understood that last sentence, read it again, because it said nothing of objective value; it was filled with weasel words of no specific meaning: "thick," "black," "bitter," "light brown," and "delicate." Each of those words has no specific, objective meaning, because each of us can interpret them differently.

Try this slogan: "Looks, smells, tastes like ground-roast coffee." So, are you now going to buy Taster's Choice instant coffee because of this ad? "Looks," "smells," and "tastes" are all words with no specific meaning and depend on your interpretation of them for any meaning. Then there's that great weasel word "like," which simply suggests a comparison but does not make the actual connection between the product and the quality. Besides, do you know what "ground-roast" coffee is? I don't, but it sure sounds good. So, out of seven words in this ad, four are definite weasel words, two are quite meaningless, and only one has any clear meaning.

Remember the Anacin ad—"Twice as much of the pain reliever doctors recommend most"? There's a whole lot of weaseling going on in this ad. First, what's the pain reliever they're talking about in this ad? Aspirin, of course. In fact, any time you see or hear an ad using those words "pain reliever," you can automatically substitute the word "aspirin" for them. (Makers of acetaminophen and ibuprofen pain relievers are careful in their advertising to identify their products as nonaspirin products.) So, now we know that Anacin has aspirin in it. Moreover, we know that Anacin has twice as much aspirin in it, but we don't know twice as much as what. Does it have twice as much aspirin as an ordinary aspirin tablet? If so, what is an ordinary aspirin tablet, and how much aspirin does it contain? Twice as much as Excedrin or Bufferin? Twice as much as a chocolate chip cookie? Remember those Unfinished Words and how they lead you on without saying anything.

Finally, what about those doctors who are doing all that recommending? Who are they? How many of them are there? What kind of doctors are they? What are their qualifications? Who asked them about recommending pain relievers? What other pain relievers did they recommend? And there are a whole lot more questions about this "poll" of doctors to which I'd like to know the answers, but you get the point. Sometimes, when I call my doctor, she tells me to take two aspirin and call her office in the morning. Is that where Anacin got this ad?

READ THE LABEL, OR THE BROCHURE

Weasel words aren't just found on television, on the radio, or in newspaper and magazine ads. Just about any language associated with a product will contain the doublespeak of advertising. Remember the Eli Lilly case and the doublespeak on the information sheet that came with the birth control pills. Here's another example.

In 1983, the Estée Lauder cosmetics company announced a new product called "Night Repair." A small brochure distributed with the product stated that "Night Repair was scientifically formulated in Estée Lauder's U.S. laboratories as part of the Swiss Age-Controlling Skincare Program. Although only nature controls the aging process, this program helps control the signs of aging and encourages skin to look and feel younger." You might want to read these two sentences again, because they sound great but say nothing.

First, note that the product was "scientifically formulated" in the company's laboratories. What does that mean? What constitutes a scientific formulation? You wouldn't expect the company to say that the product was casually, mechanically, or carelessly formulated, or just thrown together one day when the people in the white coats didn't have anything better to do. But the word "scientifically" lends an air of precision and promise that just isn't there.

It is the second sentence, however, that's really weasely, both syntactically and semantically. The only factual part of this sentence is the introductory dependent clause—"only nature controls the aging process." Thus, the only fact in the ad is relegated to a dependent clause, a clause dependent on the main clause, which contains no factual or definite information at all and indeed purports to contradict the independent clause. The new "skincare program" (notice it's not a skin cream but a "program") does not claim to stop or even retard the aging process. What, then, does Night Repair, at a price of over $35 (in 1983 dollars) for a .87-ounce bottle do? According to this brochure, nothing. It only "helps," and the brochure does not say how much it helps. Moreover, it only "helps control," and then it only helps control the "*signs* of aging," not the aging itself. Also, it "encourages" skin not to *be* younger but only to "look and feel" younger. The brochure does not say younger than what. Of the sixteen words in the main clause of this second sentence, nine are weasel words. So, before you spend all that money for Night Repair, or any other cosmetic product, read the words carefully, and then decide if you're getting what you think you're paying for.

OTHER TRICKS OF THE TRADE

Advertisers' use of doublespeak is endless. The best way advertisers can make something out of nothing is through words. Although there are a lot of visual images used on television and in magazines and newspapers, every advertiser wants to create that memorable line that will stick in the public consciousness. I am sure pure joy reigned in one advertising agency when a study found that children who were asked to spell the word "relief" promptly and proudly responded "r-o-l-a-i-d-s."

The variations, combinations, and permutations of doublespeak used in advertising go on and on, running from the use of rhetorical questions ("Wouldn't you really rather have a Buick?" "If you can't trust Prestone, who can you trust?") to flattering you with compliments ("The lady has taste." "We think a cigar smoker is someone special." "You've come a long way baby."). You know, of course, how you're *supposed* to answer those questions, and you know that those compliments are just leading up to the sales pitches for the products. Before you dismiss such tricks of the trade as obvious, however, just remember that all of these statements and questions were part of very successful advertising campaigns.

A more subtle approach is the ad that proclaims a supposedly unique quality for a product, a quality that really isn't unique. "If it doesn't say Goodyear, it can't be polyglas." Sounds good, doesn't it? Polyglas is available only from Goodyear because Goodyear copyrighted that trade name. Any other tire manufacturer could make exactly the same tire but could not call it "polyglas," because that would be copyright infringement. "Polyglas" is simply Goodyear's name for its fiberglass-reinforced tire.

Since we like to think of ourselves as living in a technologically advanced country, science and technology have a great appeal in selling products. Advertisers are quick to use scientific doublespeak to push their products. There are all kinds of elixirs, additives, scientific potions, and mysterious mixtures added to all kinds of products. Gasoline contains "HTA," "F–130," "Platformate," and other chemical-sounding additives, but nowhere does an advertisement give any real information about the additive.

Shampoo, deodorant, mouthwash, cold medicine, sleeping pills, and any number of other products all seem to contain some special chemical ingredient that allows them to work wonders. "Certs contains a sparkling drop of Retsyn." So what? What's "Retsyn"? What's it do? What's so special about it? When they don't have a secret ingredient in their product, advertisers still find a way to claim scientific validity. There's "Sinarest. Created by a research scientist who actually gets sinus headaches." Sounds nice, but what kind of research does this scientist do? How do you know if she is any kind of expert on sinus medicine? Besides, this ad doesn't tell you a thing about the medicine itself and what it does.

ADVERTISING DOUBLESPEAK QUICK QUIZ

Now it's time to test your awareness of advertising doublespeak. (You didn't think I would just let you read this and forget it, did you?) The following is a list of statements from some recent ads. Your job is to figure out what each of these ads really says.

DOMINO'S PIZZA: "Because nobody delivers better."
SINUTAB: "It can stop the pain."
TUMS: "The stronger acid neutralizer."
MAXIMUM STRENGTH DRISTAN: "Strong medicine for tough sinus colds."
LISTERMINT: "Making your mouth a cleaner place."
CASCADE: "For virtually spotless dishes nothing beats Cascade."
NUPRIN: "Little. Yellow. Different. Better."
ANACIN: "Better relief."
SUDAFED: "Fast sinus relief that won't put you fast asleep."
ADVIL: "Better relief."
PONDS COLD CREAM: "Ponds cleans like no soap can."
MILLER LITE BEER: "Tastes great. Less filling."
PHILIPS MILK OF MAGNESIA: "Nobody treats you better than MOM (Philips Milk of Magnesia)."
BAYER: "The wonder drug that works wonders."
CRACKER BARREL: "Judged to be the best."

KNORR: "Where taste is everything."
ANUSOL: "Anusol is the word to remember for relief."
DIMETAPP: "It relieves kids as well as colds."
LIQUID DRANO: "The liquid strong enough to be called Drano."
JOHNSON & JOHNSON BABY POWDER: "Like magic for your skin."
PURITAN: "Make it your oil for life."
PAM: "Pam, because how you cook is as important as what you cook."
IVORY SHAMPOO AND CONDITIONER: "Leave your hair feeling Ivory clean."
TYLENOL GEL-CAPS: "It's not a capsule. It's better."
ALKA-SELTZER PLUS: "Fast, effective relief for winter colds."

THE WORLD OF ADVERTISING

In the world of advertising, people wear "dentures," not false teeth; they suffer from "occasional irregularity," not constipation; they need deodorants for their "nervous wetness," not for sweat; they use "bathroom tissue," not toilet paper; and they don't dye their hair, they "tint" or "rinse" it. Advertisements offer "real counterfeit diamonds" without the slightest hint of embarrassment, or boast of goods made out of "genuine imitation leather" or "virgin vinyl."

In the world of advertising, the girdle becomes a "body shaper," "form persuader," "control garment," "controller," "outerwear enhancer," "body garment," or "anti-gravity panties," and is sold with such trade names as "The Instead," "The Free Spirit," and "The Body Briefer."

A study some years ago found the following words to be among the most popular used in U.S. television advertisements: "new," "improved," "better," "extra," "fresh," "clean," "beautiful," "free," "good," "great," and "light." At the same time, the following words were found to be among the most frequent on British television: "new," "good-better-best," "free," "fresh," "delicious," "full," "sure," "clean," "wonderful," and "special." While these words may occur most frequently in ads, and while ads may be filled with weasel words, you have to watch out for all the words used in advertising, not just the words mentioned here.

Every word in an ad is there for a reason; no word is wasted. Your job is to figure out exactly what each word is doing in an ad—what each word really means, not what the advertiser wants you to think it means. Remember, the ad is trying to get you to buy a product, so it will put the product in the best possible light, using any device, trick, or means legally allowed. Your own defense against advertising (besides taking up permanent residence on the moon) is to develop and use a strong critical reading, listening, and looking ability. Always ask yourself what the ad is *really* saying. When you see ads on television, don't be misled by the pictures, the visual images. What does the ad say about the product? What does the ad *not* say? What information is missing from the ad? Only by becoming an active, critical consumer of the doublespeak of advertising will you ever be able to cut through the doublespeak and discover what the ad is really saying.

Professor Del Kehl of Arizona State University has updated the Twenty-third Psalm to reflect the power of advertising to meet our needs and solve our problems. It seems fitting that this chapter close with this new Psalm.

The Adman's 23rd
The Adman is my shepherd;
I shall ever want.
He maketh me to walk a mile for a Camel;
He leadeth me beside Crystal Waters
   In the High Country of Coors;
He restoreth my soul with Perrier.
He guideth me in Marlboro Country
For Mammon's sake.
Yea, though I walk through the Valley of the
   Jolly Green Giant,
In the shadow of B.O., halitosis, indigestion,
   headache pain, and hemorrhoidal tissue,
I will fear no evil,
For I am in Good Hands with Allstate;
Thy Arid, Scope, Tums, Tylenol, and Preparation H—
They comfort me.
Stouffer's preparest a table before the TV
In the presence of all my appetites;
Thou anointest my head with Brylcream;
My Decaffeinated Cup runneth over.
Surely surfeit and security shall follow me
All the days of Metropolitan Life,
And I shall dwell in a Continental Home
With a mortgage forever and ever.
Amen.

Words That Wound

EMIL SHER

Emil Sher is a Toronto-based author who writes in a variety of genres, including drama, fiction, screenplays, and the essay. In this piece, Sher ponders the emotional force and the contradictions of the word "primitive."

I lived in an African village for two years. As I search for the words that are faithful to what I experienced, words that capture the poetry of rural Botswana, there is one I won't use. On the printed page, it's an irritant to my eyes, a thorn that pricks at my skin. Spoken, it leaves a bitter taste in my mouth. The word is "primitive."

Bobonong is a sprawling village nestled between the borders of Zimbabwe and South Africa. It's blessed with the most beautiful sunsets this side of heaven, and has all the characteristics many Canadians would call primitive. The Batswana build their traditional homes as they have for centuries, with round walls moulded from mud and thatch. With few exceptions there is no indoor plumbing or electricity. Villagers fetch water from communal taps. Women with perfect posture balance buckets on their heads in regal processions that wind through a maze of huts. Tired donkeys pull carts along unpaved roads as rough as the washboards used to scrub laundry. Meals are prepared over hot coals that flicker in the night like fireflies.

It could all look so "primitive." But I've learned that there are different ways of seeing. Life in industrialized countries comes with a risk: a severe case of myopia. We gaze at the Bobonongs scattered around the world through lenses framed in rigid assumptions. We see a way of life "less developed" than ours. We see people eating with their hands and smugly wave our forks. We see people walking comfortably in barefeet and tap our leather shoes.

As we look on in judgement of others, we lose sight of ourselves. I don't know how the Batswana would say "appalled," but I do know that's how many would feel if they saw how we treat the elderly amongst us. They don't ship the older ones in their communities to homes for the aged; there aren't any. In Botswana, the word "nuclear" had only one meaning for me: communal families of three generations, tightly bound by the spirit of collective care.

Back home, where technology thrived, I knew that nuclear referred not only to families, but to weapons of destruction that could tear them apart. Mothers in Botswana would surely be puzzled and amused to learn that public breastfeeding is still taboo in Canada. They nurse their babies wherever they happen to be—on buses, in shops, in the comfort of a neighbour's yard. And no one bats an eye.

At the end of a long day, teenagers often gather in school yards. They meet not to sniff and smoke but to sing and dance. Some keep the rhythm on a goatskin stretched over an oil can. Others wear traditional rattles around their ankles. A shoeless train of feet rumbles along tracks of dry soil, and clouds of dust mingle with voices sweet and pure. Few of their younger sisters or brothers have the electronic toys sold here in suburban malls. Resourceful village children twist wire and empty beer cans into toy cars with waist-high steering mechanisms that actually work.

The word "primitive" doesn't sit well with me anymore. I need to find one that does justice to the way others live. For the pen is mightier than the sword, and words have the power to wound.

Now Here's a Bright Idea!

RICHARD DAWKINS

Richard Dawkins is an assistant professor of zoology and author of popular evolution and biology books, including *The Selfish Gene* and *The Blind Watchmaker*. Dawkins suggests that cultures have something akin to genetic material, "memes," ideas and practices that help societies survive. One such "meme" is rational skepticism, which comes across clearly in Dawkins' promotion of a positive term for "atheist."

I once read a science fiction story in which astronauts voyaging to a distant star were waxing homesick: "Just to think that it's springtime back on Earth!" You may not immediately see what's wrong with that comment, so ingrained is our unconscious Northern Hemisphere chauvinism. Unconscious is exactly right. That is where consciousness-raising comes in.

I suspect it is for a deeper reason than gimmicky fun that, in Australia and New Zealand, you can buy maps of the world with the South Pole on top. Now, wouldn't that be an excellent thing to pin to our classroom walls instead of the Ten Commandments?

What a splendid consciousness-raiser. Day after day, children would be reminded that North has no monopoly on up. The map on the wall would intrigue them as well as raise their consciousness. They'd go home and tell their parents.

The feminists taught us about consciousness-raising. I used to laugh at "him or her," and at "chairperson," and I still try to avoid them on aesthetic grounds. But I recognize the power and importance of consciousness-raising. I now flinch at the phrase "One man, one vote." My consciousness has been raised. Probably yours has, too, and it matters.

I used to deplore what I regarded as the tokenism of my American atheist friends. They were obsessed with removing the recently inserted "under God" from the Pledge of Allegiance, whereas I cared more about the chauvinistic nastiness of pledging allegiance to a flag in the first place. They would cross out "In God We Trust" on every dollar bill that passed through their hands, whereas I worried more about the tax-free dollars amassed by bouffant-haired televangelists, fleecing nice gullible people of their life savings. My friends would risk neighborhood ostracism to protest the unconstitutionality of Ten Commandments posters on classroom walls. "But it's only words," I would expostulate. "Why get so worked up about mere words, when there's so much else to object to?" Now I'm having second thoughts. Words are not trivial. They matter because they raise consciousness.

My own favorite consciousness-raising effort is one I have mentioned many times before (and I make no apology, for consciousness-raising is all about repetition). A phrase like "Catholic child" or "Muslim child" should clang furious bells of protest in the mind, just as we flinch when we hear "One man, one vote." Children are too young to know their religious opinions. Just as you can't vote until you are eighteen, you should be free to choose your own cosmology and ethics without society's impertinent presumption that you will automatically inherit those of your parents. We'd be aghast to be told of a Leninist child or a neo-conservative child or a Hayekian monetarist child. So isn't it a kind of child abuse to speak of a Catholic child or a Protestant child? Especially in Northern Ireland and Glasgow, where such labels, handed down over generations, have divided neighborhoods for centuries and can even amount to a death warrant?

Catholic child? Flinch. Protestant child? Squirm. Muslim child? Shudder. Everybody's consciousness should be raised to this level. Occasionally a euphemism is needed, and I suggest "Child of Jewish (etc.) parents." When you come down to it, that's all we are really talking about anyway. Just as the upside-down (Northern

Hemisphere chauvinism again: flinch!) map from New Zealand raises consciousness about a geographical truth, children should hear themselves described not as "Christian children" but as "children of Christian parents." This in itself would raise their consciousness, empower them to make up their own minds, and choose which religion, if any, they favor, rather than just assume that religion means "same beliefs as parents." I could well imagine that this linguistically coded freedom to choose might lead children to choose no religion at all.

Please go out and work at raising people's consciousness over the words they use to describe children. At a dinner party, say, if ever you hear a person speak of a school for Islamic children, or Catholic children (you can read such phrases daily in newspapers), pounce: "How dare you? You would never speak of a neo-conservative Republican child or a liberal Democrat child, so how could you describe a child as Catholic (Islamic, Protestant, etc.)?" With luck, everybody at the dinner party, next time they hear one of those offensive phrases, will flinch, or at least notice, and the meme will spread.

A triumph of consciousness-raising has been the homosexual hijacking of the word gay. I used to mourn the loss of gay in (what I still think of as) its true sense. But on the bright side (wait for it), gay has inspired a new imitator, which is the climax of this article. Gay is succinct, uplifting, positive: an "up" word, whereas homosexual is a down word, and queer, faggot, and pooftah are insults. Those of us who subscribe to no religion; those of us whose view of the universe is natural rather than supernatural; those of us who rejoice in the real and scorn the false comfort of the unreal, we need a word of our own, a word like gay. You can say, "I am an atheist," but at best it sounds stuffy (like "I am a homosexual") and at worst it inflames prejudice (like "I am a homosexual"). Paul Geisert and Mynga Futrell of Sacramento, California, have set out to coin a new word, a new gay. Like gay, it is a noun hijacked from an adjective, with its original meaning changed, but not too much. Like gay, it is catchy: a potentially prolific meme. Like gay, it will offend sticklers for punctilious rectitude such as me, but it might be worth it nevertheless. Like gay, it is positive, warm, cheerful, bright.

Bright? Yes, bright. Bright is the word, the new noun. I am a Bright. You are a Bright. She is a Bright. We are the Brights. Isn't it about time you came out as a Bright? Is he a Bright? I can't imagine falling for a woman who is not a Bright. http://www.celebatheists.com/ suggests that numerous intellectuals and other famous people are Brights. Brights constitute 60 percent of American scientists, and more than 90 percent of those scientists good enough to be elected to the elite National Academy of Sciences are Brights. Look on the bright side: though at present they can't admit it and get elected, the U.S. Congress must be full of closet Brights. As with the Gays, the more Brights come out, the easier it will be for yet more Brights to do so.

Geisert and Futrell are very insistent that their word is a noun and must not be an adjective. "I am bright" sounds arrogant. "I am a Bright" sounds too unfamiliar to be arrogant: it is puzzling, enigmatic, tantalizing. It invites the question, "What on earth is a Bright?" And then you're away:

"A Bright is a person whose worldview is free of supernatural and mystical elements. The ethics and actions of a Bright are based on a naturalistic worldview."

"You mean a Bright is an atheist?"

"Well, some Brights are happy to call themselves atheists. Some Brights call themselves agnostics. Some call themselves humanists, some freethinkers. But all Brights have a worldview that is free of supernaturalism and mysticism."

"Oh, I get it. It's a bit like 'Gay.' So what's the opposite of a Bright? What would you call a religious person?"

"What do you suggest?"

Of course, even though we Brights will scrupulously insist that our word is a noun, if it catches on it is likely to follow gay and eventually re-emerge as a new adjective. And when that happens, who knows, we may finally get a bright president.

IBM Emancipates 8,000 Wage Slaves

THE ONION

The Onion is a satiric newspaper published weekly out of Madison, Wisconsin. An excellent mimic, *The Onion* often uses the language of government, business, and journalism against itself, as it does in this piece where a massive layoff appears as a boon to workers. The euphemistic language is exaggerated, but like most satire, contains much truth.

ARMONK, NY—In a move hailed by corporation owners as a forward-thinking humanitarian gesture, IBM emancipated more than 8,000 wage slaves from its factories and offices Monday.

"You are all free, free to go!" said IBM CEO Samuel J. Palmisano to the 600 men and women freed from the corporation's Essex Junction, VT, location. "No more must you live a bleak, hand-to-mouth existence, chained to your desks in a never-ending Monday-through-Friday, 9-to-5 cycle. Your future is wide-open. Now, go!"

The 600 newly freed workers cleared out their desks and were escorted from the building within an hour. In spite of Palmisano's jubilance, the emancipated wage slaves were strangely quiet as they filed into the parking lot, carrying their work possessions in cardboard boxes.

"I'll miss them," said Jim Tallman, manager of IBM's plant in Rochester, MN.

Tallman, who was ordered to set 150 of his factory's wage slaves free, added, "They were hard workers. Many of them were extremely intelligent. Some were like members of the family. But I know in my heart that having them here was a crime against human resources. The world is changing, especially the economy, and no decent businessman could look at the cost-benefit analysis and not see that turning them loose was the only thing to do."

Palmisano explained that, while IBM posted profits for its second quarter, its microelectronics sector lost money due to a sharp downturn in the industry. The corporation also freed wage slaves from plants in Endicott, NY; Austin, TX; and Raleigh, NC.

Public response to the emancipation has been largely positive, particularly among the company's shareholders. Value of IBM stock jumped 7.5 percent in the hours following the historic corporate-emancipation proclamation.

Business leaders have enthusiastically praised the wage-slave release.

"In these days of streamlined, modern business, wage slavery is an increasingly peculiar institution," CNN national business correspondent and arbitrage guru Mike Boettcher said. "We owe these poor, exploited people a chance to try to make it on their own merits. It's not right to work them to their deaths, or even to the usual retirement age of 67."

Palmisano said the move, although sudden, came at the right time.

"There is no reason for a modern-day John Henry to spend his life trying to out-spreadsheet an IBM business machine," Palmisano said. "Especially since our computers, properly programmed and equipped, can handle the accounting workload of hundreds of human beings."

Upon hearing the news, many of the liberated wage slaves expressed trepidation over their uncertain futures.

"I don't know what I'm even supposed to do now," said Essex Junction's Anne Porter, 36. "I was born into a family of wage slaves. I've never known anything but wage slavery. I barely own anything more than the clothes on my back and the other, almost identical business-casual pantsuits hanging in the closet of my studio apartment."

"On the other hand, I'll never have to see that whip-cracking quality-assurance overseer again," Porter added.

President Bush hailed IBM's decision in an address to the White House press corps Monday.

"No one said freedom was easy," said Bush, who in recent months has praised wage-slave-emancipation programs initiated by Eastman Kodak, Sun Microsystems, AT&T, General Motors, Daimler-Chrysler, Ford, Boeing, General Mills, and Oracle. "But doing what's best for the corporation as a whole eventually benefits us all. This is what America is all about. I wish all the newly freed wage slaves the best of luck in their bright new futures."

Wall Street Journal analyst J. Craig Hoffman praised the emancipation.

"In a truly modern capitalist nation, letting people go is the only right thing to do," Hoffman said. "Certainly, IBM could have kept those poor wretches slaving away for the company, as some have been doing for the past 30 years. But, we must ask, at what cost?"

"Actually, $47,643 average annual overhead per worker, counting salary, benefits, and projected cost of pension or 401K co-payments, adjusted for inflation over the wage-slaves' useful lifespan, as it turns out," Hoffman added.

Definition

> *"When I use a word,"* Humpty Dumpty said, *in rather a scornful tone,* *"it means just what I choose it to mean—neither more nor less."*
>
> *"The question is,"* said Alice, *"whether you can make words mean so many different things."*
>
> *"The question is,"* said Humpty Dumpty, *"which is to be master— that's all."*
>
> —Lewis Carroll, *Through the Looking-Glass*

The previous chapter looked at the gap between a word's connotation and its literal meaning. Unfortunately, denotative language isn't a trouble-free guide to truth. A definition from a dictionary, government, medical journal, or legal text may be as subjective and misleading as its connotative counterpart. What's worse, we tend to accept definitions as objective facts and so are less aware of potential bias—a situation that makes definitions a tricky bit of linguistic waters.

ARBITRARY DEFINITIONS

The first feature to recognize in definition is its arbitrary nature. A dictionary seldom spells out an objective and eternal truth. On the contrary, things change radically depending on *how* they're defined. Consider something as common and familiar as the kilogram. We use this unit everyday, but what is it? How was it set? Originally, scientists conceived of the kilogram as the weight of 1 litre of water, but abandoned this reference as unstable. In 1889, they commissioned the construction of a platinum-iridium cylinder to become the new universal standard for the kilogram. They chose the inert metal block partly because of its stability, but to a great degree their choice of material, size, and shape was arbitrary, as was the choice of a litre of water. The kilogram could be defined as anything, as long as the definition remained a fixed referent point for all to follow. In 2003, scientists again changed the standard for the kilogram (the platinum-iridium cylinder is losing microscopic amounts of weight), but it matters little, for the kilogram has no intrinsic or natural meaning. Neither does the second, the metre, or the other metric units, all of which have changed over the years. They work purely as an arbitrary choice, a steady benchmark for scientists (Pohl).

Many cultural definitions work in the same way—not as a reflection of pre-existing reality, but as a royal decree, an official "Make it so." Such definitions aren't *descriptive* so much as *prescriptive*— they work as rules in a game that guide and allow play, behaving like rules in a hockey game. The hockey community grants the referee a limited infallibility to call goals, penalties, and infractions, so that the game can continue without endless harangue and bickering. The infallibility of the referee enables the play of the game. In a similar manner, the definition of a universal and stable kilogram allows scientists to play the research and measurement game. The infallibility of the Pope forms one game rule of Catholicism, just as the authority of the judge is a condition of the legal game. And if one wants to enjoy the communication game, one uses the communal, dictionary meaning of words. Such decrees, rulings, fiats, and declarations allow for the smooth functioning of society.

While definitions by decree might be socially useful, they're not necessarily true in any physical sense. They remain arbitrary, sometimes even random impositions. In such cases, we need to remember that referees make bad calls from time to time, and such decisions can be overturned.

SUBJECTIVE DEFINITIONS

"How many legs does a dog have if you call the tail a leg? Four. Calling a tail a leg doesn't make it a leg."

—Abraham Lincoln

Students tend to consider reference works as sources of objective information, but such texts often have a set point of view, personality, or bias. A British dictionary such as *Oxford's* spells words differently than an American one such as *Webster's*, different again from a Canadian one such as *Gage*. The national dialects create alternative yet equally "authoritative" spellings. This point-of-view invariably affects the meanings listed in any dictionary, encyclopedia, or reference work, despite their reputation for objectivity and neutrality. Samuel Johnson was hardly impartial when his dictionary (the first in history) defined oats as "a grain, which in England is generally given to horses, but in Scotland supports the people" (Crystal 209). Today the definitions of vital terms such as pornography, madness, terrorism, pollution, and harassment differ significantly depending upon which authority you cite. Rather than accept definitions as an authoritative answer, we should ask, "Who defined this?" Or more specifically, "What influence has the author's character, interests, finances, and culture had on the definition?"

The subjective nature of definition becomes painfully clear when we look at national sovereignty. In the Middle East, Palestinians claim that Israel has no right to the historic lands of Palestine and its people. In contrast, Israel refuses to recognize the existence of Palestine, suggesting that it's not a people, a land, or a nation. The definition of sovereignty in the Middle East depends greatly on *whom* you ask, and *what* authority is evoked. Similar disputes have happened in Canada, as Aboriginal groups have questioned the legitimacy of colonial rule.

The subjective spirit of definition appears even in the supposedly objective disciplines of science and medicine. Fans of gay-themed TV shows such as *Queer Eye for the Straight Guy* are surprised to discover that the medical community considered homosexuality a mental illness for most of the 20th century. As late as the 1990s, the American Psychiatric Association (APA) listed homosexuality as a sexual deviancy in its encyclopedic reference work, *The Diagnostic Statistical Manual of Mental Disorders* (DSM). The DSM acts as the bible of the psychiatric industry; once this authoritative text lists a condition, the medical community largely accepts it as a legitimate illness. Labelled as sick by the DSM, many gay men and women received medical therapy for their sexual orientation, including counselling, drug regimes, confinement, negative reinforcement, and in the first part of the century, electro-shock treatment or lobotomy.

Not surprisingly, gay people tended to disagree with the APA's classification of homosexuality as a disease. Unlike a real mental illness, they argued, homosexuality doesn't impair a person's ability to function in society. Furthermore, most queer people are happy with their sexual orientation, not distressed by it. Most discomfort associated with homosexuality comes from the homophobic culture that persecutes gays.

If homosexuality harms none, why did the APA classify it as pathology? In part, the answer lies in the dubious assumptions and biases of those early psychiatrists. Using the cultural norm as a reference, scientists tended to see heterosexuality as natural, and homosexuality as an aberration; they saw gays as "abnormal" not just in the numerical sense as a minority population; statistical deviation became confused with moral and physical deviancy. Certain passages in the Bible further encouraged medical professionals to see homosexuality as an abomination, a defilement of the flesh. In the end, researchers wrongly concluded that homosexuality was a sickness based on cultural, personal, and religious discrimination.

Such bias shows the need to scan every definition for chauvinism, presumption, and outright bigotry, even the scientific ones. In 1994, the APA recognized its own mistake and removed any reference to homosexuality as an illness from the fourth edition of DSM. Other sexualities haven't been so lucky. Debate still rages today whether or not categories such as "gender identity disorder" and "transvestic fetishism," are real mental illnesses, or yet another medical prejudice against alternative sexual lifestyles.

These muddles demonstrate the mutability of a definition, the protean manner in which a single word can take on radically different meanings in different contexts, according to different people. In the end, the meaning of a word may well depend on who defines it and which authority backs it up.

In this way, definition can't be separated from various forms of power. As different definitions compete for currency and legitimacy, the ones backed with power, influence, and resources tend to win out. And power doesn't always act with truth or justice.

DEFINITIONS WITH PURPOSE

"Every definition is dangerous."

—Erasmus

In addition to personal bias, definitions tend to have specific political ends. That's to say, definitions are designed with purpose to achieve tangible results. People use the power of definitions to bend circumstances to their will, as in the following odd version of a "truck."

In the 1980s, governments started to impose strict guidelines on the automotive industry, mandating smaller size, lower emissions, and greater fuel economy in all cars. The government exempted trucks from these restrictions, because industry argued that it needed the powerful, if dirty, engines of a conventional truck to haul loads and perform commercial work.

Auto manufacturers grimaced. The new laws called for changes in their most lucrative lines—the sport and luxury models. Even worse, the restrictions targetted the signs of prestige, opulence, and power that distinguish luxury and sports vehicles from cheaper economy cars. How could a sports car with a two-stroke engine attract adrenaline-addicted young men? What car could they offer the rich that still brazenly declared rank and affluence?

The answer is none: instead they offered a "truck." As powerful as a Camaro, as elegant as a Lincoln, as roomy as a Seville, the SUV filled the market niche left vacant by the sports and luxury cars.

Of course, SUVs are light trucks only in the technical sense of the word. In day-to-day life, people use them as personal or family vehicles, driving them to and from work, no different from a Volvo or a Taurus. In fact, 90 percent of all sport utilities remain firmly on asphalt their entire lives ("Ultimate Poseur"). Although they may be classified on paper as a truck, SUVs are used, overwhelmingly, as cars—bigger, more powerful, and opulent cars.

Here then is a dark example of definition with a purpose. By defining their new line of vehicles as light trucks, the automotive manufacturers continued to make luxury sedans as big as they want, despite the restrictions on car size. They still cranked out gas-wasting sports models with over-sized engines, even though all other cars must meet minimum standards of fuel efficiency. Perhaps worst of all, they still make commuter vehicles that spew out unac-ceptable levels of toxins, despite pollution restrictions. By labelling their vehicles "all terrain," auto manufacturers escaped the trouble-some legislation that forced them to conserve natural resources and improve air quality.

We learn an important lesson here: definitions can be manipu-lated to achieve private, corporate, or political agendas. Rather than accept such definitions, we must begin to question their motives, asking who defined this, who gains, and who loses.

HOW TO COPE WITH PROBLEMATIC DEFINITIONS

When faced with a definition, don't accept it as fact; examine and question it.

- Who defined this? From what point of view?
- Is the definition biased?
- Is it a prescriptive or descriptive definition?
- If prescriptive, why is this definition needed?

- Can the thing in question be defined in another way?
- What purpose is served? Who gains by this definition?
- What potential problems arise?
- What authority is evoked? Can we trust the authority?
- What power backs up the definition?

By accepting someone's definitions, we let others set the game rules. If we question or create a new definition, we radically alter the game.

CASE STUDY: PORNOGRAPHY

We know pornography when we see it, but a censor board must use more objective standards. Historically, the attempts to define pornography fall into three different broad strategies.

CONTENT

A content-based approach defines pornography according to the subject matter appearing on the screen, magazine, canvass, or text. This strategy declares something pornographic based upon the depiction of specific body parts and sexual acts: breasts, vaginas, penises, intercourse, fellatio, etc.

Problems with this line of thinking begin when we try to decide what body parts and acts make their way onto that checklist of the forbidden. Early attempts at a content definition of pornography focused on the naked human form, a category that catches "skin" magazines such as *Penthouse*, but also hauls in all sorts of unwanted by-catch. If we equate pornography with nudity, for instance, we classify a huge portion of world art as pornographic.

Some censors refined the nudity premise, limiting it to specific organs. For a while, Canadian censors defined pornography as anything showing an erect penis, a definition that exempted most (but not all) museum nudes, yet applied to explicit movies like *Deep Throat*. According to this provision, the human body itself was not pornographic, only the aroused male member.

However, this version again created problems. The definition erroneously equates pornography with a man's erect penis, and so doesn't address instances of women's sexuality. Consequently, filmmakers could show graphic scenes of lesbian sexuality and still escape censure. In contrast, gay male sex became almost impossible to document.

Given these flaws, the definition of pornography shifted focus away from the human body to acts of sexuality themselves: censors declared a work pornographic if it showed vaginal or anal penetration, oral genital contact, oral digital contact, etc. This policy allowed censors to correct its male bias, and address a broader range of indulgences, gay and straight, alternative and mainstream.

As with the focus on the body, a sex-based definition created inconsistencies and controversies. In particular, this definition targetted any sexually explicit work, regardless of purpose, merit, or effect. Great writers such as D. H. Lawrence, James Joyce, and Vladimir Nabokov had novels seized because they described human sexuality in realistic detail. Non-fiction works such as *The Joy of Sex* were banned for providing information, counselling, instruction, and medical advice in a no-nonsense style. When censors applied the criterion of graphic content, a major problem arose: this definition banned works that were educational and artistic.

INTENT

A content-based definition of pornography fails, because it doesn't discriminate between serious and puerile works. It ignores the purpose of the text, photo, or video, whether to inform, inspire, or merely titillate. This led some people to think that a better definition of pornography rests in the *intent* of its makers: a work is pornographic when its only goal is sexual arousal.

This approach avoids the thorny field of subject material, concentrating instead on the sobre or lewd style. This new method solves many difficulties found in the content-based strategy. Adult videos receive a pornographic classification because they're preoccupied with sexuality, at the expense of character, dialogue, and coherent plot. Expository texts such as *The Joy of Sex* escape censorship because their purpose is scholarly and instructional. Similarly, great works of painting, literature, and sculpture receive no censure, for their intent is to reflect human nature, to fashion a mirror that entertains, educates, and explores in a creative manner. Today, the concept of *artistic merit* still stands, exempting sexually graphic works from censorship because they have aesthetic value.

The problem with an intent-based definition of pornography is that the purpose of a work is not always clear, nor objectively measurable. The slippery nature of intent leads to some obvious contradictions: in the hands of a responsible parent, a photo of a naked child is acceptable; in the hands of a pedophile, it magically becomes contraband. The smut peddler selling explicit pictures produces porn, but the artist depicting sex makes art, thanks to the serious and aesthetic intent. For example, multimedia artist Jeffrey Koons photographed himself and his ex-porn star wife Cicciolina as they engaged in intercourse and fellatio. In one picture, Koons even ejaculates across Cicciolina's face. Because Koons declares his material as "art," he can produce material as explicit as any adult video. With intent, any smut is okay, as long as it is highbrow smut.

EFFECT

The capricious nature of the content/intent definitions led to a new approach to the pornography debate: effect. This strategy shifts attention away from the pornographers and their products, and looks at the consequences of pornography, asking "What harm does erotic material do?" According to this reasoning, a film showing healthy lovemaking can be distributed freely, for it creates no tangible injury to anyone. In contrast, a film that glorifies rape or degrades women is banned if the film encourages real violence or discrimination. Similar to Canadian hate crime legislation restricting racist material, this version of pornography forbids work that fosters discrimination, aggression, cruelty, and debasement of humanity.

One of the advantages of this approach is the way it avoids the arbitrary definitions of sexuality that hamstrung content-based approaches. Any sex goes, as long as no one gets hurt. Likewise, censors no longer worry about the artist's "meaning," and base decisions upon the category of external harm.

Despite these advantages, this method has also been applied in a rather discriminatory and capricious manner.

The problem lies with the term "harm," a category as arbitrary as any previous measure. Harm is not used in its physical sense (such as broken bone), but in a more nebulous sense of spiritual, philosophical, or cultural damage: an ambiguous premise. Consider the classic feminist argument against pornography that it dehumanizes and objectifies women. This accusation contains a rather obvious contradiction: sex is perfectly healthy if it takes place in the privacy of a darkened bedroom, but magically becomes a threat once recorded on videotape. In addition, the charge does not satisfactorily explain why the depiction of sexual congress dehumanizes women, but not men engaged in the same act. Porn movies usually treat men as little more than mere appendages, while women at least have the luxury of receiving star billings.

Today, the harm-based definition continues to make suspect cases for obscenity. Some feminists label fashion magazines like *Cosmopolitan* as pornographic because they contribute to anorexia in women. Other feminists such as Andrea Dworkin suggest that heterosexuality itself conveys a secret male hatred of women, a desire to violate and possess the female space. Some fundamentalist Christians echo Dworkin, arguing that sexuality outside of marriage poses a threat to the sanctity of the family. Others suggest that sexual materials are harmful when they defy community standards—an obvious problem for alternative lifestyles.

Defined in this slippery manner, it seems pornography can be anything you don't like.

CASE STUDY: NATIVES

When the Canadian government recognizes a person as a "status Indian," the title brings tangible benefits, such as free tuition, tax exemption, housing, fishing, and hunting prerogatives. These special dispensations are costly, and intended for Aboriginal peoples alone. To avoid abuse, the Canadian government determines very precisely what constitutes an "authentic" Aboriginal.

Native "blood" or ancestry is the most obvious criterion for establishing an authentic First Nations identity, yet is far from a simple matter. If the government restricts its definition to children of "pure blood" parents, then it rejects countless mixed ancestry natives, including entire groups, such as the Métis. Some dilution of "pure blood" criterion seems appropriate, given the amount of interbreeding between First Nations and colonists over the past 500 odd years. But then new problems arise. How much First Nations blood does a person have to have to qualify as a real Indian? One half? One eighth? One sixteenth? No matter where one draws the line, the decision seems arbitrary.

Perhaps more interesting is the variety of ways that the federal government has denied official recognition to Indian people (a loss that the government euphemistically called "enfranchisement"). Indian status has been withheld or retracted for a variety of reasons, including

- Marriage to a non-Native man
- Acceptance of money in exchange for status, a bribe known as "half-breed scrip"
- The desire to vote, own land, consume alcohol, live off the reserve, live outside of Canada, become a professional such as a lawyer or priest
- Birth out of wedlock or in a non-Native community
- Exclusion from official band lists or registry
- Children of Canadian parents born in the United States
- Children of a Native who meet any of these conditions (Congress of Aboriginal Peoples)

These criteria strip Natives of their identity, in ways never applied to Europeans. They also force Native people to make a brutal choice: retain your Native identity or feed your family.

In retrospect, the federal definition of Indian has an obvious purpose: to reduce the official count of First Nations peoples and so to decrease the cost of financial support. Historically, the definition helped in the process of colonization and settlement of the country, forcing Native people to relinquish territory and accept reservation life. The reserve criterion was particularly useful for forcing Plains Indians into permanent homes, ending migrant lifestyles that threatened settlement of the prairies.

Until very recently, the official policy of the federal Canadian government towards First Nations people was assimilation, a policy that encouraged Natives to abandon traditional culture and integrate into Canadian society. The government forced assimilation upon Native communities with a variety of different tactics, including the banning of Aboriginal customs and languages, as well as the kidnapping and re-education of Native children in residential schools. One of the best weapons in the federal arsenal was its very strict definition of a First Nations person, a biased and narrow definition that stripped untold thousands of legitimate Aboriginal peoples of official recognition.

Works Cited

Congress of Aboriginal Peoples. "Indian Act/Bill C-31 – Part 1." *CAP Online.*
    Sept. 19, 2001. <http://www.abo-peoples.org/programs/c-31-1.html>.

Crystal, David. *The English Language.* London: Penguin, 1988.

Pohl, Otto. "Scientists Struggling to Make the Kilogram Right Again." *New York
    Times* May 27, 2003. Nov. 11, 2003. <http://www.physics.capcollege.bc.ca/
    phys108/kilogram_standard.htm>.

"The Ultimate Poseur Sport Utility Page." Nov. 11, 2003. <http://poseur.4x4.org>.

Exercises

1. Read the following questions and devise a definition for the following.

    a) Define a *human life.* At what point does a person come into existence? At birth? At conception? How does your definition apply to abortion? Cloning?

    b) Define *harassment* to prevent abuse but allow free expression.

    c) Define *artistic merit* so that you will protect legitimate art works, but criminalize the stuff that goes "just too far."

    d) Define "child abuse." Would it include spanking? Church attendance? Emotional neglect? Circumcision?

    e) Write a definition of *child* and *work,* to prevent exploitation, yet allow traditional jobs such as babysitting or paper delivery.

f) Define *essential service*, remembering such professions can't strike. Does your definition cover sanitation workers? Ferry workers? Teachers?

g) Define a dietary term such as *fat free*, *light*, *low sugar*, or *healthy*.

h) Define *marriage*. Does it apply to gays? Common-law relationships?

2. Create a definition for the following terms. Then discuss with your class the authority, interests, and bias that may lie behind the definition.

Canadian content
Community standards
Discrimination
Drug
Family
Feminist
Genocide
Multiculturalism
Intellectual property
Organic
Politically correct
Pollutant
Prostitution
Psychosis
Public good
Purebred
Race
Religion
Restricted/PG/Family
Sexual relations
Slander/Libel
Vegetarian
Weapons of mass destruction

3. Define the following medical conditions. Where do you draw the line between a normal and abnormal amount of the behaviour? Are all of these illnesses legitimate?

Addiction
Anorexia
Antisocial personality disorder
Attention deficit hyperactivity disorder
Chronic fatigue syndrome
Cross-dressing
Depression

Fibromyalgia
Gender identity disorder
Oppositional defiance disorder
Recovered memory syndrome
Sadomasochism
Yuppie flu

4. Invent a disease. Take any trait (such as the following) and describe it as a psychosis.

- Faith in economic growth
- Excessive consumption
- Need for love, belonging, or esteem
- Pursuit of career, health, or wealth
- Belief in religion or spirituality
- Political apathy
- Dedication to family or church

What would happen if these were included in the DSM?

What Is Terrorism?

MICHAEL MOORE

Michael Moore is a reporter, author, comedian, personality, filmmaker, and political activist. He has written best-selling books (*Downsize This*, *Stupid White Men*, and *Dude, Where's My Country?*); launched award-winning TV shows (*TV Nation* and *The Awful Truth*); and won Oscars for his documentaries *Roger and Me* and *Bowling for Columbine*. His film *Fahrenheit 911*, a damning appraisal of the Bush administration, is the most successful documentary in movie history. Moore focuses on a variety of social justice issues, paying particular attention to the problems of globalization and outsourcing, which devastated the economy of his hometown, Flint, Michigan.

What is terrorism? There is no question that, when an individual rents a Ryder Truck, loads it with explosives, and blows up a building, it is an act of terrorism and should be severely punished.

But what do you call it when a *company* destroys the lives of thousands of people? Is this terrorism? *Economic* terrorism? The company doesn't use a homemade bomb or a gun. They politely move out all of the people before they blow up the building. But as I pass by the remnants of that factory there in Flint, Michigan, looking eerily like the remnants of the Alfred P. Murrah Federal Building in Oklahoma City, I wonder: What will happen to *those* people? A few will kill themselves, despondent over the loss of their livelihood. Some will be killed by their spouse—an argument over the lack of a new job or the loss of money at the racetrack turns suddenly violent (the woman is the one who usually ends up dead). Others will be killed more slowly through drugs or alcohol, the substances of choice when one needs to ease the pain of his or her life being turned upside down and shoved into an empty, dark hole.

We don't call the company a murderer, and we certainly don't call their actions terrorism, but make no mistake about it, their victims will be just as dead as those poor souls in Oklahoma City, killed off in the name of greed.

There is a rage building throughout the country and, if you're like me, you're scared shitless. Oklahoma City is the extreme extension of this rage. Though most people are somehow able to keep their wits through these hard times, I believe thousands of Americans are only a few figurative steps away from getting into that Ryder Truck. How terrifyingly ironic that the vehicle now chosen for terrorist acts is the same one used by that vast diaspora of working-class Americans who have spent the last decade moving from state to state in the hopes of survival.

This moving van, this symbol of their downsized lives, has become a means to an end. Eighty pounds of fertilizer and a fuse made of ammonium nitrate and fuel oil now fill the trusty Ryder instead of the kids' bunk beds and the dining room set.

Timothy McVeigh couldn't get a decent job in Buffalo, so he joined the army and got the "first kill" of his unit in Iraq during the Gulf War. We gave him a medal for that kill, that taking of a human life. That murder was sanctioned because he was doing it on behalf of Uncle Sam for the oil companies.

The next year, he was unemployed, hanging around Niagara Falls, New York. A photo of him that has been widely published shows him and fellow defendant Terry Nichols horsing around on the ledge at Niagara Falls. I was there at the Falls, writing and prepping my film *Canadian Bacon*, at the time that photo was taken. I, of course, have no recollection of seeing McVeigh there, because who was he then? Just another son of a GM worker who couldn't get a job, not even as a toll-taker on the bridge to Canada (he had scored second highest on the test; there just weren't any openings). In the first scene we filmed a few months later at the Falls, the character "Roy-Boy" is a laid-off worker (also a veteran of the Gulf War) and is on that same ledge, preparing to jump and end it all.

McVeigh and Nichols had met in the Army. The day that Nichols decided to join the Army he drove through the decimated downtown of Flint, Michigan, walked into the recruiter's office, and signed up for a better life—better than whatever Flint could offer.

After the war (and their stint looking for work around Niagara Falls), McVeigh and Nichols then moved to a farm Nichols' brother owned an hour northeast of Flint. They went to Michigan Militia meetings. They blew up "things" in the backyard. It was no surprise to me that McVeigh and Nichols found themselves on a road that led from Flint, Michigan to Oklahoma City, Oklahoma.

How was it that Timothy McVeigh became so confused and filled with so much anger? What struck me most about his alleged act was that he had decided to *kill his own people* to make his point. This was a strange twist for those on the extreme Right who had always used their violence against blacks, Jews, and immigrants. But McVeigh is not accused of taking that Ryder Truck to the place where his "enemies" were—the Capitol Building, the World Trade Center, a Jewish temple, the headquarters of the NAACP, or other potential targets of his hate. No. He blows up his own people! In mostly white, Christian conservative, Republican-voting, redneck-lovin' Oklahoma City! Talk about the final insanity.

I do not like guns. I am a pacifist at heart. As a member of that minority of Americans who are unarmed, I am committed to finding a way to combat the downsizing tide that seems to be rising against us. So I have written this book. I have no college degree, so take what I say with that in mind. I'm not even supposed to be writing this book right now, because I'm under contract to produce a sitcom I've been hired to write for Fox. A sitcom! What am I doing with my life? Hell, I still owe Mr. Ricketts an English paper from twelfth-grade Shakespeare! How did I ever get here from Flint?

Oh, yeah. In a Ryder Truck.

From *The Corporation*

JOEL BAKAN

A Rhodes scholar and legal expert, Joel Bakan is a law professor at the University of British Columbia. His book *The Corporation: The Pathological Pursuit of Profit and Power* became the basis of a Mark Achbar's highly touted documentary of the same name. Behind the book and movie lies a simple observation: if the corporation is a legal person, it seems to behave like a destructive and heartless sociopath.

America's nineteenth-century railroad barons, men lionized by some and vilified by others, were the true creators of the modern corporate era. Because railways were mammoth undertakings requiring huge amounts of capital investment—to lay track, manufacture rolling stock, and operate and maintain systems—the industry quickly came to rely on the corporate form for financing its operations. In the United States, railway construction boomed during the 1850s and then exploded again after the Civil War, with more than one hundred thousand miles of track laid between 1865 and 1885. As the industry grew, so did the number of corporations.[1] The same was true in England, where, between 1825 and 1849, the amount of capital raised by railways, mainly through joint-stock companies, increased from £200,000 to £230 million, more than one thousand-fold.[2]

"One of the most important by-products of the introduction and extension of the railway system," observed M. C. Reed in *Railways and the Growth of the Capital Market*, was the part it played in "assisting the development of a national market for company securities."[3] Railways, in both the United States and England, demanded more capital investment than could be provided by the relatively small coterie of wealthy men who invested in corporations at the start of the nineteenth century. By the middle of the century, with railway stocks flooding markets in both countries, middle-class people began, for the first time, to invest in corporate shares. As *The Economist* pronounced at the time, "everyone was in the stocks now . . . needy clerks, poor tradesman's apprentices, discarded service men and bankrupts—all have entered the ranks of the great monied interest."[4]

One barrier remained to broader public participation in stock markets, however: no matter how much, or how little, a person had invested in a company, he or she was *personally* liable, without limit, for the company's debts. Investors' homes, savings, and other personal assets would be exposed to claims by creditors if a company failed, meaning that a person risked financial ruin simply by owning shares in a company. Stockholding could not become a truly attractive option for the general public until that risk was removed, which it soon was. By the middle of the nineteenth century, business leaders and politicians broadly advocated changing the law to limit the liability of shareholders to the amounts they had invested in a company. If a person bought $100 worth of shares, they reasoned, he or she should be immune to liability for anything beyond that, regardless of what happened to the company. Supporters of "limited liability," as the concept came to be known, defended it as being necessary to attract middle-class investors into the stock market. "Limited liability would allow those of moderate means to take shares in investments with their richer neighbors," reported the Select Committee on Partnerships (England) in 1851, and that, in turn, would mean "their self-respect [would be] upheld, their intelligence encouraged and an additional motive given to preserve order and respect for the laws of property."[5]

Ending class conflict by co-opting workers into the capitalist system, a goal the committee's latter comment subtly alludes to, was offered as a political justification for limited liability, alongside the economic one of expanding the pool of potential investors. An 1853 article in the *Edinburgh Journal* stated:

> The workman does not understand the position of the capitalist. The remedy is, to put him in the way by practical experience. . . . Working-men, once enabled to act together as the owners of a joint capital, will soon find their whole view of the relations between capital and labour undergo a radical alteration. They will learn what anxiety and toil it costs even to hold a small concern together in tolerable order . . . the middle and operative classes would derive great material and social good by the exercise of the joint-stock principle.[6]

Limited liability had its detractors, however. On both sides of the Atlantic, critics opposed it mainly on moral grounds. Because it allowed investors to escape unscathed from their companies' failures, the critics believed it would undermine personal moral responsibility, a value that had governed the commercial world for centuries. With limited liability in place, investors could be recklessly unconcerned about their companies' fortunes, as Mr. Goldbury, a fictitious company promoter, explained in song in Gilbert and Sullivan's sharp satire of the corporation, *Utopia Ltd*:

> Though a Rothschild you may be, in your own capacity,
> As a Company you've come to utter sorrow,
> But the liquidators say, "Never mind—you needn't pay,"
> So you start another Company Tomorrow!

People worried that limited liability would, as one parliamentarian speaking against its introduction in England said, attack "The first and most natural principle of commercial legislation . . . that every man was bound to pay the debts he had contracted, so long as he was able to do so" and that it would "enable persons to embark in trade with a limited chance of loss, but with an unlimited chance of gain" and thus encourage "a system of vicious and improvident speculation."[7]

Despite such objections, limited liability was entrenched in corporate law, in England in 1856 and in the United States over the latter half of the nineteenth century (though at different times in different states). With the risks of investment in stocks now removed, at least in terms of how much money investors might be forced to lose, the way was cleared for broad popular participation in stock markets and for investors to diversify their holdings. Still, publicly traded corporations were relatively rare in the United States up until the end of the nineteenth century. Beyond the railway industry, leading companies tended to be family-owned, and if shares existed at all they were traded on a direct person-to-person basis, not in stock markets. By the early years of the twentieth century, however, large publicly traded corporations had become fixtures on the economic landscape.[8]

Over two short decades, beginning in the 1890s, the corporation underwent a revolutionary transformation. It all started when New Jersey and Delaware ("the first state to be known as the home of corporations," according to its current secretary of state for corporations[9]), sought to attract valuable incorporation business to their jurisdictions by jettisoning unpopular restrictions from their corporate laws. Among other things, they

- Repealed the rules that required businesses to incorporate only for narrowly defined purposes, to exist only for limited durations, and to operate only in particular locations
- Substantially loosened controls on mergers and acquisitions; and
- Abolished the rule that one company could not own stock in another

Other states, not wanting to lose out in the competition for incorporation business, soon followed with similar revisions to their laws. The changes prompted a flurry of incorporations as businesses sought the new freedoms and powers incorporation would grant them. Soon, however, with most meaningful constraints on mergers and acquisitions gone, a large number of small and medium-size corporations were quickly absorbed into a small number of very large ones—1,800 corporations were consolidated into 157 between

1898 and 1904.[10] In less than a decade the U.S. economy had been transformed from one in which individually owned enterprises competed freely among themselves into one dominated by a relatively few huge corporations, each owned by many shareholders. The era of corporate capitalism had begun.

"Every tie in the road is the grave of a small stockholder," stated Newton Booth, a noted antimonopolist and railroad reformer, in 1873, when he was governor of California. Booth's message was clear: in large corporations stockholders had little, if any, power and control. By the early twentieth century, corporations were typically combinations of thousands, even hundreds of thousands, of broadly dispersed, anonymous shareholders. Unable to influence managerial decisions as individuals because their power was too diluted, they were also too broadly dispersed to act collectively. Their consequent loss of power in and control of large corporations turned out to be managers' gains. In 1913, a congressional committee set up to investigate the "money trust," led by Congressman Arsène Pujo, reported:

> None of the witnesses called was able to name an instance in the history of the country in which the stockholders had succeeded in overthrowing an existing management in any large corporation, nor does it appear that stockholders have ever even succeeded in so far as to secure the investigation of an existing management of a corporation to ascertain whether it has been well or honestly managed. . . . [In] all great corporations with numerous and widely scattered stockholders . . . the management is virtually self-perpetuating and is able through the power of patronage, the indifference of stockholders and other influences to control a majority of stock.[11]

Shareholders had, for all practical purposes, disappeared from the corporations they owned.

With shareholders, real people, effectively gone from corporations, the law had to find someone else, some other person, to assume the legal rights and duties firms needed to operate in the economy. That "person" turned out to be the corporation itself. As early as 1793, one corporate scholar outlined the logic of corporate personhood when he defined the corporation as

> a collection of many individuals united into one body, under a special denomination, having perpetual succession under an artificial form, and vested, by the policy of law, with the capacity of acting, in several respects, as an

individual, particularly of taking and granting property, of contracting obligations, and of suing and being sued, of enjoying privileges and immunities in common.[12]

In partnerships, another scholar noted in 1825, "the law looks to the individuals"; in corporations, on the other hand, "it sees only the creature of the charter, the body corporate, and knows not the individuals."[13]

By the end of the nineteenth century, through a bizarre legal alchemy, courts had fully transformed the corporation into a "person," with its own identity, separate from the flesh-and-blood people who were its owners and managers and empowered, like a real person, to conduct business in its own name, acquire assets, employ workers, pay taxes, and go to court to assert its rights and defend its actions. The corporate person had taken the place, at least in law, of the real people who owned corporations. Now viewed as an entity, "not imaginary or fictitious, but real, not artificial but natural," as it was described by one law professor in 1911, the corporation had been reconceived as a free and independent being.[14] Gone was the centuries-old "grant theory," which had conceived of corporations as instruments of government policy and as dependent upon government bodies to create them and enable them to function. Along with the grant theory had also gone all rationales for encumbering corporations with burdensome restrictions. The logic was that, conceived as natural entities analogous to human beings, corporations should be created as free individuals, a logic that informed the initiatives in New Jersey and Delaware, as well as the Supreme Court's decision in 1886 that, because they were "persons," corporations should be protected by the Fourteenth Amendment's rights to "due process of law" and "equal protection of the laws," rights originally entrenched in the Constitution to protect freed slaves.[15]

*   *   *

The corporation itself may not so easily escape the psychopath diagnosis, however. Unlike the human beings who inhabit it, the corporation is *singularly* self-interested and unable to feel genuine concern for others in any context. Not surprisingly, then, when we asked Dr. [Robert] Hare [psychologist and internationally renowned expert on psychopathy] to apply his diagnostic checklist of psychopathic traits (italicized below) to the corporation's institutional character, he found there was a close match. The corporation is *irresponsible*, Dr. Hare said, because "in an attempt to satisfy the corporate goal, everybody else is put at risk." Corporations try to *"manipulate* everything, including public opinion," and they are *grandiose,* always insisting "that we're number one, we're the best." A *lack of empathy* and *asocial tendencies* are also key characteristics of the corporation, says Hare—"their behavior indicates they don't really concern themselves with their victims"; and corporations often *refuse to accept responsibility for their own actions and are unable to feel remorse*: "if [corporations] get caught [breaking the law], they pay big fines and they . . . continue doing what they did before anyway. And in fact in many cases the fines and the penalties paid by the organization are trivial compared to the profits that they rake in."[16]

Finally, according to Dr. Hare, corporations relate to others *superficially*—"their whole goal is to present themselves to the public in a way that is appealing to the public [but] in fact may not be representative of what th[e] organization is really like." Human psychopaths are notorious for their ability to use charm as a mask to hide their dangerously self-obsessed personalities. For corporations, social responsibility may play the same role. Through it they can present themselves as compassionate and concerned about others when, in fact, they lack the ability to care about anyone or anything but themselves.[17]

Take the large and well-known energy company that once was a paragon of social responsibility and corporate philanthropy. Each year the company produced a Corporate Responsibility Annual Report; the most recent one, unfortunately its last, vowed to cut greenhouse-gas emissions and support multilateral agreements to help stop climate change. The company pledged further to put human rights, the environment, health and safety issues, biodiversity, indigenous rights, and transparency at the core of its business operations, and it created a well-staffed corporate social responsibility task force to monitor and implement its social responsibility programs. The company boasted of its development of alternative energy sources and the fact it had helped start the Business Council for Sustainable Energy. It apologized for a 29,000-barrel oil spill in South America, promised it would never happen again, and reported that it had formed partnerships with environmental NGOs to help monitor its operations. It described the generous support it had provided communities in the cities where it operated, funding arts organizations, museums, educational institutions, environmental groups, and various causes throughout the world. The company, which was consistently ranked as one of the best places to work in America, strongly promoted diversity in the workplace. "We believe," said the report, "that corporate leadership should set the example for community service."[18]

Unfortunately, this paragon of corporate social responsibility, Enron, was unable to continue its good works after it collapsed under the weight of its executives' greed, hubris, and criminality. Enron's story shows just how wide a gap can exist between a company's cleverly crafted do-gooder image and its actual operations and suggests, at a minimum, that skepticism about corporate social responsibility is well warranted.

There is, however, a larger lesson to be drawn from Enron's demise than the importance of being skeptical about corporate social responsibility. Though the company is now notorious for its arrogance and ethically challenged executives, the underlying reasons for its collapse can be traced to characteristics common to all corporations: obsession with profits and share prices, greed, lack of concern for others, and a penchant for breaking legal rules. These traits are, in turn, rooted in an institutional culture, the corporation's, that valorizes self-interest and invalidates moral concern. No doubt Enron took such characteristics to their limits—indeed, to the point of self-destruction—and the company is now notorious for that. It was not, however, unusual for the fact it had those characteristics in the first place. Rather, Enron's collapse is best understood as showing what can happen when the characteristics we normally accept and take for granted in a corporation are pushed to the extreme. It was not, in other words, a "very isolated incident," as Pfizer's Hank McKinnell described it and as many commentators seem to believe, but rather a symptom of the corporation's flawed institutional character.[19]

Reading Notes

1. Bowman, *The Modern Corporation and American Political Thought*, 41–42.

2. Paddy Ireland, "Capitalism Without the Capitalist: The Joint Stock Company Share and the Emergence of the Modern Doctrine of Separate Corporate Personality," *Journal of Legal History* 17 (1996): 63.

3. Cited in ibid., 62.

4. Cited in ibid., 65.

5. Select Committee on the Law of Partnership, 1851, B.P.P. VII, vi (as cited in Rob McQueen, "Company Law in Great Britain and the Australian Colonies 1854–1920: A Social History," Ph.D. thesis, Griffith University, p. 137). For further discussion of the relationship between limited liability and middle-class investment capital, see Ronald E. Seavoy, *The Origins of the American Business Corporation, 1784–1855: Broadening the Concept of Public Service During Industrialization* (Westport, Conn.: Greenwood Press, 1982); Phillip Blumberg,

The Multinational Challenge to Corporation Law: The Search for a New Corporate Personality (Oxford: Oxford University Press, 1993); "Report of the Select Committee in Investments for the Savings of the Middle and Working Classes," 1850, B.P.P., XIX, 169.

6. Cited in McQueen, "Company Law in Great Britain and the Australian Colonies 1854–1920," p. 75.

7. Cited in Barbara Weiss, *The Hell of the English: Bankruptcy and the Victorian Novel* (Lewisburg, Pa.: Bucknell University Press, 1986), 148.

8. Morton Horwitz, "Santa Claus Revisited: The Development of Corporate Theory," in *Corporations and Society: Power and Responsibility*, ed. Warren Samuels and Arthur Miller (New York: Greenwood Press, 1987), 13.

9. Interview with Dr. Harriet Smith Windsor.

10. Roland Marchand, *Creating the Corporate Soul: The Rise of Public Relations and Corporate Imagery in American Big Business* (Berkeley: University of California Press, 1998), 7.

11. Cited in Edward Herman, *Corporate Control, Corporate Power* (Cambridge, England: Cambridge University Press, 1981), 7 ("tie" and "witnesses").

12. Stewart Kyd, *A Treatise on the Law of Corporations* (1793), vol. 1, p. 1, as cited in Ireland, "Capitalism Without the Capitalist," 45–46.

13. John George, *A View of the Existing Law of Joint Stock Companies* (1825), p. 29, as cited in Ireland, "Capitalism Without the Capitalist," 45.

14. University of Chicago law professor Arthur W. Maschen, as quoted in Horwitz, "Santa Claus Revisited," 51.

15. *Santa Clara County v. Southern Pacific Railroad*, 118 U.S. 394 (1886). Between 1890 and 1910, business interests invoked the Fourteenth Amendment 288 times before the courts, compared to 19 times by African Americans, according to Mary Zepernick of the Program on Corporations, Law and Democracy in an interview. And in the name of the Fourteenth Amendment, beginning with its 1905 decision in *Lochner v. New York*, the Supreme Court fashioned a jurisprudence that, over the next three decades, would bar states from enacting various kinds of regulatory measures, such as maximum-hour and minimum-wage protection for workers. In 1937, President Roosevelt, fearful that the Court might thwart his New Deal with its antiregulatory bias, threatened to pack it with five new judges, all of them New Deal sympathizers, prompting it to adopt a more deferential posture toward government. More recently, however, courts have once again begun to recognize corporations'rights under the Constitution and strike down laws that, in their view, offend them.

16. Interview with Dr. Robert Hare.

17. Ibid.

18. Enron, Corporate Responsibility Annual Report, Houston, 2000.

19. Interview with Hank McKinnell.

Defining Pornography

WENDY McELROY

Wendy McElroy is a journalist, editor and author of *Sexual Correctness: The Gender Feminist Attack on Women*, *The Reasonable Woman: A Guide to Intellectual Survival*, *Queen Silver: The Godless Girl*, and *Liberty for Women*. A feminist and libertarian, McElroy champions the individual's right to choose, and so defends behaviours—such as prostitution—deemed exploitative by the mainstream feminist community. This selection comes from *XXX: A Woman's Right to Pornography*.

> If you wish to converse with me, define your terms.
>
> —Voltaire

There is no way to approach pornography without first struggling with the most fundamental question that anyone can ask: What is it?

For decades, the most common nondefinition of pornography was the one used by Supreme Court Justice Potter Stewart in his concurring opinion on *Jacobellis v. Ohio*, "I shall not today attempt further to define [hard-core pornography] . . .; and perhaps I could never succeed in intelligibly doing so. But I know it when I see it . . ."[1]

Why is it so important to define pornography?

If people were not trying to pass laws against pornography, a definition might not be so crucial. But when courts become involved, definitions become essential. Whoever controls the definition of pornography will determine which words and images the law will suppress. They will decide the framework of future debate over pornography. Definitions directly influence how people think about an issue and the attitude with which they approach it. There is no mystery as to why anti-pornography feminists have spent so much time and energy in trying to define their terms. It is a quick and effective way to control the debate.

The purpose of definitions is to sketch the legitimate boundaries within which a word can be used. The beauty of definitions lies in their ability to let people know what they are talking about. Their magic is the clarity of thought that can result from drawing distinctions. Definitions are like the focus on a camera lens, bringing the intellectual outlines of an issue into sharp relief.

ELIMINATING NONDEFINITIONS

One step toward defining anything is to determine what it is *not*. A popular approach to the word *pornography* is an appeal to its ancient Greek roots. This approach should be discarded. The word *pornography* originally meant "writing about harlots or prostitutes." But its meaning has evolved over centuries of use through dozens of different cultures. Like the Greek word *gymnasium*, which originally meant, "place of nakedness," the word *pornography* has lost its connection with the past.

Nevertheless, Andrea Dworkin, in *Pornography: Men Possessing Women*, takes this "historical" approach:

"Contemporary pornography strictly and literally conforms to the word's root meaning: the graphic depiction of vile whores, or in our language, sluts. . . . The word has not changed its meaning and the genre is not misnamed . . . the graphic depiction of the lowest whores."[2]

Even granting that it is possible to understand the contemporary use of a word by referring to ancient Greece, this definition is a vacuum waiting to be filled. For example, in today's social context, what is a "slut"—especially to a woman, such as Dworkin, who openly denounces monogamous heterosexuality?

D. H. Lawrence—the brilliant novelist who was destroyed by censorship—claimed that a purely semantic definition of pornography offered no useful information at all. "The word itself, we are told, means 'pertaining to the harlots'—the graph of the harlot. But nowadays, what is a harlot? . . . Why be so cut and dried? The law is a dreary thing, and its judgments have nothing to do with life. The same with the word *obscene*: nobody knows what it means. Suppose it was derived from *obscena*: that which might not be represented on the stage; how much further are you?"[3]

Dworkin's definition may not transmit useful information, but it does clearly show her hatred of pornography. By calling pornography "the graphic description of the *lowest* whores"—when the adjective "lowest" is not in the Greek translation, Dworkin tells us more about herself than about the word *pornography*.

Moreover, the spectacle of radical feminists leaning upon the support of etymological authority is a strange sight indeed. After all, they adamantly reject the science and history of Western civilization as manifestations of white male culture. They reject the chronicles of history, because they are not *herstory*. They rail against the hard sciences, because they spring from white male methodology. The white male study of etymology, however, is legitimate—at least, when it suits their purposes.

Enlightenment is not likely to come from anti-pornography feminists, who view the world through the lens of ideology. Their rhetoric is the linguistic equivalent of thermonuclear war. Pornography is called "genocide"; Susan Brownmiller describes it as "the undiluted essence of anti-female propaganda"; Judith Bat-Ada compares Hugh Hefner to Hitler; Andrea Dworkin's book on pornography begins by claiming "Men love death . . . men especially love murder."

Such descriptions are normative, or biased. They embody the viewers' reactions, and their desire to condemn pornography. It is important to understand why anti-pornography feminists spend so much time and energy trying to define pornography. Definitions not only control the debate, they can control what sexuality itself becomes. Radical feminists view sex as a social construct. That is, they do not believe the current expressions of sexuality are inherent in human biology; instead, they are products of culture. If women's sexuality is a blank sheet of paper, then defining it becomes tremendously important. Whoever controls the definition will determine the content. The struggle to define pornography is part of radical feminism's attempt to control sexuality itself.

The stakes are high. High enough for freedom of speech to be jettisoned. Indeed, in her recent book *Only Words,* Catharine MacKinnon argues that pornography has no connection with free speech whatsoever; it is an *act* of sexual subordination, of sexual terrorism.

"Empirically, of all two dimensional forms of sex, it is only pornography, not its ideas as such, that gives men erections that support aggression against women in particular."[4]

Over the last decade or so, the feminist position on pornography has shifted toward this definition. Pornography is no longer viewed as merely offensive; it is redefined as an *act* of violence, in and of itself. It is the sexual subordination of women, by which their victimization is eroticized and perpetuated. It is the main way patriarchy subordinates women.

Other feminists have pointed out that rape existed long before *Playboy* appeared in the racks of corner stores. Such voices of reason are lost in the wind of hysteria. Anti-pornography feminists acknowledge them only to launch an *ad hominem* attack.

For better or worse, it is necessary to treat anti-pornography feminists with more respect than they are willing to give back. It is important to consider the substance of their definitions.

The anti-pornography definitions abound with emotionally charged and highly subjective terms like "humiliation" or "subordination." And they are commonly offered as the crowning statement of horrifying stories of sexual abuse.

Consider the opening of *Only Words*: "*You* grow up with your father holding you down and covering your mouth so another man can make a horrible searing pain between your legs. When you are older, your husband ties you to the bed and drips hot wax on your nipples . . . and makes you smile through it."[5] Ms. MacKinnon springboards from this scenario into a discussion and definition of porn.

In January/February 1994, *Ms.* magazine featured the issue of pornography. In an open discussion between a group of feminists, the following definitions were offered:

> "Pornography is the use of sex to intimidate and/or control women and children. . . . It has to do with depicting something that is violent and possibly life threatening for entertainment."
>
> —Ntozake Shange

> "I look at pornography as a system and practice of prostitution, as evidence of women's second class status. It is a central feature of patriarchal society."
>
> —Norma Ramos

> "Pornography is the graphic, sexually explicit subordination of women that includes one of a series of scenarios, from women being dehumanized—turned into objects and commodities—through women showing pleasure in being raped, through the dismemberment in a way that makes the dismemberment sexual."
>
> —Andrea Dworkin[6]

Radical feminism's current definition of pornography is the logical outgrowth of its view of heterosexual sex, which was well expressed over a decade ago by Andrea Dworkin. Throughout her still-classic book *Pornography: Men Possessing Women,* Dworkin's diatribe on men and heterosexuality borders on hate mongering. "Men develop a strong loyalty to violence. Men must come to terms with violence because it is the prime component of male identity" (p. 51). "The immutable self of the male boils down to an utterly unselfconscious parasitism." (p. 13) "Men are distinguished from women by their commitment to do violence rather than to be victimized by it" (p. 53). "Men want women to be objects, controllable as objects are controllable" (p. 65).[7] Dworkin's 1988 book, *Letters from a War Zone,* continues this theme by presenting marriage as prostitution and romance as rape.

The bridge linking these two positions—the rejection of hetero-sexuality and the definition of pornography as violence was forged in 1983 with the proposed Minneapolis Anti-Pornography Ordinance. This remains the touchstone definition used by the anti-porn forces. Because it was a watershed, I quote it in full:

> (gg) *Pornography.* Pornography is a form of discrimination on the basis of sex. (1) Pornography is the sexually explicit subordination of women, graphically depicted, whether in pictures or in words, that also includes one or more of the following:
> (i) women are presented as dehumanized sexual objects, things or commodities; or
> (ii) women are presented as sexual objects who enjoy pain or humiliation; or
> (iii) women are presented as sexual objects who experience sexual pleasure in being raped; or
> (iv) women are presented as sexual objects tied up or cut up or mutilated or bruised or physically hurt; or
> (v) women are presented in postures of sexual submission; [or sexual servility, including by inviting penetration] or
> (vi) women's body parts—including but not limited to vaginas, breasts, and buttocks—are exhibited, such that women are reduced to those parts; or
> (vii) women are presented as whores by nature; or
> (viii) women are presented being penetrated by objects or animals; or
> (ix) women are presented in scenarios of degradation, injury, abasement, torture, shown as filthy or inferior, bleeding, bruised, or hurt in a context that makes these conditions sexual.[8]

Several aspects of this definition cannot pass without comment. First, the set-up to this analysis of pornography baldly and stipulatively defines it as "discrimination based on sex" and the "sexually explicit subordination of women." This is not a definition; it is a conclusion, and one that is offered without argument or evidence.

Next, the specific images that constitute pornography are described in extremely subjective and value-laden terms, such as "dehumanized," "humiliation," "degradation," and "whores by nature." What do these terms mean? Humiliation means something different to every single woman. And short of a woman's waving a handful of cash while having sex it is difficult to even imagine what the phrase "whore by nature" means.

Moreover, some of the images covered by the definition go far beyond what can reasonably be considered pornographic. For example, "women's body parts . . . are exhibited such that women are reduced to those parts." This description would include everything from blue jean commercials which zoom in on women's asses to cream ads which show perfectly manicured hands applying the lotion—the sort of advertisements that have appeared in *Ms*. magazine. Although it is commonplace to criticize such ads for using sex to sell products, it is a real stretch to call them pornographic.

Further, although pornography is predefined as a form of violence against women, several clauses of this definition have nothing to do with such abuse. Instead, they deal with explicit sexual content—e.g. women as sex objects who "invite penetration." This is more of an attack on heterosexual sex than it is on pornography. After all, if there isn't an "invitation to penetration," how can the man know that consent is present?

Other clauses merely refer to images that reflect specific erotic preferences, such as buttocks or breasts.

The ordinance's definition goes far beyond defining pornography, and well into mandating what is sexually correct to see, hear, and express.

PORNOGRAPHY VERSUS EROTICA

Words define the parameters of debate. They control thought itself. George Orwell described this process as NewSpeak in his book *1984*, which described a totalitarian societal nightmare. The ultimate goal of NewSpeak was to construct a language such that it was impossible to utter an "incorrect" sentence.

Part of the anti-porn attempt to control the debate has been the forced distinction they've drawn between pornography and erotica. Basically, pornography is nasty; erotica is healthy. What exactly constitutes erotica is never clearly expressed. It is merely described as life affirming, while pornography is decried as degrading.

In the book *Confronting Pornography*, Jill Ridington offers her dividing line between the two types of sexual expression:

"If the message is one that equates sex with domination, or with the infliction of pain, or one that denies sex as a means of human communication, the message is a pornographic one. . . . Erotica, in contrast, portrays mutual interaction."[9]

Is there a real distinction between pornography and erotica? And why does it matter?

Let me draw a parallel. A friend and I have a pleasant disagreement about whether there is a distinction between science fiction and fantasy. These two types of writing are often lumped together, with many books combining elements of both. Although the debate may be fruitless, it is good-natured and of no great consequence.

Not so with the current mania for distinguishing between erotica and pornography. The debate over where to draw the line between these two forms of literature is anything but good-natured. When that line is drawn, those who fall on the wrong side of it may well be arrested and imprisoned by those who control the definitions.

The entire process resembles a scene from Lewis Carroll's [*Through the Looking-Glass*]:

"When *I* use a word," Humpty Dumpty said, in a rather scornful tone, "it means just what I choose it to mean—neither more nor less."

"The question is," said Alice, "whether you *can* make words mean so many different things."

"The question is," said Humpty Dumpty, "which is to be master—that's all."

Humpty Dumpty was engaging in what has been called "stipulative definitions"—namely, the sort of definition which makes the word mean anything you want it to. For example, arbitrarily redefining pornography from common usage—"sex books and sex movies"—to the sexually correct meaning of "an act of rape."

Fortunately, some feminists, like Joanna Russ in *Magic Mommas, Trembling Sisters, Puritans and Perverts*, are applying common sense rather than ideology to this distinction:

"Until recently I assumed . . . that 'art' is better than 'Pornography' just as 'erotica' is one thing and 'pornography' another; and just as 'erotica' surpasses 'pornography,' so 'art' surpasses 'erotica.' I think we ought to be very suspicious of these distinctions insofar as they are put forward as moral distinctions."[10]

With such a Wonderland of definitions floating about, it is prudent to take a step backward and ask, What constitutes a proper definition of anything?

DEFINING A DEFINITION

At the risk of sounding like an instructor of Logic 101, let me run the word *pornography* through a definitional process.

A good definition consists of two basic components:

The *definiendum*. This is the word or concept being defined. In the tentative definition "pornography is sexually explicit literature," the term *pornography is* the definiendum;

The *definiens*. This is the defining part of the definition. In "pornography is sexually explicit literature," the phrase "sexually explicit literature" is the definiens.

The process of defining a word involves analyzing it in several ways:

What is the *genus?* That is, what is the general class or category to which the word belongs? In *"pornography is sexually explicit literature,"* the term *literature* is the genus. It is the wider category to which *pornography* belongs. Once the broad context for *pornography* has been established, the process of definition becomes a matter of narrowing things down. The next question becomes:

What is the *differentia?* That is, what distinguishes *pornography* from all other forms of literature? What essential characteristics make pornography different from murder mysteries or historical novels?

Establishing the differentia means following certain rules, the most basic of which are:

1. The essential characteristics—or the common denominator found in all instances of the definiendum—cannot be too broad. Consider the definition "human beings are animals that walk on two legs." Since gorillas also walk on two legs, this differentia is too broad.
2. The essential characteristics should not be too narrow. Thus, "human beings are animals that negotiate contracts" is too narrow because it excludes those people who have never signed a contract.

To state these two principles in one sentence: The definition should apply to all possible cases, and only to those cases.

By these standards, definitions can be regarded as either true or false. Competing definitions can be evaluated as better or worse.

WHAT IS PORNOGRAPHY?

I propose a value-neutral definition: *Pornography is the explicit artistic depiction of men and/or women as sexual beings.* The modifier *explicit* excludes such gray areas as women's romance novels. The modifier *artistic* distinguishes pornography from psychological analyses of sex, such as those found in Freudian textbooks. The term *depiction* includes a wide range of expression, including paintings, literature, and videos. Thus, the genus of my definition of pornography is "the explicit artistic depiction."

The differentia is "of men and/or women as sexual beings." This means that pornography is the genre of art or literature that focuses on the sexual nature of human beings. This does not mean pornography cannot present people as full well rounded human beings. *But,* in order for the piece of art to be part of the "genre" of pornography, it must explicitly emphasize their sexuality.

Two things are missing from my definition of *pornography,* which are generally found elsewhere. It is common to refer to pornography as "material intended to sexually arouse"; I have excluded the intention of the author or producer. I have also excluded the reaction of the reader or viewer.

In other words, I claim that *The Tropic of Cancer* is inherently pornographic, quite apart from Henry Miller's intentions. To put this in another way: What if Miller protested that he was doing a political commentary on fascism, not a piece of pornography? Would his intention somehow convert the book into a work of political science? By my definition, no. *The Tropic of Cancer* would be a work of pornography whether or not Miller had hoped to achieve something else.

Equally, what if a reader became tremendously aroused by *Animal Farm* and not at all by Miller's book? The reader's response would not alter the fact that Miller, not Orwell, is the one presenting pornography.

"Pornography is the explicit artistic depiction of men and/or women as sexual beings." This is not merely a working definition. It is a definition I propose as a new and neutral starting point for a more fruitful discussion of pornography.

IS PORNOGRAPHY GOOD OR BAD?

With a working definition in place, it is possible to move on to the next question, Is pornography good or bad? This question is usually asked in one of two manners:

1. Is the explicit depiction of sex, *in general,* a good or bad thing?

Opinions on this range widely. At one extreme are the Religious Right and the anti-porn feminists, who condemn any graphic expression of sexuality, including straightforward nudity. At another extreme are those people who view any sexual censorship as being far worse than pornography could ever be. Most people fall in the middle. They tend to judge pornography on a case-by-case basis.

2. Is a *specific* piece of pornography good or bad art?

This is an aesthetic question. It revolves around identifying the major themes being expressed and evaluating how well the themes have been executed.

Most pornography is bad art. Indeed, pornography probably contains less artistic value than any other genre of literature and art. The reason for this is simple. Whenever a genre is stigmatized (or criminalized), the best writers and minds tend to abandon it. Those authors—such as D. H. Lawrence or James Branch Cabell or Henry Miller—who persist in bringing their genius to bear are persecuted without mercy. No wonder the industry is dominated by those who rush to make a quick profit rather than a profound insight.

Nevertheless, I believe the quality of pornography is often maligned. Pornography tends to be judged by the worst examples within the genre. Anti-pornographers do not hold up copies of D. H. Lawrence's *Lady Chatterley's Lover* or Erica Jong's *Fear of Flying*. They choose the most repulsive examples they can find and call them "representative." What other genre could withstand being judged by its poorest instances?

CONCLUSION

To repeat: The definition used in this book is: *Pornography is the explicit artistic depiction of men and/or women as sexual beings.* No area of human psychology needs exploration and understanding as much as sexuality does. At the turn of the century, Freud revolutionized the world's view of sex. Suddenly, it became a popular topic. It became almost a social duty to discuss and examine sex. Now anti-pornography feminists are trying to turn back the clock and shut women's sexuality away behind the locked doors of political correctness. Their first line of attack is to define the debate in their own terms.

The first line of defense is to flatly reject such maneuvering.

Reading Notes

1.   *Jacobellis v. Ohio*, 378 U.S. 184, 197 (1964).

2.   Andrea Dworkin, *Pornography: Men Possessing Women* (New York, NY: Penguin USA, 1989), p. 200.

3. D. H. Lawrence, *Pornography and Obscenity* (New York, NY: Knopf, 1930), pp. 1–2.

4. Catharine A. MacKinnon, *Only Words* (Cambridge, Mass.: Harvard University Press, 1993), p. 16.

5. *Only Words*, p. 3.

6. *Ms. Magazine*, January/February 1994, p. 34.

7. *Pornography: Men Possessing Women*, p. 13, 51, 53, 65.

8. The model anti-pornography ordinance can be found in Andrea Dworkin, "Against the Male Flood: Censorship, Pornography, and Equality," *Harvard Women's Law Journal* 8 (1985).

9. Jillian Ridington, *Confronting Pornography: A Feminist on the Front Lines* (Vancouver, Can.: CRIAW/ICREF,1989), p. 27.

10. Joanna Russ, *Magic Mommas, Trembling Sisters, Puritans and Perverts* (Trumansburg, NY: The Crossing Press), p. 90.

The Bureaucrat's Indian

DANIEL FRANCIS

Daniel Francis is an editor, newspaper writer, and historian who has published extensively on Canadian history. His works include *New Beginnings: A Social History of Canada*, *Discovery of the North*, *The Great Chase: A History of World Whaling*, *Battle for the West: Fur Trades and the Birth of Western Canada*, and *Copying People: Photographing BC First Nations, 1860–1940*. In this piece, Daniel looks at the government's definition of Native status, and shows how it disenfranchised and diminished Indian populations.

The broad outline of Canadian Indian policy in the early twentieth century was an inheritance from the past. In the eighteenth and early nineteenth centuries, Britain needed Native people in its armed struggle for control of the continent. Accordingly, they received all the respect due to military allies. Following the War of 1812, however, when conflict with the United States ended and settlers began encroaching on the wilderness, British colonial officials who minded Canadian affairs recognized that a new relationship had to be worked out with Native people. No longer needed as military allies, the aboriginals had lost their value to the White intruders—and were now perceived to be a social and economic problem rather than a diplomatic one. Officials began to think in terms of civilizing the Indians so that they might assume a role in mainstream Canadian society. To this end, reserves were created as places where Indians would be taught to behave like Whites. Subsequent legislation codified the policy of civilization in a tangle of laws and regulations that would have the effect of erecting a prison wall of red tape around Canada's Native population.

The fundamental expression of the Official Indian became the Indian Act. First promulgated in 1876, amended often since then, the Indian Act consolidated and strengthened the control the federal government exercised over its aboriginal citizens. The aim of the Act, as of all Indian legislation, was to assimilate Native people to the Canadian mainstream.[1] Assimilation as a solution to the "Indian problem" was considered preferable to its only perceived alternative: wholesale extermination. There is nothing to indicate that extermination was ever acceptable to Canadians. Not only was it morally repugnant, it was also impractical. The American example showed how costly it was, in terms of money and lives, to wage war against the aboriginals. The last thing the Canadian government wanted to do was initiate a full-scale Indian conflict. It chose instead to go about the elimination of the Indian problem by eliminating the Indian way of life: through education and training, the Red Man would attain civilization. Most White Canadians believed that Indians were doomed to disappear anyway. Assimilation was a policy intended to preserve Indians as individuals by destroying them as a people.

The Indian Act defined an Indian as "any male person of Indian blood reputed to belong to a particular band," his wife and children. The Act excluded certain individuals from Indian status. The most notorious exclusion was Native women who married non-Native men. These women were considered no longer to be Indians and lost any privileges under the terms of the Act, a situation which remained unchanged until 1985. Indian became a legislated concept as well as a racial one, maintained solely through political institutions to which Native people, who had no vote until 1960, had no access.

Special status—Indian status—was conceived as a stopgap measure by White legislators who expected Indians gradually to abandon their Native identity in order to enjoy the privilege of full Canadian citizenship—a process formally known as enfranchisement. As soon as Natives met certain basic requirements of literacy, education and moral character, they would be expected to apply for enfranchisement. In return for giving up legal and treaty rights, the enfranchisement would receive a portion of reserve lands and funds and cease to be an Indian, at least in law. The government expected that in time most Indians would opt for enfranchisement, which was conceived as a reward for good behaviour. In fact, the vast majority of Native people chose not to be rewarded in this way: in the sixty-three years between 1857, when enfranchisement was first legislated, and 1920, only 250 individuals took advantage of the opportunity to shed their Native identity.[2]

The Indian Act treated Native people as minors incapable of looking after their own interests and in need of the protection of the state. "The Indian is a ward of the Government still," Arthur Meighen, then minister of the interior, told Parliament in 1918. "The presumption of the law is that he has not the capacity to decide what is for his ultimate benefit in the same degree as his guardian, the Government of Canada."[3] Indians did not possess the rights and privileges of citizenship; they couldn't vote, they couldn't buy liquor, and they couldn't obtain land under the homestead system. The government expected that Indians would abuse these rights if they had them, that they had to be protected from themselves and from predatory Whites who would take advantage of them. By the same token, status Indians did not have to pay federal taxes (if they were able to find employment) and were "protected from debt" (a condition that usually meant they could not secure loans from financial institutions). They were people apart from mainstream Canadian society. But the ultimate aim of Indian policy was not a system of apartheid. Segregationist, apartheid-like laws were sometimes imposed, but their purpose was tactical: they were intended to serve the long-term policy of assimilation.

If the government wanted to civilize the Indian, what constituted civilization in the official mind? There were several qualities which bureaucrats sought to impress on their Native charges. One was a respect for private property. The fact that Native people seemed to lack a sense of private ownership was widely regarded as a sign of their backwardness. Tribalism, or tribal communism as some people called it, was blamed for stifling the development of initiative and personal responsibility. In the hope of eradicating tribalism, the 1876 Act divided reserves into lots. Band members could qualify for location tickets which, after they proved themselves as farmers, gave them title (but not necessarily ownership) to their own piece of land.

Meanwhile, the reserve itself was an integral part of the civilizing process. Reserves were originally intended as safe havens where Native people could live isolated from the baleful influence of their White neighbours. From the Native point of view, reserves secured a land base for their traditional lifeways. But in the nineteenth century, officials increasingly thought of reserves as social laboratories where Indians could be educated, christianized and prepared for assimilation.

Agriculture was an important weapon in the war on Native culture. As game resources disappeared, farming seemed to be the only alternative way for Natives to make a living. More than that, at a time when industrialism was in its infancy, farming was seen as the profession best suited to a virtuous, civilized person: tilling the soil was an ennobling activity which fostered an orderly home life, industrious work habits and a healthy respect for private property. Farming would cause Natives to settle in one place and end the roving ways so typical of a hunting lifestyle and so detrimental to the sober, reliable routines on which White society prided itself.

Another component of civilization was Christianity. Few Whites had any sympathy for or understanding of Native religious ideas, which were dismissed as pagan superstitions. Religious training was left to missionaries, but the government did its part by banning Native traditional religious and ceremonial practices—for example, the potlatch on the West Coast and the sun dance on the Prairies.

Democratic self-government was also imposed on Native people. The ability to manage elected institutions was believed to be another hallmark of civilized society. Band members were required to elect chiefs and councillors who exercised limited authority over local matters. Indian Department officials retained the power to interfere in the political affairs of the band. The attempt to teach the Indians democracy was part and parcel of the assimilationist agenda. The elected councils were intended to replace traditional forms of Native government over which federal officials lacked control.

A property-owning, voting, hard-working, Christian farmer, abstemious in his habits and respectful of his public duties—that was the end product of government Indian policy. "Instead of having a horde of savages in the North-West, as we had a few years ago," Clifford Sifton, the minister of the interior, told Parliament in 1902, "we shall soon have an orderly, fairly educated population, capable of sustaining themselves."[4] The message the minister intended to deliver was that the Indian had gone from painted savage to yeoman farmer in one generation.

In reality it was not that simple. As time passed, officials grew impatient at the slow pace of assimilation. Native people seemed reluctant to embrace the benefits of White civilization. They resisted many of the measures the government imposed on them. As the American historian Brian Dippie put it, civilization seemed to be a gift more appreciated by the donor than the recipient.[5] Officials concluded that Indians were by nature lazy, intellectually backward and resistant to change. It seemed to be the only explanation: to blame the Indian for not becoming a White man fast enough. As a result, the government passed a series of amendments to the Indian Act in an attempt to speed up the process of assimilation. Regulations became increasingly coercive. Officials received authority to spend money belonging to an Indian band without the members' permission. They could impose the elected system of government on bands, and depose elected leaders of whom they did not approve. At the end of the century, a series of industrial and residential schools removed Native children from their families so that they could be acculturated more easily. A draconian pass system was enacted by which individual Natives could not leave their reserves without the permission of an agent. A system of permits made it difficult for Native people to sell their produce on the open market. While the government said it wanted Natives to become self-sufficient farmers, it erected a series of legal obstacles which made it very difficult for aboriginal farmers to compete with their White neighbours. Frustration at the slow pace of assimilation reached its peak in 1920, when the government took upon itself the legal power to enfranchise an Indian against his or her will; in other words, Indians could be involuntarily stripped of their status. This legislation raised such opposition that it was rescinded two years later, but it was re-enacted in the 1930s. It was a sign of just how desperate the government was to rid itself of the Indian problem by ridding itself of the Indian.

Reading Notes

1. For a discussion of the Indian Act and its predecessors, see John Leslie and Ron Maquire, eds., *The Historical Development of the Indian Act* (Ottawa: Treaties and Historical Research Branch, 1979); John L. Tobias, "Protection, Civilization, Assimilation: An Outline History of Canada's Indian Policy," Ian A. L. Getty and Antonie S. Lussier, eds., *As Long as the Sun Shines and Water Flows: A Reader in Canadian Native Studies* (Vancouver: University of British Columbia Press, 1983), pp. 38–55; John S. Milloy, "The Early Indian Acts," Getty and Lussier,

pp. 56–64; and [J.R.] Miller, *Skyscrapers: Hide the Heavens: A History of Indian-White Relations in Canada* (Toronto: University of Toronto Press, 1989), pp. 109–115.

2. Miller, p. 190.

3. House of Commons Debates, 1918, vol. II, 23 April, p. 1049.

4. Cited in E. Brian Titley, *A Narrow Vision: Duncan Campbell Scott and the Administration of Indian Affairs in Canada* (Vancouver: UBC Press, 1986), p. 19.

5. Brian W. Dippie, *The Vanishing American: White Attitudes and U.S. Indian Policy* (Middletown, Conn.: Wesleyan University Press, 1982), p. 61.

Pretty Like a White Boy

DREW HAYDEN TAYLOR

Drew Hayden Taylor is an author of Ojibway descent best known for his plays that look at Native life, including the award-winning *Toronto at Dreamer's Rock* and *Education Is Our Right*. Taylor has also worked in the film and television industries, producing material that addresses First Nations themes. Although funny, his essay raises important questions regarding Native identity.

In this big, huge world, with all its billions and billions of people, it's safe to say that everybody will eventually come across personalities and individuals that will touch them in some peculiar yet poignant way. Individuals that in some way represent and help define who you are. I'm no different, mine was Kermit the Frog. Not just because Natives have a long tradition of savouring Frogs' legs, but because of his music. If you all may remember, Kermit is quite famous for his rendition of "It's Not Easy Being Green." I can relate. If I could sing, my song would be "It's Not Easy Having Blue Eyes in a Brown Eyed Village."

Yes, I'm afraid it's true. The author happens to be a card-carrying Indian. Once you get past the aforementioned eyes, the fair skin, light brown hair, and noticeable lack of cheekbones, there lies the heart and spirit of an Ojibway storyteller. Honest Injun, or as the more politically correct term may be, honest aboriginal.

You see, I'm the product of a white father I never knew, and an Ojibway woman who evidently couldn't run fast enough. As a kid I knew I looked a bit different. But, then again, all kids are paranoid

when it comes to their peers. I had a fairly happy childhood, frol-
icking through the bullrushes. But there were certain things that,
even then, made me notice my unusual appearance. Whenever
we played cowboys and Indians, guess who had to be the bad guy,
the cowboy.

It wasn't until I left the Reserve for the big bad city that I became
more aware of the role people expected me to play, and the fact that
physically I didn't fit in. Everybody seemed to have this precon-
ceived idea of how every Indian looked and acted. One guy, on my
first day of college, asked me what kind of horse I preferred. I didn't
have the heart to tell him "hobby."

I've often tried to be philosophical about the whole thing.
I have both white and red blood in me, I guess that makes me pink.
I am a "Pink" man. Try to imagine this, I'm walking around on any
typical Reserve in Canada, my head held high, proudly announcing
to everyone "I am a Pink Man." It's a good thing I ran track in
school.

My pinkness is constantly being pointed out to me over and
over and over again. "You don't look Indian?" "You're not Indian,
are you?" "Really?!?" I got questions like that from both white and
Native people, for a while I debated having my status card tattooed
on my forehead.

And like most insecure people and specially a blue eyed Native
writer, I went through a particularly severe identity crisis at one
point. In fact, I admit it, one depressing spring evening, I dyed my
hair black. Pitch black.

The reason for such a dramatic act, you may ask? Show
Business. You see, for the last eight years or so, I've worked in various capacities in the performing arts, and as a result I'd always get
calls to be an extra or even try out for an important role in some
Native oriented movie. This anonymous voice would phone,
having been given my number, and ask if I would be interested in
trying out for a movie. Being a naturally ambitious, curious, and
greedy young man, I would always readily agree, stardom flashing
in my eyes and hunger pains from my wallet.

A few days later I would show up for the audition, and that
was always an experience. What kind of experience you may ask?
Picture this, the picture calls for the casting of seventeenth-century
Mohawk warriors living in a traditional longhouse. The casting
director calls the name "Drew Hayden Taylor" and I enter.

The casting director, the producer, and the film's director look
up from the table and see my face, blue eyes flashing in anticipa-
tion. I once was described as a slightly chubby beachboy. But even
beachboys have tans. Anyway, there would be a quick flush of

confusion, a recheck of the papers, and a hesitant "Mr. Taylor?" Then they would ask if I was at the right audition. It was always the same. By the way, I never got any of the parts I tried for, except for a few anonymous crowd shots. Politics tells me it's because of the way I look, reality tells me it's probably because I can't act. I'm not sure which is better.

It's not just film people either. Recently I've become quite involved in Theatre, Native theatre to be exact. And one cold October day I was happily attending the Toronto leg of a province-wide tour of my first play, *Toronto at Dreamer's Rock*. The place was sold out, the audience very receptive and the performance was wonderful. Ironically one of the actors was also half white.

The director later told me he had been talking with the actor's father, an older Non-Native type chap. Evidently he had asked a few questions about me, and how I did my research. This made the director curious and he asked about his interest. He replied, "He's got an amazing grasp of the Native situation for a white person."

Not all these incidents are work related either. One time a friend and I were coming out of a rather upscale bar (we were out YUPPIE watching) and managed to catch a cab. We thanked the cab driver for being so comfortably close on such a cold night, he shrugged and nonchalantly talked about knowing what bars to drive around. "If you're not careful, all you'll get is drunk Indians." I hiccuped.

Another time this cab driver droned on and on about the government. He started out by criticizing Mulroney, and eventually to his handling of the Oka crisis. This perked up my ears, until he said, "If it were me, I'd have tear-gassed the place by the second day. No more problem." He got a dime tip. A few incidents like this and I'm convinced I'd make a great undercover agent for one of the Native political organizations.

But then again, even Native people have been known to look at me with a fair amount of suspicion. Many years ago when I was a young man, I was working on a documentary on Native culture up in the wilds of Northern Ontario. We were at an isolated cabin filming a trapper woman and her kids. This one particular nine-year-old girl seemed to take a shine to me. She followed me around for two days both annoying me and endearing herself to me. But she absolutely refused to believe that I was Indian. The whole film crew tried to tell her but to no avail. She was certain I was white.

Then one day as I was loading up the car with film equipment, she asked me if I wanted some tea. Being in a hurry I declined the tea. She immediately smiled with victory crying out, "See, you're not Indian, all Indians drink tea!"

Frustrated and a little hurt I whipped out my Status card and thrust it at her. Now there I was, standing in a Northern Ontario winter, showing my Status card to a nine-year-old non-status Indian girl who had no idea what one was. Looking back, this may not have been one of my brighter moves.

But I must admit, it was a Native woman that boiled everything down in one simple sentence. You may know that woman, Marianne Jones from *The Beachcombers* television series. We were working on a film together out west and we got to gossiping. Eventually we got around to talking about our respective villages. Hers on the Queen Charlotte Islands, or Haida Gwaii as the Haida call them, and mine in central Ontario.

Eventually childhood on the Reserve was being discussed and I made a comment about the way I look. She studied me for a moment, smiled, and said, "Do you know what the old women in my village would call you?" Hesitant but curious, I shook my head. "They'd say you were pretty like a white boy." To this day I'm still not sure if I like that.

Now some may argue that I am simply a Métis with a Status card. I disagree, I failed French in grade 11. And the Métis as everyone knows have their own separate and honourable culture, particularly in western Canada. And of course I am well aware that I am not the only person with my physical characteristics.

I remember once looking at a video tape of a drum group, shot on a Reserve up near Manitoulin Island. I noticed one of the drummers seemed quite fairhaired, almost blond. I mentioned this to my girlfriend at the time and she shrugged saying, "Well, that's to be expected. The highway runs right through the Reserve."

Perhaps I'm being too critical. There's a lot to be said for both cultures. For example, on the left hand, you have the Native respect for Elders. They understand the concept of wisdom and insight coming with age.

On the white hand, there's Italian food. I mean I really love my mother and family but seriously, does anything really beat good Veal Scallopini? Most of my aboriginal friends share my fondness for this particular brand of food. Wasn't there a warrior at Oka named Lasagna? I found it ironic, though curiously logical, that Columbus was Italian. A connection I wonder?

Also Native people have this wonderful respect and love for the land. They believe they are part of it, a mere chain in the cycle of existence. Now, as many of you know, this conflicts with the accepted Judeo-Christian i.e. western view of land management. I even believe somewhere in the first chapters of the Bible it says something about God giving man dominion over Nature. Check it out, Genesis 4:?, "Thou shalt clear cut." So I grew up understanding that everything around me is important and alive. My Native heritage gave me that.

And again, on the white hand, there's breast implants. Darn clever them white people. That's something Indians would never have invented, seriously. We're not ambitious enough. We just take what the Creator decides to give us, but no, not the white man. Just imagine it, some serious looking white man, and let's face it people, we know it was a man who invented them, don't we? So just imagine some serious looking white doctor sitting around in his laboratory muttering to himself, "Big tits, big tits, hmm, how do I make big tits?" If it was an Indian, it would be "Big tits, big tits, white women sure got big tits" and leave it at that.

So where does that leave me on the big philosophical scoreboard, what exactly are my choices again; Indians—respect for elders, love of the land. White people—food and big tits. In order to live in both cultures I guess I'd have to find an Indian woman with big tits who lives with her grandmother in a cabin out in the woods and can make Fettucini Alfredo on a wood stove.

Now let me make this clear, I'm not writing this for sympathy, or out of anger, or even some need for self-glorification. I am just setting the facts straight. For as you read this, a new Nation is born. This is a declaration of independence, my declaration of independence.

I've spent too many years explaining who and what I am repeatedly, so as of this moment, I officially secede from both races. I plan to start my own separate nation. Because I am half Ojibway, and half Caucasian, we will be called the Occasions. And I of course, since I'm founding the new nation, will be a Special Occasion.

Why Multiculturalism Can't End Racism

MARLENE NOURBESE PHILIP

Marlene NourbeSe Philip is a poet, dramatist, fiction and non-fiction writer. Her works include two novels, *Looking for Livingstone: An Odyssey of Silence* and *Harriet's Daughter*, as well as three books of poetry, *She Tries Her Tongue, Her Silence Softly Breaks*; *Salmon Courage*; and *Thorns*. Born in Tobago, she now resides in Toronto, where she writes on issues of race, gender, and justice. In this piece, Philip suggests Canada's policy of multiculturalism may ironically promote rather than end discrimination.

> A national culture is the whole body of efforts made by a people in the sphere of thought to describe, justify and praise the action through which that people has created itself and keeps itself in existence.
>
> —*The Wretched of the Earth*, Franz Fanon

At its most basic, multiculturalism describes a configuration of power at the centre of which are the two cultures recognized by the constitution of Canada—the French and the English—and around which circumnavigate the lesser satellite cultures. Native culture, to date, remains unrecognized by the Constitution.

The configuration of power appears to be designed to equalize power among the individual satellite cultures, and between the collectivity of those cultures and the two central cultures, the French and English. The mechanism of multiculturalism is, therefore, based on a presumption of equality, a presumption which is not necessarily borne out in reality.

Because it pretends to be what it is not—a mechanism to equalize all cultures within Canada—it ought not to surprise us that multiculturalism would be silent about issues of race and colour.

The Ontario government in its official policy on multiculturalism, *Multiculturalism: A New Strategy for Ontario*, recognizes the special concerns that colour and race present, and addresses those concerns within their policy. The new federal bill, Bill C-18, soon to be the Department of Multiculturalism and Citizenship Act, does not even define multiculturalism, let alone mention race or colour.

A long historical overview of the formation of Canada reveals that this country was, as was the United States, shaped and fashioned by a belief system that put white Europeans at the top of society and Native and African people at the bottom. This ideology, for that is what it is, assigned more importance to European cultures and values than those of the Native or African.

The Canadian examples are numerous: its genocidal practices against Natives; its past and present treatment of the Black Empire Loyalists who fled to the Maritimes; the various immigration acts which record Canada's preference for white Europeans;

Canada's past treatment of Chinese and Indian immigrants; its refusal to allow entry to large numbers of Africans or Asians until very recently; Canada's treatment of its citizens of Japanese heritage in World War II; its present treatment of Asian refugees; and the present location and quantity of immigration offices around the world. To these must be added Canada's reluctance to allow Jews to seek refuge here during World War II.

These examples all constitute evidence of a nation founded upon a belief in white and European supremacy, of which racism, as we presently know it, is an offshoot. In his study of the right wing in Canada, *Is God a Racist?* Stanley R. Barrett writes that, "racism in Canada has been institutionalized . . . as deeply rooted as that in the United States," the difference being that Canada has always put a more polite face on its racism.

Wherever the European went, whether he was English, French, German, Spanish, Dutch or Portuguese, he took with him this particular gospel—that the Native and indigenous peoples he encountered, who were also not white, were to be brutalized, enslaved, maimed, or killed and, where necessary, used to enrich him personally and/or his particular European country.

Wherever you find the European outside Europe, there you will find this particular pattern and method of settlement. The settlement of Canada was no exception to this rule.

The source of this belief—that the light pigmentation of one's skin bespeaks one's superiority and entitles one to destroy those of a darker hue, and/or unjustly enrich one's self at their expense—is a complex one and cannot be explored here. Suffice it to say that this belief system is, historically, an integral part of the cultural fabric of Canada. It is a belief system that is still with us today in many forms, and of which South Africa presents a telling and modern example.

Some might object to the use of the expression "white supremacy" on the grounds that it is an expression commonly used to describe extreme bigots who, along with other demands, openly advocate anti-Semitism, the repatriation of African and Asian immigrants, and a keep-Canada-white policy.

It is, however, an expression that accurately describes a certain historical and present-day reality as outlined above, and one which we must understand in order to grasp how thoroughly racism—the glue that holds the edifice of white supremacy together—permeates our societies.

What we have in Canada, therefore, are the manifestations of racial and ethnic prejudices between many of the so-called multicultural groups, because racism is not restricted only to relations between white and Black people. Depending on whether the variable of power is present, these prejudices may remain just that—prejudices—but prejudices which must be eradicated through a combination of education and legal remedies.

We also have, however, a larger and overarching structure posited on the ideology of white supremacy, one of the foundation stones of this country, and within which these other manifestations of racism function. To complicate matters even further, many of the white groups within the great multicultural pool come from cultures that have espoused these beliefs of white supremacy.

The net result is that Black people of African heritage will be found at the bottom of the multicultural pool. And below them will probably be found Natives.

What do we have when schools perfunctorily dump Black and Native students into dead-end, vocational programs; when police forces in our large urban centres treat their Asian and African communities as a sub-class to be policed differently and more harshly than white communities?

What do we have when justice systems and police forces treat Native people as a sub-class which receives a lesser form of justice than do white people; when statistics reveal that Black people are refused employment three times more frequently than whites?

What is it when publishers refuse to read manuscripts because they contain African Canadian characters, or when a museum under the guise of mounting an exhibition about African cultures, glorifies the imperial conquest of Africa?

What do we have? Racism or white supremacy? Does the difference in terminology really matter? And how, if at all, does multiculturalism affect these practices?

To the Indian, Jamaican or Micmac person on the receiving end of some of the practices described above, it often matters little what words you use to describe the actions that hurt and sometimes kill them. The results, whether we call it the ideology of white supremacy or racism, are the same — poor schooling, high unemployment, and inadequate housing to name but a few. All of which add up to the greatest tragedy of racism—wasted human potential and lives.

When you are black skinned, it often matters little if the person refusing to rent to you is Polish-, Anglo- or Italian-Canadian. The result is the same. And multiculturalism, as we presently know it, has no answers to these or other problems such as the confrontations between the police forces in urban areas like Toronto and Montreal and the African Canadian communities that live there; it has no answers for the African Canadian or Native child shunted into a dead-end program in school.

In short, multiculturalism, as we know it, has no answers for the problems of racism, or white supremacy—unless it is combined with a clearly articulated policy of anti-racism, directed at rooting out the effects of racist and white supremacist thinking.

A society or nation such as Canada, founded on the principles of white supremacy and racism, cannot ever succeed in developing a society free of the injustices that spring from these systems of thought, without a clearly articulated policy on the *need* to eradicate these beliefs. And we cannot begin such an eradication by forgetting how one brutal aspect of Canadian culture was formed. It is for this reason that an understanding of the ideological lineage of this belief system is so important to any debate on racism and multiculturalism.

Despite its many critics, multiculturalism will not disappear. Too many people benefit from it, and it is far too fancy a piece of window-dressing for a government to get rid of.

However, unless it is steeped in a clearly articulated policy of anti-racism, multiculturalism will, at best, merely continue as a mechanism whereby immigrants indulge their nostalgic love for their mother countries.

At worst, it will, as it sometimes does, unwittingly perpetuate racism by muddying waters between anti-racism and multiculturalism. It is not uncommon to read material from various government departments that use these words interchangeably so as to suggest that multiculturalism is synonymous with anti-racism. It is not. It never will be.

It is possible that Canadian society may come to accept that racism and white supremacist beliefs must no longer be a part of its culture. But only if there is a collective commitment to such a goal. It cannot do so merely by a policy of multiculturalism, which is a far less difficult task than eradicating those theories, beliefs and practices that rank humanity according to colour and race. Valuing people of all races and colour equally is a much wider, and infinitely more difficult, project than multiculturalism. Until this is accomplished, Canadians will not be able to derive the full benefits of multiculturalism—even in the limited sense in which this is ever possible.

Born to Shop

ADBUSTERS

Adbusters is a Vancouver-based magazine that raises awareness about the perils of capitalism. Founded by Kalle Lasn, it uses parody to make serious points about the spiritual emptiness of our consumer culture. Using the language of psychiatry, this selection suggests that impulsive shopping may constitute a mental disorder.

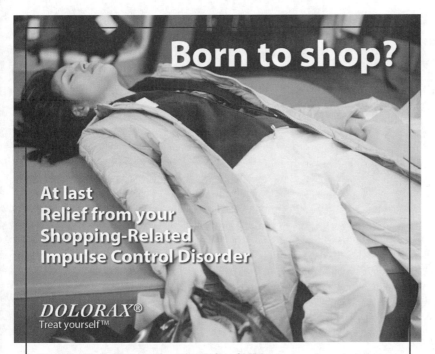

Born to shop?

At last
Relief from your
Shopping-Related
Impulse Control Disorder

DOLORAX®
Treat yourself™

How Do I Know If I Have Shopping-Related ICD?

- Recurrent failure to resist impulses to buy objects that are not needed and which contribute to personal financial or psychological harm and/or social or environmental harm.
- Increasing sense of tension or arousal immediately before committing the purchase.

- Pleasure, gratification, or relief at the time of committing the purchase.
- The purchase may be in response to a delusion, but must not be in response to a hallucination.

Experts now know that Shopping-Related ICD is an epidemic condition in North America, Europe and Japan. If you experience these symptoms, it's time to talk to your doctor about non-drowsy, 24-hour DOLORAX, the Shopping Solution™ most recommended by medical professionals.*

*Of those surveyed.

Metaphors

"All that is, is metaphor."

—Norman O. Brown

Metaphors and figurative speech are statements that make comparisons between objects, some literally spelled out, others implied. Greater than poetry, figurative speech makes up a huge chunk of daily language. For example, the phrase "walking on thin ice" doesn't literally describe a trip across a newly frozen lake, but rather risky business in general. The present danger resembles the icy one. Such metaphors are so deeply ingrained that we often overlook them (as you might have now overlooked the metaphor "ingrained"). If we ignore metaphors, however, we neglect the profound effect they have on thought and action.

KINDS OF FIGURATIVE SPEECH

"All perception of truth is the detection of an analogy."

—Henry David Thoreau

As with any large population, figurative language has distinct types. Here follow some major tropes in this family.

Simile compares two distinct objects using "like" or "as." An overt form of figurative speech, the simile honestly declares its comparison, using the "like" or "as" to suggest a parallel between two objects, while keeping them distinct. In other words, a simile argues only for a resemblance, not a substitution. So when someone says "a smoking section in a restaurant is like a peeing section in a pool," he or she suggests that the two experiences share certain features (the even dissipation of a liquid or a gas in a confined space), but remain, thankfully, separate.

Metaphor creates an identity between two distinct objects. It presents the first object as if were synonymous with the second, both the same thing. More drastic than a simile, the metaphor goes beyond resemblance, and creates an out-and-out substitution, as can be seen in Lana Turner's line "A gentleman is simply a patient wolf." This metaphor literally equates gentlemen with wolves, as if they were one and the same, even though they're physically different. The similarity between the two objects (their cunning, predatory nature, viciousness) becomes exaggerated until they become synonyms: the man *is* a wolf. Because a metaphor doesn't announce the comparison it makes, it can be tricky to spot, as one term of comparison may be implied or missing entirely. The line "the pigs threw me in jail," for example, is a metaphor in which the term "pigs" has completely erased the physical subject, the police.

Personification imbues inanimate objects or abstractions with human or living qualities. "Time devours us all" uses personification, because the abstract dimension of time appears as a ravenous person rather than a unit of measurement.

Synecdoche describes a figure of speech in which a part of an object stands for the whole. We refer to a car with the synecdoche "a set of wheels"; a rake refers to women as "skirts"; Brits use the "White Cliffs of Dover" as a synecdoche for all England.

Metonymy uses a closely related word, object, or attribute to substitute for the thing itself. Movie directors typically use eyeglasses to metonymically suggest a character's intelligence.

Imagery refers to statements that provide visual information, and an image becomes figurative when it stands for something else. George Bush's famous campaign slogan "I see a thousand points of light" provides a metaphorical image. The feel-good line doesn't refer to any real illumination, but represents Bush's social programs and policies. Think of imagery as picture language, and to use another metaphor, you get the picture.

Allegory describes a story in which every narrative element stands for something else in the real or spiritual world: an extended and sustained metaphor. Jesus Christ's parables of fig trees, shepherds and sheep are simple allegories; the characters and crises dramatize the tenets of Christianity. George Orwell's *Animal Farm* is an allegory that uses barnyard creatures to portray the failure of the Communist revolution.

Symbol is an object that represents something else in a formal and conventional manner. Canada uses the beaver as a national symbol; Great Britain, the bulldog; and the USA, the eagle. The meaning of a symbol depends on the culture using it. Consider another animal token, the raven. In European traditions, the raven appears as an omen of death and evil, yet the Salish Indians consider the raven a benign creator.

Archetype, coined by the psychoanalyst Carl Gustav Jung, is a universal symbol, whose meaning remains constant in all cultures. Most societies ascribe life-giving meaning to water, and fertility to a mother figure. An archetype is a symbol that's gone global.

These tropes shouldn't be mistaken for a comprehensive taxonomy, for figurative language is constantly evolving, mutating, and adding new species.

HOW METAPHORS WORK

"Words, like Nature, half reveal
And half conceal the Soul within."

—Lord Tennyson

All metaphoric language encourages us to consider one thing in terms of another, to discuss "apples" in terms of "oranges." For example, we metaphorically express "knowledge" as "illumination"; understanding with an "I see"; smart people as "bright" or "visionaries." Such commonplace expressions present a mental state (intelligence) in terms of a physical sense (sight). These metaphoric dislocations are useful because the two experiences are similar, and the first informs our understanding of the second. If we're to decode metaphoric language, we begin by recognizing the likeness between the two comparatives.

Literary critic I. A. Richards introduced some helpful terms for analyzing metaphors. The subject of the metaphor, the real beastie, idea, or thing referred to, Richards terms the "tenor," and the object of comparison or substitute, he names the "vehicle." Lastly Richards suggests the term "ground" to describe the points in common between the tenor and vehicle, the similarity that energizes the metaphor. More recently, linguists have introduced the terms "target domain" (for tenor), "source domain" (for vehicle), and "mapping" for the shared terrain (the ground).

Think of a metaphor as a football field: if the vehicle and tenor mark the metaphor's perimeter (the out-of-bound lines), then the ground represents the playing field where the action occurs and meaning unfolds. The ground is the centre of any figure of speech, for it provides the similarity that justifies the comparison. We cannot properly understand or evaluate any metaphor without fully appreciating the parallels between vehicle and tenor.

Unfortunately, metaphors don't declare their ground, but leave these common points for readers to deduce. Metaphoric similarities between vehicle and tenor are embedded within a metaphor, obliquely suggested or implied, but never overtly stated. To understand a metaphor, readers must "map out" this ground, identifying the parallels between the source and target domain.

Consider Robbie Burns' famous simile "My love is like a red, red rose." To fully understand the poet's meaning, we must deduce the qualities of Burns' beloved mirrored in the rose.

GROUND

Vehicle/Source Domain	Tenor/Target Domain
Rose	Beloved
Red colour	Passion, blush, fertility
Beauty of flower	Beauty of woman
Fragrance	Perfume
Thorns	Pain of love
Insect infestation	Syphilis
Brevity of bloom	Brevity of youth/infatuation
Folds of petals	Folds of vulva
Care needed to grow roses	Devotion needed to maintain affection

In eight words, Burns suggests a constellation of ideas, both positive and negative. His metaphor captures love's splendor, yet its hidden pricks as well; he suggests passion, pleasure, and rapture, but danger, frailty, and brevity too. Tracing the parallels between the rose and the beloved makes these ideas clear. To grasp metaphors, readers must "unpack" them, laying out the full range of similarities between the vehicle and tenor. A good metaphor resembles a children's pop-up book, constantly delighting us with unexpected possibilities that spring up.

As Burns' poem shows, metaphors are powerful tools for expressing complex information in a simple manner. They condense intricate and contradictory ideas into the space of a few words—intellectual shorthand. Parents often speak to children in metaphors, presenting new concepts in familiar terms: "skipping breakfast is like forgetting to put gas in your car." Such metaphors make new information accessible and familiar, for both child and adult.

Similarly, Apple computers made the confusing world of computer programming more manageable through a visual metaphor—the desktop. In this analogy, computer users carry out commands with everyday objects like documents, folders, and trashcans. Now standard, the desktop has been joined by viruses, gateways, worms, surfers, and bookmarks—all metaphors that make computer operation intuitive and recognizable.

But a metaphor is more than a potent communicator; it's a necessity of thought itself, a basic tool in our cognitive processes. We use metaphors to articulate emotions and ideas, giving a concrete form to intangible thoughts and feelings ("He was shattered," "I feel like a million bucks"). Hardly a poetic frill, metaphor is a primary activity of consciousness.

A lens on the world, metaphors affect our perceptions. A figure of speech encourages us to see the world in a specific way, and discourages alternate possibilities. Consider the different metaphors describing the relationship between Earth and humanity listed below. Each suggests a different reality, and places humanity in contradictory roles.

Earth as Home—This image presents Earth as a giant house, tenanted by plants and animals, yet managed by human landlords. Of course, a house uses municipal services (such as electricity, sewage, and garbage collection) that have no parallels on a planetary scale.

Earth as Family—This feel-good image highlights the inter-related nature of all living creatures, but can't deal with such aspects as predation or reproduction.

Earth as Treasure Chest—This image focuses attention on the mineral wealth, and presents Earth as a vault that can make people rich, if they're clever enough to unlock it. Resource extraction is represented as a simple matter of picking a lock, not as something messy like strip-mining.

Earth as Person—An environmental metaphor, this personification makes the planet a sentient being, "wounded" by activities such as mining, fishing, and forestry. This personification appears in two common guises.

- Mother Earth—emphasizing the nurturing and feminine aspects of the planet, transforming humanity into a child.
- A spirit (Gaia)—presenting Nature as a source of mysticism and meaning.

Earth as Paradise—This metaphor emphasizes the pleasant aspects of the planet, yet neglects the unpleasant ones such as earthquakes and pestilence. It also carries religious connotations, making man an interloper in a divine plan.

Earth as Spaceship—Buckminster Fuller coined the phrase "Spaceship Earth" to emphasize our small size in the cosmos, our precarious existence, and the need for cooperation. Unlike a spaceship, however, we have little control over the course.

Earth as Kingdom—The medieval mind conceived of Earth as the Kingdom of God, and Mankind as His steward. This hierarchical metaphor makes humanity *somewhat* special, ranking higher in the chain of being than plants or animals, but lower than angels. The Earth fares less well, becoming Man's vassal to be used and exploited.

Each metaphor configures differently the relationship between man and the planet. None is right or wrong, but rather each focuses our awareness on select features of the relationship. An ecologist employs the Earth Mother image to emphasize human dependency on nature; a mineralogist uses the treasure trope to encourage mineral extraction. At the same time, each metaphor suppresses aspects of the relationship. The image of the Earth as a family evokes a sense of kinship between life forms, but only by ignoring predation. In this respect, a metaphor works like a frame over a painting, drawing our attention to a central portrait, removing the undesirables that don't "fit the picture." In other words, metaphors conceal as much as they reveal.

In addition to misdirection, metaphors also introduce unwanted "noise" into our thoughts, transferring qualities in the vehicle *that don't exist in the tenor*. Indeed, distortion is inevitable, for metaphors occur only between different objects. One could not say "a Honda is like a car," for the Honda more than resembles a car: it is one. Accordingly, comparisons only work when terms are suitably divergent. Because tenor and vehicle differ, all metaphors deform and misrepresent their subjects to a degree. This is a critical point. Metaphors purport to inform, but by presenting one thing in terms of another, by speaking of X in terms of Y, they also distort, warp, and disfigure. Linguists haven't yet fashioned a term for this crucial difference between vehicle and tenor, so I would like to suggest one: the rift.

The rift is as critical to understanding metaphor as the ground, for the rift marks places where a metaphor breaks down, and potentially misleads.

Let's take a simple example. A husband complains his marriage "suffocates" him. He doesn't mean literal asphyxiation, but rather the feelings of confinement that occur in any relationship. While this metaphor dramatizes the husband's aggravation, it misrepresents and exacerbates his problem. First, suffocation is lethal, while marriage isn't, and so the metaphor exaggerates psychic pain until it becomes bodily death. Second, suffocation is almost always intentional, with a clear aggressor and victim. In contrast, marital discord typically lacks simple villains. The husband's metaphor conceals his contribution to the marital turmoil, and ascribes to the wife a masochistic intent *that might not exist.* Yet, with the image of suffocation fixed in mind, the husband sees his partner as brutal, and marriage as a death trap.

As the husband's pessimistic metaphor contributes to his domestic woes, our collective metaphors may determine our social realities. Unfortunately, we have many metaphors that increase suffering in the real world.

Feminists worry about metaphors that present women as "foxes," "bunnies," or "chicks," fearing that such animal imagery dehumanizes. Terms such as "babes," "playmates," or "girls" further rob women 'of adult status. Just as worrisome are the "Battle of the Sexes" metaphors, where good looks appear as a weapon (she's "devastatingly beautiful," a "knockout," a "bombshell"), and sex becomes aggression (he "hit on" her, she resisted his "advances," she "banged" him).

Some environmentalists feel that the "Earth as Kingdom" model encourages us to exploit the planet with the ruthless disregard of a cruel lord. Filled with a false sense of dominion, Man treats Earth as his vassal, leading to real harm such as extinction, deforestation, desertification, and pollution.

In the article "Metaphors That Kill," George Lakoff analyzes the reasons for the 1991 Gulf War (that killed an estimated 500,000 people), and finds the invasion based upon a series of metaphoric dodges, exaggerations, and distortions that exist linguistically, but not in reality. If Lakoff is right, we have an obligation to spot our society's "sick" metaphors and forge healthier ones. It's literally a matter of life and death.

HOW TO INTERPRET METAPHORS

When reading metaphor, carry out these steps.

1. Identify Tenor and Vehicle

   Restate the figure of speech in the form of a simile: X is compared to Y. This identifies the target and source domains, and clarifies the comparison—a necessary step in metaphors with implied subjects. For example, the phrase "The Prime Minister has charted a new economic course for Canada" contains an implied comparison, better understood as "The new economic policy is like the course of a ship."

2. Map the Metaphor's Ground

List similarities between vehicle and tenor. These resemblances enable the vehicle to model and explain the tenor. The more a vehicle coincides with its tenor, the more persuasive a metaphor appears. In our metaphor, many parallels appear.

GROUND

Vehicle/Source Domain	Tenor/Target Domain
Ship's course	Economic policy
Ship	Canada
Captain	Prime Minister
Sailors	Citizens
Ocean	International trade
Journey	Economic activity
Destination	Prosperity

3. Recognize Differences Between Tenor and Vehicle

List the differences between target and source domain. Such divergences help identify the limitations of a metaphor and reduce the chances of misdirection. In our example, the metaphor of the nation-as-ship collapses when we recognize that a Captain commands his sailors, but in a democracy, the citizens command the Prime Minister. Without such analysis, we might accept the Prime Minister's plan as if it were a Captain's order.

4. Find New Metaphors

A collapsed metaphor provides opportunity to invent new figures of speech. For example, one could describe an economic policy as seeding a field, finetuning an engine, or squeezing the poor. Notice how these metaphors emphasize features suppressed in the original. With a plurality of metaphors, we get a more accurate picture of reality. As the poet Wallace Stevens suggests, truth may be 13 ways of looking at a blackbird.

CASE STUDY: THE INVASION OF AFGHANISTAN

"What then is truth? A mobile army of metaphors, metonyms, and anthropomorphism."

—Friedrich Nietzsche

Shortly after September 11, 2001, the United States prepared to invade Afghanistan, which it believed was harbouring terrorists. In the battle of public opinion, one Bush administration official fostered support for the invasion with this metaphor:

> We see this war as one against the virus of terrorism. If you have bone marrow cancer, it's not enough to just cut off the patient's foot. You have to do the complete course of chemotherapy. And if that means embarking on the next Hundred Years' War, that's what we're doing. (Rose and Vulliamy)

This metaphor presents war as a medical procedure, where the disease is terrorism, and the patient, the planet Earth. The metaphor gains credibility through a series of parallels between war and medicine, as summarized below.

GROUND	
Vehicle/Source Domain	**Tenor/Target Domain**
Medical treatment	War
Patient	Planet
Virus/Cancer	Terrorists
Visible damage	Terrorist acts
DNA	Terrorist message
Diseased limbs/organs	Terrorist states
Death of patient	Global catastrophe
Health	Absence of terrorism
Doctor	United States
Multi-staged treatment: surgery, radiation, chemotherapy	Multi-staged response to terrorism; invasion, regime change, surveillance
Surgery	Invasion of Afghanistan
Breaking skin	Crossing Afghani border
Amputation of diseased tissue	Removal of Taliban
Healthy tissue hurt during treatment	Civilian casualties
Chemotherapy/Radiation	Planet wide policing
Post-op watch for reinfection (10 years)	Global surveillance of terrorism (100 years)
Withholding medical treatment	Political inaction

The metaphor makes several other parallels between war and medicine. Terrorism resembles cancer, for both are unpleasant, difficult to wipe out, and lethal if unchecked. Famously, the cancer cell can metastasize (reproduce quickly); terrorist organizations likewise swell rapidly. Cancer can lie dormant, invisible on the surface, but active underneath a healthy surface. So too may terrorists groups lurk under the veneer of a peaceful society. Cancer treatment is painful and complicated, requiring several stages. So too will the battle against terrorism be harsh, requiring a coordinated effort across several fronts. Although both procedures are unsettling, they save lives. This is perhaps the strongest parallel in the metaphor—war may be a "bitter pill," but it preserves life.

Given these similarities, the metaphor is insightful, allowing us to understand a complex situation (the American response to global terrorism) by means of a familiar scenario (treatment of disease). Unfortunately, this metaphor also misrepresents its topic in a distressing fashion.

Perhaps the biggest problem is the way this metaphor reduces terrorists to cancer cells, transforming human beings into an infection. Such dehumanization serves the purpose of invasion, for killing is easier if your enemy is a mere bug.

The metaphor further reduces terrorism to a force of nature, and so ignores the political motivation behind the assault of September 11. Diminished to a viral infection, Muslims are robbed of their voices, histories, and legitimate grievances. The metaphor not only pardons any past American offences against Islamic nations, it condones future ones (for what crime can be committed against cancer?). Finally, it renders any negotiation pointless: the only reasonable response to infection is annihilation.

The metaphor also substitutes a single person for the entire planet, a synecdoche that allows one individual to represent the opinions of over 6 billion. Of course, earth isn't so unified, and the metaphor clouds the fractious disagreement behind the invasion. And Muslim terrorists—citizens of the planet—aren't part of the patient, but alien invaders.

This metaphor also presents us another misleading synecdoche, where renegade terrorists stand for the entire Afghani state, a handful of suspects replacing 25 million innocent civilians. Naturally, the metaphor encourages this slip, for it's easier to bomb a guilty few, than an innocent majority.

Although terrorism has taken many lives, it probably won't kill its host—the planet. Nonetheless, this bureaucrat encourages us to perceive terrorism as a terminal threat that will destroy the Earth. By raising the stakes to dire levels, the metaphor persuades listeners to accept the "tough medicine" of war and invasion. In contrast, failure to invade is equivalent to withholding medical treatment from the sick. And so, the metaphor precludes peaceful options like extradition, prosecution, and imprisonment of the terrorists. We must kill in order to be kind.

If the metaphor casts terrorists as germs, then it presents the U.S. as a benevolent physician, a philanthropist acting in the interest of the planet. Of course, this statement presents another defective synecdoche in the figure of "America" (300 million, bitterly divided on the war) acting with a singular will. More interestingly, this metaphor portrays the invasion of Afghanistan as a charitable act, rather than a military aggression in the name of national security. The U.S. can't be faulted for protecting itself, but it's a fraud to suggest the invasion was a selfless gesture.

The metaphor shows another fracture, for the U.S. becomes both a diseased organ *and* the doctor. In parallel fashion, the U.S. presents itself as part of the international community, and somehow above it.

The metaphor presents violence conducted by U.S. forces as healthy, and violence conducted against the U.S. as diseased—a double standard, where American brutality is necessary, while Islamic aggression is sick.

Patients have the choice of doctors and the right to refuse treatment. No such choice applies here, for the U.S. forced the invasion of Afghanistan onto the world.

And the basic metaphor, war-as-medical-treatment, is a twisted bit of doublespeak that equates carpet bombing and depleted uranium shells with the promotion of health. Certainly some medical treatments are painful, but their unwavering purpose is to preserve—not extinguish—life.

The metaphor finally proposes the treatment of chemotherapy and radiation, stressful procedures that suggest nauseating levels of real violence. Chemotherapy and radiation therapy also flood the entire body—so the metaphor implies that the American military solution will flood every nation, every home. In the name of health, the metaphor conditions us to accept American sovereignty across the planet.

Works Cited

Richards, I. A. *The Philosophy of Rhetoric*. New York: Oxford UP, 1936.

Rose, David and Ed Vulliamy. "Iraq 'behind US anthrax outbreaks.'" *The Guardian* October 14, 2001. Oct. 23, 2003. <http://observer.guardian.co.uk/international/story/0,6903,573893,00.html>.

Turner, Lana. "Creative quotations from Lana Turner (1920–1995)." *Creative Quotations*. Dec. 16, 2003. <http://www.creativequotations.com/one/2091.htm>.

Exercises

1. Identify the vehicles and tenors of these metaphors.
    a) Primitive people are close to the earth.
    b) Carrot-Top grates on my nerves.
    c) You are the cream in my coffee.
    d) Luke is feeling blue today.
    e) Einstein was the father of relativity.
    f) Schizophrenia is a chemical storm in the brain.
    g) "Language is the dress of thought" (Samuel Johnson).

2. Identify the vehicles, tenors, and ground of these metaphors. How do these metaphors influence perception?
    a) Justice is blind.
    b) "Hope is a thing of feathers" (Emily Dickinson).
    c) The Crown wishes its red children to follow the light of the white man.
    d) In the Dark Ages, the chains of faith shackled the human spirit.
    e) The Trojan virus crippled my computer.
    f) General Leland performed a cost/benefit analysis of the war.
    g) A university education is an investment in your future
    h) Communism is a dead, politically bankrupt philosophy.
    i) *Hustler* is a filthy magazine.
    j) "As a white candle/In a holy place,/So is the beauty/Of an aged face" (Joseph Campbell).
    k) The Liberal Party has lost its moral compass.
    l) The poor suck at the teat of society, draining its milk until it is near death.

3. Think up at least two appropriate metaphors to explain the following items.
      The mind
      A boyfriend
      A child
      Civilization
      A corporation
      The DNA chain
      The economy
      Education
      Immigrants
      The Internet
      Marriage
      Medicine
      Parenting
      Religion

    What do your metaphors emphasize? Do you foresee problems or distortions?

You Fit into Me

MARGARET ATWOOD

Margaret Atwood is arguably Canada's most famous poet and novelist. A prolific writer, winner of the Booker Prize, Atwood released her latest novel *Oryx and Crake* in 2003.

> You fit into me
> like a hook into an eye
> A fish hook
> An open eye

all my seasick sailors

LYNN CROSBIE

Magazine editor and critic, Lynn Crosbie is a poet and non-fiction writer. She has released five poetry collections, *Miss Pamela's Mercy*, *Pearl*, *VillainElle*, *Missing Children*, and *Queen Rat*, as well as two novels, *Paul's Case* and *Dorothy L'Amour*.

> Sly and second-sighted, my friends have abandoned ship. Rats,
>   escaping in small grey
> lifeboats, their annular tails turn the tide, their lambent eyes, like the
>   moon, dictate its flow.
> The violinist plays *Autumn* as the masts unfold, water lilies in the
>   pitch of the sea.
>
> A message in semaphore, what I have always longed to know—to stand
>   by the stern, and
> with courage, let go. Nostalgia's poison
>
> love spreads out like a sheaf of photographs, memory without blood,
>   a fluked anchor,
> undone. The line that breaks when the storm comes, the truth that
>   sailors know:
> red skies without delight,
>
> a bad sign. To navigate you must know where you are going, with an
>   exact chart,
> pin-stuck with ellipses. Accidents, typhoon, the fibrous stakes of sea
>   monsters, the diamond ice caps,

miracles that have changed course, carved passages into the new
    worlds, where sailors
arise. In white militia,

letters come like gulls flat on the crest of waves, infatuation coursing,
    like a science of chaos,
they appear in envelopes of ice, intermittent ghosts—to remind me
    that love is spectral,
unforeseen.

The rapids were turbulent toward the Asian corridor, sailing into
    Lachine. It is China, after all.
Rare and fragile, esteemed from a great distance,

protected in shelf-ice.

I touch this china from rim to stem, and feel its raised flowers,
    brought to me from the ocean's
floor. *In spite of the danger*, the mariners have garlanded the stingray
—as the lashings narrowed,

they retrieved me from the wreck.

Canada: Case History

EARLE BIRNEY

Earle Birney was a vital force in Canadian literature for decades, producing plays, radio dramas, and novels, including *Turvey, A Military Picaresque*, and *Down the Long Table*. Author of such classic poems as "Vancouver Lights," "Bushed," "David," and "Anglosaxon Street," Birney often explores archetypes of the Canadian identity.

This is the case of a high-school land,
deadset in adolescence,
loud treble laughs and sudden fists,
bright cheeks, the gangling presence.

This boy is wonderful at sports
and physically quite healthy;
he's taken to church on Sunday still
and keeps his prurience stealthy.

He doesn't like books except about bears,
collects new coins and model planes,
and never refuses a dare.

His Uncle spoils him with candy, of course,
yet shouts him down when he talks at table.

You will note he's got some of his French mother's looks,
though he's not so witty and no more stable.

He's really much more like his father and yet
if you say so he'll pull a great face.

He wants to be different from everyone else
and daydreams of winning the global race.

Parents unmarried and living abroad,
relatives keen to bag the estate,
schizophrenia not excluded,
will he learn to grow up before it's too late?

Leather and Naughahyde

MARILYN DUMONT

Of Métis descent, Marilyn Dumont is the author of *green girl dreams Mountains* and *A Really Good Brown Girl*. A poet, critic, and educator, Dumont often examines the issues of race and identity in her poetry.

So, I'm having coffee with this treaty guy from up north and we're laughing at how crazy "the mooniyaw" are in the city and the conversation comes around to where I'm from, as it does in underground languages, in the oblique way it does to find out someone's status without actually asking, and knowing this, I say I'm Metis like it's an apology and he says, "mmh," like he forgives me, like he's got a big heart and mine's pumping diluted blood and his voice has sounded well-fed up till this point, but now it goes thin like he's across the room taking another look and when he returns he's got "this look," that says he's leather and I'm naughahyde.

Primitivism

GEORGE ELLIOTT CLARKE

Descended from black Loyalist settlers in Nova Scotia, George Elliott Clarke is a poet, dramatist, critic, and screenwriter who examines the African-Canadian experience. His poetical works include *Saltwater Spirituals and Deeper Blues*, *Whylah Falls*, *Lush Dreams, Blue Exile: Fugitive Poems*

1978–93, *Beatrice Chancy*, *Blue*, and *Execution Poems*, which won a Governor General's Award.

> He could not escape
> the wilderness. Bark
> encrusted his wine bottles.
> His pencils grew fur
> and howled. Sentences
> became wild eagles
> that flew predatory patterns,
> swooping out of a white sky-
> page to tear apart field
> mice-images, scurrying
> for meaning. A carcass-
> manuscript rotted on a shelf
> or a hillside. He could
> not tell the difference.
> A bear-trap of ideas
> snared him: he could
> not poeticize
> the country
> and not become it;
> his poems filling
> with neanderthal nudes,
> prowling punctuation,
> snarling sounds, guttural.

untitled three

PEI HSIEN LIM

Pei Hsien Lim was an artist, poet, dancer, and activist, who lobbied for gays and people with AIDS. He died in 1992.

> I love and hate
> Cherry blossoms
> So beautiful
> So short-lived

> AIDS has stripped me raw
> Down to the marrow of my bones
> Thousands of soft pink petals
> Fallen onto cold concrete

> I remember
> How a mother wept

At her gay son's funeral
And the father sat
Like a stone
In the wall
Of the old church

Metaphors That Kill

GEORGE LAKOFF

Professor of linguistics at University of California, Berkeley, George Lakoff
writes books that explore the intersection between politics and language,
including *Metaphors We Live By*, *Moral Politics*, *Women, Fire and
Dangerous Things: What Categories Reveal About the Mind*, and *More
Than Cool Reason: A Field Guide to Poetic Metaphor*. Lakoff holds that
figures of speech such as metaphor have a profound influence on our
thought and culture, and even lead to war.

Metaphors can kill.
That's how I began a piece on the first Gulf War back in
1990, just before the war began. Many of those metaphorical ideas are back, but within a very different and more dangerous context. Since Gulf War II is due to start any day, perhaps
even tomorrow, it might be useful to take a look before the
action begins at the metaphorical ideas being used to justify Gulf
War II.

One of the most central metaphors in our foreign policy is that
A Nation Is a Person. It is used hundreds of times a day, every time
the nation of Iraq is conceptualized in terms of a single person,
Saddam Hussein. The war, we are told, is not being waged against
the Iraqi people, but only against this one person. Ordinary
American citizens are using this metaphor when they say things
like, "Saddam is a tyrant. He must be stopped." What the metaphor
hides, of course, is that the **3,000 bombs to be dropped in the
first two days will not be dropped on that one person**. They
will kill many thousands of the people hidden by the metaphor,
people that according to the metaphor we are not going to war
against.

The Nation as Person metaphor is pervasive, powerful, and
part of an elaborate metaphor system. It is part of an International
Community metaphor, in which there are friendly nations, hostile

nations, rogue states, and so on. This metaphor comes with a notion of the national interest: Just as it is in the interest of a person to be healthy and strong, so it is in the interest of a Nation-Person to be economically healthy and militarily strong. That is what is meant by the "national interest."

In the International Community, peopled by **Nation-Persons**, there are **Nation-adults** and **Nation-children**, with **Maturity metaphorically understood as Industrialization**. The children are the "developing" nations of the Third World, in the process of industrializing, who need to be taught how to develop properly and to be disciplined (say, by the International Monetary Fund) when they fail to follow instructions. "Backward" nations are those that are "underdeveloped." Iraq, despite being the cradle of civilization, is seen via this metaphor as a kind of defiant armed teenage hoodlum who refuses to abide by the rules and must be "taught a lesson."

The international relations community adds to the Nation as Person metaphor what is called the "**Rational Actor Model**." The idea here is that it is irrational to act against your interests and that nations act as if they were "rational actors"—individual people trying to maximize their "gains" and "assets" and minimize their "costs" and "losses." In Gulf War I, the metaphor was applied so that a country's "assets" included its soldiers, materiel, and money. Since the U.S. lost few of those "assets" in Gulf War I, the war was reported, just afterward in the *NY Times* Business section, as having been a "bargain." Since Iraqi civilians were not our assets, they could not be counted as among the "losses" and so there was no careful public accounting of civilian lives lost, people maimed, and children starved or made seriously ill by the war or the sanctions that followed it. Estimates vary from half a million to a million or more. However, public relations was seen to be a U.S. asset: excessive slaughter reported on in the press would be bad PR, a possible loss. These metaphors are with us again. A short war with few U.S. casualties would minimize costs. But the longer it goes on, the more Iraqi resistance and the more U.S. casualties, the less the U.S. would appear invulnerable and the more the war would appear as a war against the Iraqi people. That would be a high "cost."

According to the Rational Actor Model, countries act naturally in their own best interests—preserving their assets, that is, their own populations, their infrastructure, their wealth, their weaponry, and so on. That is what the U.S. did in Gulf War I and what it is doing now. But Saddam Hussein, in Gulf War I, did not fit our government's Rational Actor Model. He had goals like preserving his power in Iraq and being an Arab hero just for standing up to the Great Satan. Though such goals might have their own rationality, they are "irrational" from the model's perspective.

One of the most frequent uses of the Nation as Person metaphor comes in the almost daily attempts to justify the war metaphorically as a "just war." The basic idea of a just war uses the Nation as Person metaphor plus two narratives that have the structure of classical fairy tales: The Self-Defense Story and The Rescue Story.

In each story, there is a Hero, a Crime, a Victim, and a Villain. In the **Self-Defense story**, the Hero and the Victim are the same. In both stories, the Villain is inherently evil and irrational: The Hero can't reason with the Villain; he has to fight him and defeat him or kill him. In both, the victim must be innocent and beyond reproach. In both, there is an initial crime by the Villain, and the Hero balances the moral books by defeating him. If all the parties are Nation-Persons, then self-defense and rescue stories become forms of a just war for the Hero-Nation.

In Gulf War I, Bush I tried out a self-defense story: Saddam was "threatening our oil life-line." The American people didn't buy it. Then he found a winning story, a rescue story—The Rape of Kuwait. It sold well, and is still the most popular account of that war.

In Gulf War II, Bush II is pushing different versions of the same two story types, and this explains a great deal of what is going on in the American press and in speeches by Bush and Powell. If they can show that Saddam = Al Qaeda—that he is helping or harboring Al Qaeda, then they can make a case for the Self-defense scenario, and hence for a just war on those grounds. Indeed, despite the lack of any positive evidence and the fact that the secular Saddam and the fundamentalist bin Laden despise each other, the Bush administration has managed to convince 40 per cent of the American public of the link, just by asserting it. The administration has told its soldiers the same thing, and so our military men see themselves as going to Iraq in defense of their country.

In the **Rescue Scenario**, the victims are (1) the Iraqi people and (2) Saddam's neighbors, whom he has not attacked, but is seen as "threatening." That is why Bush and Powell keep on listing Saddam's crimes against the Iraqi people and the weapons he could use to harm his neighbors. Again, most of the American people have accepted the idea that Gulf War II is a rescue of the Iraqi people and a safeguarding of neighboring countries. Of course, the war threatens the safety and well-being of the Iraqi people and will inflict considerable damage on neighboring countries like Turkey and Kuwait.

And why such enmity toward France and Germany? Via the Nation as Person metaphor, they are supposed to be our "friends" and friends are supposed to be supportive and jump in and help us when we need help. Friends are supposed to be loyal. That makes France and Germany fair-weather friends! Not there when you need them.

This is how the war is being framed for the American people by the Administration and media. Millions of people around the world can see that the metaphors and fairy tales don't fit the current situation, that Gulf War II does not qualify as a just war—a "legal" war. But if you accept all these metaphors, as Americans have been led to do by the administration, the press, and the lack of an effective Democratic opposition, then Gulf War II would indeed seem like a just war.

But surely most Americans have been exposed to the facts—the lack of a credible link between Saddam and al Qaeda and the idea that large numbers of innocent Iraqi civilians (estimates are around 500,000) will be killed or maimed by our bombs. Why don't they reach the rational conclusion?

One of the fundamental findings of cognitive science is that people think in terms of frames and metaphors—conceptual structures like those we have been describing. The frames are in the synapses of our brains—physically present in the form of neural circuitry. When the facts don't fit the frames, the frames are kept and the facts ignored.

It is a common folk theory of progressives that "The facts will set you free!" If only you can get all the facts out there in the public eye, then every rational person will reach the right conclusion. It is a vain hope. Human brains just don't work that way. Framing matters. Frames once entrenched are hard to dispel.

In the first Gulf War, Colin Powell began the testimony before Congress. He explained the rational actor model to the congressmen and gave a brief exposition of the views on war of Clausewitz, the Prussian general: War is business and politics carried out by other means. Nations naturally seek their self-interest, and when necessary, they use military force in the service of their self-interest. This is both natural and legitimate.

To the Bush administration, this war furthers our self-interest: controlling the flow of oil from the world's second largest known reserve, and being in the position to control the flow of oil from central Asia as well. These would guarantee energy domination over a significant part of the world. The U.S. could control oil sales around the world. And in the absence of alternative fuel development, whoever controls the distribution of oil throughout the world controls politics as well as economics.

My 1990 paper did not stop Gulf War I. This paper will not stop Gulf War II. So why bother?

I think it is crucially important to understand the cognitive dimensions of politics—especially when most of our conceptual framing is unconscious and we may not be aware of our own metaphorical thought. I have been referred to as a "cognitive activist" and I think the label fits me well. As a professor, I do analyses of linguistic and conceptual issues in politics, and I do them as accurately as I can. But that analytic act is a political act: Awareness matters. Being able to articulate what is going on can change what is going on—at least in the long run.

This war is a symptom of a larger disease. The war will start presently. The fighting will be over before long. Where will the anti-war movement be then?

First, the anti-war movement, properly understood, is not just, or even primarily, a movement against the war. It is a movement against the overall direction that the Bush administration is moving in. Second, such a movement, to be effective, needs to say clearly what it is for, not just what it is against. Third, it must have a clearly articulated moral vision, with values rather than mere interests determining its political direction.

As the war begins, we should look ahead to transforming the anti-war movement into a movement that powerfully articulates progressive values and changes the course of our nation to where those values take us. The war has begun a discussion about values. Let's continue it.

Tax Haven in the Snow

LINDA McQUAIG

Author and journalist, Linda McQuaig is an investigative reporter who tackles controversial issues in the Canadian and global landscape. She has written on everything from free trade (in her book *The Quick and the Dead*) to corporate greed (*Shooting the Hippo*), to the American invasion of Iraq (*It's the Crude, Dude*). This selection comes from her book *Behind Closed Doors*, a critique of the Canadian tax system.

"I am a brigand: I live by robbing the rich."

"I am a gentleman: I live by robbing the poor."

—from George Bernard Shaw's *Man and Superman*

If the words "rich" and "poor" have become taboo, the reality of wealth and poverty in our country has not. We may not talk about it much anymore, but an enormous gulf remains between the rich and the poor. While there is plenty of data on the poor, there are few hard figures on the rich, who tend to be less forthcoming about their financial situations. From the data available, however, some striking discrepancies leap out. In this country there were an estimated 3,950,000 people living in poverty in 1985—one in every six Canadians. More than half a million people joined the ranks of the poor in the last five years in Canada. Meanwhile, at the very top, we have produced six billionaires—possibly more, depending on the measurement used—and dozens who count their fortunes in the tens of millions.

The tax system has played a role in perpetuating this situation. Even after Wilson's tax reform, many Canadians living below the poverty line will still pay income taxes, and many well-to-do individuals will continue to pay little or no income tax. Indeed, although few people are aware of it, Canada's taxation of wealth ranks among the lowest in the western world.

Every now and then statistics appear that suggest the size of the gap between the rich and the poor in Canada. In July 1986, for instance, Statistics Canada released a study of high-income families which revealed that the top 1 percent—some 63,250 families—earned an average of $212,000 a year (in 1986 dollars). *The Toronto Star* ran a banner story about the study across the top of its front page, noting that the remaining 6.3 million Canadian families had an average income of $39,626.

While the gap between $212,000 and $39,000 is obviously large, these figures actually misrepresent the real extent of the gulf. The $39,000 is particularly misleading in that it suggests this is the income of the average Canadian family. This may be true in a statistical sense, but not in any meaningful sense. The figure is derived from adding the income of all families in Canada and then dividing by the number of families. The very large incomes of those at the top distort the results, creating an "average" family income that is much higher than what is actually enjoyed by the majority of Canadians. More than half of Canadian families, for instance, have incomes below $33,000. Furthermore, the Statistics Canada study, in calculating the $212,000 figure, did not include a number of key sources of income for the rich, such as capital gains, which would have pushed up the average income for the top-earning Canadians even higher.

All this is very hard to visualize. In an effort to bring the picture into focus, Dutch statistician Jan Pen came up with the idea of presenting the distribution of income as a parade in which everyone in the country marches and in which everyone's size is proportional to his or her income. The taller the marcher, the greater the income. After figuring out the relative heights for a parade of this sort in Britain, Pen described it as "a parade of dwarfs (and a few giants)." Roughly here's what the parade would look like in Canada.

The whole parade is only going to take an hour, so everyone will be moving quickly, flashing by us as we stand watching at the side of the road. Like any school parade, this one will begin with the smallest marchers—that is, the poorest Canadians—and the heights will gradually rise until we see the tallest marchers—the highest-income Canadians.

As the parade begins, we notice some extremely tiny people at the front. Masses of people less than a foot tall hurry past us. These tiny individuals are a mixed group of all ages. They include some welfare recipients, unemployed individuals, old age pensioners, part-time workers, struggling farmers—all earning less than $7,000 a year. Although they are moving quickly, it takes at least six minutes for this group of miniature people to pass.

For the next twelve minutes, we see a horde of very small dwarves, people less than three feet in height. Marching in this group are more people on public assistance; but we also now see a large number of full-time workers as well, people working at extremely low-paying jobs. There are building cleaners, day-care workers, bank tellers, salesclerks, etc. We can't help being struck by the preponderance of women in this group of very short marchers.

The parade has been going on for more than twenty minutes before we start to see taller dwarves who reach about four feet high. This group includes somewhat better-paid blue collar workers: parking lot attendants, maintenance and factory workers, as well as some individuals collecting unemployment insurance.

The parade reaches the halfway mark, and even at this point we are still seeing people only about five feet tall. Among them are skilled industrial workers, electricians, plumbers, as well as nurses and executive secretaries.

Another few minutes and adults of normal height start appearing. This group includes teachers, civil servants, computer programmers and factory supervisors. It is not really until the last twelve minutes of the parade that we begin to see business executives and professionals—doctors, lawyers, accountants, engineers. These people are really quite tall, well over eight feet.

As the parade nears its end, the marchers become ever larger. With about six minutes to go, we see more and more doctors, lawyers and business executives, all with incomes over $100,000. Fourteen feet tall, they tower over the dwarves at the front of the parade. There are some well-known faces in this crowd: Quebec Premier Robert Bourassa standing almost fifteen feet tall and Prime Minister Brian Mulroney, measuring more than nineteen feet.

In the last minute, the height of the marchers rises dramatically. With about 25 seconds remaining, they have reached 30 feet. Ian Sinclair, the retired president of Canadian Pacific Enterprises stands 37 feet tall—in retirement. Then, in the final few seconds, some real giants walk by. Among these, standing 75 feet tall, we will find J. L. Dunlap, president of Texaco Canada Inc. with a 1986 income of $538,308. Then there is W. W. Stinson, president of Canadian Pacific Limited, with an income of $677,418, measuring 96 feet tall. Looming in this crowd is Edgar Bronfman, chairman of Seagram Company, with a salary of $1.8 million and standing 257 feet high. But towering even above him is Frank Stronach, president of Magna International, with an income of $2.2 million and reaching a commanding height of 314 feet.

But this parade only tells part of the story, because these figures deal exclusively with *income.* In many ways, the more meaningful measure is *wealth.* When *The Financial Post Moneywise* magazine does its semi-annual survey of the richest men and women in the country, it isn't talking about their income. It is talking about their wealth—the real measure of economic power and command over the country's resources.

Someone could have significant wealth, for instance, in the form of stocks, bonds or land holdings, but receive relatively little in the way of income. This, in fact, would be the logical way for wealthy people to arrange their financial affairs, to minimize their income tax bills. Indeed, the men and women in *The Financial Post* survey employ some of the highest-priced talent in the country to come up with ways for them to avoid receiving huge incomes— incomes which would leave them vulnerable to substantial income taxes. By receiving only as much in the way of dividends as is needed for living expenses, a wealthy individual can keep the rest of the money tied up in ever-growing assets, where it is better sheltered from tax. But in the government income statistics, a wealthy person living on a dividend income, of say, $80,000 a year would resemble an employee receiving a salary of $80,000, even though the two individuals may have vastly different resources.

The gap between the wealth of the rich and the poor in Canada is far greater than the gap in their incomes. Consider the following statistics, all from Statistics Canada. In 1981, the top-earning 20 percent of Canadians enjoyed 45 percent of national *income,* while the bottom-earning 20 percent enjoyed a mere 4 percent of that income. But if one looks at *wealth,* the disparities grow dramatically larger.

The wealthiest 20 percent of the population enjoyed a massive 68 percent of the national wealth. The bottom 20 percent owned less than 1 percent. Indeed, this bottom group owned less than 0, their debts being greater than their assets. The numbers are in some ways even more striking when one looks at the wealth of the top 1 percent or the top one-tenth of 1 percent, rather than the top 20 percent, since wealth is so heavily concentrated in a very small group. In Canada, the top 10 percent own more than half of the country's wealth.

Let's now watch the same parade of Canadians, this time with their heights reflecting their holdings of wealth rather than income.

This second time around, the parade has been going for about ten minutes before we realize it has even started. That's because, despite our rapt attention, we can't see anyone. The marchers who've gone by during the first ten minutes aren't just miniscule in size, they are actually underground. These underground people represent Canadians who own nothing of value, have no savings and are, in fact, overall in debt.[1] They include university graduate students who have gone into debt to finance their education as well as young families with consumer loans.

At last, we start seeing the first signs of life above ground, tiny people a few inches high. They include the same low-income people we saw in the early stages of the last parade. It's not till fifteen minutes have passed that we begin to see dwarves—people about three feet high who have net wealth of about $18,000, mostly in the form of equity in their homes or savings that will be put towards buying a home.

The rest of the parade proceeds in much the same way as the first parade . . . until the end. By the last minute, we are encountering wealthy giants as large as Toronto's CN Tower.

But it is what happens in the last *second* which is truly astonishing. Indeed, with less than a tenth of a second left, some of the most prominent Canadian businessmen and investors suddenly appear, boasting assets of more than $100 million and ranging up into the billions.[2] These individuals are so tall that their heads disappear into the clouds. To mention only a few, there is Vancouver real estate developer Charles "Chunky" Woodward, a little over 3 *miles* high. Chatty Toronto financier Conrad Black, who, along with brother Montegu, has assets of $200 million, stands 6 miles high. There's even a tall woman—Mitzi Steinberg, heiress of the Steinberg grocery store fortune, 7 miles high. Calgary oil man Ronald Southern is more than 8 miles high; Toronto real estate magnate Robert Campeau, almost 12 miles high; Toronto shoe baron Thomas Bata, a little more than 12 miles high; Montreal entrepreneur Paul Desmarais, 18 miles high; Galen Weston, head of the Weston food empire, 29 miles high; Charles Bronfman, who inherited the Seagram's liquor fortune, 32 miles high; Paul Reichmann, 195 miles high; and finally, the richest man in Canada, Kenneth Thomson, head of the Thomson newspaper empire, 198 miles high.

Reading Notes

1. Most Canadians have debts, such as a mortgage on a house. But their assets, including equity in their homes, outweigh their debts.

2. This only includes assets they own. In addition, many of them control a far more extensive range of assets. For example, Peter and Edward Bronfman own $650 million worth of assets, but they control a corporate empire worth about $47 billion.

Don't Fence Us In

NAOMI KLEIN

Naomi Klein is a journalist and documentary filmmaker. Her seminal work, *No Logo*, investigates the world of branding, multinational capitalism, and outsourcing, becoming something of a bible of the anti–free trade movement. She followed this up with *Fences and Windows* and *The Take*, a documentary on worker-run factories in Argentina.

A few months ago, while riffling through my clippings searching for a lost statistic, I noticed a recurring theme: the fence. The image came up again and again: barriers separating people from previously public resources, locking them away from much needed land and water, restricting their ability to move across borders, to express political dissent, to demonstrate on public streets, even keeping politicians from enacting policies that make sense for the people who elected them. Some of these fences are hard to see, but they exist all the same. A virtual fence goes up around schools in Zambia when an education "user fee" is introduced on the advice of the World Bank, putting classes out of the reach of millions of people. A fence goes up around the family farm in Canada when government policies turn small-scale agriculture into a luxury item, unaffordable in a landscape of tumbling commodity prices and factory farms. There is a real if invisible fence that goes up around clean water in Soweto when prices skyrocket owing to privatisation, and residents are forced to turn to contaminated sources. And there is a fence that goes up around the very idea of democracy when Argentina is told it won't get an International Monetary Fund loan unless it further reduces social spending, privatises more resources and eliminates support to local industries, all in the midst of an economic crisis deepened by those very policies. These fences, of course, are as old as colonialism. "Such usurious operations put bars around free nations," Eduardo Galeano wrote in *Open Veins of Latin America*. He was referring to the terms of a British loan to Argentina in 1824.

Fences have always been a part of capitalism, the only way to protect property from would-be bandits, but the double standards propping up these fences have, of late, become increasingly blatant. Expropriation of corporate holdings may be the greatest sin any socialist government can commit in the eyes of the international financial markets (just ask Venezuela's Hugo Chavez or Cuba's Fidel Castro). But the asset protection guaranteed to companies under free trade deals did not extend to the Argentine citizens who deposited their life savings in Citibank, Scotiabank and HSBC accounts and now find that most of their money has simply disappeared. Neither did the market's reverence for private wealth embrace the US employees of Enron, who found that they had been "locked out" of their privatised retirement portfolios, unable to sell even as Enron executives were frantically cashing in their own stocks.

Meanwhile, some very necessary fences are under attack: in the rush to privatisation, the barriers that once existed between many public and private spaces—keeping advertisements out of schools, for instance, profit-making interests out of healthcare, or news outlets from acting purely as promotional vehicles for their owners' other holdings—have nearly all been levelled. Every protected public space has been cracked open, only to be re-enclosed by the market.

Another public-interest barrier under serious threat is the one separating genetically modified crops from crops that have not yet been altered. The seed giants have done such a remarkably poor job of preventing their tampered seeds from blowing into neighbouring fields, taking root and cross-pollinating that, in many parts of the world, eating GM-free is no longer even an option—the entire food supply has been contaminated. The fences that protect the public interest seem to be fast disappearing, while the ones that restrict our liberties keep multiplying.

When I first noticed that the image of the fence kept coming up in discussion, debates and in my own writing, it seemed significant to me. After all, the past decade of economic integration has been fuelled by promises of barriers coming down, of increased mobility and greater freedom. And yet 13 years after the celebrated collapse of the Berlin Wall, we are surrounded by fences yet again, cut off—from one another, from the earth and from our own ability to imagine that change is possible. The economic process that goes by the benign euphemism "globalisation" now reaches into every aspect of life, transforming every activity and natural resource into a measured and owned commodity. As the Hong Kong–based labour researcher Gerard Greenfield points out, the current stage of capitalism is not simply about trade in the traditional sense of selling more products across borders. It is also about feeding the market's insatiable need for growth by redefining as "products" entire sectors that were previously considered part of "the commons" and not for sale. The invading of the public by the private has reached into categories such as health and education, of course, but also ideas, genes, seeds, now purchased, patented and fenced off, as well as traditional aboriginal remedies, plants, water and even human stem cells. With copyright now the US's single largest export (more than manufactured goods or arms), international trade law must be understood not only as taking down selective barriers to trade but more accurately as a process that systematically puts up new barriers—around knowledge, technology and newly privatised resources. These Trade Related Intellectual Property Rights are what prevent farmers from replanting their Monsanto patented seeds and make it illegal for poor countries to manufacture cheaper generic drugs to get to their needy populations.

Globalisation is now on trial because on the other side of all these virtual fences are real people, shut out of schools, hospitals, workplaces, their own farms, homes and communities. Mass privatisation and deregulation have bred armies of locked-out people, whose services are no longer needed, whose lifestyles are written off as "backward," whose basic needs go unmet. These fences of social exclusion can discard an entire industry, and they can also write off an entire country, as has happened to Argentina. In the case of Africa, essentially an entire continent can find itself exiled to the global shadow world, off the map and off the news, appearing only during wartime when its citizens are looked on with suspicion as potential militia members, would-be terrorists or anti-American fanatics.

In fact, remarkably few of globalisation's fenced-out people turn to violence. Most simply move: from countryside to city, from country to country. And that's when they come face to face with distinctly unvirtual fences, the ones made of chain link and razor wire, reinforced with concrete and guarded with machine guns. Whenever I hear the phrase "free trade," I can't help picturing the caged factories I visited in the Philippines and Indonesia that are all surrounded by gates, watchtowers and soldiers—to keep the highly subsidised products from leaking out and the union organisers from getting in. I think, too, about a recent trip to the South Australian desert where I visited the infamous Woomera detention centre. At Woomera, hundreds of Afghan and Iraqi refugees, fleeing oppression and dictatorship in their own countries, are so desperate for the world to see what is going on behind the fence that they stage hunger strikes, jump off the roofs of their barracks, drink shampoo and sew their mouths shut.

These days, newspapers are filled with gruesome accounts of asylum seekers attempting to make it across national borders by hiding themselves among the products that enjoy so much more mobility than they do. In December 2001, the bodies of eight Romanian refugees, including two children, were discovered in a cargo container filled with office furniture; they had asphyxiated during the long journey at sea. The same year, the bodies of two more refugees were discovered in Eau Claire, Wisconsin, in a shipment of bathroom fixtures. The year before, 58 Chinese refugees suffocated in the back of a delivery truck in Dover.

All these fences are connected: the real ones, made of steel and razor wire, are needed to enforce the virtual ones, the ones that put resources and wealth out of the hands of so many. It simply isn't possible to lock away this much of our collective wealth without an accompanying strategy to control popular unrest and mobility. Security firms do their biggest business in the cities, where the gap between rich and poor is greatest—Johannesburg, São Paulo, New Delhi—selling iron gates, armoured cars, elaborate alarm systems and renting out armies of private guards. Brazilians, for instance, spend US\$4.5bn a year on private security, and the country's 400,000 armed rent-a-cops outnumber actual police officers by almost four to one. In deeply divided South Africa, annual spending on private security has reached US\$1.6bn, more than three times what the government spends each year on affordable housing. It now seems that these gated compounds protecting the haves from the have-nots are microcosms of what is fast becoming a global security state—not a global village intent on lowering walls and barriers, as we were promised, but a network of fortresses connected by highly militarised trade corridors.

If this picture seems extreme, it may only be because most of us in the west rarely see the fences and the artillery. The gated factories and refugee detention centres remain tucked away in remote places, less able to pose a direct challenge to the seductive rhetoric of the borderless world. But over the past few years, some fences have intruded into full view—often, fittingly, during the summits where this brutal model of globalisation is advanced. It is now taken for granted that if world leaders want to get together to discuss a new trade deal, they will need to build a modern-day fortress to protect themselves from public rage. When Quebec City hosted the Summit of the Americas in April 2001, the Canadian government took the unprecedented step of building a cage around not just the conference centre, but the downtown core, forcing residents to show official documentation to get to their homes and workplaces. Another popular strategy is to hold the summits in inaccessible locations: the 2002 G8 meeting was held deep in the Canadian Rocky Mountains, and the 2001 WTO meeting took place in the repressive Gulf State of Qatar, where the emir bans political protests. The "war on terrorism" has become yet another fence to hide behind, used by summit organisers to explain why public shows of dissent just won't be possible this time around or, worse, to draw threatening parallels between legitimate protesters and terrorists bent on destruction.

But what are reported as menacing confrontations are often joyous events, as much experiments in alternative ways of organising societies as criticisms of existing models. The first time I participated in one of these counter-summits, I remember having the distinct feeling that some sort of political portal was opening up—a gateway, a window, "a crack in history," to use subcomandante Marcos's beautiful phrase. This opening had little to do with the broken window at the local McDonald's, the image so favoured by TV cameras; it was something else: a sense of possibility, a blast of fresh air, oxygen rushing to the brain. These protests—which are actually week-long marathons of intense education on global politics, late-night strategy sessions in six-way simultaneous translation, festivals of music and street theatre—are like stepping into a parallel universe. Overnight, the site is transformed into a kind of alternative global city, where urgency replaces resignation, corporate logos need armed guards, people usurp cars, art is everywhere, strangers talk to each other, and the prospect of a radical change in political course does not seem like an odd and anachronistic idea but the most logical thought in the world. Even the heavy-handed security measures have been co-opted by activists into part of the message: the fences that surround the summits become metaphors for an economic model that exiles billions to poverty and exclusion. Confrontations are staged at the fence—but not only the ones involving sticks and bricks: tear-gas canisters have been flicked back with hockey sticks, water cannons have been irreverently challenged with toy water pistols and buzzing helicopters mocked with swarms of paper aeroplanes. During the Summit of the Americas in Quebec City, a group of activists built a medieval-style wooden catapult, wheeled it up to the 3m-high fence that enclosed the downtown and lofted teddy bears over the top. In Prague, during a meeting of the World Bank and the International Monetary Fund, the Italian direct-action group Tute Bianche decided not to confront the black-clad riot police dressed in similarly threatening ski masks and bandanas; instead, they marched to the police line in white jumpsuits stuffed with rubber tyres and Styrofoam padding. In a standoff between Darth Vader and an army of Michelin Men, the police couldn't win. These activists are quite serious in their desire to disrupt the current economic order, but their tactics reflect a dogged refusal to engage in classic power struggles: their goal is not to take power for themselves but to challenge power centralisation on principle.

Other kinds of windows are opening as well, quiet conspiracies to reclaim privatised spaces and assets for public use. Maybe it's students kicking ads out of their classrooms, or swapping music online, or setting up independent media centres with free software. Maybe it's Thai peasants planting organic vegetables on over-irrigated golf courses, or landless farmers in Brazil cutting down fences around unused lands and turning them into farming cooperatives. Maybe it's Bolivian workers reversing the privatisation of their water supply, or South African township residents reconnecting their neighbours' electricity under the slogan Power to the People. And once reclaimed, these spaces are also being remade. In neighbourhood assemblies, at city councils, in independent media centres, in community-run forests and farms, a new culture of vibrant direct democracy is emerging, one that is fuelled and strengthened by direct participation, not dampened and discouraged by passive spectatorship.

Despite all the attempts at privatisation, it turns out that there are some things that don't want to be owned. Music, water, seeds, electricity, ideas—they keep bursting out of the confines erected around them. They have a natural resistance to enclosure, a tendency to escape, to cross-pollinate, to flow through fences and flee out open windows.

It is not clear what will emerge from these liberated spaces, or if what emerges will be hardy enough to withstand the mounting attacks from the police and military, as the line between terrorist and activist is deliberately blurred. The question of what comes next preoccupies me, as it does everyone else who has been part of building this international movement. As I look again at these article clippings, I see them for what they are: postcards from dramatic moments in time, a record of the first chapter in a very old and recurring story, the one about people pushing up against the barriers that try to contain them, opening up windows, breathing deeply, tasting freedom.

Simple Words

"Good. Bad. I'm the guy with the gun."

—Ash, *Army of Darkness*

The difficult words of any language aren't complex ones, but small, everyday words such as good and evil, right and wrong. These simple terms appear in every discipline of thought, but signify radically different things. If Tim Hortons raises the price of doughnuts based upon the "law of supply and demand," it evokes a different authority from the "second law of thermal dynamics," which differs from "Mendel's Laws" in genetics, different again from a speed limit on the highway, although the word "law" applies to each. A painting declared a "real" Picasso has a criterion of authenticity different from the historical revisionist who argues the Holocaust a "fake," or the metallurgist separating pyrite from gold. When a diplomat says it's "right" to send troops to Afghanistan, he or she doesn't use the same principles as an English teacher grading spelling, or a math teacher marking equations.

Whenever a simple word appears, we should be wary of its use and potential misuse. In physics, for example, scientists use "law" as a *description* of the universe, one that reflects experiment and observation. In contrast, a law in the legal sense isn't descriptive, but *prescriptive*: it limits human behaviour. Descriptive and prescriptive laws mark out different concepts: we easily break human law, but can't defy Newton's Law of Gravity.

People who confuse these two kinds of law make serious gaffes. Creationists wrongly argue that physical laws prove the existence of a designer God, arguing "every law presupposes a law-giver." Unfortunately, they've confused prescriptive laws (requiring a creator) with descriptive laws (requiring none).

Similarly, economists like to think the marketplace obeys laws immutable and invisible as the laws of nature; and like an ecosystem, the economy works best with the least amount of human interference. Unfortunately, this free trade dogma confuses physical law (amoral) with human law (moral). The fantasy of a self-governing economy removes ethics from business and allows the market to determine what's right—a scary prospect.

Equally important is the authority behind these words. Physical laws root themselves in empirical observation, testing, and logic. Prescriptive laws draw authority from the issuing body, such as city council or federal government. Religious laws have scriptural source, binding only to believers. Military law constrains soldiers, while something like "Murphy's Law" ("Everything that can go wrong will") has small credibility beyond pessimistic folklore. The foundation of "law" varies wildly, backed by authorities as divergent as prejudice, common sense, social custom, and the universe itself.

This chapter provides a short study of some challenging words that have power in our culture. People boost credibility by using words such as "law," "reason," and "truth," yet their authority is often dubious, self-referential, circular, mystic, aristocratic, and bigoted. And yet, these ethereal, misunderstood words map out central concepts of our society.

MORALITY

"There is no good and evil; there is only power and those too weak to seek it."

—Harry Potter and the Philosopher's Stone

The concepts of good and evil are not limited to pulpits and fairy tales; they lie at the heart of any legal system. But what do they mean?

Let's tackle this thorny ethical issue by addressing a small example: McDonald's French fries. *Bad* for me, they taste *good*. How can something be both good and bad?

This statement looks contradictory because it confuses two different scales of measure, sliding imperceptibly from the criteria of health into the taste scale. Depending on which standard is used, French fries become good or evil. And indeed, we can put French fries through more ethical gyrations.

> To a vegetarian, French fries seem bad because they contain beef tallow.

> To an economist, McDonald's French fries appear good because they create employment and tax revenue.

To a Marxist, McDonald's French fries look bad because the chain fosters low-wage jobs.

To a cash-strapped student, McDonald's French fries seem good because they offer sizeable portions at discount prices.

This shows that good and evil aren't hard facts, but rather subjective and relative terms, that change according to philosophies and preferences. As Hamlet suggests, "There is nothing good or bad but thinking makes it so."

If good and evil are arbitrary, are they also meaningless? Should we jettison them entirely?

Surely, such a move is too drastic, for the relativity of good and evil doesn't make them empty concepts. After the scientific community accepted the theory of relativity, scientists still measured time, distance and velocity. Thanks to Einstein, scientists measured these units more precisely. So too does the recognition of ethical relativity help situate the scope of ethical claims. We can better process claims of good and evil if we carry out a few precautions.

A. Identify the value system

Good and evil don't exist in physical reality as a cow or toaster exists. Rather, they're value judgments created by belief systems. Not always obvious, these value systems must come to the surface. A blanket claim such as "Euthanasia is wrong," should be restated so its moral basis becomes clear: "According to Prov. 6:16–17, the Lord hates those who take innocent lives; thus Euthanasia is wrong." Here, the claim becomes a statement of Christian belief, rather than a universal edict. While persuasive to the Christian community, the argument holds less sway to the atheist, Muslim, Jew, or Hindu.

When the value system is identified, the authority of any claim becomes clearer. Just as importantly, good and evil appear not as permanent metaphysical entities, but as perceptions—tentative and changeable.

B. Consider the claim from another position

If good and evil are perceptions within particular value systems, then they change when belief systems switch. Pain appears bad to hedonists, but good to weightlifters ("no pain, no gain!"), even pleasurable to masochists. Before declaring something good or evil, consider the issue from a variety of angles and belief systems.

If we look at an issue from various viewpoints, we're less tractable and committed to a single "right" answer.

C. Negotiate and choose between value systems

If good and evil are subjective, our challenge is to negotiate between sundry meanings, such as when we balance the good of workers against corporate profit sheets, or economic good against environmental good.

Sometimes we have to choose one value system over another, for example favouring health over taste, or a secular over a religious government.

NATURE

In his essay "What Is 'Against Nature'?" Robert Anton Wilson suggests that appeals to natural law are little more than moral commands in scientific clothing. To Wilson's deconstruction of "law" and "nature," let's add another potent word: *genetic*.

Genetic research promises enormous benefits to mankind, but scientists often overstate its potential. They boast of the genetic code as a "master program" that determines everything from body shape, to behaviour, to sexual orientation. To them, DNA has become a God-like arbitrator of life itself, almost a synonym for fate. And like ancient priests, scientists place themselves in a very privileged caste as the only ones able to decipher this central text. Perhaps this is why geneticists use the same sacred metaphors as church fathers—the life script, the holy code, the Bible, the great book, and such. They see the double helix as organic destiny.

Unfortunately, such claims not only exaggerate DNA's role, but also downplay our free will and responsibility.

While genes may determine something simple such as eye colour, they're not the sole cause of complex matters, such as personality, intelligence, or disease. Genes may pass on a *proclivity* to develop an illness, but a disease like cancer arises in combination with other factors, such as diet, lifestyle, mindset, and environment. Given these variables, the boast that genes cause cancer is reductive and misleading. We could as well say the government caused the disease for failing to regulate industrial pollution, or parents for failing to instill good eating habits.

When scientists describe the genome as destiny, they diminish human ability to affect meaningful change. If we accept the existence of the "cancer gene," for example, we're less willing to eat well, exercise, legislate against pollution, educate citizens, and fund health centres, for these efforts seem in vain when facing a genetic fate. And this is particularly true for intangibles like intelligence, which thrives on stable homes, healthy food, schools, and love, as much as good genes. If we give credence to the "smart gene," don't we lessen the importance of public education? We must ensure that DNA hoopla doesn't distract us from social responsibility and agency.

PROPERTY

"Property is the creation of the law. Whoever makes the law has the power of appropriating the national wealth. If they did not make the law, they would not have the property."

—*Poor Man's Guardian*, 1835

Few notions are so central to society as property. Throughout history, private ownership has helped create wealth, abundance, and security. Yet, the idea of ownership emerges as a large social fiction, and a dodgy one at that.

Historically, societies had no concept of land ownership—villages worked cooperatively, sharing meadows for grazing, fields for agriculture, forests for hunting, and oceans for fishing. In England, private ownership began around 1200 AD with the "land enclosure movement" that transformed free territories to privately held tracts. Lands were hedged, fenced, divided, and allotted to individuals; village commons became the possession of kings and lords. Herders who relied on open fields were deprived of traditional means of subsistence. The birth of "property" marked a transition from communal to private ownership, and benefited a few aristocrats at the expense of many peasants—a move that resembled theft more than law.

This pattern of dispossession repeated itself when Europeans colonized the "New World." Most native societies consider themselves part of nature, not owners of it. When European settlers began to declare sovereignty over their colonies, Aboriginal cultures dismissed European claims as lunatic. Over time, natives lost access to traditional lands, as the countryside became the legal property of the Crown.

This land grab continued throughout the colonial period, claiming oceans, airways, icecaps, continental shelves, and even radio and TV frequencies. Now that the planet's geography has been snatched up, the race to privatize the commons continues in new forms, swallowing up public interests.

RESOURCES

Water: Corporations are seeking control over rivers, lakes, and even rainwater.

Minerals: In Canada, land tenure now applies only to the surface, not the minerals underground.

Space: Moon Estates, a U.K. company, has filed deeds for the Moon, Mars, and Venus.

PUBLIC SPACE

Advertisers are claiming public spaces, such as sidewalks, schools, bathrooms, freeways, parks and hospitals, as venues for commercials.

ARTS AND CULTURE

In the medieval age, texts circulated freely, and "the author" didn't exist. Eventually, copyright laws emerged to protect artists and inventors. Today, publishers press for more ownership laws, transferring art and culture from the common domain, to private hands. Some recent acquisitions include

- Family names (McDonald's has sued competitors using the "Mc" prefix)
- "Happy Birthday to You" (owned by AOL Time-Warner)
- The Royal Canadian Mounted Police (formerly licensed by Disney)
- Colours (Pepsi copyrighted its shade of blue)
- The lion's roar (MGM)
- Silence (copyrighted by John Cage's estate)

The surge in copyright legislation may spell the end of courtesy newspapers in coffee shops and perhaps even libraries.

COMMON TECHNOLOGY

Some businesses are seeking patent rights on pre-existing technologies; eBay is trying to patent thumbnail galleries, a graphic interface common to web design.

LIFE FORMS

Corporations have successfully patented naturally occurring chemicals, micro-cellular enzymes, genetically altered plants and animals, genes, DNA sequences, and even entire genomes. Two American doctors even filed a patent claim over a living person's entire genome, without the awareness or consent of the donor.

Of course this isn't the first time society has condoned ownership of human beings. Slavery thrived for centuries, but thanks to years of struggle, the West rejected it. Perhaps it's time to curtail property rights again.

CULTURE

"Culture is ordinary. That is where we must begin."

—Raymond Williams

What do we mean when we praise a person as cultured or slander someone as barbarian?

The root of "barbarian" comes from the Greek *barbaros*, meaning "foreign," "strange," or "ignorant." The ancient Attic Greeks thought those who couldn't speak their language made ridiculous sounds, "bar, bar, bar." Hence a barbarian is an outsider to Greek culture, one who doesn't know its customs. In contrast, a civilized person is an insider, a citizen who belongs to the group and knows its codes. Note: this definition has nothing to do with intelligence, imagination, education, skill, or any sign of sophistication. The civilized person is one who has integrated into Greek society, the barbarian one who differs.

The word "idiot" shows a parallel history, and traces back to the Greek *idiotes*, meaning one who speaks a private language (giving the modern word *idiom*). In this sense, an idiot isn't a fool, but one who talks differently from the rest: again, the outsider.

The problem with this definition of culture is its obvious chauvinistic bias. To be civilized, one is Greek. All other societies—regardless of achievement—are savage.

Many words still follow the same tribal prejudice, making cultural difference synonymous with barbarism. We insult enemies by calling them Cretin, Philistine, or Vandal, but these terms trace themselves back to racial slurs against competing clans.

The tendency then is to express civilization in terms of membership in a dominant group. To be sophisticated is to be Greek (or Roman or Jewish). To be primitive is to belong to another ethnic group. Civilization is a racial value. What is a traitor or subversive, except a deviant who doesn't follow national rules? What's a patriot but one who does?

REASON

"Reason is the devil's whore."

—Martin Luther

By reason and logic, most people mean rules set down by the Greeks in the 6th and 5th century BC. Logic offers formal guidelines for distinguishing truthful statement from falsehoods. In one rule, logic assumes that a statement can't be both true and false at the same time: "A" won't equal "Not A"; it's either one or the other. This is the same two-state principle as a light switch; just as a toggle can assume one of only two positions (on or off), logic limits propositions to true or false.

So good were logicians at predicting results in the real world, thinkers began to believe that logic was an underlying principle of nature. This explains why the charge of "unreasonableness" is so damning, for it suggests one is at odds with the universe itself.

Despite the enthusiastic claims of early philosophers, classical logic doesn't always fit with the world around us, and may even distort our perceptions.

Consider the Western system of gender. From childhood to adulthood, we're slotted into two exclusive streams: parents tick only the male or female box on a birth certificate; children select either Brownies or Scouts; adults choose between the Ladies and Gents bathroom. In countless ways, we're forced to confirm our identity as *either* a man *or* a woman, with no middle ground.

Unfortunately, sex and gender don't always conform to a two-state system. Mother Nature provides countless examples of hermaphroditic animals, asexual reproduction, and even creatures that physically change sex. All humans produce *both* testosterone and estrogen (the hormones responsible for secondary sex characteristics). The sex genes (XX for female, XY for male) are accompanied by XXY and XYY anomalies. Most telling, some newborns have both a vulva and a penis. Genes, genitalia, hormones, and looks—none of these clearly divide people into two distinct sexes.

Some cultures, such as the Thai, resolve this sexual ambiguity by creating three or more genders. In contrast, Western culture has resolutely, and blindly, stuck with two. An inter-sexed child who doesn't fit the binary mold is "medically reassigned," a horrific bit of jargon.

Such "inter-sexed" children appear as aberrations only when forced into the two-state system of genders. If we escape the either/or dogmatism of classical logic, such children don't seem unnatural, but fit into the unbroken continuum between genders.

Over the centuries, philosophers have developed alternative types of logic, including fuzzy logic that has multiple states between the "either" and the "or." Fuzzy logic works not with a two-state toggle switch, but with a dimmer switch that has multiple positions and settings. As well as a true and a false, it has a "maybe." Now we have a pageant of competing logical systems, each arriving at different solutions. In order to demonstrate this point, consider this riddle.

Picture in your mind the following movements: move 10 spaces up; then go 10 spaces right; finally, travel 10 spaces down. If you moved on a rectangular Cartesian coordinate system (the straight line grid with an X and Y axis taught in high school), you arrive 10 spaces to the left of your beginning position. However, if you move on a globe, starting from the South Pole, you arrive back at your starting point.

In technical terms, Euclidean geometry produces one answer, and non-Euclidean another. Logic depends upon the game rules

you play by. So when someone calls for us to be reasonable, perhaps we should ask, "whose reason do you mean?"

CASE STUDY: SNOPES

Snopes, at www.snopes.com, is an urban legends Web site that
catalogues all manner of tall tales, photoshopped pictures, fallacies, propaganda, rumour, and old wives' tales. Snopes not
only compiles pop culture fables, but also tries to determine their
veracity.

In its early phases, Snopes segregated yarns into two states,
true and false. After a while, this rating system proved insufficient,
and the Webmasters devised a new system that responds to
varying levels of believability. Now, Snopes colour-classifies stories
into four different states: green for true; red for false; yellow for
"undetermined or ambiguous veracity"; and white for "indeterminate
origin" (FAQ). In other words, Snopes found the two-state system of
classical logic inadequate, and devised a more sensitive four-state
system instead.

Although most people consider *urban legend* synonymous with
lie, Snopes defines the term differently. For Snopes, a story
becomes an urban legend when it meets the following conditions:
it is distributed widely; it has numerous versions with differing
details; it claims to be true. "Whether or not the events described in
the tale ever *actually* occurred is completely irrelevant to its classification as an urban legend" (FAQ). This leads to the illogical
situation in which a tale can be an urban legend, even if it's based
on an actual event (and vice versa, fictional stories aren't necessarily urban legends). For Snopes, the category of urban legends
represents a state neither true nor false, but beyond truth and
falsehood.

REALITY

"There are no facts, only interpretations."

—Friedrich Nietzsche

Words like "truth," "certainty," and "fact" are probably the most powerful entries in the simple words lexicon, for they imply an unwavering
"reality." A speaker who evokes these words implies that opponents
linger in delusion and ignorance.

Certainly some events have a "reality" to them: I was born
September 7, 1964 AD; Ottawa is the capital of Canada; the Toronto
Maple Leafs beat the Montreal Canadians to win the Stanley Cup in

1967. But in other claims, the "truth" isn't so clear. For example, choose the true statement from the following options:

A. The earth is flat.
B. The earth is a sphere.

This is a trick question, for both A and B are technically incorrect; the earth is more properly (C) a spheroid (flat on the poles, with equatorial love handles). If proposition B is less accurate than C, it still works well enough for most planet-locked people, and has "some truth," just as the flat-earth theory worked well enough for generations of the land-locked. "Fact" and "fiction" aren't absolutes, but blurry categories that bleed into each other.

The truth ultimately depends on how you define reality, falsehood, fact and fabrication. Let's reconsider a couple of strategies.

FACT AS SCIENTIFIC PROPOSITION

In science, a statement becomes true when verified by observation and experiment. The greater the evidence, the more credible appears the scientific theory. And when the evidence changes, so does the "truth."

GAME RULES

Some facts behave like guidelines within a group. Math and science, for example, use propositional or axiomatic truths—unproven statements that provide a foundation to build on. These aren't "realities," but conveniences that allow a game to occur.

FACT AS CONSENSUS

Some "facts" boil down to an arbitrary notion of community standards and collective values. For instance, many English teachers seem to believe in a god of grammar and spelling that sets down rules such as "Thou shall not split the infinitive." Of course, expression has no such spooky authority, other than community precedent. The "rightness" of a thing often depends upon the neighbourhood.

FACTS AS OPINIONS

Because opinions are based on emotions and belief, they're self-evident "facts" to the holder and require no exterior proof. Questions of aesthetics, taste, value, emotions, and sensation rely on personal feelings, so they're always matters of opinion, true for the individual, but limited as descriptions of objective reality.

MEANINGLESS FACTS

Some "facts" make claims that can't be tested, proved, or disproved. Statements about God, heaven, hell, the afterlife, and reincarnation evoke invisible beings, non-physical states or other dimensions that can't be confirmed, measured, or verified. Philosophers call such mystical claims as "meaningless," for we can't scientifically resolve them.

CASE STUDY: DEATH

Archimedes said, "Give me a place to stand, and I will move the world." Ever since, the search has been on for an Archimedean fulcrum, the stable fact on which to build a philosophy. Existential philosophers thought they'd found that stable point in the certainty of death.

Most people consider death a non-negotiable fact. Yet the boundaries of life and death get tangled up in each other. A body incorporates dead elements such as nails, hair, water, teeth, and bone. A virus can remain inert as rock for centuries. A "dead" crystal replicates itself and produces offspring. Legally, a person is dead only when a medical professional issues a certificate, so death is more ritual than a biological state, at least for the courts. Even if the coroner has a cold body on the slab, the fact of death is notoriously hard to establish, as history shows.

In early medicine, physicians used several indicators to deduce death, including body temperature, skin pallor, and hardening of muscles. Doctors might also hold a mirror up to the mouth, declaring death by the absence of condensation; a problematic definition given that drugs, meditation, coma, and deep sleep reduce breathing to low levels. In the search for a new benchmark, physicians often used torturous tools to diagnose death, such as needles or hot smoke blown up the anal cavity—the criteria for death becoming a corpse's inability to feel pain.

Doctors felt they'd found death in the absence of a heartbeat, but the flat-line standard proved unreliable. Thanks to cardiopulmonary resuscitation, people resume normal and healthy lives even after prolonged heart stoppage. Now, surgeons routinely stop hearts during medical procedures, even replacing them with animal and mechanical substitutes.

Today, doctors define death through the loss of higher brain functions, reflected in the absence of normal brainwaves—an improved definition, but hardly an end to the problem. Artificial respirators, dialysis machines, and other machines can keep a body alive, even without a functioning brain. And some patients recover from vegetative states after showing no brain waves for longer than an hour.

If cryogenics works, then we'll have to alter the brainwave criterion of death, find a new one, or perhaps abandon the notion of death altogether. Death seems not a fact, but a reflection of our own technological ignorance, and in the future, a scientific breakthrough may give new meaning to John Donne's line "Death, thou shalt die."

Works Cited

Mikkelson, Barbara, and David P. Mikkelson. "FAQ." *Snopes*. March 23, 2004. <www.snopes.com>.

Exercises

1. Decide whether these statements are true, relatively true, relatively false, false, meaningless, or indeterminate.

   a) Water freezes at 0° centigrade.
   b) There's no such thing as a free lunch.
   c) 2 + 2 = 4.
   d) If set A is a subset of set B, then A is smaller than B.
   e) The universe is infinite.
   f) This sentence is false.
   g) Tolkien is a better writer than Rowling.
   h) AB = BA.

2. Provide a definition of the following words.

   Necessity
   Indecency
   Freedom
   Liberty
   Labour
   Expert
   Authority
   Health
   Sickness
   Theory

What Is "Against Nature"?

ROBERT ANTON WILSON

Robert Anton Wilson is a novelist, philosopher, anarchist, former editor of *Playboy* magazine, humourist, conspiracy expert, libertarian, Joyce scholar, and icon of the counter-culture. He holds a Ph.D. in psychology, writing often about the nature of perception. However, he is best known for his underground novels, such as his trilogies *Illuminatus!* and *Schrödinger's Cat*. In this selection, Wilson responds to libertarians (such as Konkin or Rothbard mentioned in this essay) who believe in the concept of "natural law," two words that Wilson finds highly problematic.

> One is necessary, one is part of Fate, one belongs to the whole, one is in the whole; there is nothing which could judge, measure, compare or sentence our being, for that would mean judging, measuring, comparing, sentencing the whole. But there is nothing beyond the whole.
>
> —Nietzsche, *Twilight of the Idols*

Even when some Natural Law theorists, like Smith, admit the vast gulf between scientific (instrumental) generalizations and their alleged "Natural Laws" or *tabus,* they still habitually use *language and metaphor that blurs this distinction* and creates a semantic atmosphere in which they *seem* to be discussing "law" in the scientific sense. I do not want to be uncharitable and accuse such writers of dishonesty, but it certainly appears that their language habits create confusion, and I suspect that the Natural Law theorists confuse themselves even more than they confuse their readers.

The worst source of this semantic chaos appears to me to be the phrase, "Natural Law," itself, since it is rather grossly obvious that nothing can ever happen that truly violates nature, at least as the word "nature" is used in science and, I daresay, 99 percent of the time in ordinary speech.

As I mentioned earlier, while I was involved in the "Natural Law" debate in America via *New Libertarian,* I was involved in two similar debates in Ireland. In the first debate, the Catholic Church, through every pulpit in the land, was denouncing the government's attempt to legalize divorce as "against Nature" and in the second debate, less nationally publicized, some witches and Druids and neo-pagans were debating with one another, in a magazine called *Ancient Ways,* about whether machinery and anti-aging research "were" or "were not" against "nature." I created considerable confusion, hostility and incredulity, in both the Catholic and pagan camps, by simply insisting that nothing that happens in nature can be meaningfully said to be "against" nature. It seems to be very hard for Natural Law cultists of all stripes to understand this.

For instance, one shadowy philosopher writing under the name "Peter Z."—and I don't blame him for his near-anonymity; it can be dangerous to be associated publicly with paganism in Holy Catholic

Ireland—replied to each of my attempts to explain that nothing in nature "is" unnatural by compiling angry lists of things and events which *seemed to him* "unnatural"; of course, like most persons innocent of neurological science, Peter Z. assumed that whatever seems unnatural to him "really" "is" unnatural. (Natural Law cultists of all stripes share that pre-scientific framework, I think.) The "really" "unnatural" for Peter Z. ranged from cosmetic surgery to television and included most of what has happened since about 1750 C.E. In general, to Peter Z. nature was natural before industrialism and democracy appeared in the Occident but has become unnatural since then. In short, everything he disliked was "unnatural" and "it is unnatural" was in his vocabulary equivalent to "I don't like it."

To say that nothing in nature "is" unnatural is simply to say that nothing in existence is non-existent. Both of these propositions—nature does not include the unnatural, existence does not include the non-existent—are only tautologies, of course, and I do not reify them as Ayn Rand, for instance, habitually reified "existence." I am not saying anything "profound" here; I am merely saying something about semantics and communication. I am asserting that it is impossible to say anything meaningful in a language structure based on fundamental self-contradictions. This is not meant to be a scientific "law" and certainly not a "Natural Law" (whatever that is); it merely appears to be a necessary game-rule of logic and semantics.

The familiar pagan and romantic idea that machines "are" unnatural, for instance, cannot be admitted into logical discourse because it creates total chaos, i.e., destroys the logic game itself. This becomes clear when one tries to think about it, instead of just reciting it as a banishing ritual, as most pagans and romantics do. How does one define "machine" to avoid pronouncing such design-science devices as the spider's web, the termite city, the beaver dam, etc., "unnatural?" Is a chimpanzee "unnatural" in using a *tool* such as a dead branch to knock fruit from a high tree? Was the first stone axe "unnatural?" Are the bridges in Dublin, which the pagans use along with the Christians every day, "unnatural?" When one starts dividing "nature" or existence into two parts, the "natural" and "unnatural," can any line be drawn at all that is not obviously arbitrary and prejudicial? The atom bomb fills pagans (and most of us) with horror, but could it exist if nuclear fission was not a perfectly natural phenomenon?

It seems that when romantics speak of nature, they mean those parts of the universe they like, and when they speak of the unnatural, they mean those parts of the universe they don't like, but there is no possibility of logical or semantic coherence in such arbitrarily subjective language.

This cannot be called a Logical Positivist or 20th Century view; in the 18th Century already, Burke had enough logical clarity to point out, in his polemic against Rousseau, that the Apollo of Belvedere is as much a part of nature as any tribal totem pole. Since classical art is not as well-known today as it was then, Burke's point can be restated thusly: Marilyn Monroe with all her make-up on, the Empire State Building, Beethoven's Ninth Symphony, Hitler's terrible death camps, the moon rockets, Punk hair styles, the pollution of coal-burning furnaces, the lack of pollution in solar power collectors, and anything else humans have invented, whether we find such inventions wonderful or repulsive, must be in accord with the laws of nature in a scientific sense or they could not exist at all. The only things that can be meaningfully said to be unnatural are impossible things, such as drawing a round square or feeding your dog on moonbeams.

It would be clearer if Natural Law cultists gave up on the oxymoronic concept of *"Natural Laws" that can be violated in nature.* The rules they wish to enforce on us do not appear to be laws of nature—which *cannot* be violated and therefore do not need to be enforced—but rather appear to be "moral laws." It makes sense to say "Don't put a rubber on your willy because that's against moral law" (again: whether one agrees with it or not) but one cannot say "Don't put a rubber on your willy because that's against natural law" without getting involved in endless metaphysical confusions and self-contradictions—"the great Serbonian bog where armies whole have sunk," to quote Burke again—webs of words that connect at no point with sensory-sensual space-time experience.

It appears that the reason that the term "Natural Law" is preferred to "Moral Law" may be that many writers do not want to make it obvious that they speak as priests or theologians and would rather have us think of them as philosophers. But it still seems to me that their dogmas only make sense as religious or moral exhortation and do not make sense in any way if one tries to analyze them as either scientific or philosophic propositions.

It proved as hard to communicate this natural science point of view to editor Konkin as it was to communicate it to Peter Z. In his footnote of rebuttal at this point, Konkin instances examples of alleged "Natural Laws" and then engages in some guilt-by-association. He does not attempt at all to reply to my argument itself—that nothing in nature can be called unnatural for the same reason nothing in existence can be called non-existent. As one natural law, Konkin suggests that a society is impossible when no one produces and all consume. I reply that, if true, this would indeed be a natural law in the science of economics but it would have no more *moral* implications than the law of gravity, and that the way to demonstrate it would be to perform experiments, as was done to confirm the relative (statistical) accuracy of first Newton's and then Einstein's formulae for gravity, in contrast to the method of Natural Law cultists, which is to compose verbal (metaphysical) abstractions. However, I doubt very much that this "law" is valid, since a totally automated society seems theoretically possible and might be one in which nobody produces (the machines will do that) and yet everybody consumes. Konkin's second "natural law" is Heinlein's famous "There ain't no such thing as a free lunch" from the sci-fi novel, *The Moon Is a Harsh Mistress*. I think that should be considered a kind of proverb rather than a "law" and one should not use such a metaphor too literally. For instance, all the cultural heritage—what Korzybski called the time-binding activity of past generations—gives us an abundance of metaphorical "free lunches" in the form of roads, bridges, plants in operation, scientific knowledge, existing technology, music, folklore, languages, discoveries of resources, arts, books, etc., etc. If this cultural heritage of "free lunches" did not exist, each generation would start out as poor and ignorant as a Stone Age tribe.

Konkin's attempt at guilt-by-association seems even more amusing to me than his attempt at suggesting scientific laws of sociology. He writes, "I think it only fair to point out that Wilson certainly hangs around mystics a lot more than, say, professional atheist Smith." I will not comment on the similarity to the "logic" of the late Sen. Joseph R. McCarthy (R-Wis.) and I will not even remark that it is news to me that Konkin keeps me under such close surveillance that he knows how much time I spend in the company of "mystics." I will only say the man sounds rather desperate here. Perhaps he was very tired when he wrote that. In fact, I do share space-time with mystics on occasion, and also with occultists and even witches, and also with physicists, mathematicians, biologists, anthropologists, psychologists, psychiatrists, sociologists, writers, actors, nudists, vegetarians, plumbers, grocers, bartenders, homosexuals, left-handed people, atheists, Catholics, Protestants, Jews, Freemasons and I don't know who all. I travel a lot and talk to anybody who might be interesting. If Konkin means to imply that I have contracted some dread mental illness (a metaphysical AIDS perhaps) by not being a philosophical segregationist and only talking to people who already agree with me, I can merely reply that the only way to learn anything, for a person of limited intelligence like me, is to listen to as many diverse views as possible. Metaphysical wizards like Konkin and Rothbard may discover everything knowable about everything imaginable by sitting in their armchairs and "investigating by reason" the ghostly inner "natures" or "essences" of things, but a person of lower intelligence like me only learns a few things in one lifetime and only manages that much by meeting as many people as possible and asking questions of all those broad-minded enough not to hit me with a chair for such inquisitiveness.

To conclude this part of my thesis, if it were possible to violate nature—to perform an act "against nature"—that would be marvelous, and would undoubtedly be a turning point in evolution. It would certainly seem an exciting show to watch, and I would buy tickets to see it. So far, however, everything that has happened on this planet has been in accord with natural laws of physics, chemistry, etc., which have no moral implications and do not need to be enforced or even preached about.

Disease

THOMAS SZASZ

A psychoanalyst by trade, Thomas Szasz questions his own profession in a series of books, including *The Myth of Mental Illness*, *The Untamed Tongue*, *The Therapeutic State*, and *The Manufacture of Madness*. At the heart of Szasz's writings lies the belief that mental illness may be little more than a convenience designed to isolate people who behave outside the norms.

A glossary:
Disease: 1. Proven bodily lesion. 2. Putative bodily lesion. 3. Distress, disability, disadvantage, dysfunction. 4. An (ostensibly) treatable condition. 5. Irrationality. 6. Irresponsibility. 7. Crime. 8. Any human behavior or characteristic we dislike.

Treatment: 1. Intervention sought by a patient from a physician for the amelioration or cure of disease. 2. Punishment (as in "Let's give him the treatment . . ."; especially popular in psychiatric institutions and totalitarian countries).

*   *   *

Bad habits treated as diseases:
Using alcohol badly is called "alcoholism" and is treated with Antabuse.

Using food badly is called "anorexia nervosa" or "obesity"; the former is treated with electroshock, the latter with amphetamines or intestinal bypass operations.

Using sex badly is called "perversion," and is treated with electrical stimulation through electrodes implanted in the brain and with sex-change operations.

Using language badly is called "psychosis" and is treated with anti-psychotic drugs.

*   *   *

The term "illness" can mean either a disease (lesion) or the state of feeling sick (a sense of being ill or unwell). In the former case, "illness" is synonymous with "disease"; this is indeed the way these two terms are used in everyday speech. In the latter case, "illness" is an abstract noun without material or objective referent; in this sense, there is no difference between saying "I feel ill" and saying "I have an illness." Notice, however, that *feeling ill* is analogous to *feeling well*, or *happy*, or *sad*; but that it would be nonsensical to replace these expressions with *I have a wellness*, or *I have a happiness*, or *I have a sadness*.

In short, "I feel sick/ill" is what we say when we feel indisposed— because of disease or some other reason. Accordingly, feeling ill may or may not be a reason for assuming the sick role and seeking medical help.

*   *   *

Demonstrable bodily lesion is the gold standard of medical diagnosis. Without practical convertibility into gold, the value of paper money rests only on faith. Without conceptual convertibility into bodily lesion, the diagnosis of disease rests only on faith. Unbacked by gold, paper money is *fiat* money—the politically irresistible incentive for debauching the currency, called "inflation." Unbacked by lesion, diagnosis is *fiat* diagnosis—the medically irresistible incentive for debauching the concept of disease, called "psychiatry."

*   *   *

Today, disease is largely a *strategic category*. If the (American) government classifies a pattern of behavior—say, drug (ab)use—as *behavior*, then it cannot regulate it. That is why, when the government tries to regulate *behavior*—for example, the right to smoke in private—we indignantly protest: "But this is a free country!"

However, if the government can classify a pattern of behavior as an *illness*—for example, "alcoholism"—then it can regulate "it" by appealing to its powerful impact on business, health, economics, and so forth.

Finally, if the government can classify a pattern of behavior as a (serious) *mental illness*—for example, "schizophrenia"—then it can directly regulate personal behavior itself, by depriving the individual of the right to free speech, property, and liberty.

Seemingly oblivious to all this, jurists, psychologists, physicians, and scientists continue to debate whether X is or is not a disease.

*   *   *

"October 2 through 8 is Mental Illness Awareness Week, part of an ongoing effort by the American Psychiatric Association to 'reduce the stigma surrounding mental illnesses,' including schizophrenia. . . . Many social scientists say that one factor that tends to destigmatize a disorder is defining it as a medical problem. . . . "[1]

The American Psychiatric Association thus acknowledges that, ostensibly in an effort to destigmatize stigmatized (mis)behavior, it accepts such an ostensibly noble motive as a legitimate ground for counting stigmatized (mis)behavior as disease. However, this self-flattering posture evades confronting the question of whether it is desirable or undesirable to destigmatize behavior such as was exhibited by, say, John Hinckley, Jr., currently the most famous "schizophrenic" in the United States.

*   *   *

In the case of bodily illness, the patient pays, or is willing to pay, the doctor to relieve him of (being bothered by) his illness; in the case of mental illness, we (the taxpayers) pay, and are willing to pay, the psychiatrist to relieve us of (being bothered by) the patient.

*   *   *

A Canadian politician has discovered a new disease: illiteracy. Declares Senator Joyce Fairbairn (Ontario): "Honorable senators, illiteracy touches probably more than 20 percent of our population. . . . It is not a partisan issue. It affects us all . . . [it] is truly a national disease . . . [We] must understand that this is one disease that can be cured."[2] Spreading the alarm, a reporter (from Ottawa) adds: "Illiterates more commonly read the Bible and other religious material, while literates lean more to reference books, fiction, and manuals."[3]

Question: Who is illiterate?

*   *   *

Formerly, people had strong sexual desires or needs and were responsible for controlling them; now they suffer from the disease of "sex addiction." "Evangelist Jimmy Swaggart, who paid prostitutes to perform lewd sex acts, is one of 10 million Americans suffering from an addiction . . .," asserts David M. Moss, director of the Coventry Association for Pastoral Psychology in Atlanta. Victor B. Cline, a clinical psychologist at the University of Utah, agrees: "I see Swaggart as a good man but he had a secret illness going back to his teens."[4]

*   *   *

Jennifer Schneider, M.D., a specialist in internal medicine, asserts that "repeated sexual affairs may signal addictive behavior. . . . my husband admitted he had love affairs. . . . He said he couldn't control his behavior." Mr. Schneider was cured in "a program for sexual addicts modeled after Alcoholics Anonymous." Dr. Schneider recommends four such organizations: "SA (Sexaholics Anonymous), CoSA (for Co-dependents of Sex Addicts), SLAA (Sex and Love Addicts Anonymous), and SAA (Sex Addicts Anonymous)."[5]

*   *   *

"Compulsive gambling is a damaging disease for an estimated nine million Americans," asserts Amin Daghestani, professor of psychiatry at Loyola University in Chicago. "Physicians everywhere must recognize this problem as a treatable, medical condition."[6]

*   *   *

"Chronic gambling," we read in the *New York Times,* may be a chemically caused illness:

> The psychological forces that propel so many chronic gamblers to ruin marriages, lose jobs, and even turn to crime may spring from a biological need. . . . the biological findings suggest that pathological gamblers suffer from an addiction like alcoholism . . . gamblers had lower levels than usual of the brain chemicals that regulate arousal . . . they may engage in

activities like gambling to increase their levels of these chemicals in the noradrenergic system, which secretes them.[7]

Evidently, I have been mistaken: I have always thought that a pathological gambler was a gambler who lost money, not his wife; and that people gambled not because they wanted to increase the levels of certain chemicals in their brains, but because they enjoyed gambling and hoped to win.

*   *   *

Lionel Solursh, professor of psychiatry at the Medical College of Georgia, has discovered a new disease; "Combat Addiction." Supposedly occurring mainly in "intoxicant abusers and violence-addicted veterans," the diagnosis of this disease rests solely on the metaphors used by the (so-called) patients to describe their (alleged) experiences:

> ... the rush or the feeling that you get from this is one of an addiction to adrenalin, addiction to cocaine ... when I get into this high it is just like being in Vietnam, the thrill of killing, the thrill of destroying. And it's something I just cannot overcome, even with medication. ... It's hard to duplicate this high with drugs, except the only drug I know is cocaine ... [that gives you] the same type of high of killing, of destroying.[8]

Discovery of the disease manifested by the thrill of mugging, stealing, cheating, and lying must be right around the corner, requiring only more funding for psychiatric research.

*   *   *

Fact #1: Psychiatrists now maintain that the drug abuser and the pathological gambler are sick and need treatment.

Fact #2: Persons so afflicted pay for their "illness," but not for its treatment. (Such patients have no trouble finding the money for drugs or wagering, but seem never to have any money for treatment for drug abuse or pathological gambling.)

Fact #3: The psychiatrist treating such patients is paid by the State, which gives him a vested economic interest in the State's defining personal irresponsibility as impersonal illness.

*   *   *

New models of mental illnesses are now produced faster than new models of automobiles, perhaps because they sell faster. A new Italian model is "art sickness" or the "Stendhal Syndrome":

> In a 182-page book titled "The Stendhal Syndrome," [Dr. Graziella] Magherini details the cases of 106 tourists admitted to Santa Maria Nuova Hospital in Florence in the last 10 years suffering from delirium, disorientation and paranoia brought on by exposure to magnificent works of art. Hundreds of milder cases, probably thousands more, have gone unreported. . . . "The worst case had to be in the hospital 10 days," said Magherini, head of the psychiatric ward at Santa Maria Nuova and a lecturer on psychiatry at the University of Florence.[9]

"A sucker is born every minute," observed Phineas Barnum. Now the suckers are called "mental patients" (who believe they are sick) and "health insurers" (who pay for the fictitious treatments of non-existent illnesses).

*   *   *

Here is a recently discovered disease so ridiculous it defies being ridiculed:

> Psychiatrists and psychologists at Hartgrove Hospital [in Chicago] . . . are creating one of the nation's first treatment programs to wean teen-agers away from Satanism. . . . "I don't think there is any doubt Satanism is a growing problem," said social worker Dale Trahan, who has been researching Satanic beliefs for three years and was contracted to organize the program for the Treatment of Ritualistic Deviance. . . . In the program, teen-agers will spend four to eight weeks as in-patients and undergo individual and group counseling. . . . The new program will seek to undermine Satanism's underlying belief system. . . .[10]

*   *   *

The concept of disease is fast replacing the concept of responsibility. With increasing zeal Americans use and interpret the assertion "I am sick" as equivalent to the assertion "I am not responsible": Smokers say they are not responsible for smoking, drinkers that they are not responsible for drinking, gamblers that they are not responsible for gambling, and mothers who murder their infants that they are not responsible for killing. To prove their point—and to capitalize on their self-destructive and destructive behavior—smokers, drinkers, gamblers, and insanity acquittees are suing tobacco companies, liquor companies, gambling casinos, and physicians.

Can American society survive this legal-psychiatric assault on its moral and political foundations?

*   *   *

It is senseless to debate whether alcoholism or kleptomania are or are not diseases. The fact that we call drinking "too often" or "too much" alcoholism, and stealing things the thief "does not need" kleptomania are symptoms of our belief that they are diseases and of our desire to treat them as such. If we wanted to seriously consider how we ought to classify, understand, and respond to such behaviors we would have to name them in ways that do not prejudge their medical or moral character—which is virtually impossible.

Reading Notes

1. Chris A. Raymond, "Political Campaign Pinpoints 'Stigma Hurdle' Facing Nation's Mental Health Community," *Journal of the American Psychiatric Association*, 260: 1338 (September 9), 1988.

2. Joyce Fairbairn, "A Senator's Lament: 'Too Many Canadians Cannot Read the Charter of Rights,'" *Whig-Standard* (Kingston, Ontario), September 16, 1987, p. 11.

3. Norm Ovenden, "Southam Literacy Survey Contains Unsettling News for Newspaper Industry," ibid., September 17, 1987, p. 10. (I wish to thank Mark Barnes for providing these two items.)

4. Quoted in "Sexual Behavior Likened to Addiction," *Washington Post*, April 2, 1988. p. C11.

5. Jim Fuller, "Physician Offers Hope for Adulterers and Their Spouses," *Syracuse Post-Standard*, May 9, 1988, p. A14.

6. Quoted in Bill Stokes, "Gambling Is Being Treated as a Disease," *Buffalo News*, March 29, 1988, p. C7.

7. Daniel Goleman, "Biology of Brain May Hold Key for Gamblers: When the Casino Becomes an Addiction, the Condition May Be Chemical," *New York Times*, October 3, 1989, p. C1.

8. Lionel Solursh, "Combat Addiction: Post-Traumatic Stress Disorder Re-explored," *Psychiatric Journal of the University of Ottawa*, 13: 17–20 (March), 1988, p. 20.

9. "Great Works of Art Pose Health Threats to Tourists," *Syracuse Post-Standard*, July 26, 1989, p. D1.

10. "Hospital Plans to Wean Teens from Satanism," *Arkansas Democrat*, September 7, 1989, p. 3A.

From *The Doubter's Companion*

JOHN RALSTON SAUL

John Ralston Saul is an award-winning philosopher, political commentator, novelist, and essayist whose ideas have had considerable influence on society. His philosophical work includes *The Unconscious Civilization*, *Voltaire's Bastards*, *The Doubter's Companion*, and *On Equilibrium*. An advocate of common sense, Saul sees a danger in allowing reason to become the only value governing society, and so he offers here some unconventional definitions of familiar terms.

Civilization The single and shortest definition of civilization may be the word **Language**.

This is not to suggest that images or music are of lesser importance. It is simply that they have more to do with the unconscious. They are somehow part of metaphysics and religion. Civilization, if it means something concrete, is the conscious but unprogrammed mechanism by which humans communicate. And through communication they live with each other, think, create and act.

Economics The romance of truth through measurement.

An understanding of the value of economics can best be established by using its own methods. Draw up a list of the large economic problems to have struck the West over the last quarter-century. Determine the dominant strand of advice offered in each case by the community of economists. Calculate how many times this advice was followed. (More often than not it was.) Finally, add up the number of times this advice solved the problem.

The answer seems to be zero. Consistent failure based on expert methodology suggests that the central assumptions must have been faulty, rather in the way sophisticated calculations based upon the assumption that the world was flat tended to come out wrong. However, streams of economists are on record protesting that they weren't listened to enough. That the recommended interest rate or money supply or tariff policy was not followed to its absolute conclusion.

This "science" of economics seems to be built upon a non-scientific and non-mathematical assumption that economic forces are the expression of a natural truth. To interfere with them is to create an unnatural situation. The creation and enforcement of **Standards of Production** are, for example, viewed as an artificial limitation of reality. Even economists who favour these standards see them as necessary and justifiable deformations of economic truth.

Economic truth has replaced such earlier truths as an all-powerful God, and a natural Social Contract. Economics are the new religious core of public policy. But what evidence has been produced to prove this natural right to primacy over other values, methods and activities?

The answer usually given is that economic activity determines the success or failure of a society. It follows that economists are the priests whose necessary expertise will make it possible to maximize the value of this activity. But economic activity is less a cause than an effect—of geographical and climatic necessity, family and wider social structures, the balance between freedom and order, the ability of society to unleash the imagination, and the weakness or strength of neighbours. If anything, the importance given to economics over the last quarter-century has interfered with prosperity. The more we concentrate on it, the less money we make.

Facts Tools of authority.

Facts are supposed to make truth out of a proposition. They are the proof. The trouble is that there are enough facts around to prove most things. They have become the comfort and prop of conventional wisdom; the music of the rational technocracy; the justification for any sort of policy, particularly as advanced by special-interest groups, expert guilds and other modern corporations. Confused armies of contradictory facts struggle in growing darkness. Support ideological fantasies. Stuff bureaucratic briefing books.

It was **Giambattista Vico** who first identified this problem. He argued that any obsession with proof would misfire unless it was examined in a far larger context which took into account experience and the surrounding circumstances. Diderot was just as careful when he wrote the entry on facts for the *Encyclopédie*:

> You can divide facts into three types: the divine, the natural and man-made. The first belongs to theology; the second to philosophy and the third to history. All are equally open to question.[1]

There is little room for such care in a corporatist society. Facts are the currency of power for each specialized group. But how can so much be expected from these innocent fragments of knowledge? They are not able to think and so cannot be used to replace thought. They have no memory. No imagination. No judgement. They're really not much more than interesting landmarks which may illuminate our way as we attempt to think. If properly respected they are never proof, always illustration.

Reality You should not, as the Washington hostess Alice Roosevelt Longworth pointed out, trust any balding man who combs his hair up from his armpit over the top of his head. Or rather, it is the considered opinion of most members of our rational élites that, in any given difference of opinion with reality, reality is wrong.

Reason Whatever anyone says it means, someone will argue that it means something else. The one thing they will agree on is that reason is both central and essential to our civilization, which is curious since they don't know what it is.

One of the peculiar characteristics of key terms is that the more we apply them to the real world, the more we claim that we are not experiencing the real thing. A dictatorship of the proletariat, once installed, will never be the promised dictatorship of the proletariat. A true self-regulating market will somehow never be true or self-regulating enough. These arguments resemble the rhetoric of mediaeval scholastics. Those who use them seem to be on a mission to rescue their favourite abstract theory from its latest catastrophic defeat at the hands of reality.

With half a millennium of conscientious application under its belt, reason is regularly declared to be farther than ever from the revelation of its true meaning. But an annoying sort of commonsensical citizen might stick to her guns and repeat, whenever faced by this interminable kant, that reason is what reason does.

As the religious debates which preceded the rational debates demonstrated, if you treat all questioning of what is declared to be the central principle of society as a rejection of it, you leave no room for reasonable re-evaluation. Thus it is invariably suggested that those who question the way in which we use reason are actually calling for a return to superstition and arbitrary power. The unspoken basis of this argument is that there are no other important human qualities or that these other pretended qualities are not qualities at all. In this way we are denied access to what we know to be our own reality.

The hypothetical **Doubt**ing citizen could suggest that reason might make more sense if it were relieved of its monotheistic aura and reintegrated into the broader humanist concept from which it escaped in search of greater glory in the sixteenth century. In this larger view it would be balanced and restrained and given direction by other useful and perhaps also essential human characteristics such as common sense, intuition, memory, creativity and ethics. In such a generous context it would be easy to see that reason on its own is little more than a mechanism devoid of meaning, purpose or direction.

The rhetorical defender of the rationalist faith will immediately question whether these other characteristics are indeed independent qualities or whether they are merely lower-case concepts which can be dangerous if let loose. But why must we reduce our options to a choice between the true God and a golden calf?

Between our periods of purist folly, we keep coming back to the idea that we are balanced creatures. That is, we can be if we try. It may be impossible for each individual to achieve equilibrium. But when the varying strengths and weaknesses of the citizenry are combined, the idea of a balanced society becomes reasonable.

Reason detached from the balancing qualities of **Humanism** is irrational. The promise of a sensible society lies in the potential reality of a wider balance. And in that equilibrium reason has an essential place.

Taste There is no such thing as good or bad taste. As Coco Chanel pointed out, there is only taste. This suggests that moral judgements such as good and bad may have no relevance to fashion. Perhaps fashion is just fashion. To be enjoyed or ignored or, for that matter, deplored.

In late imperial Rome, the great aristocratic pagan families were horrified by the rise to power of the lower-middle-class Christians whose churches were so plain and ugly that they were scarcely more than hovels. These rustic believers knew nothing about architectural principles and, we can surmise, had heavy accents and dressed without style. No doubt they were what those with taste would call common. Gradually, however, the aristocrats themselves followed the odour of shifting power and began to convert. Eventually the law left them no choice. It was probably a few generations before they actually thought of themselves as Christians, but in the meantime they brought taste to the church: architecture, decoration, mosaics, painting, liturgy, music. At last the bishops began to wear chasubles as magnificent as their positions. At last the language of prayer and song began to sound elegant and powerful. The beauty that resulted from the participation of the great old imperial families became an integral part of our pleasure in ourselves as civilized people. The new pagan Christian taste was quickly confused with the original Christian message of moral clarity. But those links were and remain purely imaginary.

As Queen Elizabeth II replied, when asked how she felt about taste, "Well, I don't think it helps."[2] True and untrue. It does not, in any ethical sense, help. It may even confuse and weaken ethical standards. On the other hand it does help us to get through the day. "For the pleasure of your eyes," the classic Arab souk merchant will incant to draw you into his stall. And why not. We do have eyes. But not, as Ovid pointed out, for debating taste. *"De gustibus non disputendum est,"* which simply indicates that Coco Chanel knew her Roman poetry.

Reading Notes

1. FACTS–Denis Diderot, *L'Encyclopédie* vol. 2, 97. "Fait" ". . . On peut distribuer les *faits* en trois classes, les actes de la divinité, les phénomènes de la nature, et les actions des hommes. Les premiers appartiennent à la théologie, les seconds à la philosophie, et les autres à l'histoire proprement dite. Tous sont également sujets à la critique."

2. TASTE–*The Spectator*, 20 February 1993, 39.

Does Work Really Work?

L. SUSAN BROWN

Holding a Ph.D. from the University of Toronto, L. Susan Brown is an anarchist, feminist, and author of *The Politics of Individualism: Liberalism, Liberal Feminism, and Anarchism.* In this selection, Brown looks at the ambiguities of a word at the heart of every economic theory: work.

One of the first questions people often ask when they are introduced to one another in our society is "what do you do?" This is more than just polite small talk—it is an indication of the immense importance work has for us. Work gives us a place in the world, it is our identity, it defines us, and, ultimately, it confines us. Witness the psychic dislocation when we lose our jobs, when we are fired, laid off, forced to retire or when we fail to get the job we applied for in the first place. An unemployed person is defined not in positive but in negative terms: to be unemployed is to lack work. To lack work is to be socially and economically marginalized. To answer "nothing" to the question "what do you do?" is emotionally difficult and socially unacceptable. Most unemployed people would rather answer such a question with vague replies like "I'm between contracts" or "I have a few resumes out and the prospects look promising" than admit outright that they do not work. For to not work in our society is to lack social significance—it is to be a nothing, because nothing is what you do.

Those who *do* work (and they are becoming less numerous as our economies slowly disintegrate) are something—they are teachers, nurses, doctors, factory workers, machinists, dental assistants, coaches, librarians, secretaries, bus drivers and so on. They have identities defined by what they do. They are considered normal productive members of our society. Legally their work is considered to be subject to an employment contract, which if not explicitly laid out at the beginning of employment is implicitly understood to be part of the relationship between employee and employer. The employment contract is based on the idea that it is possible for a fair exchange to occur between an employee who trades her/his skills and labour for wages supplied by the employer. Such an idea presupposes that a person's skills and labour are not inseparable from them, but are rather separate attributes that can be treated like property to be bought and sold. The employment contract assumes that a machinist or an exotic dancer, for instance, have the capacity to separate out from themselves the particular elements that are required by the employer and are then able to enter into an agreement with the employer to exchange only those attributes for money. The machinist is able to sell technical skills while the exotic dancer is able to sell sexual appeal, and, according to the employment contract, they both do so without selling themselves as people. Political scientists and economists refer to such attributes as "property in the person," and speak about a person's ability to contract out labour power in the form of property in the person.

In our society, then, work is defined as the act by which an employee contracts out her or his labour power as property in the person to an employer for fair monetary compensation. This way of describing work, of understanding it as a fair exchange between two equals, hides the real relationship between employer and employee: that of domination and subordination. For if the truth behind the employment contract were widely known, workers in our society would refuse to work, because they would see that it is impossible for human individuals to truly separate out labour power from themselves. "Property in the person" doesn't really exist as something that an individual can simply sell as a separate thing. Machinists cannot just detach from themselves the specific skills needed by an employer; those skills are part of an organic whole that cannot be disengaged from the entire person. Similarly, sex appeal is an intrinsic part of exotic dancers, and it is incomprehensible how such a constitutive, intangible characteristic could be severed from the dancers themselves. A dancer has to be totally present in order to dance, just like a machinist must be totally present in order to work; neither can just send their discrete skills to do the work for them. Whether machinist, dancer, teacher, secretary, or pharmacist, it is not only one's skills that are being sold to an employer, it is also one's very being. When employees contract out their labour power as property in the person to employers, what is really happening is that employees are selling their own self determination, their own wills, their own freedom. In short, they are, during their hours of employment, slaves.

What is a slave? A slave is commonly regarded as a person who is the legal property of another and is bound to absolute obedience. The legal lie that is created when we speak of a worker's capacity to sell property in the person without alienating her or his will allows us to maintain the false distinction between a worker and a slave. A worker must work according to the will of another. A worker must obey the boss, or ultimately lose the job. The control the employer has over the employee at work is absolute. There is in the end no negotiation—you do it the boss' way or you hit the highway. It is ludicrous to believe that it is possible to separate out and sell "property in the person" while maintaining human integrity. To sell one's labour power on the market is to enter into a relationship of subordination with one's employer—it is to become a slave to the employer/master. The only major differences between a slave and a worker is that a worker is only a slave at work while a slave is a slave twenty-four hours a day, and slaves know that they are slaves, while most workers do not think of themselves in such terms.

Carole Pateman points out the implications of the employment contract in her book *The Sexual Contract*:

> Capacities or labour power cannot be used without the worker using his will, his understanding and experience, to put them into effect. The use of labour power requires the presence of its "owner," and it remains as mere potential until he acts in the manner necessary to put it into use, or agrees or is compelled so to act; that is, the worker must labour. To contract for the use of labour power is a waste of resources unless it can be used in the way in which the new

owner requires. The fiction "labour power" cannot be used; what is required is that the worker labours as demanded. The employment contract must, therefore, create a relationship of command and obedience between employer and worker. . . . In short, the contract in which the worker allegedly sells his labour power is a contract in which, since he cannot be separated from his capacities, he sells command over the use of his body and himself. To obtain the right to the use of another is to be a (civil) master.[1]

Terms like "master" and "slave" are not often used when describing the employment contract within capitalist market relations; however, this does not mean that such terms don't apply. By avoiding such terms and instead insisting that the employment contract is fair, equitable and based on the worker's freedom to sell his or her labour power, the system itself appears fair, equitable and free. One problem with misidentifying the true nature of the employee/employer relationship is that workers experience work as slavery at the same time that they buy into it ideologically.

No matter what kind of job a worker does, whether manual or mental, well paid or poorly paid, the nature of the employment contract is that the worker must, in the end, obey the employer. The employer is always right. The worker is told how to work, where to work, when to work, and what to work on. This applies to university professors and machinists, to lawyers and carpet cleaners: when you are an employee, you lose your right to self-determination. This loss of freedom is felt keenly, which is why many workers dream of starting their own businesses, being their own bosses, being self-employed. Most will never realize their dreams, however, and instead are condemned to sell their souls for money. The dream doesn't disappear, however, and the uneasiness, unhappiness, and meaninglessness of their jobs gnaws away at them even as they defend the system under which they exploitedly toil.

It doesn't have to be this way. There is nothing sacred about the employment contract that protects it from being challenged, that entrenches it eternally as a form of economic organization. We can understand our own unhappiness as workers not as a psychological problem that demands Prozac, but rather as a human response to domination. We can envision a better way of working, and we can do so now, today, in our own lives. By doing so we can chisel away at the wage slavery system; we can undermine it and replace it with freer ways of working.

What would a better way of work look like? It would more resemble what we call play than work. That is not to say that it would be easy, as play can be difficult and challenging, like we often see in the sports we do for fun. It would be self-directed, self-desired, and freely chosen. This means that it would have to be disentangled from the wage system, for as soon as one is paid one becomes subservient to whoever is doing the paying. As Alexander Berkman noted: "labour and its products must be exchanged without price, without profit, freely according to necessity."[2] Work would be done because it was desired, not because it was forced. Sound impossible? Not at all. This kind of work is done now, already, by most of us on a daily basis. It is the sort of activity we choose to do after our eight or ten hours of slaving for someone else in the paid workplace. It is experienced every time we do something worthwhile for no pay, every time we change a diaper, umpire a kid's baseball game, run a race, give blood, volunteer to sit on a committee, counsel a friend, write a newsletter, bake a meal, or do a favour. We take part in this underground free economy when we coach, tutor, teach, build, dance, baby-sit, write a poem, or program a computer without getting paid. We must endeavor to enlarge these areas of free work to encompass more and more of our time, while simultaneously trying to change the structures of domination in the paid workplace as much as we possibly can.

Barter, while superficially appearing as a challenge to the wage system, is still bound by the same relationships of domination. To say that I will paint your whole house if you will cook my meals for a month places each of us into a situation of relinquishing our own self-determination for the duration of the exchange. For I must paint your house to your satisfaction and you must make my meals to my satisfaction, thereby destroying for each of us the self-directed, creative spontaneity necessary for the free expression of will. Barter also conjures up the problem of figuring out how much of my time is worth how much of your time, that is, what the value of our work is, in order that the exchange is fair and equal. Alexander Berkman posed this problem as the question, "why not give each according to the value of his work?," to which he answers,

> Because there is no way by which value can be measured. . . .
> Value is what a thing is worth. . . . What a thing is worth no
> one can really tell. Political economists generally claim that
> the value of a commodity is the amount of labour required
> to produce it, of "socially necessary labour," as Marx says.
> But evidently it is not a just standard of measurement.
> Suppose the carpenter worked three hours to make a kitchen

chair, while the surgeon took only half an hour to perform an operation that saved your life. If the amount of labour used determines value, then the chair is worth more than your life. Obvious nonsense, of course. Even if you should count in the years of study and practice the surgeon needed to make him capable of performing the operation, how are you going to decide what "an hour of operating" is worth? The carpenter and mason also had to be trained before they could do their work properly, but you don't figure in those years of apprenticeship when you contract for some work with them. Besides, there is also to be considered the particular ability and aptitude that every worker, writer, artist or physician must exercise in his labours. That is a purely individual personal factor. How are you going to estimate its value?

That is why value cannot be determined. The same thing may be worth a lot to one person while it is worth nothing or very little to another. It may be worth much or little even to the same person, at different times. A diamond, a painting, a book may be worth a great deal to one man and very little to another. A loaf of bread will be worth a great deal to you when you are hungry, and much less when you are not. Therefore the real value of a thing cannot be ascertained if it is an unknown quantity.[3]

In a barter system, for an exchange to be fair, the value of the exchanged goods and services must be equal. However, value is unknowable, therefore barter falls apart on practical grounds.

Increasing the amount of free work in our lives requires that we be conscious of the corrupting effects of money and barter. Thus, baby-sit your friend's children not for money, but because you want to do so. Teach someone how to speak a second language, or edit someone's essay, or coach a running team for the simple pleasure of taking part in the activity itself. Celebrate giving and helping as play, without expecting anything in return. Do these things because you want to, not because you have to.

This is not to say that we should do away with obligations, but only that such obligations should be self-assumed. We must take on free work in a responsible matter, or else our dream of a better world will degenerate into chaos. Robert Graham outlines the characteristics of self-assumed obligations:

Self-assumed obligations are not "binding" in the same sense that laws or commands are. A law or command is binding in the sense that failure to comply with it will normally attract the application of some sort of coercive sanction by authority promulgating the law or making the command. The binding character of law is not internal to the concept of law itself but dependent on external factors, such as the legitimacy of the authority implementing and enforcing it. A promise, unlike a law, is not enforced by the person making it. The content of the obligation is defined by the person assuming it, not by an external authority.[4]

To promise, then, is to oblige oneself to see through an activity, but the fulfillment of the obligation is up to the person who made the promise in the first place, and nonfulfillment carries no external sanction besides, perhaps, disappointment (and the risk that others will avoid interacting with someone who habitually breaks her or his promises). Free work, therefore, is a combination of voluntary play and self-assumed obligations, of doing what you desire to do and co-operating with others. It is forsaking the almighty dollar for the sheer enjoyment of creation and recreation. Bob Black lyrically calls for the abolition of work, which "doesn't mean that we have to stop doing things. It does mean creating a new way of life based on play. . . . By "play" I mean also festivity, creativity, conviviality, commensuality, and maybe even art. There is more to play than child's play, as worthy as that is. I call for a collective adventure in generalized joy and freely interdependent exuberance."[5]

We must increase the amount of free work in our lives by doing what we want, alone and with others, whether high art or mundane maintenance. We need to tear ourselves away from thinking in strict exchange terms: I will do this for you if you will do that for me. Even outside our formal work hours, the philosophy of contract and exchange permeates our ways of interacting with others. This is evident when we do a favour for someone—more often than not, people feel uncomfortable unless they can return the favour in some way, give tit for tat. We must resist this sense of having to exchange favours. Instead, we need to be and act in ways that affirm our own desires and inclinations. This does not mean being lazy or slothful (although at times we may need to be so), but rather calls for self-discipline. Free work actually demands a great deal of self-discipline, as there is no external force making us work, but only our own internal desire to partake in an activity that motivates our participation.

While we move towards a freer world by consciously affirming free work outside the marketplace, we can also make a difference during those hours when we are paid to work. Being conscious of the fact that when we are selling our labour we are actually selling ourselves gives us self-awareness. Such self-awareness is empowering, as the first step to changing one's condition is understanding the true nature of that condition. Through this understanding, we can develop strategies for challenging the slave wage system. For instance, every time we ignore the boss and do what we want we create a mini-revolution in the workplace. Every time we sneak a moment of pleasure at work we damage the system of wage slavery. Every time we undermine the hierarchical structure of decision-making in the workplace we gain a taste of our own self-worth. These challenges can come from below or from above: those of us who achieve a measure of power in the workplace can institute structural changes that empower those below, drawing from principles like consensus decision-making and decentralization. For instance, as teachers we can introduce students to the idea of consensus by using such a method to make major class room decisions. Those of us who head up committees or task forces can advocate institutional structures, policies and constitutions that decentralize power. Of course, the wage system is inherently corrupt and unreformable; however, we can make it more bearable while at the same time trying to destroy it.

And destroy it we must. If one's identity is based on work, and work is based on the employment contract, and the employment contract is a falsehood, then our very identities have at their foundation a lie. In addition, the labour market is moving towards an ever-increasing exploitative form of work: it is predicted that by the year 2000, fifty percent of the labour force will be engaged in temp work—work which is even less selfdirected than permanent full-time jobs. Bob Black has it right when he proclaims that "no one should ever work."[6] Who knows what kinds of creative activity would be unleashed if only we were free to do what we desired? What sorts of social organizations would we fashion if we were not stifled day in and day out by drudgery? For example, what would a woman's day look like if we abolished the wage system and replaced it with free and voluntary activity? Bob Black argues that "by abolishing wage-labor and achieving full unemployment we undermine the sexual division of labor,"[7] which is the linchpin of modern sexism. What would a world look like that encouraged people to be creative and self-directed, that celebrated enjoyment and fulfillment? What would be the consequences of living in a world where, if you met someone new and were asked what you did, you could joyfully reply "this, that and the other thing" instead of "nothing?" Such is the world we deserve.

Reading Notes

1. Carole Pateman, *The Sexual Contract* (Stanford: Stanford University Press, 1988), pp. 150–151.

2. Alexander Berkman, *ABC of Anarchism* (London: Freedom Press, 1977), p. 20.

3. Berkman, p. 19.

4. Robert Graham, *The Role of Contract in Anarchist Ideology*, in *For Anarchism: History, Theory, and Practice*, edited by David Goodway (London: Routledge, 1989), p. 168.

5. Bob Black, *The Abolition of Work and Other Essays* (Port Townsend: Loompanics), p. 17.

6. Black, p. 33.

7. Black, pp. 29–30.

CHAPTER

Questions

"It's the question that drives us."

—Trinity, *The Matrix*

In the East, education is often depicted with the image of a teacup (the student) being filled with tea (wisdom) from a pot (the master). This traditional metaphor stresses that the master expects students to behave like empty vessels, passively receiving the gift of his lesson. For the novice, learning is less an act of creativity than obedience, consumption, and emptiness.

Modern educators often act like Confucian monks, stuffing students with facts, figures, and theorems, expecting them to regurgitate the curriculum whole. Regrettably, the teacup image doesn't depict a vital second step in learning, a step that requires less memory, and more imagination. After all, undergraduates aren't really teacups filled at the master's leisure. And knowledge isn't a "thing" like tea but a process, a dialogue.

If education is to be more than indoctrination, students must learn skills of critical interrogation. Certainly, they must memorize lessons, but also evaluate and challenge them. Because information is never neutral, analytical questioning is vital to a good education. As the philosopher Friedrich Nietzsche advises, we should read "with boxing gloves on."

This chapter hopes to teach students something about questions. The first half compiles a list of important questions that should be asked of all information sources. The second half looks at ways questions can be manipulated and skewed, sometimes maliciously.

PART ONE—10 BASIC QUESTIONS

"One who asks a question is a fool for five minutes; one who does not ask a question remains a fool forever."

—Chinese proverb

1. WHO'S SPEAKING?

In a famous parable, three blind men stumble upon their first elephant. One blind man feels the elephant's trunk and cries, "It's a snake!" The second blind man runs his hand along the leg and says, "No, it's a tree trunk!" The third blind man feels the bulky side, and says, "We've run into a wall!" All three are correct in a limited way, yet each is incomplete as well. The parable teaches us that knowledge depends on, and is limited by, perspective. The experience of the elephant—or the larger world—hangs on our point of view.

If we're to avoid mistaking the snout for the whole pachyderm, a critical reader needs to be aware of the storyteller. Who is speaking? How does point of view affect perception? How reliable is the narrator?

This can be a hard task, for we often know little about an author. Even if we do discover important biographical facts, we'll have trouble deciding how to use this knowledge. It's a mistake to suggest a writer's gender, race, religion, culture, history, or class *determines* his or her ideas. Yet it's an equal presumption to suggest these factors don't *influence* a work.

2. WHAT IS THE AUTHOR'S EXPERTISE?

Obviously, education boosts a person's knowledge and credibility, so we should always assess the training, qualifications, and authority of any writer. The better qualified the author, the more likely he or she is right.

However, education doesn't automatically render a person's views accurate or correct. Furthermore, education is often specialized and field-specific. A geneticist trained to understand the micro-mechanics of the DNA chain may be baffled by the macro-machinations of an ecosystem, even though genetics and ecology are both aspects of biology. Consequently, we should be wary of the "expert" who pontificates beyond his or her field. In other words, a reader should always gauge the kind of expertise, its value, range, and limitations.

3. WHAT ALLEGIANCES DOES THE AUTHOR HOLD?

You come across an article titled "Cigarettes and Health: A Smoky Relationship," an essay that refutes the link between secondhand smoke and cancer. Later, you discover the author is an avid smoker, owns a pub, lobbies for the tobacco industry, and owns stock in the Phillip Morris Company (a cigarette manufacturer). How does this knowledge affect the claims made in the essay? Clearly, he has a vested interest that calls into question his neutrality.

Obviously, a person may smoke and still present reliable, accurate information about smoking, just as a Palestinian may comment fairly on Middle East affairs. Personal involvement does not negate the validity of research or commentary. However, if readers are to properly judge an article, they need to know of such advocacy, so that they can judge whether a writer's allegiances have jeopardized his or her neutrality.

Unfortunately, a writer's affiliations and memberships are not always clear, and at times, are deliberately concealed.

4. WHO HAS PAID FOR THE WRITING?

In the marketplace of ideas, money often interferes with the quest for truth. Doctors, experts, professors, celebrities, and politicians sometimes testify to false or partisan ideas, because they've been paid to do so. Corporations pay PR firms to write press releases or articles that paint business in a favourable light. They create and fund phony grassroots citizen coalitions to make their views seem neutral and credible. They back scientific research that promotes their agendas.

Of course, a research report, an editorial, a drug report, or a policy piece isn't necessarily invalid simply because it's been paid for by special interest groups. However, we need to know the sources of funding if we wish to assess honestly any writing or research. Sadly, "follow the money" remains helpful advice.

5. WHO'S BEEN LEFT OUT?

If every text has a specific audience, then it also excludes groups of people. These excluded voices often limit a text, particularly when they try to speak for all society or declare universal truths.

Consider the example of the Meech Lake Accord. Written during the Mulroney period, the Meech Lake Accord tempted Quebec to accept the Canada Act, by declaring the English and French the founding nations of Canada.

The Accord required the approval of all the Canadian provinces, and eventually failed in Manitoba, as result of one filibustering MLA, Elijah Harper. A Métis Indian, Harper noticed that the Accord enshrined the English and French, but neglected Natives. Because of this exclusion, Harper opposed passage of the Accord, and eventually caused its failure.

In a very concrete way, the Meech Lake Accord failed to read its audience: an ethnically diverse population composed of far more than two founding races.

6. HOW HAS THE SUBJECT BEEN DEFINED?

Consider how writers define a subject, scanning for any bias. Remember definitions have purpose, not always benign. (See Chapter 2.)

7. WHO GAINS? WHO LOSES?

When investigating a crime, the police of classical Rome asked themselves *cui bono?* This Latin phrase translates as "for whose advantage," a maxim that remains useful for investigating texts, as does its converse "who loses?"

8. WHAT PROBLEMS ARE CREATED?

Persuasive writing emphasizes the benefits of a proposal, diminishing or neglecting problems. To get a balanced view, readers must expose the drawbacks that a persuasive writer minimizes or conceals.

Consider a new electric automobile that promises zero fuel emissions. While such a car produces no carbon monoxide, it may create equally harmful side effects, such as toxic batteries or increased demand for electricity. To properly assess this car, we must predict possible problems, not just accept the glossy promises of the car industry.

9. WHAT ASSUMPTIONS ARE MADE?

People's beliefs have enormous influence on their worldviews. Creationists, for example, trust in a God-created earth, despite overwhelming fossil evidence in favour of evolution. They accept only proof that supports the Bible's position, and dismiss contrary evidence. We must pay attention to both the obvious presumptions, such as those in a Creationist tract, as well as the invisible ones that a writer considers so self-evident they go undeclared.

As part of this process, readers should also challenge their own assumptions they bring to a text.

10. WHAT AUTHORITY IS EVOKED?

An argument presents proof to support its claims, but not all proof is equal. Certain kinds of proof are narrow in scope (such as a personal anecdote), while other evidence draws from a greater scale (such as a national census). Obviously, the argument built on a broad foundation has a greater authority than one based only on personal experience. A judicious reader looks not only at the quantity of evidence, but also at its quality.

In the debate on gay marriage, for example, critics frequently oppose same-sex unions based on passages in the Bible condemning homosexual behaviour. They resist gay marriages based on a religious principle.

Proponents of gay marriage, in contrast, typically cite the Canadian Constitution or Human Rights Code that protects against discrimination and guarantees equality. That's to say, they evoke a secular and legal principle.

In this case of competing authorities, gay marriage advocates have an advantage because their standard is more binding. The law applies to all Canadians, while Christian tenets apply only to believers.

CASE STUDY: HAROLD BLOOM AND *THE WESTERN CANON*

Let's see how a few questions can expose problems, even in a scholar as distinguished as Harold Bloom.

SUMMARY

In *The Western Canon*, Harold Bloom argues that today's professors neglect the classics of Western literature. In a misguided attempt to be fair, they teach works from writers of colour, women, the poor, low culture, not because they're good, but because it's politically correct to do so. As an antidote, Bloom provides a list of 500 literary masterpieces that deserve a central place in society: Plato, Dante, Shakespeare, and the like. Bloom feels academics have a duty to teach and pass on to the future this approved list of seminal books.

Bloom's program appeals to our sense of tradition, but makes little sense when we query its assumptions. Under cross-examination, Bloom's thinking emerges as flawed, sexist, even racist.

WHAT CONTEXT?

Latin for *rule*, the word "canon" has roots in Catholicism's struggle to stamp out various rival sects and emerge as the one true church. Faced with many competitors, the Catholic clergy declared their own gospels holy and disqualified as bogus all other scripture. This list of sanctioned books grew into the Bible—the final, fixed, and *only* word of God. Today, the word "canon" generally means a list of central books, but historically it's something more—it's censorship of the opposition.

WHAT ASSUMPTIONS?

The "West" in Bloom's title is a geographical problem, as it includes countries from every quadrant of the globe. The term is racially meaningless, as it includes Jews, Caucasians, Blacks, Asians, and Aboriginals. In the end, Bloom's "West" is an enigma: not a place, a country, a time, or a people, but a convenience.

WHOSE LITERATURE IS THIS?

By presenting a "canon," Bloom intimates that European literature is more important than literature from other cultures. Equally biased assumptions appear within Bloom's list. Although England forms a small part of Europe, Anglo literature dominates, taking as much space as all others (Canada gets a scant eight entries). And in terms of gender, men account for half the population, but make up 95 percent of the canon. This is a funhouse of dead, white, European (English) men.

WHO'S LEFT OUT?

Women, Blacks, Natives, most minorities, and the poor find little accommodation on Bloom's list.

HOW IS THE SUBJECT DEFINED?

For his index, Bloom considers only "masterpieces," a problem word that Bloom defines as work of uncompromising strength, virility, originality, and genius. Each of these words resists a clear explanation, yet they do have a strong masculine scent. Bloom's arbitrary definition may encourage us to overlook subtler, female forms of art, such as journals, diaries, letters, and children's stories traditionally written by women.

Bloom is an unapologetic advocate of "high culture," avoiding the "mass market" art of popular culture. Pop lyrics, movie scripts, TV shows, ad texts, and comic books—none appear in the canon, even though many show literary sophistication.

WHAT EVIDENCE?

As a matter of taste, Bloom's canon of central books amounts to personal preference, opinion, not fact.

WHAT EFFECTS ON SOCIETY?

Bloom's canon is a cultural blueprint. Unfortunately Bloom the traditionalist doesn't question the culture he inherits, but rather maintains the status quo: the dominance of culture by white men.

Women, minorities, colonized people who read this "boys' club" find only token numbers of their own, and hear that they've played little role in Western culture. In this way, Bloom's canon continues to demoralize and silence already marginalized people.

PART TWO—LEADING QUESTIONS

"You can tell whether a man is clever by his answers. You can tell whether a man is wise by his questions."

—Naguib Mahfouz

In James Joyce's novel *A Portrait of the Artist as a Young Man*, a schoolyard bully taunts the boyish hero Stephen Daedalus, asking him "do you kiss your mother before you go to bed?" Stephen initially answers yes, then no, but is teased mercilessly for either answer. Of course, there's no "right" answer. The bully phrases the question as a trap, and Stephen learns the power of questions: they allow the interrogator to set parameters. As any skillful lawyer knows, the right question can influence, even determine an answer before it is given. And like any power, questions can coerce and abuse.

This section suggests ways to recognize manipulative and biased forms of questioning.

1. BIASED LANGUAGE

Connotative language produces strong emotions that predispose or prejudice an audience. When used in a question, connotative language unduly influences readers.

Should public libraries stock anarchist and subversive materials?

The negative associations of "anarchist" and "subversive" sway people to reject this proposition. People would likely accept "libertarian" and "alternative" materials, even though these words mean roughly the same thing.

2. OVER-SIMPLIFICATION (BIFURCATION)

A question misleads when it offers only two choices to complex situations, particularly when one answer is clearly more attractive than the other. Speaking about the War on Terror, George Bush remarked, "You are either with us or with the terrorists." The president overlooked other possibilities, as he dramatically reduced options to a pair. Bifurcation reduces situations to black and white, good guys versus bad guys.

> Should Canada support the U.S. assault on Iraq, or risk damaging our economy?

This question manipulates by reducing a complex situation to only two possibilities. Given the second option contains a veiled threat, the question coerces people to choose war. If the question represented a wider range of options, fewer people opt for military action.

> What action should Canada take in response to the WTC attacks on the USA?
>
> a) Join the U.S.-led assault on Afghanistan but not Iraq
> b) Join the U.S.-led assault on Iraq, but not Afghanistan
> c) Join both the U.S.-led assaults
> d) Provide peace-keeping troops to Iraq and Afghanistan
> e) Provide non-military support to US forces
> f) Use diplomatic channels to pressure terrorist states
> g) Pursue extradition of terrorists
> h) Place economic embargoes on terrorist states
> i) Increase domestic security
> j) Take other action: _____

When stated with this range of ideas and options, the support for the U.S.-led assault on Iraq reduces dramatically. Even if a question gives more than two possibilities, it manipulates if it doesn't cover all options.

3. PLANTED INFORMATION

A question coerces when it follows a persuasive fact or two. Consider how the lead-in description before each of these questions affects perception.

> Q. Scientists estimate that B.C.'s offshore oil reserves exceed $45 billion. B.C. currently has the highest rate of unemployment in the country, as well as a budgetary crisis affecting education and health care. Given this dilemma, should B.C. develop its oil reserves?
>
> Q. The World Wildlife Fund recently ranked the B.C. coastline as one of the most sensitive yet threatened ecosystems in the world. After offshore oil derricks were introduced in the North Atlantic, oil spills increased by 1350 percent. The B.C. coast also has the greatest earthquake activity in Canada. Should we protect our delicate marine environment from oil development?

Even if true, such lead-in facts are manipulative, selective, and incomplete. They unfairly bias the reader.

4. VAGUE LANGUAGE

A fuzzy word can confuse readers, leading them towards a particular response.

Q. Isn't the government justified in restricting the rights of people with communicable diseases?

On the surface, this seems a reasonable proposition, until one considers the literal meanings of these words. What rights are involved? The right to free movement? To marry and have kids? To work in public? To hold a library card? To what diseases does this refer? SARS? AIDS? The flu? Warts? A "yes" may be interpreted as support for any number of draconian policies.

5. UNKNOWN QUANTITIES

Nobody can answer a question based on unfamiliar subjects or materials.

Q. Do you think CSIS should continue to prevent terrorist activities based on the emergency provisions set out in the Canadian Securities Bill of 2002?

The problem is that readers hear "preventing terrorism," and ignore the Canadian Securities Bill. In so doing, we may agree to a proposal without knowing the exact provisions set out in the Bill. Does the Bill grant the power of detention without representation? Reading of e-mail? Torture? Without this information, we can't answer.

6. FAULTY PREMISES

Many questions have assumptions built into them. When based on faulty premises, questions produce misleading results.

Q. What are you up to in there?
(The question presumes a transgression)
Q. What reparations should Canada make to descendants of Chinese labourers who died building the CPR?
(The question assumes reparation should be made)

Before answering a question, look at its presumptions. If the question rests upon a false idea, reject it.

7. QUESTIONS WITH OBVIOUS ANSWERS

Some questions have obvious answers:
a) Do children thrive best in stable homes?
b) Should the government encourage the self-reliance of citizens?

c) Are men and women different?
d) Should the government reach an equitable settlement with the Union?

The problem posed by self-answering questions lies in the interpretation of the results. If we answer, "yes" to question b, we don't know what consequences follow. Does our agreement permit the government to reduce unemployment payments, shorten welfare periods, close daycares? Be wary of easy, feel-good questions that may support unwanted programs and actions.

8. THE ORDER OF QUESTIONS

In a series of questions, the sequence often creates a story that predisposes readers to give a specific answer.

1. Do you believe that the biological union of a man and women is natural?
2. Should children be exposed to both male and female role models?
3. Can two same-sex parents adequately meet a child's physical, emotional and educational needs?

1. Have single parents raised healthy, successful children?
2. Should all homes provide a stable supportive environment for children?
3. Can two same-sex parents adequately meet a child's physical, emotional and educational needs?

A well-crafted poll randomizes the questions to avoid manipulative narratives.

9. OVER-COMPLICATION

Trick questions confuse readers with bafflegab, double negatives, and jargon.

Do you reject the proposition that possession of materials sexually depicting children in print, in photographs, video, sketches and other forms of art should be considered unlawful?

Far from clear, such questions produce dubious results. Answer only questions that use clear, specific, and unambiguous language.

CASE STUDY—THE QUEBEC REFERENDUM

Wishing to forge an independent nation, the Parti Québécois (PQ) launched two referendums on Quebec separation, most recently in 1995. The PQ and the Liberal parties debated the wording of the referendum, knowing that its phrasing would influence the outcome. Here are three possible versions of the referendum question.

Do you want Quebec to separate from Canada and become an independent country?

Are you in favour of the Act passed by the National Assembly declaring the sovereignty of Quebec? Yes or No? ("What Does Quebec Want?")

Do you agree that Quebec should become sovereign, after having made a formal offer to Canada for a new economic and political partnership, within the scope of the Bill respecting the future of Quebec and the agreement signed on June 12, 1995? ("1995 Quebec Referendum")

The Liberal party favoured something like the first version, because it presented the question in a clear manner, asking Quebecois to remain in the Canadian union or to separate. The Liberals hoped an emphasis on separation would frighten voters, encouraging them to reject the proposition.

The second question appears in the Quebec Constitution drafted by the PQ party. This convoluted statement doesn't directly address a national breakup, but focuses on support for the "Act passed by the National Assembly," a reference that requires specific knowledge of the Act. The crucial issue of separation is diminished by its placement in a subordinate phrase, and so, the question seems to ask a matter of principle: Do we *in theory* support the *idea* of Quebec sovereignty. Of course, the PQ would interpret a vote in favour of the principle of sovereignty as a mandate for actual separation. Moreover, the question stresses that the National Assembly has already passed the Act, making independence seem a foregone conclusion.

The second question also uses the word "sovereignty" because it retains the positive connotations of independence, without the fear associated with separation. Sovereignty suggests Quebec autonomy and self-governance, but doesn't exclude cooperation with the Canadian federation. In other words, "sovereignty" has a useful vagueness.

The third question is the most complicated and confusing. It likewise refers to legislation (the Bill and agreement), without clarifying their contents. The language around the Bill is fuzzy, a feel-good statement about "respecting Quebec's future" that's hard to reject. Using the same vague word "sovereignty," this question makes separation contingent upon Quebec's "formal offer" for a new "economic and political partnership." The language sounds as if Quebec will separate only after negotiations with Canada fail, but this isn't necessarily so. According to the literal language of this question, Quebec only has to make an offer—not a reasonable or fair one—but any offer, and it will have a mandate to separate. Separation could follow any wild and unworkable proposal.

Of the three different versions of the Referendum question, the PQ finally opted to use the third—the most confusing and leading of all. The results were incredibly close: the "No" side received 50.1 percent of the vote, "Yes" 49.9 percent. The fate of the Canadian nation hinged on this carefully worded, crafty question.

Works Cited

"1995 Quebec Referendum." *Wikipedia: The Free Encyclopedia.* July 24, 2004. <http://en.wikipedia.org/wiki/1995_Quebec_referendum>.

Joyce, James. *A Portrait of the Artist as a Young Man.* Sept. 10, 2004. <http://www. 4literature.net/James_Joyce/Portrait_of_the_Artist_as_a_Young_Man/3.html>.

"What Does Quebec Want?" *Global Economics Ltd.* July 24, 2004. <http://www. global-economics.ca/dth.chap2.htm>.

Exercises

1. Write a questionnaire to measure public opinion on the following topics.

   Legalization of marijuana
   Cigarette sponsorship of sporting/cultural events
   Genetic modification
   Deregulation of public power
   Animal testing
   Polygamous marriages
   Stem-cell research

   Rewrite your questionnaire to get the answers you want. Compare the results of the polls.

2. Evaluate the bias in the following questions.

   Q. Would you oppose a law that prevents the mutilation of children's genitalia?

   Q. Do you feel that the Canadian constitution should protect against discrimination based on religious principles?

   Q. Women on the dole tend to have 125 percent more unwanted pregnancies than working women. Welfare moms have higher levels of drug addiction, giving birth to addicted children, exposing them to a drug lifestyle. Is it reasonable to make birth control a mandatory condition of receiving welfare?

Q. Do the unemployed receive too many handouts and freebies?

Q. Don't you feel that the look and feel of user interfaces shouldn't fall under copyright protection?

Q. According to recent polls, 85 percent of Canadians support granting Most Favoured Nation status to China? Do you agree with this proposition?

Q. Should we repeal the Indian Act that guarantees race-based fishing rights?

Q. In what way does the CBC contribute to Canadian culture?

a) provide coverage of Canadian stories
b) give a venue to Canadian talent
c) offer a common voice across geographical differences
d) focus on the arts
e) all of the above

Q. Where did your teacher touch you?

Q. Would you rather be happy and stupid, or wise and sad?

"Preface and Prelude" from *The Western Canon*

HAROLD BLOOM

Harold Bloom is the Sterling Professor of Humanities at Yale University. Best known as a literary critic, Bloom has published many influential books on art, literature, and culture, including *The Anxiety of Influence*, *Map of Misreading*, and *The Western Canon*. In this last work, Bloom lays out works central to any literate person, and sets the course of post-secondary education.

This book studies twenty-six writers, necessarily with a certain nostalgia, since I seek to isolate the qualities that made these authors canonical, that is, authoritative in our culture. "Aesthetic value" is sometimes regarded as a suggestion of Immanuel Kant's rather than an actuality, but that has not been my experience during a lifetime of reading. Things have however fallen apart, the center has not held, and mere anarchy is in the process of being unleashed upon what used to be called "the learned world." Mimic cultural wars do not much interest me; what I have to say about our current squalors is in my first and last chapters. Here I wish to explain the organization of this book and to account for my choice of these twenty-six writers from among the many hundreds in what once was considered to be the Western Canon.

Giambattista Vico, in his *New Science,* posited a cycle of three phases—Theocratic, Aristocratic, Democratic—followed by a chaos out of which a New Theocratic Age would at last emerge. Joyce made grand seriocomic use of Vico in organizing *Finnegans Wake,* and I have followed in the wake of the *Wake,* except that I have omitted the literature of the Theocratic Age. My historical sequence begins with Dante and concludes with Samuel Beckett, though I have not always followed strict chronological order. Thus, I have begun the Aristocratic Age with Shakespeare, because he is the central figure of the Western Canon, and I have subsequently considered him in relation to nearly all the others, from Chaucer and Montaigne, who affected him, through many of those he influenced—Milton, Dr. Johnson, Goethe, Ibsen, Joyce, and Beckett among them—as well as those who attempted to reject him: Tolstoy in particular, along with Freud, who appropriated Shakespeare while insisting that the Earl of Oxford had done the writing for "the man from Stratford."

The choice of authors here is not so arbitrary as it may seem. They have been selected for both their sublimity and their representative nature: a book about twenty-six writers is possible, but not a book about four hundred. Certainly the major Western writers since Dante are here—Chaucer, Cervantes, Montaigne, Shakespeare, Goethe, Wordsworth, Dickens, Tolstoy, Joyce, and Proust. But where are Petrarch, Rabelais, Ariosto, Spenser, Ben Jonson, Racine, Swift, Rousseau, Blake, Pushkin, Melville, Giacomo Leopardi, Henry James, Dostoevsky, Hugo, Balzac, Nietzsche, Flaubert, Baudelaire, Browning, Chekhov, Yeats, D. H. Lawrence, and so many others? I have tried to represent national canons by their crucial figures: Chaucer, Shakespeare, Milton, Wordsworth, Dickens for England; Montaigne and Molière for France; Dante for Italy; Cervantes for Spain; Tolstoy for Russia; Goethe for Germany; Borges and Neruda for Hispanic America; Whitman and Dickinson for the United States. The sequence of major dramatists is here: Shakespeare, Molière, Ibsen, and Beckett; and of novelists: Austen, Dickens, George Eliot, Tolstoy, Proust, Joyce, and Woolf. Dr. Johnson is here as the greatest of Western literary critics; it would be difficult to find his rival.

Vico did not postulate a Chaotic Age before the *ricorso* or return of a second Theocratic Age; but our century, while pretending to continue the Democratic Age, cannot be better characterized than as Chaotic. Its key writers are Freud, Proust, Joyce, Kafka: they personify whatever literary spirit the era possesses. Freud called himself a scientist, but he will survive as a great essayist like Montaigne or Emerson, not as the founder of a therapy already discredited (or elevated) as another episode in the long history of shamanism. I wish that there were space for more modern poets here than just Neruda and Pessoa, but no poet of our century has matched *In Search of Lost Time, Ulysses,* or *Finnegans Wake,* the essays of Freud, or the parables and tales of Kafka.

With most of these twenty-six writers, I have tried to confront greatness directly: to ask what makes the author and the works canonical. The answer, more often than not, has turned out to be strangeness, a mode of originality that either cannot be assimilated, or that so assimilates us that we cease to see it as strange. Walter Pater defined Romanticism as adding strangeness to beauty, but I think he characterized all canonical writing rather than the Romantics as such. The cycle of achievement goes from *The Divine Comedy* to *Endgame,* from strangeness to strangeness. When you read a canonical work for a first time you encounter a stranger, an uncanny startlement rather than a fulfillment of expectations. Read freshly, all that *The Divine Comedy, Paradise Lost, Faust Part Two, Hadji Murad, Peer Gynt, Ulysses,* and *Canto general* have in common is their uncanniness, their ability to make you feel strange at home.

Shakespeare, the largest writer we ever will know, frequently gives the opposite impression: of making us at home out of doors, foreign, abroad. His powers of assimilation and of contamination are unique and constitute a perpetual challenge to universal performance and to criticism. I find it absurd and regrettable that the current criticism of Shakespeare—"cultural materialist" (Neo-Marxist); "New Historicist" (Foucault); "Feminist"—has abandoned the quest to meet that challenge. Shakespeare criticism is in full flight from his aesthetic supremacy and works at reducing him to the "social energies" of the English Renaissance, as though there were no authentic difference in aesthetic merit between the creator of Lear, Hamlet, Iago, Falstaff and his disciples such as John Webster and Thomas Middleton. The best living English critic, Sir Frank Kermode, in his *Forms of Attention* (1985) has issued the clearest warning I know about the fate of the canon, that is to say, in the first place, the fate of Shakespeare:

> Canons, which negate the distinction between knowledge and opinion, which are instruments of survival built to be time-proof, not reason-proof, are of course deconstructible; if people think there should not be such things, they may very well find the means to destroy them. Their defense cannot any longer be undertaken by central institutional

power; they cannot any longer be compulsory, though it is hard to see how the normal operation of learned institutions, including recruitment, can manage without them.

The means to destroy canons, as Kermode indicates, are very much at hand, and the process is now quite advanced. I am not concerned, as this book repeatedly makes clear, with the current debate between the right-wing defenders of the Canon, who wish to preserve it for its supposed (and nonexistent) moral values, and the academic-journalistic network I have dubbed the School of Resentment, who wish to overthrow the Canon in order to advance their supposed (and nonexistent) programs for social change. I hope that the book does not turn out to be an elegy for the Western Canon, and that perhaps at some point there will be a reversal, and the rabblement of lemmings will cease to hurl themselves off the cliffs. In the concluding catalog of canonical authors, particularly of our century, I have ventured a modest prophecy as to survival possibilities.

One mark of an originality that can win canonical status for a literary work is a strangeness that we either never altogether assimilate, or that becomes such a given that we are blinded to its idiosyncrasies. Dante is the largest instance of the first possibility, and Shakespeare, the overwhelming example of the second. Walt Whitman, always contradictory, partakes of both sides of the paradox. After Shakespeare, the greatest representative of the given is the first author of the Hebrew Bible, the figure named the Yahwist or J by nineteenth-century biblical scholarship. . . .

Canonical strangeness can exist without the shock of such audacity, but the tang of originality must always hover in an inaugural aspect of any work that incontestably wins the agon with tradition and joins the Canon. Our educational institutions are thronged these days by idealistic resenters who denounce competition in literature as in life, but the aesthetic and the agonistic are one, according to all the ancient Greeks, and to Burckhardt and Nietzsche, who recovered this truth. What Homer teaches is a poetics of conflict, a lesson first learned by his rival Hesiod. All of Plato, as the critic Longinus saw, is in the philosopher's incessant conflict with Homer, who is exiled from *The Republic,* but in vain, since Homer and not Plato remained the schoolbook of the Greeks. Dante's *Divine Comedy,* according to Stefan George, was "the book and school of the ages," though that was more true for poets than for anyone else and is properly assigned to Shakespeare's plays, as will be shown throughout this book.

Contemporary writers do not like to be told that they must compete with Shakespeare and Dante, and yet that struggle was Joyce's provocation to greatness, to an eminence shared only by Beckett, Proust, and Kafka among modern Western authors. The fundamental archetype for literary achievement will always be Pindar, who celebrates the quasi-divine victories of his aristocratic athletes while conveying the implicit sense that his victory odes are themselves victories over every possible competitor. Dante, Milton, and Wordsworth repeat Pindar's key metaphor of racing to win the palm, which is a secular immortality strangely at odds with any pious idealism. "Idealism," concerning which one struggles not to be ironic, is now the fashion in our schools and colleges, where all aesthetic and most intellectual standards are being abandoned in the name of social harmony and the remedying of historical injustice. Pragmatically, the "expansion of the Canon" has meant the destruction of the Canon, since what is being taught includes by no means the best writers who happen to be women, African, Hispanic, or Asian, but rather the writers who offer little but the resentment they have developed as part of their sense of identity. There is no strangeness and no originality in such resentment; even if there were, they would not suffice to create heirs of the Yahwist and Homer, Dante and Shakespeare, Cervantes and Joyce.

As the formulator of a critical concept I once named "the anxiety of influence," I have enjoyed the School of Resentment's repeated insistence that such a notion applies only to Dead White European Males, and not to women and to what we quaintly term "multiculturalists." Thus, feminist cheerleaders proclaim that women writers lovingly cooperate with one another as quilt makers, while African-American and Chicano literary activists go even further in asserting their freedom from any anguish of contamination whatsoever: each of them is Adam early in the morning. They know no time when they were not as they are now; self-created, self-begot, their puissance is their own. As assertions by poets, playwrights, and prose fiction writers, these are healthy and understandable, however self-deluded. But as declarations by supposed literary critics, such optimistic pronouncements are neither true nor interesting and go against both human nature and the nature of imaginative literature. There can be no strong, canonical writing without the process of literary influence, a process vexing to undergo and difficult to understand. I have never been able to recognize my theory of influence when it is under attack, since what is under attack is never even an apt travesty of my ideas. As the chapter on Freud in this book demonstrates, I favor a Shakespearean reading of Freud, and not a Freudian reading of Shakespeare or of any other writer.

204 CHAPTER FIVE • QUESTIONS

The anxiety of influence is not an anxiety about the father, real or literary, but an anxiety achieved by and in the poem, novel, or play. Any strong literary work creatively misreads and therefore misinterprets a precursor text or texts. An authentic canonical writer may or may not internalize her or his work's anxiety, but that scarcely matters: the strongly achieved work *is* the anxiety. This point has been well expressed by Peter de Bolla in his book *Towards Historical Rhetorics*:

> the Freudian family romance as a description of influence represents an extremely weak reading. For Bloom, "influence" is both a tropological category, a figure which determines the poetic tradition, and a complex of psychic, historical and imagistic relations . . . influence describes the relations between texts, it is an intertextual phenomenon . . . both the internal psychic defense—the poet's experience of anxiety— and the external historical relations of texts to each other are themselves the *result* of misreading, or poetic misprision, and not the cause of it.

Doubtless that accurate summary will seem intricate to those unfamiliar with my attempts to think through the problem of literary influence, yet de Bolla gives me a good starting point, here at the start of this examination of the now-threatened Western Canon. The burden of influence has to be borne, if significant originality is to be achieved and reachieved within the wealth of Western literary tradition. Tradition is not only a handing-down or process of benign transmission; it is also a conflict between past genius and present aspiration, in which the prize is literary survival or canonical inclusion. That conflict cannot be settled by social concerns, or by the judgment of any particular generation of impatient idealists, or by Marxists proclaiming, "Let the dead bury the dead," or by sophists who attempt to substitute the library for the Canon and the archive for the discerning spirit. Poems, stories, novels, plays come into being as a response to prior poems, stories, novels, and plays, and that response depends upon acts of reading and interpretation by the later writers, acts that are identical with the new works.

These readings of precursor writings are necessarily defensive in part; if they were appreciative only, fresh creation would be stifled, and not for psychological reasons alone. The issue is not Oedipal rivalry but the very nature of strong, original literary imaginings: figurative language and its vicissitudes. Fresh metaphor, or inventive troping, always involves a departure from previous metaphor, and that departure depends upon at least partial turning away from or rejection of prior figuration. Shakespeare employs Marlowe as a starting point, and such early Shakespearean hero-villains as Aaron the Moor in *Titus Andronicus* and Richard III are rather too close to Barabas, Marlowe's Jew of Malta. When Shakespeare creates Shylock, his Jew of Venice, the metaphorical basis of the farcical villain's speech is radically altered, and Shylock is a strong misreading or creative misinterpretation of Barabas, whereas Aaron the Moor is something closer to a repetition of Barabas, particularly at the level of figurative language. By the time that Shakespeare writes *Othello,* all trace of Marlowe is gone: the self-delighting villainy of Iago is cognitively far subtler and light years more refined imagistically than the self-congratulatory excesses of the exuberant Barabas. Iago's relation to Barabas is one in which Shakespeare's creative misreading of his precursor Marlowe has triumphed wholly. Shakespeare is a unique case in which the forerunner is invariably dwarfed. *Richard III* manifests an anxiety of influence in regard to *The Jew of Malta* and *Tamburlaine,* but Shakespeare was still finding his way. With the advent of Falstaff in *Henry IV, Part One* the finding was complete, and Marlowe became only the way not to go, on the stage as in life.

After Shakespeare there are only a few figures who fight relatively free of the anxiety of influence: Milton, Molière, Goethe, Tolstoy, Ibsen, Freud, Joyce; and for all of these except Molière, Shakespeare alone remained the problem, as this book seeks to demonstrate. Greatness recognizes greatness and is shadowed by it. Coming after Shakespeare, who wrote both the best prose and the best poetry in the Western tradition, is a complex destiny, since originality becomes peculiarly difficult in everything that matters most: representation of human beings, the role of memory in cognition, the range of metaphor in suggesting new possibilities for language. These are Shakespeare's particular excellences, and no one has matched him as psychologist, thinker, or rhetorician. Wittgenstein, who resented Freud, nevertheless resembles Freud in his suspicious and defensive reaction to Shakespeare, who is an affront to the philosopher even as he is to the psychoanalyst. There is no cognitive originality in the whole history of philosophy comparable to Shakespeare's, and it is both ironic and fascinating to overhear Wittgenstein puzzling out whether there is an authentic difference between the Shakespearean representation of thinking and thinking itself. It is true, as the Australian poet-critic Kevin Hart observes, that "Western culture takes its lexicon of intelligibility from Greek philosophy, and all our talk of life and death, of form and design, is marked by relations with that tradition." Yet intelligibility pragmatically transcends its lexicon, and we must remind ourselves that Shakespeare, who scarcely relies upon philosophy, is more central to Western culture than are Plato and Aristotle, Kant and Hegel, Heidegger and Wittgenstein.

I feel quite alone these days in defending the autonomy of the aesthetic, but its best defense is the experience of reading *King Lear* and then seeing the play well performed. *King Lear* does not derive from a crisis in philosophy, nor can its power be explained away as a mystification somehow promoted by bourgeois institutions. It is a mark of the degeneracy of literary study that one is considered an eccentric for holding that the literary is not dependent upon the philosophical, and that the aesthetic is irreducible to ideology or to metaphysics. Aesthetic criticism returns us to the autonomy of imaginative literature and the sovereignty of the solitary soul, the reader not as a person in society but as the deep self, our ultimate inwardness. That depth of inwardness in a strong writer constitutes the strength that wards off the massive weight of past achievement, lest every originality be crushed before it becomes manifest. Great writing is always rewriting or revisionism and is founded upon a reading that clears space for the self, or that so works as to reopen old works to our fresh sufferings. The originals are not original, but that Emersonian irony yields to the Emersonian pragmatism that the inventor knows *how* to borrow.

The anxiety of influence cripples weaker talents but stimulates canonical genius. What intimately allies the three most vibrant American novelists of the Chaotic Age—Hemingway, Fitzgerald, and Faulkner—is that all of them emerge from Joseph Conrad's influence but temper it cunningly by mingling Conrad with an American precursor—Mark Twain for Hemingway, Henry James for Fitzgerald, Herman Melville for Faulkner. Something of the same cunning appears in T. S. Eliot's fusion of Whitman and Tennyson, and Ezra Pound's blend of Whitman and Browning, as again in Hart Crane's deflection of Eliot by another turn toward Whitman. Strong writers do not choose their prime precursors; they are chosen by them, but they have the wit to transform the forerunners into composite and therefore partly imaginary beings.

I am not directly concerned in this book with the intertextual relations among the twenty-six authors under consideration; my purpose is to consider them as representatives of the entire Western Canon, but doubtless my interest in problems of influence emerges almost everywhere, sometimes perhaps without my own full awareness. Strong literature, agonistic whether it wants to be or not, cannot be detached from its anxieties about the works that possess priority and authority in regard to it. Though most critics resist understanding the processes of literary influence or try to idealize those processes as wholly generous and benign, the dark truths of competition and contamination continue to grow stronger as canonical history lengthens in time. A poem, play, or novel is necessarily compelled to come into being by way of precursor works, however eager it is to deal directly with social concerns. Contingency governs literature as it does every cognitive enterprise, and the contingency constituted by the Western literary Canon is primarily manifested as the anxiety of influence that forms and malforms each new writing that aspires to permanence. Literature is not merely language; it is also the will to figuration, the motive for metaphor that Nietzsche once defined as the desire to be different, the desire to be elsewhere. This partly means to be different from oneself, but primarily, I think, to be different from the metaphors and images of the contingent works that are one's heritage: the desire to write greatly is the desire to be elsewhere, in a time and place of one's own, in an originality that must compound with inheritance, with the anxiety of influence.

Selections from *The Rules*

ELLEN FEIN AND SHERRIE SCHNEIDER

Ellen Fein and Sherrie Schneider are authors of *The Rules: Time-tested Secrets for Capturing the Heart of Mr. Right*, an advice manual for women seeking to get married and settle down. Schneider and Fein revive the sexist strategies followed by women of previous generations, tactics such as playing hard to get or not making the first move. *The Rules* became a bestseller and spawned a series of follow-up books, including *The Rules for Marriage*.

RULE #2

Don't Talk to a Man First (and Don't Ask Him to Dance)

Never? Not even "Let's have coffee" or "Do you come here often?" Right, not even these seemingly harmless openers. Otherwise, how will you know if he spotted you first, was smitten by you and had to have you, or is just being polite?

We know what you're thinking. We know how extreme such a rule must sound, not to mention snobbish, silly, and painful; but taken in the context of *The Rules*, it makes perfect sense. After all, the premise of *The Rules* is that we never make anything happen, that we trust in the natural order of things—namely, that man pursues woman.

By talking to a man first, we interfere with whatever was supposed to happen or not happen, perhaps causing a conversation or a date to occur that was never meant to be and inevitably getting hurt in the process. Eventually, he'll talk to the girl he really wants and drop you.

Yet, we manage to rationalize this behavior by telling ourselves, "He's shy" or "I'm just being friendly." Are men really shy? We might as well tackle this question right now. Perhaps a therapist would say so, but we believe that most men are not shy, just not *really, really* interested if they don't approach you. It's hard to accept that, we know. It's also hard waiting for the right one—the one who talks to you first, calls, and basically does most of the work in the beginning of the relationship because he must have you.

It's easy to rationalize women's aggressive behavior in this day and age. Unlike years ago when women met men at dances and "coming out" parties and simply waited for one to pick them out of the crowd and start a conversation, today many women are accountants, doctors, lawyers, dentists, and in management positions. They work with men, for men, and men work for them. Men are their patients and their clients. How can a woman not talk to a man first?

The *Rules* answer is to treat men you are interested in like any other client or patient or coworker, as hard as that may be. Let's face it, when a woman meets a man she really likes, a lightbulb goes on in her head and she sometimes, without realizing it, relaxes, laughs, and spends more time with him than is necessary. She may suggest lunch to discuss something that could be discussed over the phone because she is hoping to ignite some romance. This is a common ploy. Some of the smartest women try to make things happen under the guise of business. They think they are too educated or talented to be passive, play games, or do *The Rules*. They feel their diplomas and paychecks entitle them to do more in life than wait for the phone to ring. These women, we assure you, always end up heartbroken when their forwardness is rebuffed. But why shouldn't it be? Men know what they want. No one has to ask *them* to lunch.

So, the short of it is that if you meet men professionally, you still have to do *The Rules*. You must wait until he brings up lunch or anything else beyond business. As we explain in *Rule #17*, the man must take the lead. Even if you are making the same amount of money as a man you are interested in, he must bring up lunch.

If you refuse to accept that men and women are different romantically, even though they may be equal professionally, you will behave like men—talk to them first, ask for their phone number, invite them to discuss the case over dinner at your place—and drive them away. Such forwardness is very risky; sometimes we have seen it work, most of the time it doesn't and it *always* puts the woman through hell emotionally. By not accepting the concept that the man must pursue the woman, women put themselves in jeopardy of being rejected or ignored, if not at the moment, then at some point in the future. We hope you never have to endure the following torture:

Our dentist friend Pam initiated a friendship with Robert when they met in dental school several years ago by asking him out to lunch. *She spoke to him first.* Although they later became lovers and even lived together, he never seemed really "in love" with her and her insecurity about the relationship never went away. Why would it? *She spoke to him first.* He recently broke up with her over something trivial. The truth is he never loved her. Had Pam followed *The Rules*, she would never have spoken to Robert or initiated anything in the first place. Had she followed *The Rules*, she might have met someone else who truly wanted her. She would not have wasted time. *Rules* girls don't waste time.

Here's another example of a smart woman who broke *The Rules*: Claudia, a confident Wall Street broker, spotted her future husband on the dance floor of a popular disco and planted herself next to him for a good five minutes. When he failed to make the first move, she told herself that he was probably shy or had two left feet and asked him to dance. The relationship has been filled with problems. She often complains that he's as "shy" in the bedroom as he was that night on the dance floor.

A word about dances. It's become quite popular these days for women to ask men to dance. Lest there is any doubt in your mind, this behavior is totally against *The Rules*. If a man doesn't bother to walk across the room to seek you out and ask you to dance, then he's obviously not interested and asking him to dance won't change his feelings or rather his lack of feelings for you. He'll probably be flattered that you asked and dance with you just to be polite and he might even want to have sex with you that night, but he won't be crazy about you. Either he didn't notice you or you made it too easy. He never got the chance to pursue you and this fact will always permeate the relationship even if he does ask you out.

We know what you're thinking: what am I supposed to do all night if no one asks me to dance? Unfortunately, the answer is to go to the bathroom five times if you have to, reapply your lipstick, powder your nose, order more water from the bar, think happy thoughts, walk around the room in circles until someone notices you, make phone calls from the lobby to your married friends for encouragement—in short, anything but ask a man to dance. Dances are not necessarily fun for us. They may be fun for other women who just want to go out and have a good time. But you're looking for love and marriage so you can't always do what you feel like. You have to do *The Rules*. That means that even when you're bored or lonely, you don't ask men to dance. Don't even stand next to someone you like, hoping he'll ask you, as many women do. You have to *wait* for someone to notice you. You might have to go home without having met anyone you liked or even danced one dance. But tell yourself that at least you got to practice *The Rules* and there's always another dance. You walk out with a sense of accomplishment that at least you didn't break *The Rules*!

If this sounds boring, remember the alternative is worse. Our good friend Sally got so resentful of having to dance with all the "losers" at a particular party that she finally decided to defy *The Rules* she knew only too well and asked the best-looking man in the room to dance. Not only was he flattered, but they danced for hours and he asked her out for the next three nights. "Maybe there are exceptions to *The Rules*," she thought triumphantly. She found out otherwise, of course. It seems Mr. Right was in town for just a few days on business and had a girlfriend on the West Coast. No wonder he hadn't asked anyone to dance that night. He probably just went to the party to have fun, not to find his future wife. The moral of the story: don't figure out why someone hasn't asked you to dance—there's always a good reason.

Unfortunately, more women than men go to dances to meet "The One." Their eagerness and anxiety get the best of them and they end up talking to men first or asking them to dance. So you must condition yourself not to expect anything from a dance. View it simply as an excuse to put on high heels, apply a new shade of blush, and be around a lot of people. Chances are someone of the opposite sex will start to talk to *you* at some point in the evening. If and when he does, and you're not having such a great time, don't show it. For example, don't be clever or cynical and say, "I would have been better off staying home and watching *Seinfeld*." Men aren't interested in women who are witty in a negative way. If someone asks if you're having a good time, simply say yes and smile.

If you find all of this much too hard to do, then don't go to the dance. Stay home, do sit-ups, watch *Seinfeld*, and reread *The Rules*. It's better to stay home and read *The Rules* than go out and break them.

RULE #31

Don't Discuss *The Rules* with Your Therapist

You're used to telling your therapist everything, so it's only natural that you want to tell him or her about *The Rules*. We strongly suggest you don't go into great detail for the following reasons:

1. Some therapists will think that *The Rules* are dishonest and manipulative. They will encourage you to be open and vulnerable in your relationships with men, to talk things out, not to keep your feelings of love or hurt inside. That, of course, is the basis of the therapeutic process. It's great advice for resolving issues with family and friends, but it doesn't work in the initial stages of dating. Unfortunately, you have to be mysterious in the beginning of a romantic relationship, not an open book.

2. Some therapists don't realize women's capacity for forcing themselves on men who don't want them and/or trying to make relationships happen. If they only knew how we wandered around campus hoping to run into men. If they only knew about the love poetry we've sent men, the interests we've pretended to have in order to make men like us (of course that never works), and if only they knew the lengths we've gone to get friendly with men's parents so that they would make their sons propose. If any therapist knew all these things—perhaps we never told them the whole story—they too would encourage us to focus on ourselves and not force things to happen. A woman in love with a man who is not in love with *her* can be dangerous to herself and him. Her only hope is to do *The Rules*.

3. Another reason not to discuss this book with your therapist is that you don't want to debate the merits of doing or not doing *The Rules*, otherwise you might lose your resolve to do them. It's hard enough to do *The Rules* when you believe in them, it's even harder when you talk to people who are downright against them. You should also not read any books that go counter to this philosophy or preach another method, particularly books that encourage women to pursue men or express their inner child.

   Self-improvement is great—we all can be better in many areas. But self-improvement still won't get you the relationship you want. You may feel "whole" and "ready" after years of inner work and wonder why you still haven't snagged Mr. Right. The reason is you're not doing *The Rules*! Simply being a better person won't get you the man of your dreams. You have to do *The Rules*!

We suggest you try *The Rules* for six months before doing anything else. You can't do *The Rules* and something else at the same time. It just doesn't work!

If there's anything your therapist should be helping you with regarding *The Rules*, it's helping you develop the discipline and self-control necessary to do them!

Marriage Between a Man and a Woman

REAL WOMEN

REAL Women is a Canadian feminist group that advocates family values. An acronym standing for "Real, Equal, Active for Life," REAL Women lobbies for marriage, motherhood, and the conventional female roles neglected by other feminist groups. Their dedication to tradition leads them to oppose gay marriage in this statement.

Marriage between a man and a woman is different from all other human relationships.

It is a unique relationship of infinite value to the individuals themselves, who benefit from the integration of the potential and strength generated by their gender differences. It is also of great social value because of its stability, which is necessary for the continuity of the nation.

Other relationships can provide intimacy, economic support, children (who, because of biological necessity, are propagated outside of a same-sex partnership), but they do not constitute a *marriage*, because they do not affect the public interest, but only a private lifestyle preference of the individuals.

The public interests which heterosexual marriages provide include:

1. THE STABILITY OF THE RELATIONSHIP

Marriage is the most stable of all relationships. In 1998, Statistics Canada released statistics indicating that 63% of couples living common law, with children, break up within 10 years. This is compared to only 14% of legally married couples with children, who break up within ten years.

Marital fidelity is not expected or even characteristic of same-sex relationships, especially among homosexual men. Even in so-called "monogamous" homosexual relationships, sexual fidelity is almost unknown.

2. CHILDREN ARE PROCREATED ONLY THROUGH THE UNION OF ONE MAN AND ONE WOMAN

Mr. Justice La Forest, in the Supreme Court of Canada in the *Nesbit and Egan* case in 1995, stated:

> [marriage] is the social unit that uniquely has the *capacity* to procreate children and generally cares for their upbringing, and as such, warrants support by Parliament to meet its needs. . . . This is the only unit in society that expends resources to care for children on a routine and sustained basis. . . . this is the unit in society that fundamentally anchors other social relationships and other aspects of society. (Page 538)

Legally married couples who struggle and sacrifice to bear and raise children must be given every encouragement to support this unique and priceless contribution to Canada's future. It is an insult to them and their tremendous effort, to have their unions equated to other relationships such as same-sex, which *cannot* make the same contribution because of biological impediments.

It is irrelevant whether the couple actually has children—only that, as a *social policy*, traditional marriage *must* be encouraged.

3. CHILDREN THRIVE BEST WITHIN A COMMITTED MARITAL UNION

In 1996, Statistics Canada released the results of its longitudinal study of 23,000 children, which disclosed that those raised in their biological two-parent family experienced far fewer problems. Children who do not have this advantage are far more likely to experience out-of-wedlock pregnancy, poor school performance, early school dropout and difficulties with the law, etc.

Dual-gender parenting provides the best environment for children to acquire knowledge as to how to relate to persons of their own and the opposite gender, and to understand inter-gender relations on which society is based.

Moreover, one of the most important functions of traditional marriage is to assure the future by providing well-socialized children by passing on social knowledge and skills, which is best achieved by dual-gender parenting.

4. PROTECTION, SECURITY AND THE STATUS OF WOMEN

Women take the greatest risks and invest the greatest personal effort in maintaining families. Marriage protects them from abuse. According to a Statistics Canada Survey on Violence Against Women, released in November 1993, women living in a common-law relationship are four times more likely to experience violence from their partners than are legally married women.

Further, domestic violence rates, according to studies, are also exceptionally high among same-sex partners.

5. TRADITIONAL MARRIAGE DISTINCT FROM ALL OTHER RELATIONSHIPS

The characteristic that defines *same-sex* partners as a group and, as couples, is not belief or biology, but *behaviour*—a particular kind of erotic behaviour. Sexual and sex-like *behaviour* is not an inherent personal characteristic such as race or gender, nor is it an exercise of conscience, like religion or speech. Homosexual behaviour is not comparable to race as a basis of marriage, since race is irrelevant to marriage.

If the guiding rule to marriage is *behaviour*, then there can be no valid or reasoned argument to exclude *other* sexual relationships, from the definition of "marriage," such as a brother and a sister, a father and adult daughter, or perhaps even three individuals together as a marriage. In short, if we accept behaviour as the guide, then there can be no meaningful limits to such "marriages," which can only lead society to social and moral chaos.

6. INTERNATIONAL RECOGNITION OF MARRIAGES

English, American and European law, with the single exception of the Netherlands, have all confined marriage to a union between a man and a woman. This is also the position taken by the European Court of Human Rights and the European Commission of Human Rights. In addition, the *UN Universal Declaration of Human Rights*, the *UN International Covenant on Civil and Political Rights*, and the *European Convention for the Protection of Human Rights and*

Fundamental Freedoms all recognize that the legal status of marriage and spousal relationships applies exclusively to married couples.

That is, marriage between a man and a woman has remained, internationally, the greatest constant over thousands of years of recorded history and crosses religious, cultural and ethnic divisions. If Canada were to recognize other relationships as legal marriages, it would place Canada outside the international norms of the world. This would lead to complications, both internally and externally for Canada, in law, immigration and to society, and in our relationships with other countries.

Mr. Justice Pitfield of the Supreme Court of British Columbia, in upholding the traditional definition of marriage, in October, 2001 stated:

> Other than the desire for public recognition and acceptance of gay and lesbian relationships, there is nothing that should compel the equation of a same-sex relationship to an opposite-sex relationship when the biological reality is that the two relationships can never be the same. That essential distinction will remain no matter how close the similarities are by virtue of social acceptance and legislative action.
>
> ... The core distinction between same-sex and opposite-sex relationships is so material in the Canadian context that no means exist by which to equate same-sex relationships to marriage while at the same time preserving the fundamental importance of marriage to the community.

MARRIAGE CAN NEVER BE A PRIVATE LIFESTYLE CHOICE, BUT MUST REMAIN BETWEEN A MAN AND A WOMAN AND BE SINGLED OUT FROM ALL OTHER ADULT RELATIONSHIPS BECAUSE OF ITS UNIQUE SERVICE TO SOCIETY.

Our Purpose

NARTH

NARTH is an acronym that stands for National Association for Research & Therapy of Homosexuality, an organization that helps gay people change their sexual orientation. In this piece, NARTH explains why it still considers homosexuality a treatable mental disorder.

"The multicultural project will never fully succeed if 'diversity' is defined as one's own preferred ideologies and political groups."

—Richard E. Redding, "Grappling with Diverse Conceptions of Diversity," *American Psychologist*, April 2002, p. 301.

In April 2001, the *American Psychologist*—the journal of the American Psychological Association—published a lead article entitled, "Sociopolitical Diversity in Psychology: The Case for Pluralism." The author, Richard Redding, argued that the psychological profession lacks political diversity.

The April 2002 issue of the *American Psychologist* followed up with published commentaries to the Redding article. Here are some of those clinicians' comments:

"Those charged with guiding students during [the clinical training] process have a responsibility to ensure that they do not impose their own worldview on students. . . . It is critical that students be able to honestly express their feelings and concerns without fear of ridicule, sanction, or retribution by those in power."

". . . although many in the field of multicultural supervision and training write about the need to 'provide trainees with a highly supportive environment,' trainees' differing ideas about such sensitive issues as gay rights . . . could unfortunately lead those directly responsible for their therapy training to label them as problematic or otherwise clinically 'impaired.'. . ."

". . . psychology needs to court a greater diversity of voices. . . ."

"What justification has psychology to identify moral principles or social policies that are right for society?"

"Supporters (such as me) of psychology's efforts to promote diversity, inclusiveness, and multi-cultural approaches to research and practice should embrace an expanded definition of diversity that includes socio-political values."

Since its 1992 founding, NARTH has been calling for just what those clinicians agree is absolutely essential within the profession: *an openness to differing worldviews, values and philosophies.*

The American Psychological Association has assumed an authority it cannot rightly claim. The group claims that science has somehow "proven" that homosexuality and heterosexuality are qualitatively indistinguishable. Thus A.P.A. advocates in the political arena for a broad array of social policies—telling our lawmakers that science supports, if not in fact mandates, gay marriage and adoption—as if any particular social policy could flow directly from the facts (from an "is" to an "ought") *without* an intervening philosophical judgment.

NARTH has responded to the mental-health professions' refusal to open itself up to socio-political diversity by advocating here for another view of sexuality and gender. No philosophical position—ours or the A.P.A.'s—is, *or can be,* scientifically "neutral."

NARTH's function is to provide psychological understanding of the cause, treatment and behavior patterns associated with homosexuality, within the boundaries of a civil public dialogue.

THE RIGHT TO SELF-DETERMINATION

We respect others' right to differ with us. We do not support coercive therapy—indeed, the basic human rights of *dignity, autonomy and free agency* require that it be *the client* who chooses whether to embrace life as gay or lesbian, or to work toward change.

But the fact that we respect and welcome intellectual diversity does not mean that we have no opinions—or that we consider all conflicting viewpoints to be equally valid. Toleration of difference does not require intellectual apathy. A respect for *pluralism* does not mandate *relativism.*

And so on these pages, we will make our case for what we believe to be the truth—as indeed, gay advocates also do, with equal intensity and conviction—in the public forum.

During the last 25 years, powerful political pressures have done much to erode scientific study of homosexuality. As a result, there is now great misunderstanding surrounding this issue. Because of the angry tenor of the debate, many researchers have been intimidated, we believe, into trading the truth for silence.

WHAT IS "NORMAL"?

Fifty years ago, researcher C. D. King offered a very useful definition of "normal." The practical wisdom of that definition is still apparent. Normality, he said, is "that which functions according to its design."

As clinicians, we have witnessed the intense suffering caused by homosexuality, which many of our members see as a "failure to function according to design." Homosexuality distorts the natural bond of friendship that would naturally unite persons of the same sex.

It threatens the continuity of traditional male-female marriage—a bond which is naturally anchored by the complementarity of the sexes, and has long been considered essential for the protection of children.

In males, homosexuality is associated with poor relationship with father; difficulty individuating from mother; a sense of masculine deficit; and a persistent belief of having been different from, and misunderstood by, same-sex childhood peers. In adulthood we also see a persistent pattern of maladaptive behaviors and a documented higher level of psychiatric complaints.

WHO JOINS NARTH?

Professionals who belong to NARTH comprise a wide variety of men and women who *defend the right to pursue change of sexual orientation.* This right-to-change is currently under threat by all of the leading mental-health professional organizations. Students writing doctoral dissertations on sexual reorientation are being discouraged from pursuing their projects; researchers are silenced and cannot find funding; and clinicians are concerned about harassment from their professional associations.

Most NARTH members consider homosexuality to represent a developmental disorder. Some of our clinician-members, however, do not consider the condition disordered, but simply defend the right to treatment for those who desire it. They have joined NARTH because they know that *the client's right to choose his own direction of treatment* must be protected.

There is also a wide range of religious and life philosophies represented among our members, including Catholic, Jewish, Mormon, Bah'ai, Protestant, Muslim, and secular humanist/atheist.

WHAT WE HOPE TO DO

Today, children from kindergarten through college are being taught that homosexuality is a normal, healthy lifestyle option with no disadvantages other than society's disapproval. Sexually confused teenagers are encouraged to investigate homosexual relationships when they are too young to make critical lifestyle decisions. If they seek counseling, they are told that change from homosexuality is impossible.

Gender-disturbed children are no longer helped to become more comfortable with their own biological sex, or with the same-sex peers they have been avoiding. Instead, counselors tell their parents, "Your child is fine—the only problem is with society."

It is NARTH's aim to provide a different perspective. Particularly, we want to clarify that homosexuality is not "inborn," and that gays are not "a people," in the same sense that an ethnic group is "a people"—but instead, they are (like all of us) simply individuals who exhibit particular patterns of feelings and behavior.

When gay advocates reframed the public debate as a discussion about "who one *is*" rather than "what one *does*," they successfully intimidated dissenters by casting them as *personally bigoted and hateful*. As a result, most people who defend the reality of male-female design have been embarrassed into public silence.

NARTH stands ready to advise government, educational, and mental-health agencies as well as the media and religious groups on issues pertaining to homosexuality.

Sympathetic individuals are asked to join our organization as a "Friend of NARTH." With your help, we will deepen and expand the level of public debate.

Declaration of War Against Exploiters of Lakota Spirituality

WARD CHURCHILL

Ward Churchill is a professor of ethnic studies at the University of Colorado, and an outspoken activist for Native causes. A prolific scholar, Churchill has published numerous books on the Native American experience, including *Fantasies of the Master Race*, *On the Justice of Roosting Chickens*, *Indians R Us?*, and *A Little Matter of Genocide: Holocaust and Denial in the Americas*. At times controversial, Churchill forces his audience to confront the brutal treatment of Indians in North America.

(Ratified by the Dakota, Lakota and Nakota Nations, June 1993)

WHEREAS we are the conveners of an ongoing series of comprehensive forums on the abuse and exploitation of Lakota spirituality; and

WHEREAS we represent the recognized traditional spiritual leaders, traditional elders, and grassroots advocates of the Lakota people; and

WHEREAS for too long we have suffered the unspeakable indignity of having our most precious Lakota ceremonies and spiritual practices desecrated, mocked, and abused by non-Indian "wannabes," hucksters, cultists, commercial profiteers, and self-styled "New Age Shamans" and their followers; and

WHEREAS our precious Sacred Pipe is being desecrated through the sale of pipestone pipes at flea markets, powwows, and "New Age" retail stores; and

WHEREAS pseudo-religious corporations have been formed to charge people money for admission to phony "sweat lodges" and "vision quest" programs; and

WHEREAS sacrilegious "sun dances" for non-Indians are being conducted by charlatans and cult leaders who promote abominable and obscene imitations of sacred Lakota Sun Dance rites; and

WHEREAS non-Indians have organized themselves into "tribes," assigning themselves make-believe "Indian names" to facilitate their wholesale expropriation and commercialization of our Lakota traditions; and

WHEREAS academic disciplines have sprung up at colleges and universities institutionalizing the sacrilegious imitation of our spiritual practices by students and instructors under the guise of educational programs in "shamanism"; and

WHEREAS non-Indian charlatans and "wannabes" are selling books that promote the systematic colonization of our Lakota spirituality; and

WHEREAS the television and film industry continues to saturate the entertainment media with vulgar, sensationalist, and grossly distorted representations of Lakota spirituality and culture which reinforce the public's negative stereotyping of Indian people and which gravely impair the self-esteem of our children; and

WHEREAS individuals and groups involved in the "New Age Movement," the "Men's Movement," in [other] "neo-pagan" cults, and in "shamanism" workshops all have exploited the spiritual traditions of our Lakota people by imitating our ceremonial ways and by mixing such imitation rituals with non-Indian occult practices in an offensive and harmful pseudo-religious hodgepodge; and

WHEREAS the absurd public posturing of this scandalous assortment of pseudo-Indian charlatans, "wannabes," commercial profiteers, cultists, and "New Age Shamans" comprises a momentous obstacle in the struggle of traditional Lakota people for an adequate public appraisal of the legitimate political, legal, and spiritual needs of real Lakota people; and

WHEREAS this exponential exploitation of our Lakota spiritual traditions requires that we take immediate action to defend our most precious Lakota spirituality from further contamination, desecration, and abuse;

THEREFORE WE RESOLVE AS FOLLOWS:

1. We hereby and henceforth declare war against all persons who persist in exploiting, abusing, and misrepresenting the sacred traditions and spiritual practices of our Lakota, Dakota, and Nakota people.
2. We call upon all Lakota, Dakota, and Nakota brothers and sisters from reservations, reserves, and traditional communities in the United States and Canada to actively and vocally oppose this alarming take-over and systematic destruction of our sacred traditions.
3. We urge our people to coordinate with their tribal members living in urban areas to identify instances in which our sacred traditions are being abused, and then to resist this abuse, utilizing whatever specific tactics are necessary and sufficient—for example, demonstrations, boycotts, press conferences, and acts of direct intervention.
4. We especially urge all our Lakota, Dakota, and Nakota people to take action to prevent our people from contributing to and enabling abuse of our sacred ceremonies and spiritual practices by outsiders; for, as we all know, there are certain ones among our own people who are prostituting our spiritual ways for their own selfish gain, with no regard for the spiritual well-being of the people as a whole.
5. We assert a posture of zero-tolerance for any "white man's shaman" who rises from within our own communities to "authorize" the expropriation of our ceremonial ways by non-Indians; all such "plastic medicine men" are enemies of the Lakota, Dakota, and Nakota people.
6. We urge traditional people, tribal leaders, and governing councils of all other Indian nations, as well as the national Indian organizations, to join us in calling for an immediate end to the rampant exploitation of our respective American Indian sacred traditions by issuing statements denouncing such abuse; for it is not the Lakota, Dakota, and Nakota people alone whose spiritual practices are being systematically violated by non-Indians.
7. We urge all our Indian brothers and sisters to act decisively and boldly in our present campaign to end the destruction of our sacred traditions, keeping in mind our highest duty as Indian people: to preserve the purity of our precious traditions for our future generations, so that our children and our children's children will survive and prosper in the sacred manner intended for each of our respective peoples by our Creator.

CHAPTER

6

Genres

"Poetry without rules is like a tennis match without a net."

—Robert Frost

All writing has rules and customs. Newspaper columns have head-lines, legal contracts signatures, and poems line breaks. Even something as private as a diary has conventions: dated entries, episodic structure, first person narration, that "Dear Diary." These game rules not only guide and shape a text, but also brand it as a specific type of writing—a genre. To understand any text, we must become familiar with its generic features, as well as the times when those rules can be broken.

Let's take a look at three short clips of writing and see if we can identify the types of writing, as well as their formulas.

A. THERE once lived a poor tailor, who had a son called Aladdin, a careless, idle boy who would do nothing but play ball all day long in the streets with little idle boys like himself. This so grieved the father that he died; yet, in spite of his mother's tears and prayers, Aladdin did not mend his ways.

B. There was a desert wind blowing that night. It was one of those hot dry Santa Anas that come down through the moun-tain passes and curl your hair and make your nerves jump and your skin itch. On nights like that every booze party ends in a fight. Meek little wives feel the edge of the carving knife and study their husbands' necks. Anything can happen. You can even get a full glass of beer at a cocktail lounge.

C. My wife ran off with my best friend
I'm sure gonna miss him
Yeh my wife ran off with my best friend

Lord I'm sure gonna miss him

They took off driving in my pickup truck
Lord a man just ain't got no luck
Yeh they took off driving in my pickup truck
Lord a man just ain't got no luck

Well my dog was sleepin in the back of that truck
Now my dogs gone too
Yeh My dog was sleepin in the back of that truck
That's why I'm singin these dog-gone blues

Most people easily identify such pieces, for they contain linguistic tics that mark each as a member of a literary family: the fairy tale, detective potboiler, and the country and western song. So predictable are these, we can deduce a generic recipe.

A. The first quote comes from "Aladdin and the Wonderful Lamp," in *The Arabian Nights*. The "Once upon a time" opening is the ritualistic beginning of the fairy tale genre, one of many earmarks, including simple diction for a young audience, blemished heroes, moral lessons, and a preoccupation with violence, cruelty, death, and the supernatural.

B. The second quote opens Raymond Chandler's novel *Red Wind*, an example of the hard-boiled detective genre. Narrated in a laconic yet witty drawl, these novels follow a solitary hero as he investigates crimes in a dirty, mean, and incomprehensible universe. He deadens himself with scotch, trusts his gun, and there's a dame; there's always a dame.

C. A lovely bit of agony, "My Wife Ran Off with My Best Friend" comes from country and western singer Mickey Newbury. Many typical elements of a country and western song appear: loss, trucks, dogs, cheating wives, and a sense of cruel fate. The country and western song is an expression of male camaraderie and sincere emotion, but is done excessively so that the sentiments seem comic, hence permissible.

WHAT IS GENRE?

Coming from the French word for kind or type, the term *genre* describes a mode of expression with distinctive requirements, features, and expectations. In some communities, genre rules are obvious, affecting everything from shape to content to style. Consider this Haiku poem, written by Japanese poet Issa.

A world of trials,
and if the cherry blossoms,
it simply blossoms.

The structure of Issa's poem identifies it as Haiku: three lines containing precisely 17 syllables arranged in a 5-7-5 pattern. The poem also depicts typical Haiku subjects (the seasons), themes (detachment), and technique (unexpected contrast). A Western equivalent to the Haiku is the sonnet—a poem of 14 lines, each with 10 syllables. More popular is the limerick, a verse that follows a predictable a/a/b/b/a rhyme scheme, concluding with a risqué joke. Limericks are fun because we know the structure and anticipate its rude climax. Here's a fairly clean, but still irreverent one inspired by the film *The Matrix*.

> If Morpheus offers to you
> a choice between red pill or blue—
> then what's your conclusion:
> to stick with illusion,
> or wake in a pod full of goo? (*Matrix Essays*)

Most people discover genres through their video stores, where they find familiar forms such as drama, comedy, horror, romance, as well as genres unique to film (the documentary, 3-D film, martial arts flick). More than artistic forms, genres appear throughout society, wherever communication has been ritualized into a regular practice. Lab reports, business letters, greeting cards, résumés, horoscopes, marriage proposals, sermons, advertisements, eulogies—all have linguistic features that tag them as a distinct genre.

DESCRIPTIVE GENRES

Some genres are traditions inherited from the past, no more binding than hanging lights on a Christmas tree. Genre, in this sense, is nothing but inherited habits and customs, a set of elastic practices that don't dictate the direction of future writers. Aristotle thought the rules for tragedy were universal and permanent, but playwrights showed how flexible the tragic genre is by breaking each and every one of Aristotle's rules. The poet Gerard Manley Hopkins similarly broke convention by composing sonnets that were 10 instead of 14 lines. Mary Shelley's *Frankenstein* tells a horror tale in which the "monster" is more likeable than the "hero." Hardly a problem, such playfulness with genre conventions constitutes a major source of artistic creativity.

A genre may be flexible, but it must contain at least some typical qualities to qualify as a genre. That is, a writer may bend generic conventions, but not abandon them entirely. If I rent a horror DVD, I expect it to have *at least one* familiar horror trait: a demon, chainsaw wielding maniac, cannibal clan, or whatever. None of these is absolutely necessary, but a DVD in the horror section makes a promise that it has some resemblance to the genre family.

The "promise" points to another key feature of genre: audience. A generic piece must satisfy the expectations of its consumers. A parent who rents a children's video expects the story to avoid certain adult themes and topics. That's to say, a genre is, to some extent, what the audience expects it to be.

PRESCRIPTIVE GENRES

Other genre customs are formal and strict, behaving like game rules that define purpose, form, and play. Any greenhorn who breaks the genre rules of formal language games may earn a penalty, even disqualification. Every year, a few shocked students receive "F" grades or expulsions, because they didn't realize academic writing has a zero tolerance policy on plagiarism.

Genre, in other words, depends partly upon the *place* of practice. A college campus expects students to write according to standards of the scholarly community; a court requires lawyers to follow law society codes; Parliament forces politicians to keep tongues civil; the newsroom scrupulously edits to avoid libel. In this respect, prescriptive genres constitute the rules of the community or institution.

Newcomers to a community must familiarize themselves with its conventions and become genre competent. We enter the business world, for example, by producing an application letter, a finicky bit of genre writing that requires professional tone and precise handling of dates, names, addresses, and salutations. Those who successfully imitate the conventions of business speech stand a chance of winning a job. Those who break form won't even receive an interview. Such genres are prescriptive in the sense that membership is denied to those who can't model proper writing conventions.

CASE STUDY: THE ACADEMIC GENRE

Students enrolling in university enter a new community with strict guidelines designed to keep scholarly writing honest, accurate, and accountable.

Academic writing is a prescriptive genre that penalizes rule-breakers. Professors routinely dock marks, fail, or even expel students who breach the following academic conventions.

CLEAR EXPRESSION

Academic essays are composed in a clear style, free from grammatical mistakes. Error-filled, awkward essays strike readers as sloppy, unprofessional, and confusing.

CLEAR ORGANIZATION

Ideas are laid out in an orderly and accessible manner with a clear statement of purpose (in academic parlance, a thesis) near the beginning. Papers that repeat or scatter ideas offer a bewildering reading experience.

OBJECTIVITY

"Justice is blind," goes the old proverb, and for a reason. Just as judges favour neither plaintiff nor defendant, so scholars write in an impartial manner.

To foster neutrality, many professors require students to write in the third person rather than the first. When we drop the subjective "I think" or "I believe" from an essay, we discuss the subject impersonally, with less interference from our own feelings and beliefs.

PROFESSIONALISM

The academic paper speaks in a formal manner, avoiding slang and sexist speech.

DEPTH

An essay covers all evidence relevant to a subject. Papers based on partial data reach invalid conclusions.

AUTHORITY

Quotation and citation lend papers credibility. A quote not only offers evidence, but also creates the impression of thorough research.

DOCUMENTATION

A good scholar provides accurate documentation so readers can trace evidence back to its source. Without citation, quotations have no more legitimacy than rumour, gossip, and hearsay.

Documentation has become a vital requirement in academic writing. Papers that don't meet MLA or APA standards are routinely failed, and worse, students are expelled for plagiarizing.

CONFRONTING GENRE

"Learn the Rules. Then forget them."

—Basho

Because genres form the basis of much social and institutional conduct, students need to master them to become culturally and professionally literate. While genre fluency is often necessary, we should be *genre wary* too. Some conventions have hardened into inflexible rules, and we must remind ourselves that they're capricious, changeable, and at times, even dangerous.

Genres aren't "real" in any physically compelling sense; they're merely handy thought patterns for organizing information. As such, they can change, thus altering our impression of what's "out there." For example, anthologies routinely organize literature into three genres: drama, poetry, and fiction. These seem "real," yet the literary field can be organized very differently. Aristotle saw a meagre two genres, tragedy and comedy; Canadian critic Northrop Frye expanded these categories, adding romance and irony; Nietzsche divided literature into the Apollonian and Dionysian; G.W.F. Hegel split it into the symbolic, classical, and romantic. New systems of organization crop up all the time—women's, post-colonial, children's lit—with no foreseeable limit, as literature may be classified and reclassified endlessly.

Given its flexible nature, a genre becomes dangerous when it's elevated into an unbreakable rule or permanent fixture. The rejection letter has no mystical, ideal form, only examples of previous practice. Even something as strict as academic documentation has undergone a complete retooling, with the APA and MLA formats largely replacing the older Chicago style. The authority behind these genres boils down to the cadres of people who choose and enforce them: in this case, a small band of academics that formalized the citation process. The rightness of such prescriptive genres really depends upon *who* scripts it.

Secondly, we should recognize that genres are also ideological and shape a reader's feelings, thoughts, hopes, and political views. The more we uncritically consume genres, the more we are indoctrinated into their belief systems.

Consider Gothic romance, a popular genre during the 18th and 19th centuries, pioneered by novels like *Jane Eyre*. The now formulaic plots follow a plain but plucky heroine, who takes a nanny job at a mysterious castle. There, she meets her new boss, an obstreperous nobleman. She gradually transforms her callous master through a display of unwavering kindness, morality, patience, and loyalty. Changed by her good soul, the lord marries his servant. As this plot reincarnates itself in various novels, movies, and plays, the Gothic romance reinforces some questionable lessons: bad men need a good woman to change them; cruelty is misdirected love; marriage crowns a woman's life. A female fantasy, the genre romanticizes women's mistreatment, servitude, and social inferiority.

In contrast, a masculine genre such as the action adventure movie (think *Rambo* or *Dirty Harry*) follows a taciturn loner who resorts to vengeance after the law fails to exact justice. Almost always male, the protagonist trains men to resolve problems with a rocket launcher; to divide the world into heroes and villains; to favour personal vendetta; to feel no empathy; to believe that violence has few consequences.

The more that such genres spread through society, the more we accept their troublesome messages as commonplace, desirable, even natural. This is a precarious situation, as a famous example demonstrates.

In 1939, Orson Welles broadcast a radio play about a Martian attack on Earth. Although the story was fictional, Welles made it realistic by telling the tale via a series of urgent bulletins that mimicked news radio conventions. Many hallmarks of radio journalism appear in Welles' play: a weather report; the gravel voiced anchorman; eyewitness interviews; reporters on the scene; appeals to experts, politicians, and military. The first bulletin even interrupts a "regularly scheduled" music program, and the entire broadcast contains deliberate glitches that add to the authenticity.

The rest is history: hordes of listeners became hysterical, mistaking fiction for fact.

This incident demonstrates the enormous influence genre has over our minds. Thousands of people believed in the alien invasion because the story *sounded like real journalism*. The audience's acceptance of the news format *as truth* becomes more shocking when we realize that Welles made several disclaimers during the broadcast, declaring the performance a bit of theatre. Yet, even when the illusion was broken, some listeners chose to believe the "reporters."

Today, books, movies, and television make regular use of news conventions to create bogus credibility. The pseudo-documentary *The Blair Witch Project* deluded thousands into searching for a fictional witch. Television commercials disguise themselves as consumer tests. Shows like *Unsolved Mysteries* use the veneer of investigative journalism to lend integrity to paranormal topics.

The genre of news has percolated so deeply into modern consciousness that we must take care not to confuse its style with truth.

HOW TO READ GENRE

When you read any text, ask yourself the following.

- What genre is it?
- What are its conventions and rules?
- Is it prescriptive or descriptive?

- Who mandated it?
- What is its authority?
- What useful purpose do the conventions serve?
- What values does the genre carry?
- Can you imagine alternatives to the rules?
- Is the genre claiming to be true, natural, or real?

These few questions can help us master genres, rather than be mastered by them.

CASE STUDY: "DEAR ABBY" AND "ANN LANDERS"

Most North Americans recognize the advice column genre: people describe personal problems and receive counsel from an "expert." Such columns are so commonplace that we seldom reflect on them. Yet we might consider investigating their values, authority, and influence, given the advice genre is a huge cultural phenomenon; "Dear Abby," the prototype, is the world's largest syndicated column, carried by over 1400 newspapers, with a daily audience of 110 000 000 people ("Dear Abby"). However, beneath the formula of "Dear Abby" or "Ann Landers" lie some problematic assumptions.

QUESTION AND ANSWERS

The question and answer format gives the columnist a subtle power advantage, forcing letter writers into the role of befuddled ignoramus; in contrast, the columnist seems an informed expert, as she dishes out answers. The Q&A format preempts discussion, overlooks other perspectives, and prevents rebuttals.

BREVITY

Most personal problems are complex matters, yet advice columnists can't respond in depth, because discussion is limited to a few inches of text. Worse, the columns are based on a single, one-sided letter, and so offer counsel that lacks balance and depth.

PSEUDONYMS

Advice columns run anonymous letters or use a cute synonym. In this way, they echo the confidentiality of a legitimate therapist, and create a safe atmosphere for revealing shocking, sordid secrets (which are then published).

MAINSTREAM READERS

To increase circulation, "Ann Landers" and "Dear Abby" run letters from a mainstream group, one that's mostly white, working, religious, middle-aged, and family-oriented. Because this group forms the readership base, columns cater to their needs, fears, and prejudices. Left out are the concerns of marginal groups such as the poor, minorities, gays, and anarchists. The content reflects the market.

MIDDLE-CLASS MORALS

Landers and Abby reaffirm the values of people with homes, kids, and jobs. They don't encourage criticism of this lifestyle, but give readers the regurgitated truisms they want to hear: marriage is hard work, but worth it; promiscuity is empty and dangerous; honesty is the best policy.

"FEMALE" PROBLEMS

Women form the largest chunk of Abby's readership, so she appeals to them with topics such as dating, marriage, infidelity, parenting, and sex. With lurid content, the column offers socially acceptable voyeurism, making private life a public spectacle. Like a soap opera, the advice column presents emotional issues such as betrayal and suicide, drawing readers in with pain and tragedy.

By presenting women predominantly in their roles as wife, girlfriend, or mother, Landers and Abby tend to reinforce popular prejudice, and so cater to stereotypes of women as emotional creatures obsessed with relationships.

NO BIZARRE SUBJECTS

Abby's column concentrates on sex and relationships, but avoids scenarios from alternative lifestyles. She offers few testimonials about S&M, orgies, polygamy, wife-swapping, anal sex, or other unconventional practices, because these alienate her mainstream audience, advertisers, and editors.

Occasionally, Abby prints a letter from one of these subcultures, usually to recommend counselling. In this way, readers receive a double pleasure: the vicarious thrill of deviance, the satisfaction of helping a lost soul.

NO POLITICS

Focused on relationships and families, these columns shun letters dealing with political problems, such as pollution, globalization, sexism, militarization, or the disparity between rich and poor. In other words, they refuse to look at large issues requiring social change.

Abby and Landers *do* tell readers they can make a difference, but limit discussion to the personal realm. Readers are told they *can* change—their outlook, relationship, friends, attitude, or appearance—but never the system.

EMPATHY

The advice column legitimizes its preoccupation with sex under the guise of professional counselling. Thus, Abby and Landers present the persona of a clinical therapist, a warm, compassionate listener.

NO PERSONAL CONTRIBUTIONS

A therapist doesn't give out personal information. By remaining silent on their own lives, Landers and Abby not only sound professional, but also deprive readers of a potential source of criticism. An anonymous voice is more authoritative.

CLEAR SOLUTIONS

An advice columnist gives readers unequivocal solutions, alleviating readers of adult responsibilities for thought and choice. An escape from ambiguity, advice columns reassure people that clear moral answers are still possible.

THERAPY

Who reads advice columns? Obviously people who trust the counselling profession form the bulk of readers. When stuck, Abby sends readers to a real professional. Think of it as another aspect of her persona: the referral.

CASE STUDY: "SAVAGE LOVE"

Dan Savage is an advice columnist whose writing largely subverts rather than preserves the rules of his profession. Appearing in small alternative publications that appeal to subcultures, "Savage Love" breaks many rules associated with the genre.

"Savage Love" has enough recognizable features to mark it as a member of the advice column family. It offers genuine advice on sex and relationships, keeps the Q&A format, as well as the pseudonyms for correspondents (although they're hilariously contrived). Yet, within this customary frame, readers sense something's amiss.

The first shock is his blunt style. Savage strips away journalistic decorum, and describes sex in a blunt, unromantic, even mechanical manner. He uses slang and invective, foregoing the role of empathetic counsellor; if something strikes Savage as stupid or dangerous, he says so. Until a few years ago, readers played along with this tough-talk, greeting their host with "Dear Fag." The insults are comical rather than hurtful, but serve an important function: they break the pall of sincerity, and push the discussion onto a more objective level. Savage's rudeness forces people out of the tragic mode of feeling into critical thought.

Savage further breaks the advice-giver's code by expressing opinions and feelings. Openly gay, Savage details not only his private life, but also pet peeves and predilections. He foregoes psychiatric detachment, presenting himself as an involved citizen, not a "scientist" with the "facts." If readers ask him something that he doesn't know, he admits ignorance and consults a professional. This is a generic convention, but Savage gives such referrals an added twist: he names the consultant, and leaves a visible paper trail for readers to trace. Savage's deferrals don't appear as disembodied voices of authority, but more modestly as confirmation.

In addition to showing a personal side, Savage discusses political issues. He launches diatribes against politicians, the church, medicine, and law. Unlike typical advice columns, Savage refuses to separate the personal and political, bedroom and boardroom. If someone asks for advice on an unwanted pregnancy, he may link it to the government's policies on contraception and abortion; if a teenager seeks advice on coming out of the closet, Savage may rail upon the criminalization of homosexuality; if a wife wants to escape an abusive relationship, he may start a letter campaign to oppose the closure of women's centres. For Savage, sex *is* political, and he counsels private problems by connecting them to the big picture.

In this expanded universe, Savage discusses a broader menu of sexual practices, consisting of the taboo sexuality shunned by Ann Landers: homosexuality, fisting, S&M, orgies, rape fantasies. Geared to the alternative market, "Savage Love" provides a forum for people excluded by Ann Landers' sense of good taste and mainstream morality. In this way, "Savage Love" is more libertarian and inclusive than "Dear Abby," for it has no commitment towards traditional mores, marriage, or the straight life. He has recommended lying, cheating, and divorce to his readers, a disregard for family values anathema in Ann Landers' world.

Yet Savage doesn't lack values; his morality merely differs from Abby's or Ann's. While Abby bases herself in God, family, and tradition, Savage behaves more pragmatically, offering advice that's useful rather than "moral." He condones infidelity, for example, because, for him, it isn't a "sin" to satisfy a biological urge in a sexually sterile relationship. For Savage, Darwin wins out over God.

And Savage does limit his readers' conduct, reprimanding them for causing harm. For example, Savage slams people who practise sex without a condom, not because it breaks a holy principle, but because it spreads disease. Savage's ethics are bounded by tangible consequences, not metaphysical abstractions.

If a hot topic generates controversy, Savage prints a range of dissenting opinions, letting readers speak in town-hall fashion. He doesn't impose a "right" answer, and routinely prints hostile, withering criticism. He also publishes a series of letters and follow-up replies, so his column resembles dialogue more than a catechism. His column works not as a single opinion piece, but as a forum, a democracy where people disagree and ideas compete for acceptance.

Works Cited

"Aladdin and the Wonderful Lamp." *The Arabian Nights.* May 30, 2004. <http://www.web-books.com/Classics/Fiction/Youth/Aladdin/AladdinP1.htm>.

Chandler, Raymond. *Red Wind.* May 30, 2004. <http://www.stormpages.com/starrbooks/chandler.htm>.

Newbury, Mickey. "My Wife Ran Off with My Best Friend." May 30, 2004. <http://mobyswebpage.com/SongBook/My%20Wife%20Ran%20Off%20With%20My%20Best%20Friend.htm>.

Matrix Essays. Weblog. Nov. 18, 2003. <http://matrixessays.blogspot.com>.

"Dear Abby." Homepage. Aug. 20, 2003. <http://www.amuniversal.com/ups/features/dearabby/phillips.htm>.

Exercises

1. Draw a tree diagram of *all genres*, including fiction and non-fiction, sub-genres and sub-sub-genres.
2. Describe the rules behind the following genres. What are their audiences? What values do they hold?

   Star Trek
   Cyberpunk
   Horror
   Disney cartoons
   Mystery
   Adventure
   Romance
   Fairy tale
   Soap opera
   Documentary

3. Write a passage for the above genres, displaying their rules and conventions.
4. Play with the conventions of a genre. How far can you bend the rules before the genre becomes unrecognizable?
5. What are the conventions of "reality" in a reality TV show?

Image Slaves

ALISON HEARN

Alison Hearn is an assistant professor who teaches media literacy courses in the Information and Media Studies department at the University of Western Ontario. In "Image Slaves," Hearn explores the unstated conventions and potential harm of "reality TV."

PART ONE

> The question isn't "are they the right color to be slaves?" but "are they vulnerable enough to be enslaved?" The criteria of enslavement today do not concern color, tribe or religion; they focus on weakness, gullibility and deprivation. . . .
>
> —Kevin Bales, *Disposable People*

1.

I'm in Boston at a popular bar called The Rack. The bar is full of young adults, only they're not drinking or eating or chatting each other up. They are all sitting at tables writing intently. These 18 to 24 year olds are not studying for exams in this famous college town; they are filling out applications to audition for an MTV "real movie" called *The Real Cancun*.

I slide in next to some kids at a booth and introduce myself. I have a tape-recorder with me, am middle-aged and, I assume, reasonably legitimate-looking. But, before I get a chance to explain my project and directly ask for their consent, one of them says "YES! I'd love to be interviewed, what do you want to know?" The others perk up and pay attention. I sense they think this is part of the audition. What the hell, I figure, so I turn the recorder on and ask for their names. They all reply eagerly, sitting up straight, flipping their hair, and, with cadences down pat, like car salesman trying to close a deal, they offer me their best pitch:

"My name's John and I'm a 20 year old Boston native with a great sense of humor and an adventuresome spirit."

"I'm Jenny. I'm planning to be a nurse, but being in this movie is my destiny! It would be a dream come true . . ."

"Hi, I'm Matt. I'm 19 years old and I really feel I have something special to share with the world. . . ."

I feel assaulted by shiny happy people; these guys are showing me their well-rehearsed personas and offering them up to me for my own use. I hesitate and then set the record straight. "Okay look, I'm an academic," I confess, "chances are really good it will be a few years until any of the results of this research sees the light of day, if at all. Any quotes I use will be anonymous, and, sadly, there won't be any photos in the book I'm working on."

Beat. "Oh. Ummm. Well that's cool. What do you want to know?" says John. And the interview begins.

2.

"Reality" now sits alongside "comedy" or "drama" as a major genre in broadcast television. The networks have entire divisions devoted to "reality" with VPs in charge. Six out of the twelve toprated programs last season in US primetime were "reality" shows; with *American Idol*'s Tuesday and Wednesday night shows repeatedly capturing the top two spots. "Reality" is now an Emmy category.

Never mind that no one really knows what, exactly, the generic term "reality" refers to—game show, soap opera, action-adventure, drama, sports. "Reality" has made over the industry in an incredibly short period of time, economically, textually and culturally. Industry people recognize that the term "reality television" signifies, not generic coherence, but common modes of production: these shows use "real people" or "non-actors" as their talent, in some instances "real contexts" for sets, and, on occasion, amateur or non-professionally produced video tapes for their content. Chad Raphael has called these things "nontraditional labor and production inputs." Producers of reality television series routinely by-pass unionized labor.

In the simplest sense, "reality television" names a set of cost-cutting measures in television production brought in by management as a response to the economic pressures faced by broadcast television trans-nationally. Some of these pressures include increased competition in media markets and growing audience fragmentation, legislative deregulation, the weakening of public broadcasting, and, specifically in the case of American-based broadcast television, spiraling costs associated with the inflated demands of already existing media celebrities. The no-brainer solution to broadcast television's economic woes involves lowering production costs by self-consciously deploying the fantasy-image economy already in place to entice "outsiders" to offer up their labor for free.

The economy of reality television is certainly the reason for its rise to prominence. It is cheap to produce and easy to sell, and the supply of labor is apparently endless. Everybody wants to be on television.

3.

Pretty much everything I do is as if I'm being watched anyway.

—Mike, a twenty-year-old student from Salem State College

Over and over again in the interviews I conduct that day in Boston, and in subsequent interviews, potential reality show contestants claim they don't really care about the money; they only want the fame. These folks line up for hours, longing for the "life-altering experience" of being a part of TV-land, hoping to generate a saleable image-commodity for themselves.

The reason for this desire for fame is clear enough. We live in the age of phantasmagoric capital, as Ernest Sternberg calls it, where image, not information, is the driving force in the market. Workers understand that our labor involves self-production in the form of persona. Just as we accept the loading up of goods with evocative emotions and meanings by advertisers, we understand that we, ourselves, must also consciously self-present in concrete and meaningful ways. It's just as important to "be seen" as a good nurse, executive, flight attendant, as to actually do the tasks that make up the job; "the capacity for calculated posing" is a routine job requirement. Sternberg argues that notoriety and recognition serve as "proxy indicators" of personal ability in this new economy of the image. If a person is well known, then their persona-producing capacity must be good; therefore they must be a good bet—a good worker, a good hire.

Since 1953 American courts have recognized fame as property with market value. A person's fame is seen not as a part of their identity, but rather as a commodity they have labored to produce; it is their "publicity right." A person's fame or "publicity right" is deemed to be fully alienable and descendible. Celebrity Joe Piscopo had to give away half of his publicity rights to his ex-wife in a divorce case. Whenever he trades on his name she gets half the profit. David Bowie issued Bowie Bonds in 1997—securities based on the very fact of his fame. Tiger Woods made 50 million dollars in endorsement deals in the year 2000. Fame is big business.

Reality television is the fast lane to fame. Why work as a wage slave when the promise of big payoff from being on TV is only an audition away?

PART TWO

[T]he new slavery appropriates the economic value of individuals while keeping them under complete coercive control—but without asserting ownership or accepting responsibility for their survival.

—Bales

4.

Welcome to the coliseum. Here's your net and your trident. Get to work.

—Reality show producer to casting agent

The first round of auditions for *The Real Cancun* are conducted in groups of eight kids. The casting agent gathers them up and initiates a modified game of "I never-ever"—a college drinking game where someone names something they haven't ever done, and, if you have done it, you must drink a shot. In this case, people are asked to simply raise their hand. The casting agent starts, "I've never ever had a threesome." Within minutes these complete strangers are revealing incredibly intimate details of their lives. One guy is obsessive compulsive and has to keep wiping himself down with wet-naps during sex. One girl once woke up naked on a beach, miles from her hotel, during spring break with no memory of what had happened. One guy confesses to having had every sexually transmitted disease possible except AIDS. These kids are locked in a pitched battle to sell their most personal stories and experiences to the casting agent.

While the kids are working on trading their mundane selves in for shiny new image-commodities, the casting agents are looking for "eye candy with issues." They see their job simply as casting good potential "characters," pretty people with good "life-story arcs"—a conflicted back-story that remains unresolved and the desire to "work through their issues" in the future, preferably in front of millions of people. "Non-pretty" people are chosen only if they are "telegenically ugly," like Kramer on *Seinfeld*.

The casting process is rigorous and involves detailed questionnaires, lengthy on-camera interviews, and psychological and background checks. The one-on-one interviews are intense, usually lasting over an hour. One casting agent confesses:

> It's a very one-way pulling of information out of people, and when someone tells you something tragic or something like that, you get this weird mixture of emotions. You think "wow that's really interesting and it'll be great for the show" and you're happy, but then you feel sorry for the person at the same time. It can be confusing. It's very intimate. You feel almost like a psychiatrist without any of the responsibility.

Reality television contestant contracts are notoriously exploitative. Participants trade away the rights to their identities almost entirely for the chance to enter the star-making machinery of the television industry. An outtake from an *American Idol* contract reads:

> I hereby grant to Producer the unconditional right throughout the universe in perpetuity to use, simulate or portray ... my name, likeness, voice, singing voice, personality, personal identification or personal experiences, my life story, biographical data, incidents, situations, events which heretofore occurred or hereafter occur. ...
>
> Other parties ... may reveal and/or relate information about me of a personal, private, intimate, surprising, defamatory, disparaging, embarrassing or unfavorable nature that may be *factual and/or fictional*.

Idol franchise king-pin Simon Fuller signs all the *Idol* finalists (in all the *Idol* competitions all over the globe) to exclusive agreements with his recording, management and merchandising companies. Contestants must agree to allow their likenesses to be used for sponsorships and endorsements, whether or not they themselves support the particular service or product. In this way 19 Entertainment manages all potential aspects of these contestants' careers. 19 Entertainment can opt-out of its agreements at any time with all but the winners of the competition.

The contestants, however, cannot. It's been estimated that Fuller earned 60 million dollars in 2003.

The confidentiality clauses on reality television contracts are also ironclad. These shows depend on contestants remaining mum about the show's outcome until the airdate. The contracts threaten severe punishment for any such breach. The contracts also prevent contestants from disclosing anything at all about the working conditions on the show, the producers, the series as a whole, or the broadcast network. In other words, they are contractually obligated to have had nothing but a "great time" during the filming. *American Idol* contestants are liable for five million dollars should they say anything about their experience on the show. *American Idol* Rueben Stoddardt: "Without the show we wouldn't be recording artists. But we did a lot of commercials, dawg. We were exploited but not exploited. It just taught us a lot about the business. *American Idol* is what we like to call a crash course on the entertainment industry."

5.

> I just don't get what makes someone else more interesting than me. I mean everyone has something valuable to offer, right? How come these TV guys get to decide?
>
> —John, a 20-year-old Boston native, after his failed audition

Humiliation is foundational to reality television. It certainly marks its current labor practices. The TV industry enacts strategies of what contemporary management literature calls "corporate seduction." These "seductive socialization programs," use status as their carrot—merely by creating categories of inclusion and exclusion—"you are one of the chosen few out of a great field of candidates, we want you." In this way loyalty is created and any number of abuses can be done to the worker once loyalty is won and the seduction is complete. As Roy Lewicki writes, "if the seduction has worked it feels like free choice, and the organization does not have to kick you; you kick yourself."

More and more of people are voluntarily "kicking themselves" for the benefit of the image industry, hoping to generate their own individualized image-token in return. Paid nothing, often asked to foot their own bills for the privilege of subjecting themselves to the colonizing gaze of the camera, and captive to the interests of the owners who generate the terms of their "fame," these "actively engaged" audience bodies have become, in a most explicit way, the sensuous raw material which the image industry cannibalizes to perpetuate its own interests.

The degree to which humiliation is blatantly enacted in the shows themselves varies. Sometimes it is simply implied. The recent spate of home and body makeover shows presumes "original humiliation" on the part of their participants and then offers deliverance from it. But, more often, the performance of humiliation is overt—such as in the recent *What's Hot* show—in which judges use laser pointers to highlight the flaws in contestant's bodies. Humiliation is clearly the draw in the recent spate of *Candid Camera*–type shows like *Punked* or the *Jamie Kennedy Experiment*, in which celebrities and regular folks get humiliated in a good natured kind of way. In other instances, such as the weekly ritual of voting off characters of both *American Idol* and *Survivor*, the humiliation involved is less obvious because it has been naturalized. The contestants who get voted off have simply been subject to the Darwinian process of survival of the fittest. They just didn't play the game well enough. These show's narratives make a virtue out of those who can successfully withstand the exclusion, judgment and heartless assessment of others, and use their own ability to manipulate to "win." More simply, they rehearse, over and over again, the story of sacrifice, pain, and exploitation required by life under capital.

Humiliation also marks the experience of watching reality television. Anecdotal responses often involve repulsion and shock at, both, the inane concepts behind the shows ("They're doing what? Chaining 50 midgets together to pull an airplane? Sending people to boot camp? Trying to break up couples? Making people live out in the bush for a year? Locking a group of strangers in portables for 3 months?") *and* at having watched them. In spite of these reactions, however, we seem to be drawn to the shows—like "flies to a glue-pot"—like passing motorists to a car wreck. Pleasure and humiliation are elided when we watch. Reality shows summon their viewers to ignore any initial shock or dismay, and to adopt, what Susan Sontag has called, a form of "professionalized looking." This kind of looking is engendered by the commodity system; it involves seeing through the lens of cold fiscal calculation. Reality television links this form of perceptual cruelty to the experience of cultural pleasure.

At the level of production, text, and reception, then, reality television shows perform, mine, and enforce a general cultural ethos of humiliation and masochism. Reality television reinforces at every level the terms of the masochistic contract offered us by techno-capital; non-unionized, mostly non-paid workers are enlisted through strategies of corporate seduction and the promise of fame, to produce stories that legitimate the broader ethos of the corporate regime that gave birth to them. Once on the shop floor workers are contractually obligated to comply with a version of reality fully delineated and controlled by their employers. Reality television programs might best be understood as the ideological sweatshops of techno-capital; their participants are its paradigmatic docile bodies.

6.

> Dear friend, I give you what you need, but you know the conditio sine qua non; you know the ink in which you have to sign yourself over to me; in providing for your pleasure, I fleece you.
>
> —Marx, *Economic and Philosophical Manuscripts*

A few weeks after the interviews at The Rack, Jenny, the student nurse calls me on my office phone: "I was just wondering whether you need anything else from me, you know, for your book thing." I explain to her that I have what I need from her, but thanks. I ask her how her audition went: "Oh, I didn't get past the first round. Some other girl in my group totally hogged all the attention. But I'm gonna go to the *American Idol* auditions in NYC, and I've sent a tape into *Real World*, so I'm still hoping. I still believe it's my destiny . . ."

NewsCorps, Viacom, Disney and General Electric all posted record profits in 2003. The television sectors of these corporations, Fox, CBS, ABC, NBC respectively, showed profit growth ranging from 6 to 14 percent. Reality shows such as *Survivor, American Idol,* and *The Apprentice* were routinely in the top 10–rated shows. Ad rates and revenues have increased. There can be no doubt that the reality television format is producing increased corporate earnings. But what else is being produced?

The phenomenon of reality television represents the increasing trend toward the corporate colonization of the "real." In the rhetorical use of the term "real" to name the process of capture by the television camera and production as its subject, these shows work to legitimate a "post-real" world—a world driven by the interests of corporate capital, mediated by new technology. In their colonization of the concepts of identity, relationship, meaningful interactivity, reality television shows work to construct and reinforce a system of cultural value, which involves the active production of the self as a saleable image-commodity. This process of self-commodification is both summoned and exploited by the media industries. In Kevin Bales' words, reality television's labor practices involve a system of control where "people become completely disposable tools for making money." In this age of image-capital, reality television produces the image slave.

The Wolf and the Lamb

AESOP

Although details of his life are murky, Aesop was a slave in Greece during the 6th century. Legend has it he gained his freedom by impressing the Greek intelligentsia with his wit, keen observations, and storytelling. His famous beast fables dramatize human problems and convey clear moral lessons.

Once upon a time a Wolf was lapping at a spring on a hillside, when, looking up, what should he see but a Lamb just beginning to drink a little lower down. "There's my supper," thought he, "if only I can find some excuse to seize it." Then he called out to the Lamb, "How dare you muddle the water from which I am drinking?"

"Nay, master, nay," said Lambikin; "if the water be muddy up there, I cannot be the cause of it, for it runs down from you to me."

"Well, then," said the Wolf, "why did you call me bad names this time last year?"

"That cannot be," said the Lamb; "I am only six months old."

"I don't care," snarled the Wolf; "if it was not you it was your father"; and with that he rushed upon the poor little Lamb and WARRA WARRA WARRA WARRA WARRA—ate her all up. But before she died she gasped out—"Any excuse will serve a tyrant."

The Crow and the Pitcher

AESOP

A Crow, half-dead with thirst, came upon a Pitcher which had once been full of water; but when the Crow put its beak into the mouth of the Pitcher he found that only very little water was left in it, and that he could not reach far enough down to get at it. He tried, and he tried, but at last had to give up in despair. Then a thought came to him, and he took a pebble and dropped it into the Pitcher. Then he took another pebble and dropped it into the Pitcher. Then he took another pebble and dropped that into the Pitcher. Then he took another pebble and dropped that into the Pitcher. Then he took another pebble and dropped that into the Pitcher. Then he took another pebble and dropped that into the Pitcher. At last, at last, he saw the water mount up near him, and after casting in a few more pebbles he was able to quench his thirst and save his life.

Little by little does the trick.

The Little Match Girl

HANS CHRISTIAN ANDERSEN

Hans Christian Andersen lived in Denmark during the 19th century. He earned lasting fame for his series of children's stories and fairy tales, such as "The Ugly Duckling," "The Tinderbox," "The Princess and the Pea," and the "The Little Mermaid." His works have been frequently adapted into film and television, but few productions capture the beauty and psychological details of Andersen's originals.

Most terribly cold it was; it snowed, and was nearly quite dark, and evening—the last evening of the year. In this cold and darkness there went along the street a poor little girl, bareheaded, and with naked feet. When she left home she had slippers on, it is true; but what was the good of that? They were very large slippers, which her mother had hitherto worn; so large were they; and the poor little thing lost them as she scuffled away across the street, because of two carriages that rolled by dreadfully fast.

One slipper was nowhere to be found; the other had been laid hold of by an urchin, and off he ran with it; he thought it would do capitally for a cradle when he some day or other should have children himself. So the little maiden walked on with her tiny naked feet, that were quite red and blue from cold. She carried a quantity of matches in an old apron, and she held a bundle of them in her hand. Nobody had bought anything of her the whole livelong day; no one had given her a single farthing.

She crept along trembling with cold and hunger—a very picture of sorrow, the poor little thing!

The flakes of snow covered her long fair hair, which fell in beautiful curls around her neck; but of that, of course, she never once now thought. From all the windows the candles were gleaming, and it smelt so deliciously of roast goose, for you know it was New Year's Eve; yes, of that she thought.

In a corner formed by two houses, of which one advanced more than the other, she seated herself down and cowered together. Her little feet she had drawn close up to her, but she grew colder and colder, and to go home she did not venture, for she had not sold any matches and could not bring a farthing of money: from her father she would certainly get blows, and at home it was cold too, for above her she had only the roof, through which the wind whistled, even though the largest cracks were stopped up with straw and rags.

Her little hands were almost numbed with cold. Oh! a match might afford her a world of comfort, if she only dared take a single one out of the bundle, draw it against the wall, and warm her fingers by it. She drew one out. "Rischt!" how it blazed, how it burnt! It was a warm, bright flame, like a candle, as she held her hands over it: it was a wonderful light. It seemed really to the little maiden as though she were sitting before a large iron stove, with burnished brass feet and a brass ornament at top. The fire burned with such blessed influence; it warmed so delightfully. The little girl had already stretched out her feet to warm them too; but—the small flame went out, the stove vanished: she had only the remains of the burnt-out match in her hand.

She rubbed another against the wall: it burned brightly, and where the light fell on the wall, there the wall became transparent like a veil, so that she could see into the room. On the table was spread a snow-white tablecloth; upon it was a splendid porcelain service, and the roast goose was steaming famously with its stuffing of apple and dried plums. And what was still more capital to behold was, the goose hopped down from the dish, reeled about on the floor with knife and fork in its breast, till it came up to the poor little girl; when—the match went out and nothing but the thick, cold, damp wall was left behind. She lighted another match. Now there she was sitting under the most magnificent Christmas tree: it was still larger, and more decorated than the one which she had seen through the glass door in the rich merchant's house.

Thousands of lights were burning on the green branches, and gaily-colored pictures, such as she had seen in the shop-windows, looked down upon her. The little maiden stretched out her hands towards them when—the match went out. The lights of the Christmas tree rose higher and higher, she saw them now as stars in heaven; one fell down and formed a long trail of fire.

"Someone is just dead!" said the little girl; for her old grandmother, the only person who had loved her, and who was now no more, had told her, that when a star falls, a soul ascends to God.

She drew another match against the wall: it was again light, and in the lustre there stood the old grandmother, so bright and radiant, so mild, and with such an expression of love.

"Grandmother!" cried the little one. "Oh, take me with you! You go away when the match burns out; you vanish like the warm stove, like the delicious roast goose, and like the magnificent Christmas tree!" And she rubbed the whole bundle of matches quickly against the wall, for she wanted to be quite sure of keeping her grandmother near her. And the matches gave such a brilliant light that it was brighter than at noon-day: never formerly had the grandmother been so beautiful and so tall. She took the little maiden, on her arm, and both flew in brightness and in joy so high, so very high, and then above was neither cold, nor hunger, nor anxiety—they were with God.

But in the corner, at the cold hour of dawn, sat the poor girl, with rosy cheeks and with a smiling mouth, leaning against the wall—frozen to death on the last evening of the old year. Stiff and stark sat the child there with her matches, of which one bundle had been burnt. "She wanted to warm herself," people said. No one had the slightest suspicion of what beautiful things she had seen; no one even dreamed of the splendor in which, with her grandmother, she had entered on the joys of a new year.

The Zebra Storyteller

SPENCER HOLST

Spencer Holst is an American short story writer who became famous by publicly reciting his tales in Greenwich Village and New York cafés. His collections include *Brilliant Silence: Sentences, Paragraphs, and Very, Very*

Short Stories, *The Zebra Storyteller*, *The Language of Cats*, and *Spencer Holst Stories*. In this parable, Holst uses Aesop's tradition of the animal fable, but withholds the clear moral message.

Once upon a time there was a Siamese cat who pretended to be a lion and spoke inappropriate Zebraic.

That language is whinnied by the race of striped horses in Africa.

Here now: An innocent zebra is walking in a jungle and approaching from another direction is the little cat; they meet.

"Hello there!" says the Siamese cat in perfectly pronounced Zebraic. "It certainly is a pleasant day, isn't it? The sun is shining, the birds are singing, isn't the world a lovely place to live today!"

The zebra is so astonished at hearing a Siamese cat speaking like a zebra, why—he's just fit to be tied.

So the little cat quickly ties him up, kills him, and drags the better parts of the carcass back to his den.

The cat successfully hunted zebras many months in this manner, dining on filet mignon of zebra every night, and from the better hides he made bow neckties and wide belts after the fashion of the decadent princes of the Old Siamese court.

He began boasting to his friends he was a lion, and he gave them as proof the fact that he hunted zebras.

The delicate noses of the zebras told them there was really no lion in the neighborhood. The zebra deaths caused many to avoid the region. Superstitious, they decided the woods were haunted by the ghost of a lion.

One day the storyteller of the zebras was ambling, and through his mind ran plots for stories to amuse the other zebras, when suddenly his eyes brightened, and he said, "That's it! I'll tell a story about a Siamese cat who learns to speak our language! What an idea! That'll make 'em laugh!"

Just then the Siamese cat appeared before him, and said, "Hello there! Pleasant day today, isn't it!"

The zebra storyteller wasn't fit to be tied at hearing a cat speaking his language, because he'd been thinking about that very thing.

He took a good look at the cat, and he didn't know why, but there was something about his looks he didn't like, so he kicked him with a hoof and killed him.

That is the function of the storyteller.

The Really Ugly Duckling

JON SCIESZKA

Jon Scieszka is a writer of children's books, including *The Stinky Cheese Man, The True Story of the Three Little Pigs, The Frog Prince Continued, Squids Will Be Squids: Fresh Morals for Beastly Fables,* and *The Book That Jack Wrote.* His work tends to twist and invert the normal expectations readers have of fairy tales.

Once upon a time there was a mother duck and a father duck who had seven baby ducklings. Six of them were regular-looking ducklings. The seventh was a really ugly duckling. Everyone used to say, "What a nice-looking bunch of ducklings— all except that one. Boy, he's really ugly." The really ugly duckling heard these people, but he didn't care. He knew that one day he would probably grow up to be a swan and be bigger and look better than anything in the pond. Well, as it turned out, he was just a really ugly duckling. And he grew up to be just a really ugly duck. The End.

Selections from "Ask Ellie"

ELLIE TESHER

Working in the genre first forged by Ann Landers and Abigail Van Buren (of "Dear Abby" fame), Ellie Tesher is an advice columnist who counsels readers on relationship, marital, personal, and family problems. Tesher has modernized the advice column somewhat, but still retains many of the familiar patterns and trademarks of the genre. Author of a bestselling book *The Dionnes*, Tesher has previously worked as journalist and a talk show host.

Workplace crush is a passing distraction

Q. I'm 32 and married to a wonderful woman. We have three daughters. There's this woman at work and every time I'm with her, I feel like I'm in high school again. My heart races and I get nervous around her. I find her attractive and I don't know if this is just a puppy-dog crush or what. I still get this way with my wife, don't get me wrong.

I just wonder if I should tell these feelings to this woman at work or hold them in? Just like a lot of things I hold in.

—Just Classic

A. Your puppy crush appears to have a bit of bite to it. But it has little to do with the woman at work. It's common to occasionally be attracted to a colleague you see every day; however, don't tell her, as it will make things awkward and complicated.

You still love your wife, and you have a full plate; there's no good reason to pursue an affair that will mess up your life. This is just a passing distraction. But your comment about "holding in" feelings suggests you're frustrated at home about other things. Perhaps it's just the normal pressure of a houseful of kids and responsibilities, and you sometimes feel crushed, yourself, by it all. Talk to your wife, she's your partner, the person with whom you're spending a life. She undoubtedly feels stressed, too. The more you communicate your feelings to each other, the more you'll understand each other and share compassion as well as passion.

Why isn't being a prude ever in vogue?

Q. What do you think of guys who want to "kiss passionately" on the first date? Is that a signal that they could do the same with other girls? My problem is trust, though we're both adults.

—Taken Aback

A. Personally, I'd rather lick this problem than a stranger's tonsil! Here's my summation of first-date passion: It isn't real. Not unless you two have been getting to know each other as friends and suddenly realized there's huge chemistry between you, such that this "first" date is the result of a build-up of mutual excitement, with many more dates ahead. But most first dates are usually a beginning. So, yes, of course, yours is not the only dental site with which he's making contact. Yech! Turn your cheek and say, "Later". . . if ever.

The ripple effect of infidelity won't go away

Q. My husband and I have been together for three years; last year he had to go away for work for six months. We've been through a lot together and I think that put me over the edge. I asked if he'd mind if I slept with one of our friends, once. I was feeling lonely and sad. He agreed. Instead of feeling better, it made me feel a lot worse. Our sex life hasn't been the same since. He's my absolute world and I can't picture my life without him. I know it bugs him because he's told me it does. It breaks my heart to see him upset over my selfishness. What can I do?

—Foolish in Fredericton

A. Here's where I could wish for Dr. Phil's incredulous, drawling voice behind these words: "What were you thinking?" You've learned several lessons, but that doesn't mean school's out; your hubby is the one who still feels punished. Just because the one-night stand didn't feel so good doesn't mean its impact is over. It's no different from an affair to your husband, as he's left unsure he can trust you if work ever takes him away again. He also doesn't understand how you could do this, when it was bound to put a wedge into your intimacy. And he's wondering about comparisons to this so-called "friend." Get to marriage counselling together. He needs to vent his feelings, hurts, disappointments about this and you need to listen. You, too, should express why a necessary absence made you so insecure and needy. Give him plenty of time to get past this . . . since "once" is one time too many.

Girlfriend's appetite for porn causing rift

Q. My live-in girlfriend has many email contacts, most of them men friends and teammates from sports. She's apparently never had a romantic connection with any of them. She receives from them many humorous/graphic emails containing male and female nudity, and passes them onto others, including me. One particular attachment would only appeal to a male, so I questioned why this friend sent it, saying it disrespected her. She got defensive, then suggested she wouldn't forward those emails to me in future since they offended me. I said perhaps she was sending the wrong message to her friends with this material. Since, she's continued to handle the same types of emails and shuts down her screen when I'm around. She says women can have male friends and I shouldn't be over-reacting or feel threatened. In the intimate portion of our lives, she's become unenthusiastic. I'm usually put off with some reason or other and the disappointment is getting me down. Frustration is giving way to resentment. Am I being the "prude" or does somebody have a problem?

—Frustrated

A. Double problem here—your relationship is in trouble, and your girlfriend acts inappropriately with male friends. If you break up, that's her business and may not change. But while together, it's *your* business if these nude emails bother you, especially because there's a disconnect between her enjoyment of salacious material, and her rejection of intimacy with you. The main message is to you: She's no longer a team player with you. Instead, she's hanging on to the old gang by acting like a jock and, even if I personally didn't find her taste for porn out of line, I'd still say she's the one dissing you.

"Sweetie" is ducking truth about her marriage

Q. I'm 20, in a sexual affair with a married female, 37, who's a mother of two. We met online and talked for several months before meeting. She said she wanted to be satisfied by a younger guy. She told me her marriage wasn't working out. She doesn't want to divorce because of their daughters. We continue to see each other. She knows I'm with her just to satisfy her. Should I continue seeing her? She really is a sweetie inside and out. I love her attitude and the way she is, but I'm confused on what to do now.

—Mother's Helper

A. You give new meaning to the phrase "Secret Service," but not one that's nearly so admirable as the original. You see yourself as the silent helper in her marriage, yet you're not really *satisfied*. That shows you have better instincts than to just be someone else's toy boy. This is NOT a healthy situation for you, her or her daughters, and you're disturbed because you know it. At some point you'll be discovered, which will create a huge mess all around. At some point she has to face up to the truth, which is she's only distracting herself from her marriage, never working to improve it or take an honest stand. Get out of this. She's no "sweetie," just an unhappy woman taking the sleazy route.

Selections from "Savage Love"

DAN SAVAGE

Dan Savage is the journalist behind the weekly sex advice column "Savage Love." Uncharacteristically frank for an advice columnist, Savage has made a reputation by addressing not only heterosexual problems, but also those from gay and alternative lifestyles. Openly gay himself, Savage has published several collections of his columns, including *Savage Love* and *Skipping Towards Gomorra*, as well as *The Kid*, his story of the adoption process.

Q: Here's the sitch: I was married for 4.5 years; for 3.5 of those years, I had a dog who gave me no trouble. However, now that I'm a single girl again, my dog is incredibly jealous of my lovers. It began with him breaking into my room during intercourse and making an embarrassing ruckus. He growls menacingly at my lovers as well. Lately my dog has been picking through my laundry basket, retrieving my underwear, which he proceeds to destroy and/or eat. This isn't so funny when you're dropping $14 on a thong. So my dog (a precious terrier-heeler mix) is the jealous type, and I don't know what to do to reassure him.

—Doggie Comes First

P. S. He's fixed, but he still gets hard-ons.

A: Oh, Lord. If I wasn't already feeling queasy after I read your letter, that P. S. sure would've done the trick.

Anyway, advice: Despite the fact that your dog is doing you a favor when he destroys those $14 thongs (butt floss is now and forever a fashion don't), you can solve your problem by having your dog destroyed. It's a drastic step, I realize, but the Godlike power of life and death is one of the thrills of pet ownership. Good luck.

Q: The girl I'm seeing is a stripper and an escort. I'm fine with the stripping, but the idea of her alone in hotel rooms with old horny men bothers me. A woman who used to be a stripper has been filling my head with horror stories, trying to convince me that 80 percent of escorts have sex with their clients. I asked my girlfriend about her job, and she got hella pissed. Now I feel awful that I inadvertently implied she has sexual contact with her clients. Do you know anyone in the business that might be able to give me a heads up on how frequently sex does occur?

—David

A: Personally, I've never heard of an escort who doesn't sleep with her clients, and I assumed your girlfriend was lying when she denied that she had any physical contact with creepy men in hotel rooms. However, your letter arrived on the same day as a press release promoting *Turning Pro: A Guide to Sex Work for the Ambitious and the Intrigued* (Greenery Press). The author, Magdalene Meretrix, "has worked as a prostitute, escort, phone sex worker, professional submissive, and porn film actress," which means Ms. Meretrix is better qualified to answer your question.

"His girlfriend might work for an agency where there's no physical contact with clients," Meretrix said. "There are agencies that send girls out to do lap dances, or touch themselves while clients watch, or use toys on themselves but with no sexual contact with the client. It's possible his girlfriend is working for one of these agencies."

Since I'm the suspicious type, I asked her why your girlfriend was so touchy and defensive. If she's not hiding anything, why does she get pissed when her boyfriend asks perfectly reasonable questions about her job? "She may well be lying," Meretrix conceded. "A sneaky way to find out if she's telling the truth is to call the agency on a night his girlfriend's not working. If he calls a girl and she agrees to have sex, it's a pretty good indication that his girlfriend is lying to him."

Q: After years of trying to make a living in the "straight" world of office drudgery, I've decided to pursue a career as a professional dominatrix. After exhausting the Internet, asking everyone I know, and scanning classified ads, I hit a brick wall. I finally realized that you, Dan, would be the perfect person to give me advice on this subject.

How can I get into this line of work? Can I apprentice under an experienced pro dom? How can I connect with pro doms and let them know I'm eager and ready to go to work? I think I would make a great dominatrix. I've always attracted men who want me to dress them up like little girls and spank them, so why shouldn't I get paid for doing it?

—Looking for Work

A: Being a professional dominatrix isn't something you do on a whim—and the money isn't as easy as you seem to think it is. "The equipment costs are high—$10,000 or more to set up a real dungeon," said Meretrix. "The doms who are any good aren't doing it to work through their anger toward men or because they think it's easy money. If you want to make easy money, be a prostitute. There's a high level of skill involved in being a dom, and the expenditure for costumes can be steep. Working under another dom is an excellent idea. Some cities, like Atlanta, have communal dungeons with several doms, and those places are often willing to train new doms. It will be much harder to find an independent dom willing to train you. There's one in California, Mistress Cleo Dubois. She'll train people for money."

Q: I am thinking about becoming a professional escort (transvestite). I see a lot of ads come and go here in Toronto—not too many people seem to stay in the business very long. Are there not enough clients to go around?

—Wondering About Sex Work

A: Ads come and go because there's a high burnout rate among sex workers, but Meretrix says you'll find plenty of work in a city like Toronto. "There's a huge demand in major cities, and most is for people who aren't totally through with the change," she said. "Your clients will want someone with breasts and a functional penis." So if you've still got your dick, you're set up.

A Modest Proposal for Preventing the Children of Poor People in Ireland from Being a Burden to Their Parents or Country, and for Making Them Beneficial to the Public

JONATHAN SWIFT

An Irish writer of the 18th century, Jonathan Swift is best known for satiric works such as *Gulliver's Travels* and *A Tale of a Tub*. A political activist, Swift used his literary skills to expose hypocrisy and injustice of power, particularly the British treatment of Ireland. In "A Modest Proposal," his most scandalous piece, he imitates the style of a businessman to highlight the heartlessness that lies within cool reason.

It is a melancholy object to those who walk through this great town or travel in the country, when they see the streets, the roads, and cabin doors, crowded with beggars of the female sex, followed by three, four, or six children, all in rags and importuning every passenger for an alms. These mothers, instead of being able to work for their honest livelihood, are forced to employ all their time in strolling to beg sustenance for their helpless infants: who as they grow up either turn thieves for want of work, or leave their dear native country to fight for the Pretender in Spain, or sell themselves to the Barbadoes.

I think it is agreed by all parties that this prodigious number of children in the arms, or on the backs, or at the heels of their mothers, and frequently of their fathers, is in the present deplorable state of the kingdom a very great additional grievance; and, therefore, whoever could find out a fair, cheap, and easy method of making these children sound, useful members of the commonwealth, would deserve so well of the public as to have his statue set up for a preserver of the nation.

But my intention is very far from being confined to provide only for the children of professed beggars; it is of a much greater extent, and shall take in the whole number of infants at a certain age who are born of parents in effect as little able to support them as those who demand our charity in the streets.

As to my own part, having turned my thoughts for many years upon this important subject, and maturely weighed the several schemes of other projectors, I have always found them grossly mistaken in the computation. It is true, a child just dropped from its dam may be supported by her milk for a solar year, with little other nourishment; at most not above the value of 2s., which the mother may certainly get, or the value in scraps, by her lawful occupation of begging; and it is exactly at one year old that I propose to provide for them in such a manner as instead of being a charge upon their parents or the parish, or wanting food and raiment for the rest of their lives, they shall on the contrary contribute to the feeding, and partly to the clothing, of many thousands.

There is likewise another great advantage in my scheme, that it will prevent those voluntary abortions, and that horrid practice of women murdering their bastard children, alas! Too frequent among us! sacrificing the poor innocent babes I doubt more to avoid the expense than the shame, which would move tears and pity in the most savage and inhuman breast.

The number of souls in this kingdom being usually reckoned one million and a half, of these I calculate there may be about two hundred thousand couple whose wives are breeders; from which number I subtract thirty thousand couples who are able to maintain their own children, although I apprehend there cannot be so many, under the present distresses of the kingdom; but this being granted, there will remain an hundred and seventy thousand breeders. I again subtract fifty thousand for those women who miscarry, or whose children die by accident or disease within the year. There only remains one hundred and twenty thousand children of poor parents annually born: the question therefore is, how this number shall be reared and provided for, which, as I have already said, under the present situation of affairs, is utterly impossible by all the methods hitherto proposed. For we can neither employ them in handicraft or agriculture; we neither build houses (I mean in the country) nor cultivate land: they can very seldom pick up a livelihood by stealing, till they arrive at six years old, except where they are of towardly parts, although I confess they learn the rudiments much earlier, during which time, they can however be properly looked upon only as probationers, as I have been informed by a principal gentleman in the county of Cavan, who protested to me that he never knew above one or two instances under the age of six, even in a part of the kingdom so renowned for the quickest proficiency in that art.

I am assured by our merchants, that a boy or a girl before twelve years old is no salable commodity; and even when they come to this age they will not yield above three pounds, or three pounds and half-a-crown at most on the exchange; which cannot turn to account either to the parents or kingdom, the charge of nutriment and rags having been at least four times that value.

I shall now therefore humbly propose my own thoughts, which I hope will not be liable to the least objection.

I have been assured by a very knowing American of my acquaintance in London, that a young healthy child well nursed is at a year old a most delicious, nourishing, and wholesome food, whether stewed, roasted, baked, or boiled; and I make no doubt that it will equally serve in a fricassee or a ragout.

I do therefore humbly offer it to public consideration that of the hundred and twenty thousand children already computed, twenty thousand may be reserved for breed, whereof only one-fourth part to be males; which is more than we allow to sheep, black cattle or swine; and my reason is, that these children are seldom the fruits of marriage, a circumstance not much regarded by our savages, therefore one male will be sufficient to serve four females. That the remaining hundred thousand may, at a year old, be offered in the sale to the persons of quality and fortune through the kingdom; always advising the mother to let them suck plentifully in the last month, so as to render them plump and fat for a good table. A child will make two dishes at an entertainment for friends; and when the family dines alone, the fore or hind quarter will make a reasonable dish, and seasoned with a little pepper or salt will be very good boiled on the fourth day, especially in winter.

I have reckoned upon a medium that a child just born will weigh 12 pounds, and in a solar year, if tolerably nursed, increaseth to 28 pounds.

I grant this food will be somewhat dear, and therefore very proper for landlords, who, as they have already devoured most of the parents, seem to have the best title to the children.

Infant's flesh will be in season throughout the year, but more plentiful in March, and a little before and after; for we are told by a grave author, an eminent French physician, that fish being a prolific diet, there are more children born in Roman Catholic countries about nine months after Lent than at any other season; therefore, reckoning a year after Lent, the markets will be more glutted than usual, because the number of popish infants is at least three to one in this kingdom: and therefore it will have one other collateral advantage, by lessening the number of papists among us.

I have already computed the charge of nursing a beggar's child (in which list I reckon all cottagers, laborers, and four-fifths of the farmers) to be about two shillings per annum, rags included; and I believe no gentleman would repine to give ten shillings for the carcass of a good fat child, which, as I have said, will make four dishes of excellent nutritive meat, when he hath only some particular friend or his own family to dine with him. Thus the squire will learn to be a good landlord, and grow popular among his tenants; the mother will have eight shillings net profit, and be fit for work till she produces another child.

Those who are more thrifty (as I must confess the times require) may flay the carcass; the skin of which artificially dressed will make admirable gloves for ladies, and summer boots for fine gentlemen.

As to our city of Dublin, shambles may be appointed for this purpose in the most convenient parts of it, and butchers we may be assured will not be wanting; although I rather recommend buying the children alive, and dressing them hot from the knife, as we do roasting pigs.

A very worthy person, a true lover of his country, and whose virtues I highly esteem, was lately pleased in discoursing on this matter to offer a refinement upon my scheme. He said that many gentlemen of this kingdom, having of late destroyed their deer, he conceived that the want of venison might be well supplied by the bodies of young lads and maidens, not exceeding fourteen years of age nor under twelve; so great a number of both sexes in every country being now ready to starve for want of work and service; and these to be disposed of by their parents, if alive, or otherwise by their nearest relations. But with due deference to so excellent a friend and so deserving a patriot, I cannot be altogether in his sentiments; for as to the males, my American acquaintance assured me, from frequent experience, that their flesh was generally tough and lean, like that of our schoolboys by continual exercise, and their taste disagreeable; and to fatten them would not answer the charge. Then as to the females, it would, I think, with humble submission be a loss to the public, because they soon would become breeders themselves; and besides, it is not improbable that some scrupulous people might be apt to censure such a practice (although indeed very unjustly), as a little bordering upon cruelty; which, I confess, hath always been with me the strongest objection against any project, however so well intended.

But in order to justify my friend, he confessed that this expedient was put into his head by the famous Psalmanazar, a native of the island Formosa, who came from thence to London above twenty years ago, and in conversation told my friend, that in his country when any young person happened to be put to death, the executioner sold the carcass to persons of quality as a prime dainty; and that in his time the body of a plump girl of fifteen, who was crucified for an attempt to poison the emperor, was sold to his imperial majesty's prime minister of state, and other great mandarins of the court, in joints from the gibbet, at four hundred crowns. Neither indeed can I deny, that if the same use were made of several plump young girls in this town, who without one single groat to their fortunes cannot stir abroad without a chair, and appear at playhouse and assemblies in foreign fineries which they never will pay for, the kingdom would not be the worse.

Some persons of a desponding spirit are in great concern about that vast number of poor people, who are aged, diseased, or maimed, and I have been desired to employ my thoughts what course may be taken to ease the nation of so grievous an encumbrance. But I am not in the least pain upon that matter, because it is very well known that they are every day dying and rotting by cold and famine, and filth and vermin, as fast as can be reasonably expected. And as to the young laborers, they are now in as hopeful a condition; they cannot get work, and consequently pine away for want of nourishment, to a degree that if at any time they are accidentally hired to common labor, they have not strength to perform it; and thus the country and themselves are happily delivered from the evils to come.

I have too long digressed, and therefore shall return to my subject. I think the advantages by the proposal which I have made are obvious and many, as well as of the highest importance.

For first, as I have already observed, it would greatly lessen the number of papists, with whom we are yearly overrun, being the principal breeders of the nation as well as our most dangerous enemies; and who stay at home on purpose with a design to deliver the kingdom to the Pretender, hoping to take their advantage by the absence of so many good protestants, who have chosen rather to leave their country than stay at home and pay tithes against their conscience to an Episcopal curate.

Secondly, the poorer tenants will have something valuable of their own, which by law may be made liable to distress and help to pay their landlord's rent, their corn and cattle being already seized, and money a thing unknown.

Thirdly, whereas the maintenance of an hundred thousand children, from two years old and upward, cannot be computed at less than ten shillings a-piece per annum, the nation's stock will be thereby increased fifty thousand pounds per annum, beside the profit of a new dish introduced to the tables of all gentlemen of fortune in the kingdom who have any refinement in taste. And the money will circulate among ourselves, the goods being entirely of our own growth and manufacture.

Fourthly, the constant breeders, beside the gain of eight shillings sterling per annum by the sale of their children, will be rid of the charge of maintaining them after the first year.

Fifthly, this food would likewise bring great custom to taverns; where the vintners will certainly be so prudent as to procure the best receipts for dressing it to perfection, and consequently have their houses frequented by all the fine gentlemen, who justly value themselves upon their knowledge in good eating: and a skilful cook, who understands how to oblige his guests, will contrive to make it as expensive as they please.

Sixthly, this would be a great inducement to marriage, which all wise nations have either encouraged by rewards or enforced by laws and penalties. It would increase the care and tenderness of mothers toward their children, when they were sure of a settlement for life to the poor babes, provided in some sort by the public, to their annual profit instead of expense. We should see an honest emulation among the married women, which of them could bring the fattest child to the market. Men would become as fond of their wives during the time of their pregnancy as they are now of their mares in foal, their cows in calf, their sows when they are ready to farrow; nor offer to beat or kick them (as is too frequent a practice) for fear of a miscarriage.

Many other advantages might be enumerated. For instance, the addition of some thousand carcasses in our exportation of barreled beef, the propagation of swine's flesh, and improvement in the art of making good bacon, so much wanted among us by the great destruction of pigs, too frequent at our tables; which are no way comparable in taste or magnificence to a well-grown, fat, yearling child, which roasted whole will make a considerable figure at a lord mayor's feast or any other public entertainment. But this and many others I omit, being studious of brevity.

Supposing that one thousand families in this city would be constant customers for infant's flesh, besides others who might have it at merry meetings, particularly weddings and christenings: I compute that Dublin would take off annually about twenty thousand carcasses, and rest of the kingdom (where probably they will be sold somewhat cheaper) the remaining eighty thousand.

I can think of no one objection that will possibly be raised against this proposal, unless it should be urged that the number of people will be thereby much lessened in the kingdom. This I freely own, and it was indeed one principal design in offering it to the world. I desire the reader will observe, that I calculated my remedy for this one individual Kingdom of Ireland, and for no other that ever was, is, or, I think, ever can be upon earth. Therefore let no man talk to me of other expedients: Of taxing our absentees at five shillings a pound: Of using neither clothes, nor household furniture, except what is our own growth and manufacture: Of utterly rejecting the materials and instruments that promote foreign luxury: Of curing the expensiveness of pride, vanity, idleness, and gaming in our women: Of introducing a vein of parsimony, prudence, and temperance: Of learning to love our country, wherein we differ even from Laplanders, and the inhabitants of Tompinamboo: Of quitting our animosities and factions, nor act any longer like the Jews, who were murdering one another at the very moment their city was taken: Of being a little cautious not to sell our country and consciences for nothing: Of teaching landlords to have at least one degree of mercy towards their tenants. Lastly, of putting a spirit of honesty, industry, into our shopkeepers, who, if a resolution could now be taken to buy only our native goods, would immediately unite to cheat and exact upon us in the price, the measure and the goodness, nor could ever yet be brought to make one fair proposal of just dealing, though often and earnestly invited to it.

Therefore I repeat, let no man talk to me of these and the like expedients, till he hath at least some glimpse of hope that there will ever be some hearty and sincere attempt to put them in practice. But as to myself, having been wearied out for many years with offering vain, idle, visionary thoughts, and at length utterly despairing of success, I fortunately fell upon this proposal, which as it is wholly new, so it hath something solid and real, of no expense and little trouble, full in our own power, and whereby we can incur no danger in disobliging England. For this kind of commodity will not bear exportation, the flesh being of too tender a consistence to admit a long continuance in salt, although perhaps I could name a country that would be glad to eat up our whole nation without it.

After all, I am not so violently bent upon my own opinion as to reject any offer proposed by wise men, which shall be found equally innocent, cheap, easy, and effectual. But before something of that kind shall be advanced in contradiction to my scheme, and offering a better, I desire the author or authors will be pleased maturely to consider two points. First, as things now stand, how they will be able to find food and raiment for an hundred thousand useless mouths and backs. And secondly, there being a round million of creatures in human figure throughout this kingdom, whose whole subsistence put into a common stock would leave them in debt two millions of pounds sterling, adding those who are beggars by profession to the bulk of farmers, cottagers, and laborers, with their wives and children who are beggars in effect: I desire those politicians who dislike my overture, and may perhaps be so bold as to attempt an answer, that they will first ask the parents of these mortals, whether they would not at this day think it a great happiness to have been sold for food, at a year old in the manner I prescribe, and thereby have avoided such a perpetual scene of misfortunes as they have since gone through by the oppression of landlords, the impossibility of paying rent without money or trade, the want of common sustenance, with neither house nor clothes to cover them from the inclemencies of the weather, and the most inevitable prospect of entailing the like or greater miseries upon their breed for ever.

I profess, in the sincerity of my heart, that I have not the least personal interest in endeavoring to promote this necessary work, having no other motive than the public good of my country, by advancing our trade, providing for infants, relieving the poor, and giving some pleasure to the rich. I have no children by which I can propose to get a single penny; the youngest being nine years old, and my wife past child-bearing.

White Peril

TARAS GRESCOE

Taras Grescoe is a Montreal author and journalist. He has published *Sacré Blues: An Unsentimental Journey Through Quebec* and *The Devil's Picnic*. In his satire "White Peril," Grescoe allows white readers to feel the pain of racial profiling, by making them the target of media fear mongering.

As he walks past the small, carefully tended gardens of Strathcona, Vancouver's oldest residential neighbourhood, Mr. Sang Lee can recall a time when he didn't have to knock used condoms out of the rosebushes or flick syringes into the gutter with the tip of his umbrella. During the past year, the president of the Strathcona Property Owners and Tenants Association—one of Canada's oldest neighbourhood-rights groups—has watched drug-related crime hit the streets in earnest, an overflow from the incessant dealing at the nearby intersection of Hastings and Main. "The selling of drugs seems to be very active over the last year. Some people who are not residents of this area are trying to bring drugs and prostitution to this neighbourhood."

Who are these arrivals, the dealers, pimps, and burglars poisoning life for the residents of Strathcona? Mr. Sang Lee doesn't have to think twice. "Most people involved in local criminal activities are Caucasians."

It's one of the tragedies of Vancouver's urban geography that the city's oldest residential neighbourhood, peopled by the founders of the city—farmers from China's Guangdong province, whose families have prospered in the New World—is also bordered by one of Canada's hotbeds of white crime. On any given day, Mr. Sang Lee can watch Irish- and Scottish-Canadian dealers on Hastings Street peddling heroin outside the bars and welfare hotels. When their clients run out of cash for their habits (and statistics show that drug addiction in Canada is an overwhelmingly white problem), they break into the respectable homes of Strathcona—then sell what they've stolen to pawnshops on Hastings. Not coincidentally, many of these shops are owned by other Caucasians. . . .

When Mr. Sang Lee came to Vancouver in 1967, he—like many other settlers—was looking for a safe and prosperous place to raise his children. But it's becoming clear that in this paradise on the Pacific, all is not as advertised. The tourist brochures and magazine articles that have attracted settlers from Hong Kong, India, and Singapore may dwell on the city's scenery, but they inevitably fail to mention that it is also home to a burgeoning Caucasian underclass. What's at work is a disturbing social trend: while 41,252 immigrants from around the world came to B.C. in 1994—by far the nation's wealthiest immigrants—almost as many, 38,649, came from other Canadian provinces. Many of these "in-migrants" were poor—and most of them were white. Alongside peaceful residential neighbourhoods, the city's swollen welfare rolls and overflowing skid-road bars are breeding a Caucasian criminal class with no scruples about the race of their victims.

It's long been a truism among criminologists that, in Canadian prisons, white faces tend to outnumber those of visible minorities. Statistics released by the Correctional Service of Canada show that Caucasian Canadians are regularly overrepresented in federal pens. In British Columbia's penitentiaries, where 2,114 prisoners are incarcerated, 1,573—or 74 percent—are Caucasian. People of Asian descent, who account for 11 percent of B.C.'s population, account for only four percent of the province's federal prisoners. Nationwide, the figures are even more telling: although only one in a hundred prisoners is Asian, fully 80 percent are white. These unsettling statistics are finally forcing observers and experts to ask some tough questions. Why do so many whites turn to crime, and in numbers out of all proportion to their representation in the population at large? Is it merely a cultural failing—a lack of morality in a group for whom family values and tradition are falling by the wayside—or, more ominously, is it something genetic, an innate propensity toward crime?

Can anything be done about these monsters in our midst? . . .

The Writing Workshop

ANONYMOUS

This following gem has been making the rounds on the Internet humour sites for years. It purports to be a chain exercise between two creative writing students; Rebecca writes an introductory paragraph to a story that Gary continues. After a few minutes, Gary returns the story to Rebecca, who fashions another link in the chain, until a story is slowly built just as a tennis game is created through the volleys between its players. Whether real event or fiction, it nicely dramatizes the differences between two hard-to-reconcile genres: the women's novel and science fiction. The first is introspective, emotional, domestic in scope, structured around memory, designed for a feminine audience; the second is extroverted, action oriented, futuristic, technological, galactic in scale, geared for a masculine readership. The humour arises partly because Gary and Rebecca each emulate their styles particularly well, but the real kick comes as each refuses to bend the rules of their preferred genre to make a coherent story. They remain, unapologetically, genre purists.

Each person will pair off with the person sitting to his or her immediate right. One of you will then write the first paragraph of a short story.

The partner will read the first paragraph and then add another paragraph to the story. The first person will then add a third paragraph, and so on back and forth. Remember to reread what has been written each time in order to keep the story coherent. The story is over when both agree a conclusion has been reached.

At first, Laurie couldn't decide which kind of tea she wanted. The chamomile, which used to be her favorite for lazy evenings at home, now reminded her too much of Carl, who once said, in happier times, that he liked chamomile. But she felt she must now, at all costs, keep her mind off Carl. His possessiveness was suffocating, and if she thought about him too much, her asthma started acting up again. So chamomile was out of the question.

Meanwhile, Advance Sergeant Carl Harris, leader of the attack squadron now in orbit over Skylon 4, had more important things to think about than the neurosis of an air-headed asthmatic bimbo named Laurie whom he had spent one sweaty night with over a year ago. "A.S. Harris to Geostation 17," he said into his transgalactic communicator. "Polar orbit established. No sign of resistance so far . . ." But before he could sign off, a bluish particle beam flashed out of nowhere and blasted a hole through his ship's cargo bay. The jolt from the direct hit sent him flying out of his seat and across the cockpit.

He bumped his head and died almost immediately, but not before he felt one last pang of regret for psychologically brutalizing the one woman who had ever had feelings for him. Soon afterwards, Earth stopped its pointless hostilities towards the peaceful farmers of Skylon 4. "Congress Passes Law Permanently Abolishing War and Space Travel," Laurie read in her newspaper one morning. The news simultaneously excited her and bored her. She stared out the window, dreaming of her youth—when the days had passed unhurriedly and carefree, with no newspapers to read, no television to distract her from her sense of innocent wonder at all of the beautiful things around her. "Why must one lose one's innocence to become a woman?" she pondered wistfully.

Little did she know, but she has less than 10 seconds to live. Thousands of miles above the city, the Anu'udrian mothership launched the first of its lithium fusion missiles. The dim-witted wimpy peaceniks who pushed the Unilateral Aerospace Disarmament Treaty through Congress had left Earth a defenseless target for the hostile alien empires who were determined to destroy the human race. Within two hours after the passage of the treaty the Anu'udrian ships were on course for Earth, carrying enough firepower to pulverize the entire planet. With no one to stop them, they swiftly initiated their diabolical plan. The lithium fusion missile entered the atmosphere unimpeded. The President, in his top-secret mobile submarine headquarters on the ocean floor off the coast of Guam, felt the inconceivably massive explosion which vaporized Laurie and 85 million other Americans. The President slammed his fist on the conference table. "We can't allow this!! I'm going to veto that treaty!! Let's blow 'em out of the sky!!!"

This is absurd. I refuse to continue this mockery of literature. My writing partner is a violent, chauvinistic, semi-literate adolescent.

Yeah? Well, you're a self-centered, tedious, neurotic whose attempts at writing are the literary equivalent of Valium.

Asshole.

Bitch.

—The end.

CHAPTER

7

Media

"The medium is the message."

—Marshall McLuhan

We gather information through a cornucopia of sources, including books, public forums, television, DVDs, newspapers, radio and the Internet. Each of these forms has a physical character that influences and limits the data it contains. If we want to better understand our world, we have to recognize the way each medium distorts and influences our perceptions.

This chapter starts by examining two media institutions: the newspaper and the evening TV news. Although vital arteries of information, these media have built-in biases that distort the facts. In contrast, the Internet holds the potential to challenge the current news monopoly, but it's a medium with its own troubles. This chapter concludes by offering some ways to evaluate Internet sources.

TELEVISION AND NEWSPAPERS

"Early in life I had noticed that no event is ever correctly reported in a newspaper."

—George Orwell

A robust press safeguards a free society, for it provides citizens with the intelligence needed to make informed decisions. Just as importantly, the press monitors government and industry, a watchdog that makes our culture more transparent, accountable, and democratic.

The news works best when it reports in an impartial manner, yet the structure of television and newspapers often warps the ideas mirrored there. The most obvious wrinkle is the profit incentive: the news business selects content that maximizes revenues and minimizes loss. Private ownership also gives the news a subjective bent. The brevity of column space or airtime further limits their ability to provide fair representation. Taken together, these influences make the news a rather dirty lens with which to view the world.

CONSTRAINTS OF SPACE AND TIME

A typical newspaper story runs between 400 and 800 words, a cap that limits its ability to present background, counterpoint, or analysis. Written according to the inverted pyramid schema, columns tend to place important facts near the top, so readers can get the gist in the first paragraph, without having to read the entire piece. In other words, journalistic news is designed to be superficial and disposable.

Televised news further constrains information, cutting stories down to as little as 30 seconds. This small window allows anchors to identify key names and dates, but precludes detailed discussion. TV reporters look for "sound bites"—punchy quotes with high intensity and low information.

Photos and video take more space away from analysis. Chosen for dramatic value, such imagery provokes a visceral response that biases rational judgment. In the case of television, the ratio of pictures to information becomes significantly lopsided.

The format of both televised and print news resembles MuchMusic: a rapid-fire collage of glossy visuals and lyrical riffs that stimulate and titillate, but don't cohere into an understandable narrative.

MARKET SHARE

TV and paper news strive to reach the widest possible audience, so they may justify high advertising fees (which forms the largest chunk of revenue streams). Market share represents the economic lifeblood of television and print, and both media scramble to increase their portions.

The drive for market share tends to degrade news quality in several ways.

1. In order to attract viewers, the news emphasizes stories of war, crime, assault, murder, and suffering. As the saying goes, if it bleeds, it leads.

    However, the focus on violence creates a very unrealistic version of society, making it seem more dangerous and criminal than it is. While the media gives undue prominence to tales of violence, Statistics Canada in contrast reports that our crime rate reached a 25-year low.

Fixated on mayhem, the media tends to overrepresent blue-collar crime, while underreporting white-collar and corporate crime. Embezzlement or tax fraud doesn't offer images as dramatic as assault or murder, so editors play down these stories.

While violence dominates the headlines, journalists and anchors seldom explain these crimes in a meaningful way. Typically, the news offers heartbreaking images, but little explanation or accountability. Instead, the news shows the calamity as random and unpredictable, a force of nature.

The recent coverage of the SARS epidemic exemplifies media scare tactics. In the first half of 2003, SARS received a phenomenal amount of news attention, with the *New York Times* running over 300 pieces on it in one month. *Time* magazine made SARS a cover story with the inflammatory headline "How scared should you be?" Although the media painted SARS as a global crisis, the facts around SARS proved more humble. The World Health Organization (WHO) reports 6903 cases of SARS worldwide between mid-November 2002 and May 7, 2003, with 495 deaths. In contrast, the WHO claims the yearly flu epidemic affects 3 to 5 million people, with 250 000 to 500 000 fatalities. Malaria and TB both kill as many as 15 000 people a day, and pneumonia claimed 62 000 victims in America in 2001 (Fumento). Yet, none of these familiar diseases received suitable media attention. SARS was new, mysterious, and exotic, so journalists turned it into a media event.

2. Entertainment has replaced information as the main substance of the news. The typical news-hour or newspaper fills space with movie reviews, crosswords, comics, relationship forums, horoscopes, gardening advice, lifestyles, travel tips, and weather reports. The sports report alone may take up one third of the entire news product. Such features engross, but distract from social issues.

3. In order to reach a wider audience, the news stays simple and accessible, tailored to a consumer with basic skills, but little technical or historical knowledge. The quest for a large market share "dumbs down" the discussion.

4. The news counters its horror and violence with fluffy feel-good stories, designed to reassure viewers that the world remains benign. Such cat-up-the-tree stories typically appear at the end of the news, leaving the viewer with a sweet rather than sour

taste. Local in scope, they create the illusion that home is fine, even if the rest of the world is falling apart.

5. Few people buy products that insult or depress them. Thus, news seldom examines the poor habits of its audience, let alone encourages meaningful reflection, especially about consumption. Consider the case of David Suzuki, a scientist who wrote an environmental column for *The Globe and Mail*. In it, Suzuki tended to make gloomy predictions, and press Canadians to change their wasteful ways. His column suffered a double whammy: it alarmed the audience and provoked guilt. When Suzuki's message affected the paper's market share, the truth was irrelevant. He was released.

6. Just as news dilutes its content for the average reader, so too does it pander to public morality, avoiding discussion of controversial topics that challenge community standards. The search for market share enforces a kind of normalization on the possible voices in the news.

ADVERTISERS

"Advertising is the rattling of a stick inside a swill bucket."

—George Orwell

Some newspapers have become so dependent upon advertising revenue that ads dominate their pages. Television and radio stations are in a worse state, almost entirely reliant on commercial sponsors for income. This dependence gives advertisers powerful leverage.

Afraid of losing ad revenue, papers, magazines, and TV stations seldom investigate stories critical of their sponsors. Kalle Lasn knows from experience that TV stations won't bite the hand that feeds them. Founder of the countercultural magazine *Adbusters*, Lasn produced a public awareness commercial critical of the automotive industry and tried to run it on CBC. To his dismay, the network refused to accept Lasn's money or air his commercial.

Lasn's case demonstrates the newsroom's ability to self-censor, but companies have been known to directly influence the news, squelching stories with the threat of pulled commercials or even lawsuits. Fox TV reporters Steve Wilson and Jane Akre discovered the extent of corporate influence over the news when they tried to run a story critical of rBGH, a synthetic hormone that stimulates milk production in cattle. Their report was never broadcast, because the manufacturer of rBGH, Monsanto, pressured Fox to drop the story ("We Paid").

News can't be independent if it relies upon sponsors' money.

NEWS SERVICES AND PUBLIC RELATIONS FIRMS

A newsroom churns out its product in great volume and at a hasty rate (up to four daily editions for a major paper; 24 hours a day for TV news such as CNN). This rapid-fire assembly constrains reporters to a fairly superficial coverage, and encourages owners to streamline production, lower costs, and centralize management. Budget constraints and profit incentive force newspapers to reduce staff, especially costly national and foreign correspondents, leaving a core of local reporters. To pick up the slack, newspapers use news services, such as United Press (UP), Associated Press (AP), the Canadian Press (CP), CanWest News Service, or Canada Newswire. These services provide stories, images, editorials, and even video news releases (VNRs) to newsrooms lacking resources.

The drawback of these services is the homogenization of the news. With a wire story, the public gets one version of events, rather than a healthy dose of competing viewpoints. Indeed, a newswire story may be repeated verbatim from coast to coast, becoming a *de facto* national account. By relying on news services rather than independent investigation, the press loses perspective and diversity.

Newswire stories have another problem: they're often anonymous and originate with public relations (PR) firms paid to promote corporate interests. These PR firms disguise their propaganda as news, because marketing seems more credible if it comes from a neutral source, such as an anchorperson or journalist. In this shill game, the public consumes promotional materials, believing it's disinterested journalism.

And the problem is big: a full 40 percent of all broadcast news can be traced back to PR firms or corporations themselves (Cutlip 210). Such a situation marks a shocking failure of journalistic integrity. Imagine if Exxon wrote the news reports on the *Valdez* oil spill in Prince William Sound, or Union Carbide the account of the disaster in Bhopal. Yet this happens almost half the time.

PRIVATE OWNERSHIP

The news is a public trust, but it's run as a private business that follows owners' interests. The control begins when the boss selects likeminded editors and reporters. If a journalist creates problems, the owner can discipline or fire the troublemaker, as former media mogul Conrad Black makes clear: "I am ultimately the publisher of these papers, and if the editors disagree with us, they should do so when they are no longer in our employ" (Russell).

Owners dictate not only staff, but news content as well, giving extensive coverage to stories in ownership's interests, and little or no time to undesirable reports. At times, the bias is subtle—in story selection, spin, and space allotment. According to Noam Chomsky, the news "manufactures consent" by offering a biased representation of the facts that lulls people into cooperation. Canada has a clear record of manufactured news. Owners of CanWest, the Asper family, directed its newspaper chains to print editorials in favour of Israel and big business. Owner of 55 B.C. newspapers, David Black ordered his staff to write no editorial favourable of the Nisga'a Treaty. And it happens abroad too. During the prelude to the 2003 invasion of Iraq, all 175 of Rupert Murdoch's newspapers printed editorials supporting military intervention ("Rupert Murdoch").

Only the very wealthy can afford to own a media conglomerate, so the news tends to take a pro-business perspective. This capitalist bias affects the representation of everything from the environment to technology, from socialized medicine to education, from nuclear power to militarization.

Not surprisingly, the chain of command discourages reporters from investigating stories critical of their parent corporation. The multinationals that own NBC and CBS, for example, also manufacture weapons and nuclear devices, so few journalists explore these taboo subjects. If passive dissuasion proves ineffective, the head office may directly order a journalist to drop troublesome stories. When ABC merged with Disney, for example, executives ordered the news department to stop investigating alleged pedophilia at a Disney theme park, as well as unfair labour practices at a Disney factory in Haiti (Sullivan).

The problem has worsened lately because of media concentration (euphemistically called "convergence" or "synergy"). After 15 years of mergers and takeovers, local news outlets are disappearing, swallowed up by larger, Borg-like media conglomerates. We now have more media choices, but ironically these rest in fewer hands. The independent daily newspaper has vanished entirely from the Canadian market, taking with it the benefits of competition and diversity. In Canada, the three largest newspaper chains control 74 percent of daily distribution, with CanWest Global controlling 40 percent of all circulation ("Campaign"). The situation doesn't improve when we include other news forms. A mere five companies own 84 percent of all media in Canada ("Journalists Question"). The FCC recently relaxed regulations preventing corporations from owning both newspapers and television networks—a change that accelerates the rate of media concentration. In the U.S., a meagre four corporations control the major TV news: General Electric, Westinghouse, ABC/Disney, and AOL/Time Warner. While not yet a monopoly, such concentration means a reduction in voices—more people reading the same ideas.

RECOGNIZING MEDIA BIAS

Here's a short list of the ways media "massages" facts.

CENSORED AND UNREPORTED STORIES

Editors choose to cover or ignore stories. They bury reports harmful to corporate interests in the back pages, or don't print them at all. The day's most important news often receives no coverage at all.

REPEATED ATTENTION

If controversial stories are given scant attention, minor stories can become central questions in the public's mind, if an editor gives them enough space or time. No matter how trivial, a story can become a public concern—and a distraction from real issues—if covered repeatedly.

SELECTIVE REPRESENTATION

Reporters create misleading stories if they offer only a portion of the facts or amplify inflammatory details. For example, coverage of the protests at the G-8 conference in Quebec emphasized the few acts of vandalism and glossed the vast majority of peaceful protest, creating a distorted view of demonstrators.

LACK OF CONTEXT

News reports, headlines, and sound bites frequently foreground dramatic elements, without providing background necessary to understanding a story.

MANIPULATIVE IMAGERY

Pictures have a powerful emotional force and often influence readers more than facts, especially if the picture presents a distorted image.

EMOTIONAL LANGUAGE

Connotative language creates unfair portraits. If a journalist describes the finance minister as "gutting" social programs, he or she uses a negative phrase that prejudices perception.

BIASED HEADLINES

Headlines have an undue influence on our perception of events because of their early placement, their oversized type, and brevity. Such sloganeering can be inflammatory and misleading.

LIES, ERRORS, OPINION, OR INNUENDO

Sometimes the news simply prints false statements. Before the first Gulf War, newspapers across North America ran stories about Iraqi soldiers stealing Kuwaiti incubators, leaving babies to die. Later, the story was revealed as a hoax, designed to foster support for the invasion. In the second Gulf War, stories of the heroic rescue of Private Lynch also turned out to be fabrications.

Opinion columns are good indicators of a paper's bias, for owners use them to directly manipulate public sentiment.

PERSON-ON-THE-STREET INTERVIEWS

Person-on-the-street interviews or "talking heads" columns create bias through the selection of speakers, who may voice a slanted range of ideas. People on the street aren't bound by journalistic constraints, so editors use these "talk-back" segments to say things journalists can't. Too small to be statistically meaningful, these samplings lack sufficient data to gauge public opinion.

INTERVIEWS

An interview can create bias if only one side of the debate speaks, or if one side receives a disproportionate amount of time.

THE EXPERTS

Bias can manifest itself in the choice of experts, specialists, or pundits. If the news allows one kind of expert to dominate discussion, the audience receives a lop-sided perspective. In its coverage of the 1991 Iraqi invasion, for example, TV news overwhelmingly turned to armed forces personnel for analysis. In the five months before the invasion, American news stations spent 2855 minutes covering the topic. Generals and other military experts dominated airtime, pointing out the strategic aspects of the battle, staying mum on human casualties and political alternatives. In contrast, news stations gave dissidents and conscientious objectors only 29 minutes of airtime (Briemberg 57).

The news tends to present "experts" as disinterested, but in reality they often have close ties to corporations, trade associations, or governments, and may receive money in exchange for testimony. The expert's opinion may be valid, but the public needs to know that his statement is a paid endorsement, not an impartial evaluation.

Obviously corporations and PR firms downplay the purchase of expert testimony, for an endorsement is more convincing if it seems unsolicited. Big money even sets up and funds phony research institutes—front groups—that pretend to be neutral players, but do little more than propagandize for business interests.

Even governmental experts aren't immune from market forces, as many public watchdogs receive funding from the businesses they supposedly monitor.

THINK TANKS

A new voice of authority comes from a creature called the "think tank," a term that describes a group of private individuals investigating and issuing papers on public policy. While the name conjures an image of free and fair-minded research, think tanks almost always have an ideological bent.

On the left appear think tanks such as the Canadian Centre for Policy Alternatives and Council of Canadians, which tend to pursue socially minded agendas. On the right, arise organizations such as the Fraser Institute and C. D. Howe Institute that extol free trade.

Think tanks are dangerous when the news presents their findings as disinterested. Many are little more than corporate front groups with a mandate to manufacture findings favourable to industry.

Thanks to ample corporate funding, right-wing think tanks vastly outnumber left-wing ones, swamping the airwaves with their findings.

THE INTERNET

If corporate megaliths dominate traditional media, then hope remains in the Internet. Designed to survive a nuclear assault, the Web is notoriously difficult to censor. With only a PC, an amateur can access vast caches of information, and circulate materials to millions of readers. The Internet offers the possibility of smashing the media monopoly over information, and realizing the dream of a democratic, informed society.

At least that's the theory. In practice, the Internet hasn't yet realized its potential.

Part of the problem rests in the Net's open and uncensored nature. Because anyone can speak in this virtual town hall, the Web has grown into a cacophony of voices, not all good. Some Internet materials are informed and professional; others are inaccurate, incomplete, and hateful. The challenge for the Web-surfer is to distinguish between reliable and unreliable information.

EVALUATING INTERNET SOURCES

Use the following factors to help distinguish trustworthy Web materials.

1. URL DOMAIN NAME

The URL domain name is the series of letters at the end of a Web site's home address. These domain names provide useful clues regarding the quality of information on any Web site.

> .com—commercial site run for profit
> .org—an organization, usually non-profit
> .net—computer network
> .edu—educational institution
> .gov—government site
> .gc—Canadian government site
> .mil—American military site
> .int—international site
> .ca, .uk, .jp, etc.—national domains (here, Canada, United Kingdom, and Japan)
> .bc, .nb, .on, etc.—provincial sites (here, British Columbia, New Brunswick, and Ontario)

Texts from government sites represent officially sanctioned sources, while texts from educational sites have academic safeguards. A paper from an .org listing isn't swayed by the profit incentive as a .com posting might be.

2. AUTHORSHIP

The credibility of an author is important in evaluating Web material.

- Is the material anonymous? Can it be confirmed or refuted?
- What biographical information does the site provide?
- Does the author have expertise?
- What affiliations does the author hold?
- Does the author provide contact information?

Author indexes, employment listings, bibliographies, periodical databases (such as Academic Search Premier), government databases, reference guides (like *Who's Who*), and Google searches can provide helpful biographical information.

3. HOSTS, SPONSORS, AND ENDORSEMENTS

Many Web sites receive funding or endorsements from other institutions or companies. Such relationships say much about a Web site's credibility, especially if it's affiliated with problematic groups. Keep in mind the following.

- Who's hosting or sponsoring the site?
- What's the relationship between sponsor/host and author?
- Is the host or sponsor reputable?
- Does the sponsorship jeopardize the site's neutrality?

4. PURPOSE

The purpose of a Web site provides crucial information for evaluating quality.

- Is the purpose informative, persuasive, expressive, entertaining, commercial, or other?
- Is the page selling something?
- Is the page opinion disguised as fact?

5. QUALITY OF INFORMATION

A skeptical reader appraises the quality evidence on a Web site, asking basic questions such as:

- Does the Web site offer sufficient proof?
- Are all facets of the topic addressed?
- How extensive is the database?
- How was the data gathered?
- How many primary vs. secondary sources are used?
- Can the information be verified?
- Is the information current?
- Has the material been reviewed or peer-edited?

One should view warily Web texts that use the following:

- Generalizations and vague claims
- Name calling or bias
- Missing dates or documentation
- Dated information
- Dubious sources or referrals
- Anonymous sources
- One-sided reporting
- More images than information
- More secondary than primary sources

A new Internet genre, blogs, are online diaries that record people's thoughts, feelings, experiences and opinions. The power of a blog lies in its availability to everyone. The drawback of the blog lies in its limited scope and single perspective.

6. LINKS

The "links" or "friends" section of a Web site provides a glimpse into an author's affiliations and community.

- Does the author link to reputable or problematic sites?
- Is the author repeating ideas from another site?

Works Cited

Briemberg, Mordecai. "More Than Censorship, More Than Imbalance." *It Was, It Was Not: Essays & Art on the War Against Iraq.* Vancouver: New Star Books, 1992. 57–60.

The Campaign for Press and Broadcasting Freedom. "Campaign Statement." Mar. 28, 2004. <http://www.presscampaign.org/statement.htm>.

Cutlip, Scott. *The Unseen Power: Public Relations: A History.* Hillsdale, New Jersey: Lawrence Erlbaum Associates, Inc., 1994.

Fumento, Michael. "SARS Hysteria Must End." May 8, 2003. <http:/www.fumento.com/disease/scrippsars.html>.

"Journalists Question Media Ownership in Canada." *The Dominion.* Nov. 10, 2003. April 5, 2004. <http://dominionpaper.ca/accounts/2003/11/10/journalist.html>.

"Rupert Murdoch." *Wikipedia: The Free Encyclopedia.* April 29, 2004. <http://en.wikipedia.org/wiki/Rupert_Murdoch>.

Statistics Canada. "Crime in Canada." April 5, 2004. <http://142.206.72.67/04/04b/04b_002_e.htm>.

Sullivan, Barry. "Update—ABC Pulls Disney Pedophile Story." April 5, 2004. <http://www.cnsnews.com/indepth/archive/199810/IND19981014g.html>.

Russell, Frances. "Laying Down the Liberal law." *Winnipeg Free Press* July 5, 2002. May 14, 2004. <http://www.canadiandimension.mb.ca/extra/d0716fr.htm>.

"We Paid $3 Billion for These Stations. We'll Decide What the News Is." *Extra! Update* June 1998. May 14, 2004. <http://www.fair.org/extra/9806/foxbgh.html>.

Exercises

1. List the local and global stories you feel a newspaper should address. Rank them. Next, bring in a daily newspaper such as *The National Post* and judge how it covers these issues. Are stories omitted or given undue prominence? Why?
2. Choose a news story that demonstrates bias. Document the various ways in which the story places a spin on events.
3. Choose a think tank such as the Fraser Institute or Heritage Foundation and research it. Evaluate its policy positions and

papers for bias. Is there a consistent pattern in their rhetoric and findings? Where does the group receive its funding?
4. Trace an anonymous news service story back to its source. If possible, find out who wrote it and what influenced the story.
5. Research a local news issue. When you've attained a level of expertise on the issue, choose a newspaper article or TV show on the same subject. Evaluate the news story, paying attention to its depth of information. Is it complete? Fair? Balanced?
6. Investigate the ownership of a news conglomerate. What companies do they own? What might their interests be? Who advertises with them? How does the paper filter content according to corporate interests?

Deception

DAVID MODEL

A professor of political science and economics, David Model works at Seneca College. He is also author of *People Before Profits*. In this selection from his book *Corporate Rule*, Model looks at the adverse effect that the profit incentive, private ownership, and media concentration have on the news industry.

> The media serve the interests of state and corporate power, which are closely interlinked, framing their reporting and analysis in a manner supportive of established privilege and limiting debate and discussion accordingly.
>
> —Noam Chomsky

One of the major challenges of the corporate elite is to win approval for neoliberal policies that are not in the public interest. By winning approval, powerful interests are able to avoid an uprising from those who are harmed by these policies.

In totalitarian states, the State controls information either through force or through control of all sources of information. The population can be easily indoctrinated through the propaganda of the state. For example, in the former Soviet Union, the State owned all the newspapers and television stations and those caught with banned books were imprisoned. Hitler's youth is another example of the power of propaganda. The irony is that people in Canada and the United States are also subject to propaganda but in a much subtler form. Those who seek to indoctrinate us are invisible and the means is not force but an almost monopolistic control over the channels through which we obtain our information.

There are major differences between a totalitarian State and a democracy such as Canada. In a totalitarian state, force is used to suppress dissenting points of view and those caught with underground literature are imprisoned. In Canada, enormous amounts of capital are needed to start a newspaper or television network capable of reaching a mass audience. Those with sufficient capital are members of the corporate elite and their newspapers and television networks expose us to the propaganda of neoliberalism. A major difference between Canada, or the United States, and a totalitarian State is that there are alternate sources of information for those who seek a comprehensive, accurate view of issues.

The problem is that few people are aware of the one-sidedness of the mass media and are not aware of the alternate sources. The result is that most people are exposed to a narrow range of opinions and are easy targets for propaganda. James Winter, in *Democracy's Oxygen,* observes that:

> Despite the fact that the news media are owned by a small portion of the corporate elite, members of the public generally do not view media content as reflecting corporate interests . . . people tend to regard the media as reasonably objective entities, which, in most instances, present a fairly diverse spectrum of views.

In fact, the range of opinions found in the mass media is fairly narrow. As members of the corporate elite, the owners of media conglomerates have a vested interest in persuading the public to accept neoliberal policies. The following characteristics of the mass media deny the public the opportunity to have a comprehensive, accurate, and in-depth understanding of issues:

- Filtering of news: only allowing some information to reach the public.
- Framing information: giving a story a particular slant.
- Underreporting stories: important news stories that do not receive coverage proportional to the significance of the story.
- Missing stories: important stories that are not reported at all.
- News value: the need to attract a large readership or audience and therefore the need to make news entertaining.

- A lack of investigative stories: a shortage of reporters to investigate important issues.
- Reliance on other sources: most news outlets cannot afford foreign correspondents and hence rely on large newspapers such as the *New York Times* or news services.

Although reporting the news is very one-sided in Canada and the United States, some of the major newspapers offer alternate points of view in the editorial sense, but overall the propaganda machine of the corporate elite shapes the public's views. I am not suggesting, however, a conspiracy theory that is often invoked to challenge the idea of corporate propaganda. Such challenges are guilty of the "straw man" fallacy in which a false argument is set up that can be easily shot down. If indoctrination depended on a conspiracy among the ruling class, then the argument for a systematic bias in the media is an easy argument to refute. It would be silly to postulate that corporate barons meet behind closed doors to plot their strategy. The fact is that the owners of the mass media conglomerates all have the same vested interest in maintaining the status quo that serves their interests. They have no need to conspire. Their common interest results in more or less the same news stories. There are differences of opinion in different newspapers and television networks but the differences are often about tactical issues or about side issues, but rarely about basic assumptions about the social and economic system. The point is to indoctrinate people continuously until neoliberal beliefs about the world become background assumptions. The advantage of background assumptions is that by their very nature they are not challenged, they are just assumed to be true. Such assumptions include materialism, consumerism, privatization, deregulation, the market system, and democracy in its present form. They are a major determining factor in what we are willing to believe about how our society functions.

An examination of the media must begin with the distinction between the mainstream media and the alternate media. The mainstream media are owned by large corporations and depend on large corporations for advertising. Therefore it is not surprising that the mainstream media reflects the values of the owners and advertisers. The alternate media are not owned by large corporations and do not depend on large corporations for advertising.

Two royal commissions have been appointed by the Canadian government to investigate the growing concentration of the media and its impact. In 1970 the Special Committee on Mass Media, chaired by Senator Keith Davey, concluded that "What matters, is the fact that control of the media is passing into fewer and fewer hands, and that the experts agree that this trend is likely to continue and perhaps accelerate . . . The country should no longer tolerate a situation where the public interest in so vital a field as information is dependent on the greed or goodwill of an extremely privileged group of businessmen" (Ottawa, Queen's Printer). The second royal commission appointed in 1981 and chaired by Tom Kent was called The Kent Royal Commission on Newspapers. It concluded that:

> In a country that has allowed so many newspapers to be owned by a few conglomerates, freedom of the press means, in itself, only that enormous influence without responsibility is conferred on a handful of people. (Ottawa, Ministry of Supply and Services)

Both these commissions were studying newspapers before the media behemoths of today reduced the number of major competing chains to a mere handful. One point that escapes the attention of those who believe that diversity in the media exists is the fact that as long as the media are owned by large corporations that depend on other corporations for advertising, diversity is irrelevant. Whatever diversity exists, there will be the same corporate view of the world reflected in the news.

Noam Chomsky is the Institute Professor, Department of Linguistics, at the Massachusetts Institute of Technology and extolled by the *New York Times* as "one of the greatest intellectuals of our times." Edward Herman is Institute Professor of Finance at the Wharton School of the University of Pennsylvania. In their book *Manufacturing Consent* they talk about the need of established power to persuade the public to accept policies that are not in their interest and to "manufacture consent" for these policies.

The authors created a propaganda model to understand the means by which information is filtered to only allow information favourable to the corporate owners and advertisers to reach the public. These filters are applied to the major media in the United States to demonstrate the extent to which the news reflects the values of the corporate elite. These five filters are:

- Ownership
- Advertising
- Official Sources
- Flak
- Marginalizing Dissent

I have changed their fifth filter from anti-communism to marginalizing dissent because communism is no longer a major factor in the global military and economic system. Anti-communism was a way of discrediting dissenting voices. I have simply generalized the category to all methods used to discredit dissenting voices.

As predicted by the Davey Commission, the concentration of ownership in the media is growing at an alarming pace. These empires not only reduce the number of voices but also create cross-ownership. Cross-ownership means that one company may own not only newspapers but also a television network, a publishing house, a Hollywood studio and also companies that are not part of the media or entertainment industry.

The Irving family in New Brunswick controls an empire that not only includes a huge media empire but also economic interests. The following table describes the Irving Empire (all in New Brunswick).

CANADIAN MEDIA CORPORATIONS

IRVING EMPIRE

Dailies	Radio Stations	Other Economic Interests
Telegraph Journal	CHSJ-FM	Lumber Business
The Daily Gleaner	CHTD-FM	Paper Mill
Times & Transcript	CHWV-FM	Trucking Company
Time Globe	CKBW-FM	Woodland Ownership
Carleton Victoria Advertiser		Gas Stations
L'Etoile		Inter-city Buses
Oromocto		Shipyards
This Week		Steel Mills
		Retail Building Production

How neutral and objective is the reporting of the news when control of the media and many other companies that employ one in every three working people in New Brunswick are owned by the Irving family? The Irving Empire is not unique in mixing ownership of media companies with ownership of other companies.

The media divisions of some of the other media empires in Canada are:

QUEBECOR

Dailies	Broadcasting	Printing
Le Journal de Montréal	Sun Media Corporation	Asie, America du Nord
Le Journal de Québec	TQS Inc.	Amerique Latine & Europe
The Toronto Sun		
The Calgary Sun		
The Edmonton Sun		
The Ottawa Sun		
The Winnipeg Sun		
The London Free Press		
Weeklies	More than 165 weeklies	

ROGERS

Wireless	Rogers Media Inc.	Publishing
Rogers Wireless Communications Inc.	Rogers Broadcasting Limited	*Maclean's*
		Chatelaine
Rogers Wireless Inc.	578223 British Columbia Ltd.	*L'Actualité*
	CHEZ-FM Inc.	*Canadian Business*
	Rogers (Toronto) Ltd.	*Profit*
	Wright, John P. (OBCI)	*Flare*
	Rogers (Alberta) Ltd.	
	Rogers (Toronto) Ltd.	
	Wright, John P. (OBCI)	

Specialty Services	Rogers Cable Inc.
Viewer's Choice Canada Inc.	Rogers Cable Atlantic Inc.
Outdoor Life	Rogers Cable Inc.
CTV Sports Net Inc.	Rogers Cable System Ontario Limited
Mystery	
The Shopping Channel	Rogers Ottawa Limited
	Rogers Cable System Georgian Bay Limited
	CPAC

CHUM

CHUM Radio

CFCA-FM Kitchener	CKLW-AM Windsor
CKKW-AM Kitchener	CKWW-AM Windsor
CFJR-AM Brockville	CKPT-AM Peterborough
CJPT-FM Brockville	CKQM-FM Peterborough
CFLY-FM Kingston	CFUN-AM Vancouver
CKLC-AM Kingston	CHQM-FM Vancouver
CFRA-AM Ottawa	NEW-TC Victoria
CKKL-FM Ottawa	CFST-AM Winnipeg
CHST-FM London	CHIQ-FM Winnipeg
CHUM-AM Toronto	CJCH-AM Halifax
CHUM-FM Toronto	CIOO-FM Halifax
CIDR-FM Windsor	CKGM-AM Montreal
CIMX-FM Windsor	CHOM-FM Montreal

(Continued)

CHUM (Continued)

CHUM Television

CFPL-TV London	City-TV Toronto
CHRO-TV Pembroke	CKNX-TV Wingham
CHWI-TV Pembroke	CKVR-TV Barrie

CANWEST GLOBAL

CanWest Global Communications Corp.

The National Post	*Windsor Star*
Halifax Daily News	*Saskatoon Star Phoenix*
Montreal Gazette	
St. Catharines Standard	*Calgary Herald*
St. Johns Telegram	*Edmonton Journal*
Ottawa Citizen	*Vancouver Sun*
Regina Leader Post	*Vancouver Province*
Charlottetown Guardian	*Victoria Times-Colonist*

CanWest owns 120 daily and weekly newspapers and shoppers in smaller communities. What follows is a partial list:

Halifax Daily News Group (6)
The Atlantic Group (21)
The Charlottetown Guardian Group (6)
The Summerside Group (6)
Montreal Gazette Group (2)
The Windsor Star Group (4)
The SOCN Group (14)
The Niagara Group (7)
The St. Catharines Group (12)
Vancouver Group (16)

[(x) = number of dailies, weekly newspapers and shoppers]

CANWEST TELEVISION BROADCASTING

Global Toronto	Global Calgary
Global Ottawa	Global Edmonton
Global Atlantic	CHEK Victoria
Global Winnipeg	CHTV Hamilton
Global Regina	CHBC Okanogan
Global Saskatoon	

BELL CANADA ENTERPRISES (BCE)

Teleglobe—World's largest international Internet backbone

Bell ExpressVu—Canada's leading satellite TV service

CTV—Canada's leading TV network

The Globe and Mail—Canada's leading national newspaper

Source: CRTC

AMERICAN MEDIA CORPORATION: AOL TIME WARNER

Networks	Publishing	Music
Turner Broadcasting*	Time Inc.	Warner Music Group
Home Box Office	AOL Time Warner Book Group	

Filmed Entertainment	Cable Systems	Interactive Video
Warner Bros.	Time Warner Cable	AOL Time Warner
New Line Cinema		Interactive Video

*includes TBS, Superstation, TNT, The WB, Cartoon Network, Turner Classic Movies, CNNRadio, CNN Headline News etc.

There are only a few media empires in Canada that dominate the propagation of news and information and cross-ownership is very common. The significance of "other economic interests" is that media conglomerates have an even greater vested interest in maintaining the status quo and advancing neoliberal ideology. In *The Canadian Corporate Elite*, Walter Clement analyzes the overlap of the corporate elite and media elite and concludes that:

> Actually, the overlap with the economic elite is extensive, almost one-half the members are the same people. Moreover, those not overlapped resemble very closely the economic elite. The conclusion must be that together the economic and media elite are simply two sides to the same upper class; between them they hold two of the key sources of power— economic and ideological—in Canadian society and form the corporate elite.

Furthermore, Clement wrote his book in 1986 long before the huge takeovers of the media by massive conglomerates.

Owners of these media empires indirectly exercise control over the content of news and commentary. The top executives in these media conglomerates hire publishers and news producers who share the same basic worldview. In *The Missing News*, the authors note that:

> Because commercial media are privately owned, profit-oriented corporations, it is no surprise that ownership ultimately determines key hiring and resource allocation decisions, and that management is accountable primarily to the dominant shareholders rather than to the audience or the working journalists.

One of the classic studies of the media, *The Media Monopoly*, written by Ben H. Bagdikian reports that "it is a rare corporation that appoints a leader considered unsympathetic to the desires of the corporation." Publishers often hire or promote editors who reflect their views and journalists who write "unacceptable" reports or columns risk their careers. These reporters are less likely to be promoted, get the good assignments, or even remain on the job.

Reporters often exercise self-censorship in the knowledge that certain stories or perspectives would be unacceptable to the owners. During the Free Trade debate in Canada preceding and during the 1988 federal election, reporters for the *Toronto Star* knew very well that their newspaper strongly opposed negotiating an agreement. On the other hand, reporters for *The Globe and Mail* knew that their newspaper strongly supported the negotiations. The *Star* was peppered with articles criticizing the agreement while the *Globe* was peppered with articles extolling the virtues of such an agreement.

An organization called NewsWatch conducted a study of journalists to evaluate their perceptions of media filters and blind spots. The directors of NewsWatch are also two of the authors of *The Missing News*. The study, based on a questionnaire of various groups in the media, found that among journalists:

> Nearly 52% of our respondents cited "Direct Pressure: Owners" as a factor that "often" or "occasionally" has the effect of "filtering the news" . . . almost half (45%) of respondents indicated the fear of reprisals from owners "occasionally" or "often" leads reporters to censor themselves . . . Viewed collectively, these results suggest—despite the profession's image of beholden-to-no-one autonomy—that many journalists do admit to feeling pressured to write and research their stories within certain constraints. The fear of alienating sources, owners, or advertisers can create a powerful "internal" self-censoring mechanism that can potentially influence which issues get covered and how such issues are framed.

Conrad Black is an example of ownership indirectly interfering with the production of the news. When he owned Hollinger before he sold it to CanWest Global, Conrad Black owned almost one-half of the daily newspapers in Canada. David Radler, president of Hollinger International, admitted that "I am ultimately the publisher of all these newspapers, and if editors disagree with us, they should disagree with us when they're no longer in our employ" (*Maclean's Magazine*, Peter C. Newman, February 3, 1992).

Another example of ownership interference involves an editor who worked for the Thomson newspaper *Cambridge Reporter*. Hollinger purchased Thomson. The editor phoned into *CBC Ontario's Radio Noon* phone-in to criticize the changes that occurred after the takeover. Although she had been an editor for six years under Thomson, she was demoted to reporter.

The media also play a major role in shaping the public's view toward changes in public policy. For example, the mainstream media played a significant role in frightening the public into accepting cutbacks to social programs to balance the budget. CTV's *W5* aired a documentary in February of 1993 comparing the debt crisis in Canada to the alleged debt crisis in New Zealand and warned the public that Canada was heading in the same direction. Also in 1993 the C. D. Howe Institute, a think tank created, directed by, and funded by large corporations, organized a forum for mostly bankers and brokerage houses to discuss the debt crisis. *The Globe and Mail* followed up with a front-page story "Debt Crisis Looms." The article further fanned the flames of fear about an imminent debt crisis with horrendous consequences. To add to the growing drumbeat for solving the debt by slashing social programs, *Maclean's Magazine* also ran a cover story. Between the media's coverage of the so-called debt crisis and business leaders warning of the dangers of not balancing the budget the public became convinced that it was necessary to slash social programs to avoid a debt crisis. Big business and their propaganda machine, the mainstream media, had sold an important element of neoliberal policies to the public.

The second filter, advertising, is the major source of revenue for broadcasting, newspapers, and magazines. All of the revenue for private broadcasting and 78–80 per cent of revenue for daily newspapers comes from advertising. The competition for advertising rates is partly responsible for the near media monopoly. As media corporations begin to earn high profits, they become attractive investments for other corporations. The need to appeal to mass markets "lends itself to increasing amounts of 'lifestyle journalism,' 'infotainment,' and celebrity-focused 'junk-food news,' at the expense of investigative and analytical journalism" (*The Missing News*). In *The Media Monopoly*, Bagdikian writes that the unseen hand of the corporation produces an "enormous increase in material of superficial content and minimal interest to readers but of maximum interest to advertisers."

The second problem caused by the dependence on advertising is the need to create a positive response to the advertiser's products. Advertisers want the media to create a buying mood that will induce the readers and viewers to be more receptive to the message in the ads and to eliminate controversy or partisanship to avoid offending the readers and viewers. "In the 'Total Newspaper,' [Doug] Underwood concludes, there is less space for nonconformity. When MBAs take over newsrooms, news outlets in the future 'will be less tolerant of oddballs and erratic visionaries—brilliant though they may be . . . The emphasis will be on collaboration, on building compatible teams, on taking fewer risks'" (*The Missing News*). Dissenters, critics and those who challenge conventional wisdom will not be invited to express their opinions. Dissenters will be effectively marginalized.

Another reason for the marginalization of dissenters and critics of the status quo is the fact that advertisers are also big corporations and the top management in these corporations will refuse to advertise in newspapers that threaten their wealth, privilege, and power.

Andre Prefontaine, publisher of the *Windsor Star*, pulled a column written by Gord Henderson which posed some questions about the fairness of Chrysler Corp. granting American executive bonuses ranging from 75 to 100 per cent of their salaries while workers were only allowed 1.5 per cent (*Democracy's Oxygen*). In 1994, the *Sunshine Coast News*, a British Columbia newspaper, published an editorial accusing local businesses of being lazy and one-dimensional. Following the cancellation of advertising, the editor and the reporter were fired and the paper apologized for printing hate literature, after which the advertising was restored (*The Missing News*).

Journalists have acknowledged that advertising has an influence on which stories they write and how they write them. In the study "NewsWatch," journalists believed that they:

> . . . increasingly have the feeling that their profession is under siege . . . it is also a question of changing priorities, for example, from serious news to less expensive "features" that are tailor made for advertising . . . It is also notable that a majority of journalists identified external pressures from owners, advertisers . . . This was followed by a 43% rating for "Direct Pressures": Advertisers. . . . Note that we are talking not about direct or open pressure from owners and advertisers, but something more insidious—journalists censoring themselves for fear of reprisals.

Objectivity and balance of news stories depends to a significant extent on the sources of information on which the story is based. If a reporter only interviews people with the same bias, the story will be one-sided. For example, if there is an accident at a nuclear power plant and reporters only interview people who work in the plant, the resulting reports would be very one-sided. To provide balance and objectivity, reporters would have to interview people from environmental groups and groups that monitor the safety of nuclear-power plants.

The "official sources" for much of the news in the mainstream media are people who accept conventional wisdom and the neoliberal philosophy. These sources include political leaders, business leaders, conservative academics, and corporate think tanks. There are a number of explanations described below for this propensity to depend on these sources.

Downsizing in media conglomerates has reduced the number of reporters available for investigative reporting. A lack of resources and the heavier load on reporters encourages them to rely on easily available sources such as government agencies, corporations, and think tanks that have a conservative bias. Government and corporations are recognizable, credible, authoritative, and appear to lend objectivity to news stories. The public is very hesitant to accept opinions from dissenting voices that need substantial proof to penetrate the background assumptions created by the mainstream media.

In the NewsWatch study, 80 per cent of journalists reported that "Too Narrow Range of Sources" is either "often" or "occasionally" a factor that leads to omission of news. Therefore a number of factors contribute to a dependence on business and political leaders as a source of information. The public is infrequently exposed to dissenting voices and is easily manipulated into accepting the corporate agenda.

In the campaign to persuade the public that the budget needed to be balanced by slashing social programs, official sources were an important factor. The Howe Institute contributed by holding a forum on the debt crisis that led to a front-page story in *The Globe and Mail*.

There are a number of think tanks in Canada including the business-friendly Howe and Fraser Institutes and the dissenting Canadian Centre for Policy Alternatives (CCPA). Both the Howe and Fraser Institutes are supported, funded, and directed by big business and promote the neoliberal agenda. They engage in research, publish papers, submit columns to newspapers, hold workshops on university campuses, and frequently appear as guests on panel shows. The Canadian Centre for Policy Alternatives "offers an alternative to the message that we have no choice about the policies that affect our lives." The board of directors includes activists, union leaders and authors such as Tony Clarke, Murray Dobbin, Earl Manners, Nancy Riche, and Heather-Jane Robertson. One of their most important projects is the Alternative Budget that receives input from a broad spectrum of civil society.

NewsWatch Canada conducted a study in 1997 to compare the access of right-wing and left-wing think tanks to the media. The study concluded that right-wing (business-friendly) think tanks had a:

> ... disproportionate amount of news coverage, more than three times as much as left-wing think tanks . . . In the second stage of research, coverage of the Fraser Institute (right-wing) and The Canadian Centre for Policy Alternatives (left-wing) was analyzed for the type and quality of coverage in the *Vancouver Sun* and *The Globe and Mail*. There were five times more articles about the Fraser Institute than about the CCPA, but the quality of coverage was similar.

The efforts of the Howe Institute were complemented by the *W5* documentary on CTV comparing Canada's economy to that of New Zealand. The *W5* program compared Canada to New Zealand in order to show that slashing social programs was the most effective strategy for resolving the debt crisis. In 1984, New Zealand had experienced a short-term currency crisis and was never in danger of "hitting the debt wall" or going bankrupt as Eric Malling of *W5* had suggested. "Its international credit rating by Moody's, one of New York credit rating agencies, never dropped below Aa3—the rough equivalent of an A–" (*Shooting the Hippo*). *W5* never allowed the truth to interfere with its determination to show that Canada was heading for the same debt crisis as New Zealand. The government of New Zealand had recently implemented the same neoliberal agenda as we did a few years later. The impact was disastrous for the people of New Zealand. When Eric Malling traveled to New Zealand to find the truth, he only interviewed those politicians and officials who were responsible for implementing the new agenda. These sources claimed that slashing social programs had been beneficial to New Zealand. Eric Malling did not interview anyone who could have reported on the negative impact of neoliberal policies in New Zealand such as increasing unemployment and poverty.

The fourth filter, flak, is a means of disciplining the media or reporters who dare to raise a dissenting voice, challenge conventional wisdom, or criticize the established order. The intent of flak is to create a deterrent to any further aberrant behaviour. James Winter, in *Democracy's Oxygen*, suggests that "one purpose . . . is to harass the media and put pressure on them to follow the corporate agenda." Think tanks such as the Howe and Fraser Institutes and the Business Council on National Issues monitor the media in the search of a left-wing bias. The purpose in accusing the media of being too critical of power or too oppositional leaves the public with the impression that they can rely on the media to monitor the establishment. The result is that the media gain in credibility and authority and the public is persuaded that they need search no further for alternate points of view.

One of the major weapons of flak is the threat of a libel suit. The fear of a libel suit tends to act as a constraint on the media leading to "libel chill" which encourages the media to be very cautious in what it reports. In *The Missing News*, this form of flak is defined as:

> One of the most important legal constraints which sometimes filter out public information . . . Even the threat of a libel suit can result in "libel chill" in the press, as media

lawyers advise extreme caution in stories that reflect nega-
tively on particular individuals . . . It is worth noting that it
is the wealthy and the powerful who have both public
reputations to protect and the resources to engage lawyers
to "chill" their critics.

An example of this type of flak involves the publisher Macmillan
Canada who asked Kimberley Noble, a *Globe and Mail* business
reporter, to write a book about companies owned by the Bronfman
family. The book was to be based on the award-winning story
about Hees International Bancorp Inc., a Bronfman company. The
president of Hees sent a letter to the president of Macmillan suggesting that some parts of the book would be actionable if published. The president of Macmillan quickly responded to Hees
International promising not to publish the book.

In a similar incident, the Reichmann family filed a multi-
million dollar libel action against *Toronto Life* magazine and writer
Elaine Dewar who had written an article about the history of the
family. The article was never published.

The first four filters are very effective in filtering out information in the media that opposes the power structure, dissents from
conventional wisdom, or criticizes neoliberal policies. There are
columnists with dissenting points of view who write columns in
the editorial section in many Canadian newspapers but they have
little impact on the public perception of the news. The reporting of
the news and the majority of opinion pieces in the editorial section
overshadow these columns.

As long as dissenting points of view or criticisms of the established order are only reaching small audiences, they pose no threat
to corporate rule. The reporting in the mainstream media still influences most Canadians and therefore corporate interests are safe.
The problem arises when one of these critics or dissenters is able to
reach a large segment of the public. If their arguments expose
neoliberal policies as an ideology that benefits only a few people at
the expense of the majority of people in Canada, then those with
power, wealth, and privilege will legitimately feel threatened.

The challenge in attacking the ideas and arguments of critics is
that their arguments may make sense. Challenging conventional
wisdom is a daunting task because of the need to convince people to
reject ideas that have been propagated repeatedly by authoritative
and credible sources. Nevertheless, well documented arguments
and sound reasoning pose a powerful threat. Since it may not be
possible to discredit the arguments of a critic who is reaching a mass
audience, those threatened can resort to ad hominem arguments

attacking the credibility of the critic. These sorts of attacks on the individual are very effective because the onus is on the subject of the attack to prove that it is not true. In other words, guilty until proven innocent.

The objective of these attacks is to convince the public not to pay attention to the dissenting points of view because their author is not credible. This strategy is referred to as marginalizing dissent, the fifth filter. For example, when Rachel Carson wrote *Silent Spring* in 1962 attacking the use of pesticides and DDT in particular, she posed a significant threat to the chemical industry. Her studies were sound but she was the first person to speak out on this issue and was therefore an easy target. *Reader's Digest* reprinted an article from *Time Magazine* with the title "Are We Poisoning Ourselves with Pesticides—Here are the reasons why 'many scientists . . . fear that her emotional outburst in *Silent Spring* may do more harm than good'" (Eleanor MacLean, *Between the Lines*). In 1962, women had not yet achieved equality with men. The reference to her "emotional outburst" was an attempt to create the impression of a hysterical woman expressing irrational views. Today, her book is considered a classic in the environmental movement.

A more recent example involves Linda McQuaig in her book *Shooting the Hippo: Death by Deficit and Other Canadian Myths*. In her book she documents very carefully how the monetary policies of the government and the Bank of Canada and their zero inflation policy which was initiated in 1987 were the real cause of the debt and not social programs. She also refers to a number of studies which confirm her conclusion. The government's policy to slash social programs to balance the budget was called into question by Linda McQuaig with well-documented arguments. Anthony Wilson-Smith wrote a review of *Shooting the Hippo* in *Maclean's Magazine* (April 10, 1995) in which he resorted mainly to ad homenem arguments. In the review, she is referred to as a member of:

> . . . a baby boomer generation that has wallowed in every kind of nostalgia . . . The 43-year-old author . . . will have to do better than repeat theories that were in vogue when boomers were younger, but which like mood rings, bell-bottoms and pet rocks have been discarded and discredited.

There is not one reference to any of her arguments or evidence in the review but only references to Linda McQuaig the person. The nearest Anthony Wilson-Smith comes to challenging an argument was his comment "but McQuaig . . . appears to see nothing wrong with the spending habits that led to the present situation." His comment misses the whole point of the book, namely that spending did not cause the debt. What is the relevance of mood rings, bell-bottoms, pet rocks, or the attitudes of her generation when they were young? In fact, the reference to pet rocks and mood rings is an attempt to make her appear silly. Also, to what theories of her generation was he referring? The entire review is an attempt to discredit Linda McQuaig, not her ideas so that people would not read her book. Bear in mind, that *Maclean's* ran a cover story on the debt crisis and the need to slash social programs. All these filters result in a very one-sided perspective of important issues and events. There is barely a dissenting voice or a critical murmur.

Other factors may also inhibit readers or viewers from being well informed and from having an in-depth understanding of issues. There was a time when news programs on television were not expected to earn money. As media conglomerates become a part of corporate empires, profits and capturing markets overrode the objective of informing the public. The predominant news value may no longer be an in-depth examination of events but a need to maximize profits and markets by enhancing the entertainment value of the news. Television news is packaged as a kind of show with handsome news readers, exciting music, and dynamic film footage, all of which contributes, to the entertainment value of the news. Neil Postman, in *Amusing Ourselves to Death*, concludes that "if you were a producer of a television news show . . . It would be demanded of you that you strive for the largest possible audience, and . . . you would arrive at a production very nearly resembling MacNeil's description [short, no complexity, no difficult concepts, bite-sized, and visual stimulation as a substitute for thought]." The result of the entertainment imperative in the production of the news is that complex issues such as deficits, trade agreements, tax policy are only covered superficially for fear that the audience will change channels. Drama, conflict, war, tragedies and celebrities are newsworthy. According to the NewsWatch study, "55% of respondents [journalists] felt that pressure to 'Attract Particular Audiences' for their employers 'occasionally' or 'often' limits the kinds of stories which get covered."

Other problems interfere with a comprehensive, in-depth coverage of the news. Downsizing has affected many newsrooms with the result that there are not enough reporters to do in-depth coverage of events or to engage in investigative reporting. *The Toronto Star*, one of the last holdouts in retaining a labour beat, finally dropped it resulting in a less balanced reporting on labour issues.

One-sided or inadequate reporting on serious issues poses a serious threat to a democratic society. Issues which have a major impact on peoples' lives are underreported, not reported, or reported from only one perspective. Without full and balanced information, it is impossible for citizens in a democratic society to make intelligent political choices. Noam Chomsky, in his book *Necessary Illusions*, added the subtitle "Thought Control in Democratic Societies" referring to the exposure of people to a narrow range of opinions which, in his words, is equivalent to "thought control."

There have been several studies in Canada that identify over-reported stories and under-reported stories. The over-reported stories tend to have more entertainment value and are often about celebrities. The under-reported stories often involve points of view that are threatening to the corporate elite. Project Censored Canada was created in 1993 to study the news that the media excludes or under-reports. A very rigid process was established to identify the 10 most under reported and over-reported stories of the year.

OVER-REPORT STORIES: "JUNK FOOD NEWS" (1995)

The O.J. Simpson Trial
Actor Hugh Grant Nabbed with Prostitute
Release of Microsoft's Windows 95
Dick Assman Promoted by Dave Letterman
Princess Diana's BBC Interview
The Information Superhighway
The Beatles' Anthology
The Paul Bernardo Trial
The 1995 Hockey and Baseball Strikes
The Toronto Raptors and Vancouver Grizzlies Join the NBA

Project Censored Canada identified the following under-reported stories in 1996:

• Social spending was not the cause of the deficit or debt. The extensive coverage of the need to slash social spending to balance the budget completely overwhelmed the critics of this analysis. Big business, including the media conglomerates, were campaigning for the cutbacks.
• The garment industry in Canada was exploiting home-based garment workers. Asian women and other Third-World women

were working in their homes in the garment industry for an average of $4.64 per hour with no benefits.

- The Canadian government and military hold arms bazaars where weapons manufacturers have an opportunity to display their military hardware for prospective buyers from other countries. The Biennial Abbotsford International Air Show, with 70 countries in attendance, was billed as family entertainment. Calling an Arms Bazaar "family entertainment" could be subject to criticisms for several reasons. Firstly, associating a fun event with the trade in weapons might send the wrong message to children. Secondly, it might raise questions about to whom Canada is selling arms. There were 300,000 visitors to the bazaar including 104 military participants. Canadians take pride in the role Canada plays in peace-keeping missions around the world but most are probably not aware of the fact that Canada is also one of the leading arms suppliers internationally, in fact, Canada ranks 7th in sales to Third-World countries and 10th overall in the world. For example, in Indonesia, General Suharto, a brutal dictator, killed 600,000 of his own people and committed genocide in East Timor. Canada developed strong economic ties to Indonesia and was more than willing to over-look his brutality for the sake of business. Furthermore, we sold arms to General Suharto who used his military to kill innocent people. In 1990, export permits for arms totaled $3.7 million dollars [and] included parachutes, aircraft engines, and airborne radar/electronic equipment. In 1996, Foreign Affairs Minister, Lloyd Axworthy, approved $32 million worth of military goods for export to Indonesia including armoured vehicles, aircraft components, and specialized military training equipment. In the case of Indonesia, we were selling arms to a brutal dictatorship that regularly violated the rights of its own citizens, and com-mitted genocide in East Timor. The Canadian media's coverage of the invasion and subsequent occupation of East Timor was shameful. When General Suharto visited Canada to represent Indonesia at the APEC conference, protestors were not allowed near him for fear of causing him discomfort and police used pepper spray on protestors. That was a big story. The record of Suharto was not a story. Business at all costs, even if it means supporting brutal dictators.
- A proposed U.S. environmental law that would lift protection for wetlands could harm Canada's air and water.
- When the federal government cutback transfer payments to the provinces, it opened the door for American-style health care in Canada.

- The U.S. was planning to conduct high frequency radio energy experiments in the northern ionosphere. These tests could have serious consequences for human health, the environment, wildlife, and the weather.
- New Zealand embarked on a campaign to balance the budget by slashing social programs and was held up as a model of debt reduction. The doubling of the public debt and rising unemployment in New Zealand were not reported.
- The violence at Kanaesatake between the Mohawk First Nations and various police forces was great drama for the television cameras but the root cause of the problem, the Indian Act, was not covered.
- The violation of Mexican human rights two years after signing the NAFTA agreement was largely ignored by the Canadian media.
- The Canadian Government undertook an expensive modernization program of its CF-5 jets costing $300 million and then scrapped them.

The need to protect political and economic interests largely explains why these stories were under-reported. There is no question that their impact on the audience is greater than the junk news stories, yet they were hardly a blip on the radar screen. Also the complexity and blandness of these stories detracted from their entertainment value and rendered them less newsworthy. Princess Diana is much more interesting than an arms bazaar.

Preface to *MediaThink*

JAMES WINTER

A professor of communications at the University of Windsor, James Winter is a media watchdog. Author of *Democracy's Oxygen: How the Corporations Control the News*, *Common Cents: Media Portrayal of the Gulf War and Other Events*, *The Big Black Book: The Essential Views of Conrad and Barbara Amiel Black*, and *Lies the Media Tell Us*, Winter also runs an online news service called Flipside. This selection from his book *MediaThink* looks at the way the media fostered support for an illegal and immoral war.

As the page proofs for this book were being prepared, two hijacked planes destroyed the World Trade Center in New York, while another crashed into the Pentagon in Washington.

Mainstream news coverage of the so-called "Attack on America" provided a classic example of the MediaThink phenomenon detailed in this book. Everywhere, Canadian news media emulated their American cousins, competing to be the best allies for the global policies of U.S. President George W. Bush.

Because of the grave consequences and ramifications of war, when one appears imminent it is the role of the news media to hold governments accountable to a considerable burden of proof. Possibly more so than at any other time, this is when news media must perform their much-vaunted "watchdog" function over governments. The press and the airwaves should be filled with questioning, challenges, and diverse viewpoints. In the public interest, no effort should be spared with respect to a full exploration of justifications and alternatives. This is if the media are to serve the public interest. If instead, they serve other interests, then things will be different.

In the aftermath of September 11, so uniform was the media perspective that it hardly matters which corporation you study. The *Windsor Star*, for example, carried barely a single critical word of objection (except for an occasional letter) versus literally hundreds of pages filled with faithful columnists, editorials and news stories championing the cause of war. The Montreal *Gazette* refused to run a mildly critical piece by regular columnist Lyle Stewart, who said in an email that it was cut "for reasons I don't completely understand."

The Globe and Mail carried a huge, 72-point headline the day after September 11, calling it "A Day of Infamy," using Franklin Delano Roosevelt's words about Pearl Harbour and indicating this was an act of war. The media drum beating saw them adopt a uniform logo ("Attack on America") and subsequent bellicose themes such as "America Fights Back," "America's New War," then "Operation Infinite Justice," and finally "Operation Enduring Freedom," much as they did in the Gulf War with "Operation Desert Storm." With the other topics in this book I have intentionally delayed my analysis for at least one or two years, to augment the potential for greater perspective. The publisher and I felt that owing to the importance of these latest events, some instant analysis is in order. An examination of the ways in which the media justified the policies of the U.S. Administration, is instructive. I will discuss these under six categories, beginning with:

WORLD WAR III

The media response was sensational, emotional, and repetitive, soon lapsing into persistent warmongering, clamouring for vengeance. Eventually, a few commentators called for calm and a measured

response: but most wanted blood. The same national security appa-
ratus which couldn't detect anything coming, could, within just a
few hours, identify Osama bin Laden as the culprit. Within a week,
George Bush was demanding bin Laden's head, as "Wanted Dead or
Alive." It was the return of the wild west. Soon, he would be heading
up a posse of high tech vigilantes, with a national lynching on the
horizon and nary a courtroom in sight.

Lorne Gunter of Southam wrote that "retaliatory measures
should be brutal against those directly involved, as well as against
those, like, for example, the Afghan government if bin Laden is
responsible."[1] Marcus Gee of *The Globe and Mail* wrote that the U.S.
wrath would "shake the world."

"Expect an all-out war on terrorism that will almost certainly
include some kind of U.S. military strike. Expect a far more
assertive United States, far more willing to throw its weight around
and far less likely to listen to the doubts of its allies on the United
Nations,"[2] Gee wrote. The way they listened to UN doubts over
Kosovo, for instance. Peter Worthington of *The Toronto Sun* attacked
George Bush's weak-kneed response. "Except for one line, George
Bush was more grief counsellor than warrior leader . . . Americans
want to fight back. So should we all . . . Damn caution. Fight
back!"[3] A column by Richard Gwyn of the *Toronto Star* was head-
lined, "Expect Americans to launch powerful anti-terrorist war."[4]
A *Toronto Star* editorial the day after referred to "an unparalleled
act of barbarism that Americans took as an act of war."

And the enemy was built up, just as Saddam Hussein's "battle-
hardened Elite Republican Guard" was built up before the Gulf War.
Toronto Star columnist Stephen Handelman wrote September 12,
"[the] U.S. administration will have to mobilize effectively for war
against an enemy that has proved himself as well-organized and as
efficient as any this country has seen before."

The media indicated that this calculated atrocity could only
have been carried out by one man: Osama bin Laden. Within just a
few hours they had zeroed in on him, and were running photos and
accounts of his alleged terrorism. The analogies to the Japanese
attack on Pearl Harbour, which drew the U.S. into World War II,
were rampant. While *The Globe and Mail* headline read, "A Day of
Infamy," *The Toronto Star* reprinted FDR's entire speech to Congress
after Pearl Harbour. Within the week, Defence Minister Art
Eggleton was quoted as saying, "I think [Canada is] going to play a
major role, a frontline role" in any military strike against terrorism.[5]
Later, as Jean Chretien scurried down to Washington to confer with
Bush, columnist Gord Henderson complained bitterly that Bush
didn't solicit Canadian military aid.[6] With "one of the world's most

illustrious military legacies," Henderson lamented, Canada has been "reduced by decades of government negligence" to just a "helpless bystander" during the "first great showdown between good and evil in the 21st century."

The presumption had been that any war would include Canada, of course. Graham Greene, an editor at *The Ottawa Citizen*, wrote, "the United States needs to know that its allies will stand with it, including militarily, if its retaliatory actions provoke a wider conflict."[7] *The Globe and Mail* editorialized that "Prime Minister Jean Chrétien should establish a 'war cabinet' of senior ministers and officials."[8]

The U.S. media were even more warlike. *USA Today* declared an "Act of War," while *The New York Times* proclaimed "World War III." And, it wasn't just a headline. Thomas Friedman asked in *The Times*, "Does my country really understand that this is World War III?" Detroit TV news anchor Carmen Harlan commented, "If this isn't war, I don't know what war is."[9] Within two days, *The Washington Times* decided it was "Time to Use the Nuclear Option." U.S. Deputy Secretary of Defense Paul Wolfowitz, spoke of "ending states who sponsor terrorism." R.W. Apple, Jr., wrote in *The Washington Post*, "In this new kind [of] war . . . there are no neutral states or geographical confines. Us or them. You are either with us or against us."[10] The analysts and commentators in the media bounced back and forth with the Pentagon, State Department and White House officials, exchanging and intensifying their hyperbole and rhetoric.

In *The Philadelphia Inquirer*, David Perlmutter demonstrated an understanding of recent historical events in Iraq, Bosnia, and Kosovo. He warned that if states allegedly harbouring terrorists do not do Washington's bidding, they must: "Prepare for the systematic destruction of every power plant, every oil refinery, every pipeline, every military base, every government office in the entire country . . . the complete collapse of their economy and government for a generation."

In other words, it will be similar to what they did in Iraq, and Kosovo. As Fairness and Accuracy in Reporting (FAIR) indicated, American media advocated pursuing civilian targets, contrary to the Geneva Conventions. Columnist Ann Coulter wrote in *The New York Daily News*, for example, that:

> This is no time to be precious about locating the exact individuals directly involved in this particular terrorist attack . . . *We should invade their countries, kill their leaders and convert them to Christianity.* We weren't punctilious about locating

and punishing only Hitler and his top officers. We carpet-bombed German cities; we killed civilians. That's war. And this is war.[11]

Over at *The Washington Times,* guest columnist Thomas Woodrow was arguing that it's "Time to Use the Nuclear Option," as to do less would be seen "as cowardice."[12]

In their thirst for vengeance and war, the media ignored or dispensed with international law. Gone were international boundaries, and the presumption of innocence until guilt is proven in a court of law. After a century of fuelling wars and coups, death and destruction abroad, a single attack on the domestic U.S. was enough to see this allegedly "civilized, free and democratic" country revert to the crude motto of: an eye for an eye.

WE ARE THE WORLD

The World War III which they anticipated was justified, according to the mainstream media, because what took place was not just an attack on three buildings in two American cities, but on the world itself. This is because the U.S. is not simply another country: it represents freedom, democracy, and civilization itself. *The Windsor Star* editorialized that:

> The real targets of the hijackers and their flying bombs were freedom, democracy, and capitalism ... It is time to draw a line in the sand. On one side lies democracy, individual freedom, and the capitalism that makes the two most essential qualities of life possible. On the other side lies terrorism.[13]

The Toronto Star said "The assault on America is a threat to every civilized nation."[14] Lorne Gunter of Southam wrote that "Nothing less than the western way of life is at stake."[15] Graham Greene of *The Ottawa Citizen* said, "this was not just an attack on American targets or U.S. citizens. It was well-planned and deliberate attack on the very essence of all truly democratic countries."[16] Playing the following week in his first game as a New York Ranger, the NHL's Eric Lindros told CNN, "We're all in this together. It affects all of us."

IT HAPPENED FOR NO REASON

In the mainstream media universe, whatever revenge would be taken was all the more justified because this was more than an act of violence: it was a senseless act of wanton destruction, gigantic in proportion. So, even though it was termed "an act of war," like Pearl

Harbour, it was an unprovoked attack which precipitated the war that would follow. The response to it would be an act of war, but not the terrorism itself, which if it was, would lend it legitimacy. In fact, it was a criminal act, for which the appropriate response was legal rather than militaristic.

There are no reasons because these people are fanatics. Paul Rosen, an invited guest on CBC radio's *Ontario Today* call-in program asked in response to a question about potential negotiations, "Can you reason with the Devil?"

To the media, like the U.S. administration, there was no precipitating act. It was unimaginable that there was any discontent with U.S. foreign policy. It was impossible that such a tragedy could be backlash for (nonexistent) U.S. aggression or economic exploitation. For example, Richard Gwyn wrote in *The Toronto Star* that, "It was done without warning, not in response to American aggression but as an act of aggression in itself." Editorially, the "liberal" and relatively "progressive" *Toronto Star* said that it's not even possible to imagine any justification. "Prime Minister Jean Chretien has rightly denounced this 'cowardly and depraved assault,' for which there can be no imaginable justification."[17]

Margaret Wente, former managing editor of the *Globe and Mail*, wrote, within 24 hours of the attack:

> Those who are responsible are most likely men from remote desert lands. Men from ancient tribal cultures built on blood and revenge. Men whose unshakable beliefs and implacable hatreds go back many centuries farther than the United States and its young ideas of democracy, pluralism, and freedom . . . Men capable . . . of giving up their lives for the greater glory of Allah. . . . Men . . . with the implacable determination of fanatics.[18]

The Globe and Mail editorialized, "This is a show of power and strength. It is a show of cold-hearted brutality perpetrated by fanatics who have discarded all pretense of humanity or morality." What's more, even if they did have "a foreign political cause, their campaign has now lost all international support and legitimacy."[19]

A *Globe* reporter in Calgary, Dawn Walton, wrote that her husband explained to their young daughter that "some bad guys . . . just wanted to hurt people" and that's why they crashed into the WTC.[20]

"Obviously [Osama bin Laden] is filled with hate for the United States and for everything we stand for . . . freedom and democracy," U.S. Vice President Dick Cheney told Tim Russert on *Meet the Press*, September 16. He went on, "It must have something to do with his background, his own upbringing." Or perhaps it was the support he received from the CIA during Afghanistan's struggle with the Soviet Union. According to the media, terrorists are merely a product of their own personal insanity. They are not seen in a global context where there are deep divisions between rich and poor; where wealth and power are concentrated in the hands of a few. Oblivious to these conditions and the true nature of U.S. intervention abroad, they can offer us no explanations.

Hence, as with Montreal Massacrist Marc Lepine, who murdered 14 women in 1989, it was an act devoid of anything other than personal context. Lepine was portrayed as a madman, rather than as being influenced by our anti-feminist culture.

ATTACK ON CANADIAN IMMIGRATION POLICY

The media renewed their ongoing campaign to get the federal government to tighten up on immigration policy. . . . Columnist Gord Henderson of *The Windsor Star* lambasted "Those weak-kneed decision-makers in the Liberal government and federal bureaucracy who let Canada become a patsy for potential mass murderers from around the globe."[21] Stewart Bell of *The National Post* said, "Through negligence and indifference, the Canadian government has permitted virtually every major terrorist organization to operate within its borders." Bell wrote that "Canada's vulnerability to infiltration by terrorists is deeply entrenched. Its refugee laws are probably the most lax in the Western world."[22]

Editorially, *The Post* said "Canada has been a porous staging area and conduit for terrorist conspiracies in the past. The Canadian government should not wait till U.S. authorities complete their investigation. They need to reform our immigration, refugee and visitor entry procedures now."[23] In its editorial, *The Globe and Mail* said that although the federal government just finished overhauling Canada's immigration rules three months earlier, and they were still before the Senate, they "should review the issue again with particular focus on the new war on terrorism."[24] The Senate was pressured to compact five weeks of debate on the new legislation into just four days. *The Toronto Star* quoted Jean Chretien, to the effect that "Perhaps there will be a need of changing some of the [immigration] legislations."[25]

REINFORCING RACISM

Media coverage was rooted in nationalism, patriotism, jingoism, but also racism. About 7000 predominantly middle and upper middle class, mostly White American lives are "worth" much more attention, grieving, and retaliation, than the 700,000 Iraqis who died during and since the Gulf War, or the 300,000 East Timorese who died since the Indonesian invasion of 1975, et cetera. Given the ease with which this information may be had, the media are willfully blind to these deaths.

In a revealing comment, a psychiatrist told *The Windsor Star,* "The people of America will now live with what the people of Israel have lived with for generations." No mention of the far greater tribulations the Palestinians have endured: they remain off the radar screen.[26] The coverage has not simply been racist: there are elements of classism and xenophobia, as well. And although some people from around the world were in the World Trade Center, and died, this event was significant not due to them but because it was an "Attack on America," and specifically on the monied, heartland of New York.

The racist coverage, lack of context, and other elements contributed to the backlash in which a Sikh Indian was murdered in Texas. *The Windsor Star* ran a wire service story which began, "Those who look like Muslims—but aren't—say they are suffering from angry fellow Americans."[27] But how do you look like a Muslim? What does someone who is Roman Catholic look like?

A DIVERSIONARY TACTIC

The glut of media coverage diverted attention away from the real "Attack on America," the attack on the working class and poor through elite policies which favour the rich. This takes the form of tax breaks, cuts to welfare, social programs, health and public education. "Right to work" laws are an attack on people, eliminating minimum wages, as are free trade policies which continually transfer jobs to the cheapest available labour market. There is also excessive corporate and individual profiteering. These policies have led to an increasing gap between the rich and poor.

The Attack coverage has rallied Americans and others to the cause, and led to a climate of emotional hysteria. In this atmosphere there is even less national and international monitoring of U.S. activities abroad. The U.S. Administration has capitalized on this hysteria to win funding and approval from Congress, and advance support around the world permitting forthcoming repressive and brutal acts which, like their antecedent actions, will far outweigh the effects of the hijackings. At this writing, the Taliban government in Afghanistan has asked Osama bin Laden to leave that country within a reasonable time period. They subsequently offered to turn him over to the U.S., in exchange for proof of his involvement in the September 11 attacks. But this response to the U.S. threats was juxtaposed against the irrepressible American war machine, which was already converging on Afghanistan, named "Operation Enduring Freedom" by the Pentagon, funded and approved by Congress, and condoned by ostensibly peace loving nations around the world. The response of the Bush administration was that they would "not negotiate" with the Taliban. They would not even provide the Taliban with the same evidence reportedly given to NATO, and other countries such as Canada.[28]

PROMOTING U.S. POLICIES

As evidenced by their early coverage of the "Attack on America," the media not only report on, but seldom stray from, the policies, statements and spin of the U.S. Administration and its client governments in Canada, Britain, and elsewhere. This may mean simply overlooking some things, or suffering from apparent historical amnesia, or adhering to what George Orwell called the "prevailing orthodoxy." This is what I have chosen to call "MediaThink." The consequences may lead, as in the current case, to amplification of the terror, horror and deaths. Rather than abetting U.S. geopolitics, in response to the attack on the World Trade Center the media might have chosen to demand that the U.S. cease and desist from the bloody international interventions it has perpetrated over the last century, from Cuba to the Philippines, from Guatamala to Kosovo.[29] Were the U.S. Administration to agree, I suspect that the violence would greatly diminish, along with the "blowback" terrorism (to use the CIA term) inflicted in response. Obviously, as the mainstream media are a crucial component of a global agenda which involves the U.S. Administration, transglobal corporations, the World Bank, International Monetary Fund, and others, it would be heretical, "suicidal" and perhaps patricidal for them to attack, criticize, or even differ with stated policy.

As with Orwell's Winston Smith in *1984*, severe penalties are in store for the foolish few who dare to stray from the one true view of the world handed down by our leaders. For example, Bill Maher, host of the TV programme *Politically Incorrect* wandered out onto thin ice when he ventured that, whatever you might think of the terrorists their actions were not "cowardly," as labelled by Bush and Co., compared with dropping bombs on civilians from great heights. Federal Express, and Sears Roebuck and Co. pulled their ads from Maher's programme, after indicating there were consumer complaints.

This censorship, trouncing of civil liberties and suppression of dissent, is nothing new. During the Gulf War, for example, at a war protest rally held at the SUNY college campus in New Paltz N.Y., professor Barbara Scott urged American military personnel not to kill innocent people. In the enormous brouhaha following the event, the media dubbed her "Baghdad Barbara," in reference to Tokyo Rose of WW2. Republican Senator Charles Cook went so far as to publicly accuse Scott of treason. Letter campaigns were aimed at the college president and then-Governor Mario Cuomo, urging them to fire Scott. Meanwhile, hate mail arrived at her office.[30]

In Canada, on October 1, 2001, University of British Columbia professor Sunera Thobani spoke out at a conference on violence against women, held in Ottawa. Dr. Thobani said the U.S. is "the most dangerous and most powerful global force unleashing horrific levels of violence." Although she empathized with the suffering caused by the September 11 attacks, she asked, "do we feel any pain for the victims of U.S. aggression?" The 500 women in the audience interrupted Thobani's speech with cheers and a standing ovation. But the media lapdogs leapt to the attack on this "feminist," and "former president of the National Action Committee on the Status of Women," condemning what they described as a "hateful, manipulative and outrageous rant."[31]

The National Post reached out to Gordon Campbell, premier of B.C., for his characterization of her remarks as "hateful, destructive and very disturbing," along with Alliance leader Stockwell Day and Gwen Landolt of Real Women of Canada, a reactionary women's group. Columnists such as Christie Blatchford and Claire Hoy attacked Thobani as "vicious" and "hate-filled" and a "bitter bit," and her audience as "collected wing-nuts." Because the conference received government funding, Stockwell Day said it was "unacceptable" for Thobani "to be saying the things that she did . . . at taxpayers' expense." He called for prime minister Chretien to inform the U.S. government that Canada repudiates Thobani's message.

Of course, there was no hatred in Thobani's talk, merely a call for peace and compassion for all victims.

In contrast to the corporate media hysteria, as did Sunera Thobani, the alternative media placed the terrorist attacks in the historical context of U.S. "interventions" abroad and aggression. While not excusing the terrorists, and also mourning the 7000 civilian lives taken, through the writings of Michael Albert and Noam Chomsky and others, Z *magazine*, Indymedia, etc., provided information which was crucial for understanding the events. In "Five Reasons Not to Go to War," for example, Michael Albert and Stephen R. Shalom argued that war would be horribly wrong for at least five reasons: 1. Guilt hasn't yet been proven; 2. War would violate International Law; 3. War would be unlikely to eliminate those responsible for the September 11 attacks; 4. Huge numbers of innocent people will die; 5. War will reduce the security of U.S. citizens.[32]

In sum, as indicated earlier, at times such as this it is the media's responsibility to hold governments accountable for their decision to go to war, to defend the public interest by providing intense scrutiny, demanding evidence and reasons, and displaying a wide range of diverse perspectives. This is a time for the adversarial journalism of the fourth estate: for watchdogs rather than lapdogs. Instead, the corporate media resorted to frenzied advocacy of an illegal vigilante war, promoting violence, hatred and blindness to reason. They have functioned, with few exceptions, as an extension of the U.S. administration, demanding a violent, vengeful and bloody war.

Reading Notes

1. Lorne Gunter, "Retaliation is a must," *The Windsor Star*, September 13, 2001.

2. Marcus Gee, "The sleeping giant wakes up angry," *The Globe and Mail*, September 12, 2001.

3. Peter Worthington, "America needs a leader," *Toronto Sun*, September 13, 2001, A7.

4. Richard Gwyn, "Expect Americans to launch powerful anti-terrorist war," *The Toronto Star*, September 12, 2001, A1.

5. Quoted in Janice Tibbetts, "What can Armed Forces contribute?" *The Windsor Star*, September 18, 2001.

6. Gord Henderson, "Canada as bystander," *The Windsor Star*, September 25, 2001.

7. Graham Greene, "Time to stand with U.S.," *The Windsor Star*, September 12, 2001, A7.

8. Editorial, "It's time to consider how best we can help," *Globe and Mail*, September 18, 2001.

9. Quoted in Ted Shaw, "TV brings terrorism home," *The Windsor Star*, September 12, 2001, A10.

10. These U.S. headlines and quotations are taken from, Jared Israel, Rick Rozoff & Nico Varkevisser, "Washington wants Afghanistan," www.emperors-clothes.com, September 18, 2001.

11. Ann Coulter, *New York Daily News*, September 12, 2001, quoted in FAIR, Media March to War, September 17, 2001.

12. Quoted in "Media pundits advocate civilian targets," FAIR, September 24, 2001.

13. Editorial, "Freedom: A struggle that involves us," *The Windsor Star*, September 13, 2001.

14. Editorial, "Democracy will prevail over barbarous hate," *The Toronto Star*, September 12, 2001, A26.

15. Lorne Gunter, "Retaliation is a must," *The Windsor Star*, September 13, 2001.

16. Graham Greene, "Time to stand with U.S.," *The Windsor Star*, September 12, 2001, A7.

17. Editorial, "Democracy will prevail over barbarous hate," *The Toronto Star*, September 12, 2001, A26.

18. Margaret Wente, "U.S. will never be the same," *The Globe and Mail*, September 12, 2001, Al.

19. Editorial, "Let loose the war on global terrorism," *The Globe and Mail*, September 12, 2001, A18.

20. Dawn Walton, "Explaining the day the bogeyman came," *The Globe and Mail*, September 12, 2001, A20.

21. Gord Henderson, "Shameful times," *The Windsor Star*, September 13, 2001.

22. Stewart Bell, "A conduit for terrorists," *The National Post*, September 13, 2001.

23. Ibid.

24. Editorial, "It's time to consider how best we can help," *The Globe and Mail*, September 18, 2001.

25. CP, "Bush summons PM to White House council," *The Toronto Star*, September 18, 2001.

26. Quoted in Don Lajoie, "Trauma to be felt for years, doc says," *The Windsor Star*, September 12, 2001.

27. Thomas Hargrove, "Backlash hits non-Arab minorities," *The Windsor Star*, September 18, 2001, A8.

28. In the article "Canada convinced," *The Windsor Star*, October 3, 2001, the newspaper quoted prime minister Jean Chretien as saying that he was convinced of Osama bin Laden's guilt, based upon the secret information provided to him by the Bush administration.

29. For a brief overview, since World War II, see William Blum, "A brief history of U.S. interventions: 1945 to the present," *Z magazine*, June 1999.

30. For more details, see James Winter, "Truth as the first casualty," in *Common Cents: Media Portrayal of the Gulf War and Other Events*, Black Rose Books, Montreal, 1992.

31. Mark Hume and Mary Vallis, "Thobani 'rant' called hateful," *The National Post*, October 3, 2001.

32. Michael Albert and Stephen R. Shalom, "Five reasons not to go to war," www.Zmag.org, September 21, 2001.

Ten Steps to the Creation of a Modern Media Icon

MARK KINGWELL

Mark Kingwell is an author, futurist, cultural critic, and professor of philosophy at the University of Toronto. He is the author of numerous award-winning books, including *The World We Want*, *Dreams of the Millennium*, *Marginalia*, *Better Living*, *Practical Judgments*, and *Catch and Release*. His writings often look at modern problems with an eye to the old Socratic question, "What is the good life?" In this piece, Kingwell suggests that television encourages us to be interested in the superficial qualities of appearance.

1. "Icon" is from the Greek *eikon*, which means "image," which is everything: The name of a camera. The word for all those little point-and-click pictures on your computer screen. Greek and Roman Orthodox religious objects. Little oil paintings of saints with elaborate gold panel coverings. Anybody who represents something to someone somewhere. The image that gives a debased Platonic suggestion of reality without ever being it. So create an image—one the cameras, and therefore we, will love.

2. The image must be drastically beautiful or else compellingly ugly. It must, for women, show a smooth face of impenetrable maquillage and impeccably "tasteful" clothing (Chanel, Balenciaga, Rykiel; not Versace, not Moschino, definitely not Gaultier), a flat surface of emotional projection, the real-world equivalent of a keyboard emoticon. Icon smiling at the cheering crowds: :-). Icon frowning bravely at diseased child or crippled former soldier in hospital bed: :-(. Icon winking slyly at the crush of press photographers as she steps into the waiting limousine: ;-). There should be only one name, for preference a chummy or faux-intimate diminutive: Jackie, Di, Barbra. Sunglasses are mandatory whenever the ambient light rises

above building-code-normal 250-foot candles. These can be removed or peered over to offer an image of blinking vulnerability. Or else the image should be, in men, so overwhelmingly tawdry and collapsed, preferably from some high-cheekbone peak of youthful beauty, that it acquires a can't-look-away magnetism, the sick pull of the human car wreck. (The only exceptions: (1) Athletes—Tiger, Michael—whose downy smoothness and transcendental physical abilities offer a male counterpoint that is almost female in appeal; they are the contraltos of the icon chorus. And (2) actors, whose malleable faces are so empty of particular meaning as to be innocent of intelligence.) Folds of leathery skin, evidence of drug use and chain-smoking, the runes of dissipation etched on the pitted skin of hard living— they all have them. Johnny Cash, Mick Jagger, Leonard Cohen, Kurt Cobain, Chet Baker, late Elvis: the musician in ruins, the iconic face as crumbling stone monument. Basic black attire is effective but must be Armani, never Gap. This suggests wisdom and sexual power, deep and bitter knowledge of the world—but with dough. The face need never change, its very stasis a sign of rich inner troubles. Sunglasses are superfluous. They smack of effort.

3. There must be a narrative structure that bathes the icon in the pure light of the fairy tale or morality play. Beautiful princess beset by ugly siblings or nasty stepmother. Lovely rich girl mistakes the charisma of power for true character. Overweening ambition turns simple boy into gun-toting, pill-popping maniac. Feisty rebel takes on the establishment of (circle one) Hollywood/big business/government/rock music/professional sports. Prodigy singled out for great things at an early age by psycho father. Indispensable words in the story: "trapped," "betray," "tragic," "love," "promise" (as both verb and noun), "happiness" (always without irony), "fame" (always with venom), and "money" (never spoken). The details of the story may change, but the overarching structure cannot: you can improvise and elaborate, but never deviate. Sometimes a new story (thrill-happy slut consorts with swarthy and disreputable jet-setter) will be temporarily substituted for an old one that no longer applies (virginal bride is unloved by philandering husband). We can't be sure which story will win out until . . .

4. Death. Already, at step four? Yes, absolutely, for iconography is very much a post mortem affair. The death ends the life but does not quite complete it: that is the business of story-tellers

and their audience, the cameras and their lights. Death is just the beginning. It should be, if possible, violent, messy and a bit mysterious. Unwise confrontations with fast-moving industrial machines—sports cars, airplanes, cargo trucks, high-speed trains, bullets. Accidents are good, having as they do an aura of adventitious innocence, followed closely in order of preference by murder, assassination, execution and suicide. If suicide it must be either a gun or an overdose of illicit drugs, usually in colorful and nasty combination: alcohol and barbiturates, crack and benzedrine, heroin and anything. In all cases, the death is "shocking" and "tragic," though in neither instance literally.

5. Now, an outbreak of hysterical mourning, baseless and all the more intense for being so. (Nobody feels so strongly about someone they actually know.) Extended retrospectives on television. Numerous panel discussions and attempts to "make sense," to "assess the life," to "provide context." Long broadcasts of the funeral or memorial service complete with lingering, loving shots of weeping crowds. Greedy close-ups of the well-known people in attendance, the bizarre fraternity of celebrity which dictates that those famous for being born in a certain family has everything in common with those famous for singing pop tunes or throwing a ball in a designated manner. News agencies and networks must spend a great deal of money sending a lot of people somewhere distant to cover the death. They must then justify that expense with hours and hours of coverage. We must see images of the iconic face, beautiful or ruined, over and over and over. "Ordinary" people must be shown, on the media, insisting that the media have nothing to do with their deep feelings of loss. They must say that they "felt they knew him (her)," that "she (he) was like a member of the family." This keeps them happy and ensures that no larger form of public participation—say, protesting a tax hike or program cut, resisting a corporate takeover—will ever cross their minds as possible, let alone desirable.

6. A small backlash must gather strength, a token gesture of cultural protest that, in pointing out the real faults and shortcomings of the dead icon, unwittingly reinforces the growing "larger-than-life" status of the image. This is the culture's way of injecting itself with a homeopathic inoculation, introducing a few strains of mild virus that actually beef up the dominant media antibodies. Those who have the temerity to suggest that the dead icon was not all he (she) is thought to be will be

publicly scorned, accused of cynicism, insulted at dinner parties, but secretly welcomed. The final storyline of the icon-life will now begin to set, rejecting the foreign elements as dead-ends or narrative spurs, or else accepting them as evidence that the icon was "after all" human—a suggestion that, in its very making, implies the opposite. The media coverage will fall into line in telling this story because individual producers and anchors will be unable to imagine doing otherwise. Tag-lines and feature-story titles will help set the narrative epoxy for good, providing catchy mini-stories for us to hang our thoughts on to. Quickie books with the same titles will begin to appear— things like Icon X: Tragic Ambition or Icon Y: Little Girl in Trouble. The producers and anchors must then claim that they are not creating this tale, simply "giving the people what they want." Most people will accept this because to do otherwise would hurt their brains.

7. The image will now be so widely reproduced, so ubiquitously mediated on television, at the supermarket, in the bookstore, that it seems a permanent feature of the mediascape, naturalized and indispensable. It will now begin its final divorce from the person depicted. Any actual achievements—touchdowns thrown, elections won, causes championed—fall away like the irrelevancies they are. The face (or rather, The Face) looms outward from glossy paper, T-shirts, fridge magnets, posters, Halloween masks and coffee mugs. Kitschification of the image is to be welcomed, not feared. It proves that the icon is here to stay. The basic unit of fame-measurement is of course, as critic Cullen Murphy once argued, the warhol, a period of celebrity equal to fifteen minutes. Kitsch versions of the image augers well: we're talking at least a megawarhol icon or better (that's 15 million minutes of fame, which is just over 10,400 days, or about 28.5 years—enough to get you to those standard silver-anniversary retrospectives). No kitsch, no staying power: a 100 kilowarhols or less, a minicon.

8. There follow academic studies, well-meaning but doomed counter-assessments, sightings, and cameo appearances of the icon on a Star Trek spinoff series or as an answer on *Jeopardy*. People begin to claim they can commune with the spirit of the dead icon across vast distances of psychic space. Conspiracy theories refuse to be settled by overwhelming evidence of a boringly predictable chain of events involving a drunk driver, too much speed, and unused seatbelts. Or whatever.

9. Television retrospectives every decade, with a mid-decade special at 25 years. The final triumph of the image: entirely cut off now from its original body, it is free-floating and richly polysemous. Always more surface than depth, more depiction than reality, the icon now becomes pure zero-degree image, a depicted lifestyle without a life, a face without a person, a spiritual moment without context or meaning. In other words, the pure pervasive triumph of cultural exposure, a sign lacking both sense and referent. In still other words, the everything (and nothing) we sought all along: communion without community.

10. Now, for a religious experience, just point. And click.

Watching the Eyewitless News

ELAYNE RAPPING

A professor of media studies at SUNY Buffalo, Elayne Rapping has published several books on television and media, including *Media-tions: Forays into the Culture and Gender Wars*, *The Looking Glass World of Non-Fiction Television*, and *Law and Justice As Seen on TV*. In "Watching the Eyewitless News," she examines how the format of the evening TV news limits and distorts the presentation of the facts.

Jimmy Cagney, the ultimate street-smart wise guy, used to snap, "Whadya hear? Whadya know?" in the days of black-and-white movies and READ ALL ABOUT IT! headlines. But that was then and this is now. Today, when gangsta rap has replaced gangster movies, and television has replaced newsprint as the primary source of information (for two-thirds of us, the *only* source), Cagney's famous question is not only antiquated, it is beside the point. What we hear when we consume "the news" has only the most marginal relationship to what we *know* about anything.

I'm not referring here to CNN or the "evening news" on the national broadcast networks. I'm referring to what passes for news in the homes and minds of the vast majority of Americans today: the *Eyewitless, Happy Talk* local newscasts that run in many cities for as much as an hour and a half to two hours a day, on as many as seven or eight different channels.

The rise of local news, the infotainment monster that ate the news industry, is a long and painful story about a key battlefront in the endless media war between capitalism and democracy, between the drive for profits and the constitutional responsibility of those licensed to use the airwaves to serve the public interest. We know who's winning, of course. The game was rigged from the start.

To make sure it stays that way, most members of the Federal Communications Commission are appointed—no matter who's in the White House—from the ranks of the industry itself. Indeed, if there is any phenomenon that gives dramatic support to Leonard Cohen's baleful lines, "Everybody knows the war is over/Everybody knows the good guys lost," it's the specter of local news, slouching roughly across a wider and wider stretch of airwave time, planting its brainless images as it goes.

Local news as we know it was invented in 1970, the brainchild of a marketing research whiz hired by the industry to raise ratings by finding out what audiences "wanted to see." The Jeffersonian notion that public media should cover what citizens "need to know" was not a big consideration. Nor was it a concern to respect the audience's intelligence or diversity.

The researchers offered a limited, embarrassingly vapid list of choices of formats and subjects, while ignoring the possibility that different groups might want different kinds of information and analysis. More annoying still, they ignored the possibility that individual views, of all kinds, might want and need different things at different times for different reasons. Nope, said the marketing whizzes, this master model of "The News" will buy us the most overall-ratings bang per buck. Wrap it up and send it out.

And it worked. Their invention has conquered the TV world. The sets, the news lineups, the anchors, the weather maps, the sports features—all developed for a New York City market—quickly became a universal formula, sent out to every network affiliate and independent station in America, complete with fill-in-the-blanks guidelines for adaptation to any community, no matter how large or small, urban or rural. Local news today is the single most profitable form of nonfiction television programming in the country and, for most stations, the only thing they actually produce. Everything else comes from the networks. As time went by, this tendency toward cookie-cutter formulas, exported far and wide from a central media source, reached ever more depressing depths. The trend has led to ever more nationally produced, generic features exported to local stations to be passed off as "local."

So today we have a phenomenon euphemistically called "local news," although it is anything but, filled with images of a pseudo-community called "America," which is actually closer to Disney World in its representation of American life. But why should that surprise us, in a national landscape now filled, from coast to coast, with identical, mass-produced shopping malls that pass for town marketplaces, and hotels and airports that pass for village inns? In postmodern America, after all, this kind of brand-name synthetic familiarity appears to be the only thing that holds us—a nation of endlessly uprooted and mobile strangers—together.

When you turn on the news, whether at home or in an airport or Holiday Inn in some totally strange locale, you see a predictable, comforting spectacle. The town or city in question, whether Manhattan or Moose Hill, Montana, is presided over by a group of attractive, charming, well-dressed performers—whose agents, salaries, and movements up and down the ladder of media success, gauged by the size of the "market" they infiltrate, are chronicled each week in *Variety*. They seem to care endlessly for each other and us. "Tsk, tsk," they cluck at news of yet another gang rampage or Congressional scandal. "Ooh," they sigh, at news of earthquakes and plane crashes, far and near.

If it bleeds, it leads is the motto of the commercial news industry and local news. Its endless series of fires, shootouts, collapsing buildings, and babies beaten or abandoned or bitten by wild dogs is the state-of-the-art showcase for the industry. As Don Henley once put it, in a scathing song about the local-news phenomenon, "It's interesting when people die." And it's especially interesting when they die in bizarre or inhuman situations, when their loved ones are on camera to moan and wail, when a lot of them die at once. And since so much of our news is indeed personally terrifying and depressing, we need to have it delivered as cleverly and carefully as possible. And so we have the always smiling, always sympathetic, always confidently upbeat news teams to sugarcoat the bad news.

Not that local news ignores the politically important stories. Well, not entirely anyway. When wars are declared or covered, when elections are won or lost, when federal budgets and plant closings do away with jobs and services or threaten to put more and more of us in jail, for less and less cause, the local news teams are there to calm our jagged nerves and reassure us that we needn't worry.

This reassurance is sometimes subtle. National news items typically take up less than two minutes of a half-hour segment. And what's said and seen in that brief interlude is hardly enlightening. On the contrary, the hole for "hard news" is generally filled with sound bites and head shots, packaged and processed by the networks, from news conferences with the handful of movers and shakers considered "newsworthy"—the President and his key henchmen and adversaries, mostly.

But even local issues of serious import are given short shrift on these newscasts. Hard news affecting local communities takes up only a minute or two more airtime than national events. And local teams are obsessed with "man-on-the-street" spot interviews. Neighbors on local TV are forever gasping and wailing the most clichéd of reflex responses to actual local horrors, whether personal or social.

"It's so horrible," they say over and over again, like wind-up dolls with a limited repertoire of three-word phrases, when asked about a local disaster. And when the crisis affects them directly—a school budget cut or neighborhood hospital closing, for example— their on-air responses are equally vapid. "I don't know *what* we're going to do without any teachers or books," they say with puzzled, frenzied expressions as they try desperately to articulate some coherent reply to a complex issue they've just heard about.

I am not suggesting that the news should not feature community residents' views and experiences. Of course it should. But the local news teams' way of presenting such community responses is deliberately demeaning and fatuous. No one could say much worth saying in such a format. And if someone managed to come up with something serious and intelligent, rest assured it would be cut in favor of a more sensational, emotional response.

But real news, even about cats in trees or babies in wells, is hardly what takes up the most airtime. "Don't bother too much about that stuff," say the guys and gals in the anchor chairs. Here's Goofy Gil with the weather, or Snappy Sam with the sports—the two features which, on every local newscast, are given the longest time slots and the most elaborate and expensive props. The number and ornateness of the weather maps on local news, and the endlessly amazing developments in special-effects technology to observe climate changes and movements of impending "fronts" is truly mind-boggling.

Who needs this stuff? But we're not forgetting that this is not the question to ask. "Who wants it?" is the criterion for news producers, and it is, understandably, the weather and sports that most people, most of the time, are likely to sit still for. If local news is meant to be a facsimile of a sunny Disneyesque community of happy, cozy campers, in which the bothersome bad guys and events of the day are quickly dealt with so that community harmony may once more reign, at least for the moment—and that *is* the intended fantasy—then what better, safer, kind of information than weather reports. Historically, after all, the weather is the standard small-talk item for people wishing to be pleasant and make contact without getting into anything controversial or heavy. It is the only kind of news we can all share in—no matter what our face, class, gender, or political differences—as members of a common community.

The researchers are not entirely wrong, after all, about what people in this kind of society want. They do want comfort, reassurance, and a community where they belong and feel safe. And why shouldn't they? They find precious little of those things in the streets and buildings they traverse and inhabit in their daily lives. In my urban neighborhood, parents warn children never to make eye contract with anyone on the street or subway; never to speak to anyone, even in case of tragedy or emergency; never to look at or listen to the pathetic souls who regularly beg for money or ramble incoherently in the hope that someone, anyone, will take pity and respond.

Remember when California was God's country, the Promised Land of Milk and Honey, to which people migrated for clean air, good jobs, and single-dwelling homes? Try to find these things in overpopulated, polluted, socially vexed and violent LA today. Don Henley, again, said it best some twenty years ago: "Call some place paradise/Kiss it good-bye."

But if we can't all dream of moving to sunny California anymore, there's always TV, where something resembling that innocent dream still exists. *Eyewitness News* and its various clones allow us to believe, just for a moment, that there really is a Santa Claus, a Mary Poppins, a Good Samaritan giving away fortunes to the needy, a spirit of Christmas Past to convert the most cold-hearted of corporate Scrooges. Indeed, this kind of "good news" is another staple of the genre. Charities, celebrations, instances of extraordinary good luck or good works by or for local residents are ever-present on local newscasts. Every day, in the midst of even the most dreadful and depressing news, there are legions of friends and neighbors to mourn and console each other, offering aid, bringing soup and casseroles to the victims of natural and man-made disasters, stringing lights and hanging balloons for festive neighborhood gatherings.

The news teams themselves often play this role for us. They march at the head of holiday parades and shake hands and kiss babies at openings of malls and industrial parks. They are the neighbors—often thought of as friends by the loneliest among us—we wish we had in real life, there to do the right thing on every occasion. That is their primary function. They are not trained in journalism. They often cannot pronounce the local names and foreign words they read from teleprompters. But they sure can smile. And joke around. And let us in on the latest bargain to seek out or scam to avoid. In fact, the "Action Line" and "Shame on You" features, in which reporters hang out at local shopping centers trying out new gadgets, testing fabrics, and trapping shady shopkeepers in their nefarious efforts to sell us junk, poison, and instant death, are among the most popular and cheery things on the air.

The news teams also bring us gossip, at a time when more and more of us are lonely and scared of each other. The gossip is not about our actual neighbors of course, those suspicious, *different*-looking folks who just moved in. We don't open the door to them for fear they will shoot us or rape us. No, no.

The news teams bring us word of our nice friends and neighbors, the celebrities we have come to know and love through their ever-present images on the TV screens that have become our virtual homes and communities. Marla and The Donald, Michael and Lisa Marie, Lyle and Julia, Richard and Cindy—we know and love these people and delight in sharing the latest bits of harmless scandals about them with co-workers and other semi-intimates.

Sociologist Joshua Gamson has suggested, in an insightful essay, that there is a lesson to be learned from the enormous popularity of tabloid television—a category in which I would certainly include local news. The lesson is not that people are stupid, venal, "addicted," or otherwise blameworthy for their fascinated interest in junk TV. On the contrary, it is those responsible for the quality of our public life who are more deserving of such terms of contempt and opprobrium. For it is, says Gamson, "Only when people perceive public life as inconsequential, as not their own, [that] they readily accept the invitation to turn news into play." And people most certainly do perceive public life as inconsequential and worse these days, whether outside their doors or in Washington or on Wall Street.

Only I don't think it is primarily the desire to "play" that drives people in droves to local newscasts, or even the trashier tabloid shows like *Hard Copy*. What people are getting from local newscasts—and here the researchers were right on the money, literally—is indeed *what they want*, in the most profound and sad sense of that phrase. They are getting what they always sought in fantasy and fiction, from *The Wizard of Oz* to *As the World Turns*. They are getting, for a brief moment, a utopian fantasy of a better, kinder, more decent and meaningful world than the one that entraps them.

It is not only that public life is inconsequential, after all. It is, far more tragically, that public and private life today are increasingly unjust, inhumane, painful, even hopeless, materially and spiritually, for many of us. And there is no relief in sight except, ironically, on the local newscasts that are a respite from reality. Only, unlike the utopian villages of soap opera and fairy tale, these "imagined communities" are supposed to be, pretend to be, real and true. And for that reason they are more troubling than the trashiest or silliest of pop-culture fictions.

Cancerous Journalism

BARBARA McLINTOCK

Barbara McLintock is a community activist and an award-winning investigative reporter from Victoria, B.C. She has also published *Anorexia's Fallen Angel*, a book that exposes problems within eating disorder clinics. In "Cancerous Journalism," she suggests that corporations often disguise their advertising as legitimate news.

Those of us in the journalism business like to think we're pretty smart in figuring out when we're being "spun"—when some "communications officer" or "public relations officer" or ministerial aide is trying to persuade us to write a story that reflects a view that will benefit their political or business cause. We like to think we're particularly careful in such cases to ensure that we are actually being given the full information available and to make every effort to reflect also the other side of the story, whatever that may be.

I suspect most readers of newspapers and magazines also would tell any pollster that asked them that they too have a high suspicion index, and are good at picking out any news stories or features that are in fact based on the spin provided by a business or political group with a specific axe to grind.

All those of us who harbour such self-beliefs, whether we be writers or readers, will be most distressed to read a detailed academic study published in this month's *American Journal of Preventive Medicine*. The study shows, without any doubt, that many of us were badly deluded in examining what might be considered one of the primary public health topics of the past couple of decades—the health consequences of exposure to secondhand tobacco smoke. The inevitable conclusion from the researchers' work, in fact, is that tobacco giant Philip Morris went to a huge amount of trouble to influence journalists to present the tobacco industry's viewpoint on the issue—and met with remarkable success in return.

BLOWING SECONDHAND SMOKE

The researchers, from such highly-respected institutions as the Mayo Clinic, not only examined the news stories that appeared in the print media on the subject, but also reviewed thousands of previously secret internal tobacco company documents made public as part of the giant lawsuit settlement in the U.S. In particular, the research team concentrated on the industry's reaction to the 1992 decision by the U.S. Environmental Protection Agency to classify secondhand smoke as a human carcinogen—the formal decision that sparked numerous efforts to restrict or ban smoking in workplaces, restaurants and bars in various communities across North America.

The main focus of the study was of events that occurred in the U.S. But it doesn't take much reading between the lines to realize exactly the same sort of media manipulation was going on here in Canada. For instance, the study cited dozens of alleged "scientific experts" who were actually paid by the tobacco industry but were trotted out to the media as "independent" scientists who had "discovered" that secondhand smoke wasn't as bad as some would have you think.

FRASER INSTITUTE BACKED INDUSTRY'S PAID "EXPERT"

One of those alleged "experts" frequently quoted was a former cancer researcher named Gio Gori. And who should turn up in British Columbia in 1999 but Gori, as co-author of a book attacking the EPA decision, entitled "Passive Smoke: The EPA's Betrayal of Science and Policy." The publisher was none other than the well-known right-wing think-tank, the Fraser Institute, which used its influence to get as much positive coverage as possible for the volume. The book was used as ammunition against a new bylaw which had just come into effect in Victoria to ban smoking in all indoor public places—exactly the sort of legislation the tobacco industry had most feared.

From the moment the EPA came down with its ruling, the tobacco industry had been well aware that those smoking bans would be a major risk to its profits. According to the industry documents the researchers studied, within weeks of the decision, Philip Morris had asked its PR firm, the world-wide giant Burson-Marsteller, to undertake a program that would "build considerable reasonable doubt . . . particularly among consumers" about what it saw as the "scientific weaknesses" of the EPA report.

It should be made clear that in the past few years, in the light of ever-increasing evidence, even the tobacco industry has mostly stopped trying to argue that secondhand smoke is not a health hazard. The U.S. National Institute for Occupational Health and Safety wrote just this month, after a review of all the relevant scientific literature: "Among blue-collar workers, workers in the restaurant, bar, and gaming industries are exposed to much higher levels of environmental tobacco smoke (ETS) than are office workers, and are at increased risk of cancer and cardiovascular diseases even if they are non-smokers themselves."

JOURNALISTS TARGETED "ONE-ON-ONE"

But back in 1993, the tobacco industry and Burson-Marsteller thought it was still worth a try to raise controversy surrounding the EPA findings. In its report back to Philip Morris, the PR firm suggested media strategies that would focus on "one-on-one opportunities with journalists and editorial writers rather than . . . on the herd of daily journalists." These "opportunities," it suggested, would be "supplemented by carefully tailored, authored, placed pieces."

The next step, the researchers found, was to hire a media and political consultant in Washington by the name of Richard Hines. A major lobbyist in Washington, D.C. whose clients include the government of Cambodia, Hines himself is an interesting addition to almost any political debate. A former South Carolina state legislator, Hines is best known in the U.S. for his "neo-Confederate" views, supporting the pro-slavery southern states from the time of American Civil War 140 years ago. He is also a very active supporter of President George W. Bush, credited by some as being the individual who ensured that Bush actually got the Republican nomination back in 2000.

But back in the mid-1990s, Hines's job was to persuade a number of prominent writers to develop articles critical of the EPA report, suggesting it was based on political considerations, and not good science. In March 1993, just three months after the report was made public, a Philip Morris vice-president wrote a memo, reporting that Hines "is responsible for a number of articles that have appeared in . . . major news publications" on the issue. Hines himself wrote that he had been able to develop "a selected network of journalists" and hence to "reach millions of the public through numerous syndicated columnists that are in our network." Most of those in the "network" were apparently columnists and editorial writers who'd already shown a pronounced opposition to what they saw as too much government regulation in the lives of citizens.

MORRIS FUNDED "NATIONAL JOURNALISM CENTER"

But Philip Morris went even further. It provided funding for a U.S. journalism school called the National Journalism Center, which was founded by a small-c conservative journalist in 1977 and works to provide training for young and student journalists in the conservative, free-enterprise view of the world. Through its support, Philip Morris was able to provide seminars on secondhand smoke to young journalists at the Center and to have access to graduates of the program, many of whom also wrote articles echoing the tobacco industry's view of the issues.

A third tactic was for Philip Morris to work with conservative think-tanks to have pieces placed on op-ed pages by writers for the think-tanks.

The study notes, for instance, that one of the "scientific consultants" quoted in many of the orchestrated studies was one Gio Gori, who was actually being paid by the tobacco industry at the time, although this was not known publicly until much later.

FRASER INSTITUTE CRIED "BETRAYAL OF SCIENCE"

Gori turned up here in British Columbia as well, as co-author of a book attacking the EPA decision, entitled "Passive Smoke: The EPA's Betrayal of Science and Policy." The publisher was none other than the Fraser Institute which used its influence to get as much positive coverage as possible for the volume.

The authors of the *Preventive Medicine* article warn that the full details of just how much the tobacco industry directly and indirectly influenced journalistic coverage will probably never be known as all the industry documents aren't available to be made public.

But even the information made available so far should be enough to warn readers of the mainstream media that if high-powered players are at work, suspicion should be the watchword of the day.

Militarism and the Media

JOEL ANDREAS

Assistant professor of sociology at Johns Hopkins University, Joel Andreas is an anti-war activist whose comic book exposé *Addicted to War: Why the U.S. Can't Kick Militarism* has sold over 200 000 copies. Using comics, Andreas exposes the links between the arms and news industries, a collusion that often hampers investigation of weapons manufacturing.

Since the days of William Randolph Hearst, the **pro-war message** has been delivered to the people by the **news media**.

New York American Editorial Page
The Mailed Fist of Uncle Sam Must Be Armed with American Dollars

Buy a Liberty Bond *Help furnish* the *Sinews* of **War**

Typical Hearst journalism, 1917

But it was after World War II that the press, the radio networks, and the fledgling television industry became fully integrated into the **newly emerging military-industrial complex.**

With the **"Cold War"** getting under way, this complex had its work cut out for it. Charles Wilson, Chairman of the Board of **General Electric** (whom Truman had just appointed to head the **Office of Defense Mobilization**), spelled out what this work was in a speech to the Newspaper Publishers Association in 1950:

"If the people were not convinced [that the Free World is in **mortal danger**] it would be impossible for Congress to vote the **vast sums** now being spent to avert this danger. With the support of public opinion, as **marshalled by the press**, we are off to a good start. It is our job — yours and mine — to **keep our people convinced** that the only way to keep disaster away from our shores is to **build up America's might.**" (125)

Charles Wilson and his cronies at GE were, of course, **very eager** to see a massive military build up.

51

GE had **major investments** around the world, which they expected the Pentagon to protect. It also was, and is, **a charter member** of the military-industrial complex.

"A member in good standing, I might add!"

GE is the country's third-largest military contractor, **raking in billions** of dollars every year. It produces parts for every nuclear weapon in the U.S. arsenal, makes jet engines for military aircraft, and creates all kinds of **profitable electronic gadgets** for the Pentagon. It's also the company that secretly released **millions of curies** of deadly radiation from the Hanford nuclear weapons facility in Washington state and produced **faulty nuclear power plants** that dot the U.S. countryside.

"We bring good things to life!"

From Wilson's time, GE has been very concerned with making use of the media. In 1954 it hired **a floundering actor** named Ronald Reagan to be its **corporate spokesman.** It furnished Ron and Nancy with an all-electric house, and Ron with his own TV show called **"GE Theater."**

It also furnished Reagan with **"The Speech,"** GE's political message for America, and sent him around the country to deliver it. He's been delivering variations of "The Speech" ever since.

(126)

Meanwhile, GE was busy **buying up** TV and radio stations across the country.

(52)

Then, in 1986, GE bought **its own TV network — NBC**

Good evening, I'm **Tom Brokaw** and this is the NBC Nightly News.

⑫⑦

Charles Wilson would be **pleased** with NBC's programming. The network is very good at marshalling public opinion along just the lines he suggested. And NBC is not alone. You get just about **the same message** no matter what channel you turn to.

Our game plan is right on schedule....

Our game plan is right on schedule....

Our game plan is right on schedule....

After the Persian Gulf War, one of the Bush Administration's top war planners spoke to a group of **prominent journalists** and thanked them for their help.

"[Television was] our **chief tool** in selling our policy."

Richard Hass, National Security Council, 1991
⑫⑧

It sure was. We were treated to live 24-hour war coverage, **sponsored by** Exxon and General Electric and **cleared by** the Pentagon.

Just **how many lives** can these new high-tech weapons **save**, Colonel?

53

NEL

When it comes to **war**, the networks discard all **pretenses** of objectivity.

Bomb 'em back! Bomb 'em back! Wwwway back!

Lawrence Grossman, who was in charge of **PBS** and **NBC News** for many years, described the role of the press this way:

"The job of the President is to set the agenda and the job of the press is to **follow the agenda** that the leadership sets."

Why do all the networks sound the same? Why are they all **consumed by war fever** every time the White House decides to send troops oversees?

Maybe it's got something to do with **who controls them**

The television news media are owned by some of the largest corporations in the country. NBC, as we have seen, is owned by GE, CBS is owned by Viacom, ABC is owned by Disney, and CNN is owned by AOL Time Warner. The members of the boards of directors of these powerful corporations also sit on the boards of **weapons manufaturers** and other companies with **vested interests** around the world such as Sun Microsystems, EDS, Lucent Technologies, Prudential, etc.

Our networks tell you everything you **need to know**

XEROX   JPMorganChase   CHRYSLER   Marriott   CITIBANK

Most of the news available to us — about war and peace and everything else - is **filtered through the perspective** of the corporate news media. The government and the news media obviously have a **powerful influence** on public opinion.

Everyone is rallying behind the President.

Hmmm...Oo

But their influence is not as complete as they **might hope**.

CHAPTER

8

Argument

"I said there was a society of men among us, bred up from their youth in the art of proving by words multiplied for the purpose, that white is black, and black is white, according as they are paid. To this society all the rest of the people are slaves."

—Jonathan Swift

Argument is writing that persuades readers to accept an idea or adopt a course of action. Certain language characteristics distinguish arguments as a distinct genre.

DISAGREEMENT

An argument is a kind of intellectual conflict where people disagree about what's true or right. The euthanasia or abortion debates, for instance, split into polarized camps, each believing earnestly in its own viewpoint.

One goal of argument is to win popular support, so argument is inherently a public discussion.

REASONS, EXAMPLES, LOGIC

Although an argument begins in disagreement, it does more than simply refute opponents. A superior argument supports its main idea with evidence and sound reasoning, working together harmoniously to establish the thesis. In fact, the evidence should dominate and form the bulk of any argumentative paper.

An argument = position + soundly reasoned evidence.

OBJECTIVE EVIDENCE

Because argument is a social process, it must offer evidence that meets a public standard. The most compelling proof in this regard is physical proof seen and shared by all. Consider the case for Bigfoot. Many people report seeing it, but the debate won't be resolved until someone produces an actual Sasquatch body. The state motto of Missouri provides a helpful guide for argumentative proof: *show me*.

Some topics are hard to argue because of their intangible nature. Discussions of the afterlife, God, the spirit realm, Feng Shui, heaven, conspiracy theories, and recovered memory, lack objective evidence, and perhaps can't be argued at all. Because of their nebulous character, these claims are difficult to disprove, so people wrongly accept them as valid.

Key point: subjective claims must be argued in objective terms.

MEASUREMENT

Measurement improves on the idea of objective proof, for evidence that can be quantified tends to be more accurate, consistent, and compelling.

Consider global warming. We find much evidence for this theory in our daily lives: hot summers, warm winters, forest fires, melting glaciers, dropping water tables. These are important clues, but unless measured against an external scale, they remain subjective and anecdotal.

When we measure climate change, a pattern emerges confirming the model. Meteorologists look at temperature readings and determine whether this summer is hotter than last; they establish a pattern over time, and calculate the rate of temperature acceleration; measurement differentiates between an anomaly and a general trend.

TESTABILITY

A good argument can be tested, and so verified or rejected. ESP makes a valid argumentative subject because researchers can devise experiments that test psychic abilities. Such trials push the debate beyond the researcher's personal beliefs, and let the experimental results indicate whether ESP exists. Testability even adds weight to arguments that are moral, ethical, or philosophical in nature.

For a test to work, it must provide a chance for either failure or success. For an argument to work, an idea must, paradoxically, permit the possibility that it's wrong.

If an idea can't be tested, it may be a belief that lies outside of the argumentative realm. Christians, for example, haven't devised a satisfying experiment to test whether God exists, because belief in God is an article of faith that can't be doubted. Arguments can be shown to be wrong, but a belief remains a belief, no matter how much evidence amounts against it.

REFUTATION

Contradiction is a feature of the argumentative genre. If all facts align on one side, no one would argue over them.

A good argument never ignores contradictory information, but recognizes and confronts it, making concessions and rebuttals. A good writer looks at all known facts—even incongruous ones— and blends them into a balanced verdict.

UNIFIED PROPOSITION

Could you imagine a judge who fails to decide whether the accused is innocent or guilty? Such a judge is incompetent and irresponsible.

Writers of argument have a similar responsibility to advance a single plan. In the capital punishment debate, it's pointless to say both sides have good points. Eventually, the author must choose whether or not to condone executions.

Key point: don't sit on the fence. Choose a position—even a moderate one—and argue it.

CONSEQUENCES AND SOCIAL CHANGE

Medieval theologians never actually debated how many angels could dance on a pinhead, but they did quarrel over inconsequential stuff. Do saints go the bathroom in heaven? Did Eve have a belly button? Will Adam ever get his rib back? These aren't creditable arguments because they're inconsequential, even for Christians.

By nature, arguments treat significant subjects that affect large segments of population, seeking to change belief or behaviour.

Key point: arguments discuss important ideas and seek change.

LIFESPAN

If argument is a public separation of truth from falsehood, then some propositions eventually fail, while others succeed. Debate eventually leads to consensus, and arguments that once split a community are laid to rest. No one seriously quarrels anymore over witches, meteors, or slavery, even though these were once subjects of furious, even murderous debate. Arguments have a lifespan and die.

THE QUALITY OF PROOF

"A proof is a proof. What kind of a proof? It's a proof. And when you have a good proof, it's because it's proven."

—Jean Chrétien

All arguments offer some proof. For example, the Flat Earth Society offers evidence verifying the earth as a two-dimensional surface. Victorian doctors provided research proving women intellectually inferior. Pharmacists declared Thalidomide safe for pregnant mothers. As such invalid claims show, proof isn't always enough for establishing truth.

If argument is a competition where ideas vie for acceptance, then the big question isn't which arguments have reasons and evidence. They all do. The question is *which argument has the superior proof*? Or better, *which theory best fits all known data*?

Consider why we believe that earth revolves around the sun, and not the other way around. Common sense favours a geocentric model (the earth-centred one), as the evidence of our senses suggests our planet stays still, while the sun, moon and stars reel through the heavens. The Alexandrine mathematician Claudius Ptolemy devised a geocentric model that explained the movement of the five known planets, stars, and moon. Ptolemy's system was a complicated matter, as the apparent retrograde motion of the planets (their tendency to apparently reverse motion) forced him to add epicycles or loops onto the perfectly circular orbits of his model. Despite these complications, Ptolemy's system predicted celestial movements and events with accuracy, higher even than the heliocentric model of Nicholas Copernicus. This is a historic shocker for many people: Ptolemy's earth-centred system works better than Copernicus' sun-centred one.

So why do we reject the evidence of our eyes, and believe that the earth rotates around the sun?

Of course, the West didn't opt for the "correct" answer right away. The Church considered geocentrism part of its doctrine, bullied Copernicus to abandon his theory, imprisoned Galileo for teaching it, and even burned Giordano Bruno. Heliocentrism had to battle religious dogma before it could be accepted.

And to top it off, all things weren't equal—Ptolemy's system worked better than his rival's. Galileo and Bruno backed a less predictive theory, at least initially.

The debate took time to resolve. When the astronomer Johannes Kepler replaced Copernicus' circular orbits with ellipses, the accuracy of the heliocentric model improved beyond Ptolemy's. With the invention of telescopes, new evidence accumulated in favour of the sun-centred model, until belief in Ptolemy's model became unten-able. Space travel introduced visual confirmation of earth's planetary motion. The geocentric system gradually won because it explains *all* of the emerging data in a more comprehensive way.

The question is partially one of depth. Flat Earthers adequately explain the experience of the average pedestrian unconcerned by a few misbehaving lights in the sky. Ptolemy adequately explains the movements of the planets seen with the naked eye. The Copernicus-Kepler hypothesis accounts for all the planetary motion seen through telescopes, as well as spacecraft. With each step, the scale of evidence broadens. The earlier theories made sense only if they ignored new evidence.

The transition from a geocentric to a heliocentric model says much about argument and the establishment of a truthful proposition.

- All arguments have evidence. Yet, this doesn't make them valid.
- Arguments are approximations, rather than eternal "truth."
- The argument that best explains all data wins the day.
- Beliefs change in response to new discoveries and information.
- Some arguments require centuries to resolve.
- Worldviews have shifted, and will shift again.
- Truth is often influenced by other values.

These lessons help us judge debates currently raging today, such as the controversies over global warming, Intelligent Design, and UFOs. These propositions offer a hefty body of "proof" and argue for a radical swing in belief systems (in Thomas Kuhn's useful phrase, a "paradigm shift").

Because proof itself is insufficient for establishing the truth of a claim, we must judge these cases in competition, and choose which one best fits all the available data—a task that requires research. And we need to keep an eye open for the places where evidence is ignored or suppressed. What biases do the proponents hold that might make them blind?

In this spirit, let's consider that perennial topic of forbidden science: UFOs. Conservative by nature, scientists tend to dismiss UFO encounters as nonsense, and so ignore difficult-to-explain data: landing impressions, burn marks, radiation trails, radar logs, and eye-witness testimony. Scientists scoff that UFOs lack evidence, but there exist reams. By discounting the data, by discrediting witnesses as fantasy-prone, scientists behave in a most unscientific manner.

On the other hand, the UFO case is far from solid. Although some data demands scientific investigation, other evidence is ques-tionable. Mistakes and hoaxes abound. The use of hypnotic regres-sion compromises testimony. Money-hungry movie executives fill the popular consciousness with tales of aliens. The UFO field has so much interference that the "truth" is never a simple matter.

LOGIC AND LOGICAL FALLACIES

"Logic is the anatomy of thought."

—John Locke

Logic is a system that builds truthful arguments and identifies false ones. While hardly perfect, logic remains a helpful guide, especially for developing persuasive points and detecting flawed reasoning.

Philosophers classify logic into two categories: inductive and deductive reasoning.

INDUCTIVE REASONING

Inductive reasoning (IR) refers to the process of reaching conclusions based on observations of the physical world. A doctor uses IR when observing symptoms and making a diagnosis.

> Patient: I have fever, aching muscles, sore throat, congestion and a cough.
>
> Doctor: You have the flu.

The particular symptoms indicate a general category of disease, the flu. IR is the process behind the scientific method itself: it begins with the collection of data and ends with an explanation.

In other words, IR moves from the specific to the general.

We frequently rely on IR to make decisions, for IR is the voice of experience.

> Mandeep bought five computers from Dell, and they all crashed. Dell makes lousy computers.

IR is a powerful form of reasoning, for its conclusions are based on observable patterns in the real world.

The trouble with IR is that the movement from a particular observation to a general conclusion is always a leap. It takes a limited experience and passes it off as a definite truth. This built-in tendency towards overstatement can produce some dodgy ideas.

A **hasty generalization** is the name given to a logical error that occurs when a conclusion is based upon insufficient evidence.

> My car won't start. It must need gas.

This reasoning uses limited observation to reach an unwarranted conclusion, for many other factors may explain the car's failure: a dead battery, missing spark plugs, extreme cold. Upon reconsideration, we see that the doctor's diagnosis from our first example is also a hasty generalization, as other illness such as pneumonia or bronchitis produce identical symptoms. So too is the conclusion regarding Dell computers based on anecdotal evidence that may be due to Mandeep's negligence not Dell's design. In each case, we lack enough evidence for absolute or even convincing conclusions.

Hasty generalizations decrease in proportion to the amount of data we have. The bigger the sampling, the more reliable are the conclusions.

Still, IR has one large caution: conclusions are only as good as the evidence.

DEDUCTIVE REASONING

Deductive reasoning (DR) describes a process of applying known truths to real situations and reaching new conclusions. Logicians call the known truth a "premise," and they distinguish between a major premise (a general principle) and a minor premise (an observation). When a major and minor premises join together, we reach a new insight.

> All humans are mortal.
> Jarome is human.
> Therefore Jarome is mortal.

This three-line progression is called a syllogism, and provides the building block of DR.

In contrast to IR, DR moves from the general to the specific.

The major problem with DR rests in the ideas it assumes as true. When DR reasons from a mistaken assumption, it produces flawed results.

> Preston is a lean and hungry man.
> Such men are dangerous.
> Preston is a dangerous man.

This sounds reasonable, except for that second line slipping by like a wolf in sheep's clothing. The premise that lean and hungry men are dangerous is dubious, and so are the conclusions drawn from it. Here's an example that drives the point home.

> All English teachers are charismatic and sexy.
> Kent Lewis is an English teacher.
> He must be charismatic and sexy.

338 CHAPTER EIGHT • ARGUMENT

The fault here, obviously, lies in the major premise.

False premise is the name given this error. An argument that begins with a doubtful statement produces tainted results.

Genetic fallacy is a particular kind of False Premise that begins with bigoted ideas about an entire race of people. Sometimes called the **Naturalistic Fallacy**, this error contends all people within a genetic or biological block share similar features.

All Caucasians lack rhythm.
Geddy is Caucasian.
Therefore Geddy has no rhythm.

People of one race don't possess the same abilities, frailties, passions, predilections, and beliefs. Genetic fallacies sound logical, but rest on prejudice.

The genetic fallacy also applies to assumptions that homogenize any large group.

All lawyers are crooked.
Homosexual men lead promiscuous lives.

These premises make generalizations that appeal more to stereotypes than reality. Whether positive or negative, such ideas wrongly characterize people who share the same profession, gender, class, or religion, and lead to mistakes.

The main flaw in DR is that its conclusions are only as good as its presumptions. Flawed ideas = flawed conclusions.

A **logical fallacy** is an argument that's formally sound, yet leads to incorrect deductions (fallacy is a $10-word meaning bad reasoning). We've already looked at two fallacies in the false premise and the hasty generalization, but philosophers have identified many more.

An **analogical fallacy** occurs when a writer compares two objects, and allows their similarity to pass as equality. For example, people often discredit an idea by comparing it to Nazism.

Just as the Nazi party blamed the Jews for German ills, so too has the anti-free trade movement found a convenient scapegoat: the CEOs.

The analogy has a grain of truth: both groups direct frustration against a minority in society. The writer here obviously wants people to see protestors as vindictive and irrational as the Nazis, and in a small way, this rings true.

However, this analogy misleads when we try to see the two terms as synonymous, and forget their overwhelming differences. The Nazis were racist, but the protestors aren't; the Nazis seized power through violence, but protestors are mostly peaceful; the

Nazis commanded a military force, but protestors have none; the Nazis committed genocide, while protestors promote justice. In fact, the differences here are so profound, they overpower the similarity and render the analogy an insult.

Analogies can be effective but must be used carefully and evaluated rigorously.

The **appeal to good character (*argumentum pro hominem*)** suggests a proposition is true because it comes from a well-regarded person or source. Translated into a syllogism, the fallacy appears like this.

> The speaker is respected.
> The speaker said X.
> X must be true.

Obviously a good reputation doesn't guarantee a belief is true, yet the appeal to good character abounds.

> One of the greatest intellectuals of the age, Noam Chomsky, says the Western news media is a propaganda machine.

The problem is that we accept a proposition based on the speaker's good character, rather than on the idea's merits. Chomsky is educated, but like any human being, he's prone to mistakes, foibles, and delusions. The quality of the speaker doesn't guarantee the validity of the statement, no matter how "authoritative" the voice.

Celebrity endorsements use pro hominem strategies to sell consumer wares, hoping that the charm, athletic prowess, or sex appeal of the star transfers to the product. Such character-based marketing exploits our trust and says nothing about the merchandise.

Appeal to bad character (*argumentum ad hominem*) suggests a proposition is false based on the bad reputation of its speaker. This fallacy pressures us to reject an idea because it originates from a disreputable or unpopular source. As a syllogism, it unfolds like this.

> The speaker has a dubious character.
> The speaker said X.
> X must be false.

Typically an ad hominem argument is subtler:

> Barbara Amiel wants to privatize medicine in Canada, just the sort of idea one expects from a billionaire's wife.

This statement coerces us to reject an idea based on a bad impression of the speaker. It bullies us into resisting privatized medicine because Barbara Amiel married rich. Private medicine may or may not be good for Canada, but this reasoning decides the issue on irrelevant grounds. Character isn't a reliable guide to truth.

Sadly, ad hominem arguments are a mainstay of political campaigning, as rivals sling muck and impugn moral character, instead of examining policies and ideas.

Based on the Latin word *antiquatum* meaning "the past," the **appeal to tradition (*argumentum ad antiquatum*)** suggests an idea is right because it's old. Filled with error, intolerance, and stupidity, tradition regrettably offers an unreliable guide to truth and moral behaviour.

> Throughout history, marriage has been a union between men and women. If we sanction gay weddings, we'll undermine a time-honoured institution.

The argument here is pure ad antiquatum: the past definition of marriage forms the future one. Yet, by this reasoning, we should revive the "time-honoured institutions" of slavery, fascism, and witch burning, for these all have past precedent. History doesn't guarantee the rightness of any proposition.

The **appeal to popularity (*argumentum ad populum*)** fallacy persuades us an idea is valid because many folk believe it (*populum* is Latin for "people"). The strength of this pseudo-reasoning rests in the large numbers of adherents, not objective standards.

> Everybody knows a private business provides services more efficiently than government.

The key words are "everybody knows," the essence of appeal to popularity. They coerce us to trust a scheme, merely because it's fashionable. Of course, an idea isn't necessarily true or gainful because a crowd says so.

Based on the dubious authority, ad populum is the herd mentality masquerading as reliable reasoning. It's mob-think.

Circular reasoning (*circulus in probando*) occurs when the conclusion appears as part of an argument's proof.

> The Bible is the word of God.
> The Bible says that God exists.
> Therefore God exists.

The problem here is that the existence of God has been settled using the word of God, the Bible. God thus vouchsafes for God— the logical equivalent of a dog chasing its own tail.

Also called **begging the question**, circular reasoning is easy to spot, particularly when the conclusion echoes the same words as the premise: "A pollutant is a polluting agent emitted by a polluter."

Circular reasoning is harder to spot when the repeated idea hides under a veil of synonyms.

All magazines displaying lascivious and licentious images are pornographic.

You'll know a treasonous idea by the way it betrays Canadian values.

These seem to say something, but merely regurgitate the conclusion in the proof, and so add no new information.

A **false dilemma** or **bifurcation** presents only two sides in a debate, even though many other perspectives exist. A fancy word meaning "to split into two," bifurcation polarizes discussion into two positions, and forces us to choose between an artificially good idea and a contrived bad one.

We stand at a crossroads: we can master the genetic code or embrace ignorance.

Sometimes called **black and white thinking**, bifurcation omits middle paths, moderate answers, and alternatives to "yea" or "nay." Fuelled by a sense of crisis, the false dilemma forces us to choose from a rigged contest.

The **appeal to force (*argumentum ad baculum*)** sways people by making a direct or veiled threat. A Latin phrase meaning "arguing with a stick," argumentum ad baculum intimidates with fear of physical, psychological, economic, or other injury.

If you reject Christ, you're going to hell.

Palestinian families must vacate their homes willingly or face a military solution.

These arguments ignore the merits and detriments of the issues at hand, resolving controversies by menacing opponents with a fist, real or otherwise. The appeal to force is the strategy of a bully.

The **appeal to pity (*argumentum ad misericordiam*)** influences us by demanding sympathy. Based on the Latin word for misery, this fallacy focuses attention on the suffering created by a course of action.

I got the wrong answer, but I'm already on Academic probation; if you fail me on this quiz, then I'll be kicked out of college, lose my scholarship, and my residence. Can't you give me a D–?

This student appeals a failure by demonstrating the havoc the mark wreaks on his life. By focusing on his pain, the student delivers an emotional punch that's difficult for a caring person to ignore.

However, his argument skirts the issue of fairness and account-ability. He admits his answers were incorrect, yet still wants marks for them. He botches his schoolwork consistently, yet feels poor con-duct merits reward. The student amplifies his suffering hoping the professor will pay attention to it, rather than his own irresponsibility.

This appeal to pity exploits human kindness but never asks whether suffering is appropriate.

A **straw person argument** sets up a deliberately weak opposi-tion, just to knock it down. Also known as **poisoning the well**, this fallacy is "straw" in the sense that it attacks a shell of the opposi-tion's real argument, an effigy that can be easily quashed, hoping to discredit the whole case.

> Homeless kids choose a life on the streets so they can enjoy the freedom, drugs, and partying. Don't feel sorry for them.

Certainly this accusation fits a portion of the street-kid population, but an extremely small, even negligible percentage. Most children flee homes to escape sexual abuse, violence, poverty, or alcoholism. While the street life has moments of pleasure, these are grossly offset by problems and perils: hunger, malnutrition, disease, lethal winters, theft, rape, assault, pimps, and prostitution. By focusing attention on a few "homeless tourists," the argument reduces sym-pathy for street kids, while neglecting the major reasons for their flight.

The fallacy of the **false cause (*post hoc, ergo propter hoc*)** occurs when we wrongly assume that one thing has caused another. Latin for "after this, therefore because of this," post hoc, ergo propter hoc usually revolves around two events happening near each other. If A and B occur closely together in time, this fal-lacy takes for granted that A causes B.

> Shortly after angora sweaters became fashionable, teenagers began bearing children out of wedlock. Angora sweaters con-tribute to teenage pregnancy.

> Every night the cicadas start singing, and then the sun sets. Cicadas make the sun go down.

> Ever since Tanner began listening to Rap music, he's been slacking off in school and talking back to his parents. Those CDs are ruining his life.

In the first case, the correlation between sweaters and preg-nancy is merely coincidental. In the second case, the observer has confused cause with effect. In the third case, the two effects show a high correlation, but have been caused by an unstated factor (teenage angst). In all of these situations, two unconnected events are causally linked.

A **slippery slope argument** discredits an idea by connecting it to ludicrous and unrelated consequences. The fallacy suggests that if A comes to pass, then so will B, C, D, and E, all falling together like a stack of dominoes. The imagery implies we stand at the edge of a cliff beyond which we mustn't advance, else we slide down a moral abyss.

> If we sanction same-sex unions today, then tomorrow we'll have to recognize polygamy, incestuous relationships, adult/ child sex, even bestiality.

In this example, the speaker rejects gay marriage based upon an aversion to polygamy, incest, pedophilia, and eventually animal abuse. Although these are all alternate sexualities, they differ strongly, marking separate issues. We can condone the first without approving the last.

EMOTIONAL APPEALS

"But reason has no power against feeling."

—Charlotte Perkins Gilman

Sigmund Freud argued that humans are irrational, driven by sub-conscious desires and fear more than reason. If Freud's right, a writer should consider emotion as much as logic, for tweaking the right feelings can be more persuasive than the facts. Rhetoricians often make a distinction between argument (that appeals to reason) and persuasion (that appeals to emotion). If argument strives to establish valid or ethical propositions, persuasion aims for a simpler goal: to sway as many people as possible. Hitler suggested that politics is the science of moving the masses, a maxim that nicely defines persuasion.

Advertising is a familiar form of persuasion that routinely exploits our passions, insecurities and fantasies. Car commercials appeal to psychological factors such as power, prestige, or freedom, rather than tangible qualities like fuel economy or reliability. Today, it's a challenge to find a commercial that provides practical information about its product. Why? Advertisers know people respond to feelings rather than intellect.

Even political campaigns target our irrational nature. Hitler tailored his messages to the suppressed anxieties of the German people, petitioning patriotism, pride, and racist phobias. Current-day politicians use the same techniques. During the 1992 elections,

George Bush Sr. ran ads that played on white America's fear of black convicts. With this strategy, Bush defeated contender Michael Dukakis, showing that an educated modern society still responds to primitive anxieties and racial allegiances. Canadian elections are little different, as our politicians regularly exploit fears of terrorists, immigrants, even the U.S.A., to win votes in the same neurotic manner.

The sociologist Abraham Maslow designed a handy classification system for categorizing emotional appeals that he called the Hierarchy of Needs. His pyramid diagram places all human needs on an ascending scale with the most powerful human needs on the bottom, and the weaker, more refined at the top. According to Maslow, we have five basic needs.

Self-Actualization Needs: the quest to fulfill the human potential, and connect with a higher cause or meaning.

Esteem Needs: the longing for mastery, dominance, status, and prestige.

Belonging Needs: the desire to feel part of an identifiable group, such as a country, company, club, family, or a romance.

Security Needs: safety requirements such as shelter, clothing, and medicine.

Physiological Needs: basic body requirements such as air, water, food, and sex.

According to Maslow, the bottom two levels of the pyramid represent essentials that have to be fulfilled for human survival, while people may survive (but not flourish) without satisfying the top three needs.

A clever writer makes sure that a persuasive essay hits some, if not all these emotional needs. The base needs motivate people more strongly than the more refined and ethereal drives at the pyramid's top, which explains why sex and food dominate advertising.

Of course, the emotional appeal is a Pandora's box that contains all sorts of psychic fantasies, bugbears, malignancies, and delusions. The ideal persuasive essay uses emotional appeals *in addition to* sound reasons, not in place of them, as a supplement, not a substitute.

Exercises

1. Can the following propositions be developed into an argument? Why or why not? If not, rewrite them as potential arguments.

   a) Man is a flawed, physical reflection of an eternal, ideal form. (Plato)

   b) Fluoridated water is safe for human consumption.

c) Immigrants often keep the cultural identity of the country they left behind.

d) Gay marriage violates God's will and Natural Law.

e) Safe injection sites save lives and reduce drug-related crime.

f) Spiderman makes a better hero than Superman.

g) American foreign policy is soaked in blood.

2. Discuss the following topics, and evaluate the quantity and quality of evidence on either side. Does the evidence on one side appear stronger? Is any evidence suppressed? What social factors influence the selection of evidence?

Creationism vs. evolution

Global warming

UFOs

Bigfoot

Holocaust denial

Any conspiracy theory

3. Identify the following logical fallacies.

a) Those hippies are blocking the logging road just so they can feel important and grab TV time.

b) Schools need to get back to basics: reading, writing, and arithmetic.

c) The government should pardon those native militants, because Aboriginals have tough enough lives as it is.

d) Any idea coming from Jack Layton has to be bankrupt.

e) Hector is black, so he must be good at sports.

f) Canada can embrace globalization, or become an economic backwater.

g) If we condone stem cell research, we open a Pandora's box leading to genetic manipulation, eugenics, human cloning, and a black market in fetuses.

h) We should not decriminalize marijuana because it's an illegal substance.

i) Three of my friends took a Literature class with Dr. Clark, and each one got an "A." He must be an easy professor.

j) Regarded scholar, Harvard professor, and Pulitzer Prize winner Dr. John Mack believes in the alien abduction phenomenon, so there must be something to it.

k) Men are more logical than women, so I tend to trust Henry's versions of events more than Eliza's.

l) Shortly after cellphones became popular, the incidence of attention deficit disorder skyrocketed. Cellphones are giving our kids ADD.

m) All the girls at school are trying the Atkins diet, so it must be safe.

n) If Canada doesn't ban the seal hunt, the Animal Liberation Front will launch a campaign of industrial sabotage and boycott Canadian goods.

o) A boyfriend is a lot like a dog; you have to speak to them firmly, use simple commands, and keep them on a short leash.

4. Choose a magazine or TV ad and analyze its persuasive techniques. How much time is devoted to identifying measurable benefits? How many ads rely on emotional appeals? Use Maslow's Hierarchy of Needs to identify different emotional needs.

5. Who has a more difficult time shaving: men or women?

Evolution as Fact and Theory

STEPHEN JAY GOULD

Stephen Jay Gould was a professor of geology and zoology at Harvard University. Author of award-winning books on evolution, natural science, and paleontology, including *The Mismeasure of Man*, *Ever Since Darwin: Reflections in Natural History*, *Hen's Teeth and Horse's Toes*, and *Bully for Brontosaurus*, Gould modified Darwin by suggesting that evolution is not slow and steady, but has stages of stagnation and rapid development. He called this the "punctuated equilibrium" theory of evolution. In this piece, Gould looks at the lop-sided evidence in favour of evolution over creationism.

Kirtley Mather, who died last year at age ninety, was a pillar of both science and Christian religion in America and one of my dearest friends. The difference of a half-century in our ages evaporated before our common interests. The most curious thing we shared was a battle we each fought at the same age. For Kirtley had gone to Tennessee with Clarence Darrow to testify for evolution at the Scopes trial of 1925. When I think that we are enmeshed again in the same struggle for one of the best documented, most compelling and exciting concepts in all of science, I don't know whether to laugh or cry.

According to idealized principles of scientific discourse, the arousal of dormant issues should reflect fresh data that give renewed life to abandoned notions. Those outside the current debate may therefore be excused for suspecting that creationists have come up with something new, or that evolutionists have generated some serious internal trouble. But nothing has changed; the creationists have presented not a single new fact or argument. Darrow and Bryan were at least more entertaining than we lesser antagonists today. The rise of creationism is politics, pure and simple; it represents one issue (and by no means the major concern) of the resurgent evangelical right. Arguments that seemed kooky just a decade ago have reentered the mainstream.

The basic attack of modern creationists falls apart on two general counts before we even reach the supposed factual details of their assault against evolution. First, they play upon a vernacular misunderstanding of the word "theory" to convey the false impression that we evolutionists are covering up the rotten core of our edifice. Second, they misuse a popular philosophy of science to argue that they are behaving scientifically in attacking evolution. Yet the same philosophy demonstrates that their own belief is not science, and that "scientific creationism" is a meaningless and self-contradictory phrase, an example of what Orwell called "newspeak."

In the American vernacular, "theory" often means "imperfect fact"—part of a hierarchy of confidence running downhill from fact to theory to hypothesis to guess. Thus creationists can (and do) argue: evolution is "only" a theory, and intense debate now rages about many aspects of the theory. If evolution is less than a fact, and scientists can't even make up their minds about the theory, then what confidence can we have in it? Indeed, President Reagan echoed this argument before an evangelical group in Dallas when he said (in what I devoutly hope was campaign rhetoric): "Well, it is a theory. It is a scientific theory only, and it has in recent years been challenged in the world of science—that is, not believed in the scientific community to be as infallible as it once was."

Well, evolution *is* a theory. It is also a fact. And facts and theories are different things, not rungs in a hierarchy of increasing certainty. Facts are the world's data. Theories are structures of ideas that explain and interpret facts. Facts do not go away when scientists debate rival theories to explain them. Einstein's theory of gravitation replaced Newton's, but apples did not suspend themselves in mid-air, pending the outcome. And humans evolved from apelike ancestors whether they did so by Darwin's proposed mechanism or by some other, yet to be discovered.

Moreover, "fact" does not mean "absolute certainty." The final proofs of logic and mathematics flow deductively from stated premises and achieve certainty only because they are *not* about the empirical world. Evolutionists make no claim for perpetual truth, though creationists often do (and then attack us for a style of argument that they themselves favor). In science, "fact" can only mean "confirmed to such a degree that it would be perverse to withhold provisional assent." I suppose that apples might start to rise tomorrow, but the possibility does not merit equal time in physics classrooms.

Evolutionists have been clear about this distinction between fact and theory from the very beginning, if only because we have always acknowledged how far we are from completely understanding the mechanisms (theory) by which evolution (fact) occurred. Darwin continually emphasized the difference between his two great and separate accomplishments: establishing the fact of evolution, and proposing a theory—natural selection—to explain the mechanism of evolution. He wrote in *The Descent of Man*: "I had two distinct objects in view; firstly, to show that species had not been separately created, and secondly, that natural selection had been the chief agent of change. . . . Hence if I have erred in . . . having exaggerated its [natural selection's] power . . . I have at least, as I hope, done good service in aiding to overthrow the dogma of separate creations."

Thus Darwin acknowledged the provisional nature of natural selection while affirming the fact of evolution. The fruitful theoretical debate that Darwin initiated has never ceased. From the 1940s through the 1960s, Darwin's own theory of natural selection did achieve a temporary hegemony that it never enjoyed in his lifetime. But renewed debate characterizes our decade, and, while no biologists question the importance of natural selection, many doubt its ubiquity. In particular, many evolutionists argue that substantial amounts of genetic change may not be subject to natural selection and may spread through the populations at random. Others are challenging Darwin's linking of natural selection with gradual, imperceptible change through all intermediary degrees; they are arguing that most evolutionary events may occur far more rapidly than Darwin envisioned.

Scientists regard debates on fundamental issues of theory as a sign of intellectual health and a source of excitement. Science is—and how else can I say it?—most fun when it plays with interesting ideas, examines their implications, and recognizes that old information might be explained in surprisingly new ways. Evolutionary theory is now enjoying this uncommon vigor. Yet amidst all this turmoil no biologist has been led to doubt the fact that evolution occurred; we are debating *how* it happened. We are all trying to explain the same thing: the tree of evolutionary descent linking all organisms by ties of genealogy. Creationists pervert and caricature this debate by conveniently neglecting the common conviction that underlies it, and by falsely suggesting that evolutionists now doubt the very phenomenon we are struggling to understand.

Secondly, creationists claim that "the dogma of separate creations," as Darwin characterized it a century ago, is a scientific theory meriting equal time with evolution in high school biology curricula. But a popular viewpoint among philosophers of science belies this creationist argument. Philosopher Karl Popper has argued for decades that the primary criterion of science is the falsifiability of its theories. We can never prove absolutely, but we can falsify. A set of ideas that cannot, in principle, be falsified is not science.

The entire creationist program includes little more than a rhetorical attempt to falsify evolution by presenting supposed contradictions among its supporters. Their brand of creationism, they claim, is "scientific" because it follows the Popperian model in trying to demolish evolution. Yet Popper's argument must apply in both directions. One does not become a scientist by the simple act of trying to falsify a rival and truly scientific system; one has to present an alternative system that also meets Popper's criterion—it too must be falsifiable in principle.

"Scientific creationism" is a self-contradictory, nonsense phrase precisely because it cannot be falsified. I can envision observations and experiments that would disprove any evolutionary theory I know, but I cannot imagine what potential data could lead creationists to abandon their beliefs. Unbeatable systems are dogma, not science. Lest I seem harsh or rhetorical, I quote creationism's leading intellectual, Duane Gish, Ph.D. from his recent (1978) book, *Evolution? The Fossils Say No!* "By creation we mean the bringing into being by a supernatural Creator of the basic kinds of plants and animals by the process of sudden, or fiat, creation. We do not know how the Creator created, what process He used, *for He used processes which are not now operating anywhere in the natural universe* [Gish's italics]. This is why we refer to creation as special creation. We cannot discover by scientific investigations anything about the creative processes used by the Creator." Pray tell, Dr. Gish, in the light of your last sentence, what then is scientific creationism?

Our confidence that evolution occurred centers upon three general arguments. First, we have abundant, direct, observational evidence of evolution in action, from both the field and laboratory. This evidence ranges from countless experiments on change in nearly everything about fruit flies subjected to artificial selection in the laboratory to the famous populations of British moths that became black when industrial soot darkened the trees upon which the moths rest. (Moths gain protection from sharp-sighted bird predators by blending into the background.) Creationists do not deny these observations; how could they? Creationists have tightened their act. They now argue that God only created "basic kinds," and allowed for limited evolutionary meandering within them. Thus toy poodles and Great Danes come from the dog kind and moths can change color, but nature cannot convert a dog to a cat or a monkey to a man.

The second and third arguments for evolution—the case for major changes—do not involve direct observation of evolution in action. They rest upon inference, but are no less secure for that reason. Major evolutionary change requires too much time for direct observation on the scale of recorded human history. All historical sciences rest upon inference, and evolution is no different from geology, cosmology, or human history in this respect. In principle, we cannot observe processes that operated in the past. We must infer them from results that still surround us: living and fossil organisms for evolution, documents and artifacts for human history, strata and topography for geology.

The second argument—that the imperfection of nature reveals evolution—strikes many people as ironic, for they feel that evolution should be most elegantly displayed in the nearly perfect adaptation expressed by some organisms—the camber of a gull's wing, or butterflies that cannot be seen in ground litter because they mimic leaves so precisely. But perfection could be imposed by a wise creator or evolved by natural selection. Perfection covers the tracks of past history. And past history—the evidence of descent— is the mark of evolution.

Evolution lies exposed in the *imperfections* that record a history of descent. Why should a rat run, a bat fly, a porpoise swim, and I type this essay with structures built of the same bones unless we all inherited them from a common ancestor? An engineer, starting from scratch, could design better limbs in each case. Why should all the large native mammals of Australia be marsupials, unless they descended from a common ancestor isolated on this island continent? Marsupials are not "better," or ideally suited for Australia; many have been wiped out by placental mammals imported by man from other continents. This principle of imperfection extends to all historical sciences. When we recognize the etymology of September, October, November, and December (seventh, eighth, ninth, and tenth), we know that the year once started in March, or that two additional months must have been added to an original calendar of ten months.

The third argument is more direct: transitions are often found in the fossil record. Preserved transitions are not common—and should not be, according to our understanding of evolution (see next section) but they are not entirely wanting, as creationists often claim. The lower jaw of reptiles contains several bones, that of mammals only one. The non-mammalian jawbones are reduced, step by step, in mammalian ancestors until they become tiny nubbins located at the back of the jaw. The "hammer" and "anvil" bones of the mammalian ear are descendants of these nubbins. How could such a transition be accomplished? the creationists ask. Surely a bone is either entirely in the jaw or in the ear. Yet paleontologists have discovered two transitional lineages of therapsids (the so-called mammal-like reptiles) with a double jaw joint—one composed of the old quadrate and articular bones (soon to become the hammer and anvil), the other of the squamosal and dentary bones (as in modern mammals). For that matter, what better transitional form could we expect to find than the oldest human, *Australopithecus afarensis*, with its apelike palate, its human upright stance, and a cranial capacity larger than any ape's of the same body size but a full 1,000 cubic centimeters below ours? If God made each of the half-dozen human species discovered in ancient rocks, why did he create in an unbroken temporal sequence of progressively more modern features—increasing cranial capacity, reduced face and teeth, larger body size? Did he create to mimic evolution and test our faith thereby?

Faced with these facts of evolution and the philosophical bankruptcy of their own position, creationists rely upon distortion and innuendo to buttress their rhetorical claim. If I sound sharp or bitter, indeed I am—for I have become a major target of these practices.

I count myself among the evolutionists who argue for a jerky, or episodic, rather than a smoothly gradual, pace of change. In 1972 my colleague Niles Eldredge and I developed the theory of punctuated equilibrium. We argued that two outstanding facts of the fossil record—geologically "sudden" origin of new species and failure to change thereafter (stasis)—reflect the predictions of evolutionary theory, not the imperfections of the fossil record. In most theories, small isolated populations are the source of new species, and the process of speciation takes thousands or tens of thousands of years. This amount of time, so long when measured against our lives, is a geological microsecond. It represents much less than 1 per cent of the average life-span for a fossil invertebrate species—more than ten million years. Large, widespread, and well established species, on the other hand, are not expected to change very much. We believe that the inertia of large populations explains the stasis of most fossil species over millions of years.

We proposed the theory of punctuated equilibrium largely to provide a different explanation for pervasive trends in the fossil record. Trends, we argued, cannot be attributed to gradual transformation within lineages, but must arise from the different success of certain kinds of species. A trend, we argued, is more like climbing a flight of stairs (punctuated and stasis) than rolling up an inclined plane.

Since we proposed punctuated equilibria to explain trends, it is infuriating to be quoted again and again by creationists—whether through design or stupidity, I do not know—as admitting that the fossil record includes no transitional forms. Transitional forms are generally lacking at the species level, but they are abundant between larger groups. Yet a pamphlet entitled "Harvard Scientists Agree Evolution Is a Hoax" states: "The facts of punctuated equilibrium which Gould and Eldredge . . . are forcing Darwinists to swallow fit the picture that Bryan insisted on, and which God has revealed to us in the Bible."

Continuing the distortion, several creationists have equated the theory of punctuated equilibrium with a caricature of the beliefs of Richard Goldschmidt, a great early geneticist. Goldschmidt argued, in a famous book published in 1940, that new groups can arise all at once through major mutations. He referred to these suddenly trans- formed creatures as "hopeful monsters." (I am attracted to some aspects of the non-caricatured version, but Goldschmidt's theory still has nothing to do with punctuated equilibrium—see essays in section 3 and my explicit essay on Goldschmidt in *The Panda's Thumb*.) Creationist Luther Sunderland talks of the "punctuated equilibrium hopeful monster theory" and tells his hopeful readers that "it amounts to tacit admission that anti-evolutionists are cor- rect in asserting there is no fossil evidence supporting the theory that all life is connected to a common ancestor." Duane Gish writes, "According to Goldschmidt, and now apparently according to Gould, a reptile laid an egg from which the first bird, feathers and all, was produced." Any evolutionists who believed such nonsense would rightly be laughed off the intellectual stage; yet the only theory that could ever envision such a scenario for the origin of birds is creationism—with God acting in the egg.

I am both angry at and amused by the creationists; but mostly I am deeply sad. Sad for many reasons. Sad because so many people who respond to creationist appeals are troubled for the right reason, but venting their anger at the wrong target. It is true that scientists have often been dogmatic and elitist. It is true that we have often allowed the white-coated, advertising image to repre- sent us—"Scientists say that Brand X cures bunions ten times faster than . . ." We have not fought it adequately because we derive bene- fits from appearing as a new priesthood. It is also true that faceless and bureaucratic state power intrudes more and more into our lives and removes choices that should belong to individuals and communities. I can understand that school curricula, imposed from above and without local input, might be seen as one more insult on all these grounds. But the culprit is not, and cannot be, evolution or any other fact of the natural world. Identify and fight our legitimate enemies by all means, but we are not among them.

I am sad because the practical result of this brouhaha will not be expanded coverage to include creationism (that would also make me sad), but the reduction or excision of evolution from high school curricula. Evolution is one of the half dozen "great ideas" developed by science. It speaks to the profound issues of genealogy that fascinate all of us—the "roots" phenomenon writ large. Where did we come from? Where did life arise? How did it develop? How are organisms related? It forces us to think, ponder, and wonder. Shall we deprive millions of this knowledge and once again teach biology as a set of dull and unconnected facts, without the thread that weaves diverse material into a supple unity?

But most of all I am saddened by a trend I am just beginning to discern among my colleagues. I sense that some now wish to mute the healthy debate about theory that has brought new life to evolutionary biology. It provides grist for creationist mills, they say, even if only by distortion. Perhaps we should lie low and rally around the flag of strict Darwinism, at least for the moment—a kind of old-time religion on our part.

But we should borrow another metaphor and recognize that we too have to tread a straight and narrow path, surrounded by roads to perdition. For if we ever begin to suppress our search to understand nature, to quench our own intellectual excitement in a misguided effort to present a united front where it does not and should not exist, then we are truly lost.

Excerpt from *Stormy Weather: 101 Solutions to Global Climate Change*

GUY DAUNCEY

An eco-activist, researcher, journalist, editor, and author, Guy Dauncey writes extensively on ecological challenges and sustainable development. This selection comes from his book on global warming, *Stormy Weather: 101 Solutions to Global Climate Change*. In this piece, Dauncey reviews the scientific evidence in favour of the climate change model.

THE GREENHOUSE EFFECT

The sun pours its energy into the entire solar system, which by nature is rather cold. If you stood on a planet such as Mars, which has almost no atmosphere and no greenhouse effect, the sun would keep you warm during the day at 98 F°, but at night, when the temperature fell to −189 F°, you would discover how cold the cosmos can be. Bye-bye life, hello deep-frozen astronaut. If you stood on Venus, however, where the atmosphere traps so much of the sun's heat that the average temperature is 860° F, you'd learn what "hot" meant. Bye-bye life, hello astronaut fricassée.

The difference is caused by an atmosphere that contains gases that trap the sun's heat, giving us the greenhouse effect. On Earth, as far as humans are concerned, the greenhouse effect happens to have got it "just right" for the past 10,000 years. With an atmosphere that's 77% nitrogen, 21% oxygen, 0.99% argon, 1% water vapor, and 0.3% trace gases (CO_2 275 parts per million, methane 700 parts per billion, nitrous oxide 275 parts per billion), we have been able to enjoy a pleasant average temperature of 59° F (15° C), just right for gardening and growing forests. It's the miniscule presence of water vapor and trace gases that makes all the difference. They create the *good* greenhouse effect. If we had no greenhouse effect, Earth's average temperature would be 0° F (−18° C), which is bad for tomatoes and trees.

It was not always so pleasant. Water vapor, CO_2, ozone, methane, and nitrous oxide all trap the Earth's heat as it is reflected back into the coldness of space, but the gas that makes the biggest difference is CO_2. Over the past 400,000 years, there have been four occasions when CO_2 levels fell below 200 ppm, causing the global average surface temperature to fall by approximately 5° C and plunging the world into an ice age. In all those years, CO_2 levels never rose above 298 ppm, and Earth's temperature was never more than 3° C above today's. By 2000, CO_2 levels had reached 370 ppm, the highest in 20 million years.[1] It is desperately important that we understand how the greenhouse effect works, and reduce our emissions to less worrying levels.

When the sun's rays hit the Earth, 30% of the incoming visible light is reflected back into space, 25% by clouds and 5% by ice; the remaining 70% is captured by the greenhouse gases warming the earth and especially the oceans. Plants, algae, and ocean phytoplankton capture the sun's energy through photosynthesis, and use it to convert carbon dioxide into carbon as part of nature's carbon cycle, a process we call carbon sequestration. The carbon

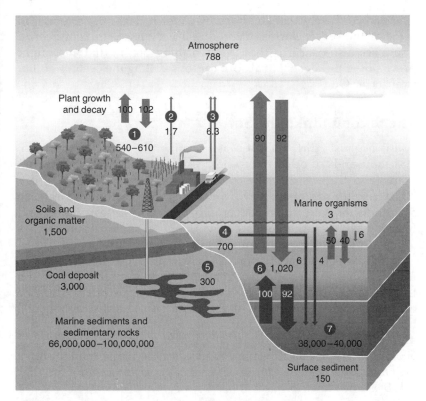

1 Terrestrial vegetation
2 Change in land use
3 Fossil fuel emissions
4 Dissolved organic carbon

5 Oil and gas deposit
6 Surface water
7 Intermediate and deep water

cycle determines how much of our excess CO_2 is absorbed and how much remains in the atmosphere to trap more heat.

The First Sink: The Oceans

In general, half of nature's photosynthesis is carried out in the oceans by phytoplankton,[2] and half on the land by bacteria, plants, and trees. Every year the oceans absorb around 92.4 billion tonnes of carbon and release 90 billion tonnes, storing 2.4 billion tonnes as dissolved inorganic carbon in the deep ocean (see diagram). Over the millennia, the oceans have socked away almost 40,000 billion tonnes of carbon, where, hopefully, it will remain. A quarter of this is stored as frozen methane hydrates, which have the potential to thaw as the ocean warms, triggering a very nasty turn of events. There are also concerns that in a warming ocean, diatoms might prevail over the algae that absorb carbon, stalling the ocean's ability to absorb CO_2.

The Second Sink: The Soil

Soil is not just "dirt." It is a mass of minerals, moisture, bacteria, and thousands of other micro-organisms that absorb carbon from plants and trees as they die. Every year, the world's soils absorb 50 billion tonnes of carbon from dying vegetation and release 50 billion tonnes through decomposition. Forest destruction and farming weaken the soil, however, causing 1.5 billion tonnes a year to be lost to the atmosphere. In western Canada, when an oldgrowth Douglas fir forest is clearcut, it can take 150 years for the soil and forest to recover the carbon they had before the trees were felled, which is why it is so important to change our methods of forestry.[3] Over the millennia, the world's soils have accumulated 1,500 billion tonnes of carbon, of which 500–800 billion tonnes is locked up in the world's peatlands, including 500 billion tonnes in the Arctic tundra, where rising temperatures are unlocking it as the snow cover disappears,[4] opening another troublesome scenario.

The Third Sink: Forests and Vegetation

The world's forests and vegetation store around 550 billion tonnes of carbon, 40% in the tropical forests. Every year, forests lose 50 billion tonnes of carbon to the soil and 50 billion tonnes to the atmosphere through respiration, but they absorb 101.5 billion tonnes from the atmosphere, reducing its load by 1.5 billion tonnes. Yes, trees matter. In our warming world, however, scientists fear that by 2050, the tropical forests will cease storing CO_2 and start releasing it, adding another factor to the scary prospect of a run-away greenhouse effect.[5]

In the balanced natural carbon cycle, approximately half of the atmospheric CO_2 is exchanging with the forests and soil, and half with the global oceans, resulting in no net atmospheric increase. In the disturbed carbon cycle that we are creating, approximately a quarter is going into the soil and vegetation, a quarter is going into the oceans, and half is accumulating in the atmosphere, trapping the sun's heat, which is why we are having this little problem.

THE GREENHOUSE GASES

Before the industrial age, we didn't have a problem with greenhouse gases. If anything, according to the pattern of the past 420,000 years, we were due for another ice age. Then we started adding greenhouse gases to the atmosphere. If we take carbon dioxide, methane, and nitrous oxide, the three main gases after water vapor, and express them as carbon-equivalents, we are adding 10 billion tonnes of carbon-equivalent to the atmosphere every year that nature would not have put there. At the present trend, this will rise to 10.6 billion tonnes per year by 2010.

The best way to measure the impact of the various gases is by their "radiative forcing." This is a measure of the extent to which a gas alters the balance of incoming and outgoing energy in the atmosphere. The sun's natural radiation is around 240 watts per square meter (240 W/m^2); the greenhouse gases are increasing this by about 1% (2.78 W/m^2). Most aerosols (such as dust) have a negative radiative forcing, though there is still much uncertainty about the data. The various gases also have different global warming potentials (GWP). GWP is the standard used to compare the radiative forcing of each greenhouse gas over 100 years, using CO_2 as a baseline, which is given a GWP of 1 (see chart . . .).

Carbon Dioxide is released by the fossil fuels we burn to generate electricity, drive the world's 530 million vehicles, and heat our homes and buildings. It is also released by the flaring of natural gas and oil, and by the production of cement. (Cement is made from limestone, the crushed shells of ancient carboniferous sea-creatures that surrender their carbon when we turn them into patio tiles.) It is released when forests and savannah grasslands are burned down,

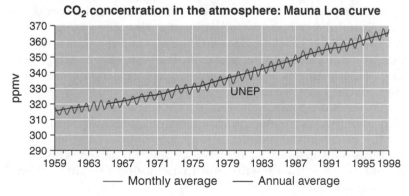

CO$_2$ concentration in the atmosphere: Mauna Loa curve

—— Monthly average —— Annual average

Source: Scripps institution of oceanography (SIO), University of California, 1998.

and when forests are clearcut, which destroys the soil they depend on. It is released by plowing and disking when farmers don't farm sustainably, and lose the carbon in their soil. In 1999, the world's carbon emissions from fossil fuels came to 6.144 billion tonnes; global forest and net biomass loss added another 1–2 billion tones. Cement production may add 100 million tonnes, and there are no clear figures for soil loss. The present concentration is probably the highest it has been for 20 million years; the rate of increase is the highest in at least 20,000 years.

To convert carbon emissions into CO_2 emissions, multiply by 3.667 to include the addition of oxygen. Most global data is expressed as carbon, while most national and local data is expressed as carbon dioxide just to keep us on our toes.

Methane comes from a variety of sources. It escapes from landfills. Cows release it during digestion, and liquid slurry ponds release it when animal wastes break down without oxygen. It is released when natural gas escapes (natural gas is 85%–95% methane), and it is released by coal mines, oil wells, sewage treatment plants, and flooded rice fields. It was recently discovered that methane is produced by rivers that have been dammed to generate hydroelectricity, when biomass in and entering the reservoir breaks down without oxygen. The present atmospheric concentration is the highest for at least 420,000 years.

Nitrous Oxide is released by the use of nitrogen-based chemical fertilizers in farming and by transportation, nitric acid production, poor manure management, and various other sources.

The CFCs, HCFCs and HFCs. Remember the CFCs (chlorofluorocarbons), the chemicals we used as coolants in fridges and air-conditioning systems and as propellants in spray cans, that are blowing holes in the ozone layer? Turns out they are potent global warming gases, too. They are being phased out, but their replacements, the HCFCs and HFCs (hydrochlorofluorocarbons and hydrofluorocarbons) are also potent greenhouse gases. (HCFCs also attack the ozone layer, but much less so.) See Solution #95 for more on this muddle. Life gets complex here, because the ozone that CFCs destroy is a natural greenhouse gas, counterbalancing some of their radiative forcing.

Other Industrial Chemicals. There's perfluorocarbons, used in the manufacture of aluminum and semi-conductors; sulfur hexafluoride, used in the production of magnesium, as a dielectric in electrical transmission and distribution and in the semi-conductor industry; and trifluoromethyl sulfur pentafluoride, that nobody knows much about.[1]

Tropospheric Ozone is also a greenhouse gas. Its accumulation in the lower atmosphere (troposphere), up to seven miles high, is caused by pollutants from burning fossil fuels. Ozone in the upper atmosphere (seven to 30 miles up) is a good thing.

Aerosols. These are very fine dust particles or liquid droplets that come from fossil fuel burning, forest and biomass burning, and industrial pollution. With the exception of black carbon, they have a negative radiative forcing, shielding Earth from the impact of the main greenhouse gases. The data on the next page is from the 2001 IPCC report, but there is not a good understanding of how the different aerosols work. James Hansen, Director of NASA's Goddard Institute for Space Studies, thinks that black carbon, or soot, may contribute 15%–30% to the overall radiative forcing.[2] If this is so, it changes the responsibility of the various greenhouse gases: CO_2—41%; Black Carbon—22%; Methane—13%; Ozone—10%; CFCs etc—10%; Nitrous Oxide—4%. 90% of black carbon comes from burning biomass and fossil fuels.

THE ENHANCED GREENHOUSE EFFECT

So what do these gases do when you add them to the atmosphere? That's what the world's climatologists and oceanographers have been looking at.

One of their projects has been to drill 3,600 meters into the ice at Vostok station in East Antarctica, retrieving frozen samples of ice that date back 420,000 years.[1] When they melt the ice and analyze the air trapped in it, they can produce readings for temperature, carbon dioxide, methane, and dust throughout the period. The record confirms that there have been four major ice ages, each lasting 65,000 to 100,000 years. During each ice age, the temperature was 6–8° C lower than it has been for the past 11,000 years, and levels of CO_2 and methane were equally low. The connection between temperature and CO_2 and methane is almost mathematical.

Each of the ice ages was followed by a relatively sudden "termination," when the temperature rose to 5° C above the recent norm, accompanied by a rise in CO_2 and methane and a fall in the amount of dust in the atmosphere. (Dust prevents solar radiative forcing, creating a shield against the sun's rays.) CO_2 rose from 200 parts per million to 280–300 (today's level is 370), while methane rose from 300–400 parts per billion to 550–800 (today's level is 1750). The warm periods lasted 6,000–10,000 years, then the world plunged back into the next ice age, accompanied by falling CO_2 and methane.

The scientists do not yet understand why the climate stabilized 11,000 years ago instead of peaking and freezing. The Vostok research shows that the recent stability (the Holocene) has been the longest in the past 420,000 years. This has been the *exception*, not the rule; without the warmer temperature, there would have been no farming, no food surpluses, no cities, no civilizations. We mess with this stuff at our peril.

The Vostok scientists believe that each warming period starts with a change in the nature of the Earth's orbit, bringing an increase in solar radiation. The warming is amplified by simultaneous increases in CO_2 and methane caused by the massive increase in flooding as the ice melts, and by a decrease in dust. As the temperature rises, the melting snow and ice lose their albedo effect, allowing the earth and oceans to absorb more heat. Albedo is the name given to the reflection of the sun's light off a surface. Snow has a very high albedo, reflecting 75%–95% of the light;

Temperature and CO_2 concentration in the atmosphere over the past 400,000 years (from the Vostok ice core)

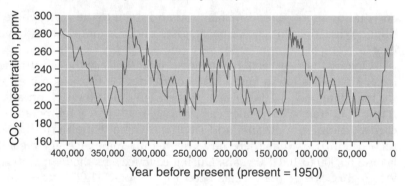

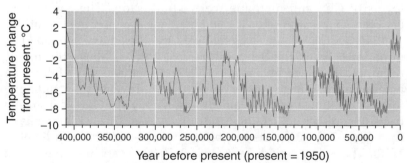

Source: J.R. Petit, J. Jouzel, et al. Climate and atmospheric history of the past 420,000 years from the Vostok ice core in Antarctica, *Nature* 399 (3 June), pp 429–436, 1999.

tundra and forest have a low albedo (15%–20%) and absorb a lot of heat. Water's albedo can be as low as 5%. The climate is also influenced by changes in the albedo of the clouds—cirrus clouds have low albedo (15%–20%) while stratus clouds have high albedo (70%)—and by particles of dust in the atmosphere from volcanoes and industrial pollution, which have a cooling effect.

So what is happening in the greenhouse today? The concentration of CO_2 in the atmosphere is the highest that it has been for 20 million years.[2] If the increase continues, in 100 years' time it will be the highest since the Eocene Epoch, 50 million years ago, when there were no ice caps at all, London (England) was a tropical swamp and there were crocodiles on today's Arctic islands.

There is no doubt that the Earth is warming. The evidence of warming has been confirmed by research that looked at 15 different records of past climate, including tree rings in Colorado, ice cores from Tibet, old English shipping records, ancient Chinese writings, and mud from the bottom of the Sargasso Sea.[3] From 1750 to 2000, the temperature in the Northern Hemisphere rose by 2° F (1.1° C). An analysis of more than 600 deep boreholes shows that temperatures rose by 1.25° F (0.7° C) from 1750 to 1990.[4] During the 1990s, temperatures rose six to seven times faster, by 0.72° F (0.4° C). Since 1990, the rate of warming has increased to 7° F (4° C) per century. Scientists have concluded that there is only a 1-in-20 chance that the current string of high temperatures is a result of natural phenomena; the evidence points overwhelmingly to human activities as the cause.[5] British scientists at the Hadley Centre for Climate Research have predicted that the global temperature could increase by as much as 14° F (8° C), as the increased warmth causes forests and oceans to stop absorbing CO_2 and begin releasing it.[6]

Climate science is like detective work, piecing together clues about the past, studying the present, and making informed guesses about the future. Climate modeling is very complex and there are many different feedback loops to consider, including the effects of changing cloud cover, albedo, solar radiation, ocean temperatures, carbon sinks, sulfate aerosols, ozone, and so on. The UN Intergovernmental Panel on Climate Change (IPCC) is an elite body of 2,500 global scientists who work together to establish a consensus on what the science is telling us. In their 2001 report, they said that "there is now stronger evidence for a human influence," and that man-made greenhouse gases "have contributed substantially to the observed warming over the last 50 years." Their estimate is that the global temperature will rise by 2.5° F to 10.4° F (1.4° to 5.8° C) by 2100, replacing their previous estimate of 1.8° F to 6.3° F (1.0° to

3.5° C). Of the ten warmest years on record since 1860, eight have occurred since 1990.

THE CLIMATE IMPACTS

What will it all mean? All over the world, people have been studying how the enhanced greenhouse effect will affect life on Earth.

Prediction: The Arctic ice will melt.

Reality: Temperatures in the Arctic have risen by more than 4° F in the past 30 years, twice as much as in the rest of the world. Some areas are up to 7° F warmer. Arctic ice is normally up to 3 meters thick, but when Russian and US submarines compared their data, they found that it had lost 40% of its depth since 1970. At this rate, the summer ice will be gone by 2040, and the polar bears will starve to death since they will be unable to hunt on the summer sea ice. In 2000, a scientific cruise ship found open water at the North Pole: the last time this happened may have been 50 million years ago. The Greenland ice sheet has thinned by a meter on its southern and eastern edges. At the other end of the world, the Antarctic ice has been melting slowly for the past 10,000 years, but the speed of melting may be increasing. On the Antarctic Peninsula, the temperature has risen by 4.5° F over the past 50 years; between 1973 and 1993, the sea ice decreased by 20%. The IPCC scientists do not foresee any loss of the grounded ice (e.g. the west Antarctic ice sheet) during the 21st century.

Prediction: The glaciers will melt.

Reality: In Glacier National Park, the number of glaciers has fallen from 150 to 50 since 1850. In Africa, Mount Kenya's largest glacier has lost 92% of its mass, and Mt Kilimanjaro has lost 75% of its ice. In Argentina, the Upsala Glacier is retreating by 60 meters a year. In New Zealand, the Tasman Glacier has retreated by 1.7 miles since 1971. Scientists predict that by 2050, a quarter of the world's mountain glacier masses will have disappeared.

Prediction: The oceans will warm.

Reality: Between the mid-1950s and mid-1990s, the overall world ocean warmed by 0.06° C to a depth of 3,000 meters. In the top 300 meters, the warming was 0.31° C, or 0.3 watts per square meter.[1] In the northern hemisphere, the ocean surface is warming by 1° F per decade, similar to the amount that the entire planet has seen over the past 100 years.[2]

Prediction: Sea levels will rise; coastal areas will flood.

Reality: As the ocean warms, it expands. The 2001 IPCC forecast is for a rise of 3.5 to 35 inches (0.09 to 0.88 meters) by 2100, and a 7–13 meter rise over the next 500 years. If global warming is halted within the century, thermal expansion will still raise the oceans by 0.5 to 4 meters as the heat reaches the ocean deeps. In 2000, floods kept two-thirds of Bangladesh under water for two months, setting back many of their social and economic gains. This much sea level rise will affect far more than Polynesia and Micronesia. Thirty of the world's largest cities are close to sea level, including London, New York, and Shanghai.

Prediction: Spring will come earlier.

Reality: In Europe, an extensive study of gardens has found that spring is arriving six days earlier and fall is arriving almost five days later.[3] In England, frogs are spawning 9–10 days earlier;[4] in the US, spring migrants are being recorded earlier as they reach Michigan's Upper Peninsula.[5]

Prediction: There will be increased precipitation and floods.

Reality: As the temperature warms, more water evaporates from the oceans, causing more downpours and more snow. In 1998, Sydney (Australia) broke all records with 12 inches of rain in two days; Texas had two rainstorms that dumped 10 and 20 inches, causing $1 billion in damage and 31 deaths; the Black Hills of South Dakota had 8.5 feet of snow in five days. In 1999, Mount Baker (WA) had 95 feet of snow between November 1998 and June 1999, a world record.[6] The NOAA data show that in stronger storms, the amount of rainfall per storm has increased by about 10% in recent decades.[7] The clearing of lands and filling of wetlands makes the flooding worse.

Prediction: More heat waves and droughts.

Reality: In 1998, Tibet had its warmest June on record; Christchurch (NZ) had its warmest February; Edmonton (Canada) had its warmest summer; Little Rock, Arkansas had its hottest May; Cairo (Egypt) had its warmest August. From April to June 1998, Florida, Texas, and Louisiana had their driest period in 104 years; in Texas, temperatures stayed over 100° F for 15 straight days. In 1999, New York had its hottest and driest July on record; the eastern US had its driest growing season on record, with agricultural disaster areas being declared in 15 states. Since 1980, droughts are visiting the US,

Europe, Africa, and Asia more frequently. There will also be much colder periods in some places.

Prediction: More forest fires and insect damage.

Reality: In 1998, Florida had its worst wildfires in 50 years, and Mexico had its worst fire season ever. In Canada, the area of forest consumed by fire each year has risen steadily since the 1970s; the Canadian Forest Service is predicting a 50% increase by 2050.[8] Scientists in Alaska have reported that 20 million hectares of forest are suffering from an unprecedented attack by spruce budworms as a result of warmer weather.

Prediction: Ecosystems will be disrupted.

Reality: From Bermuda to the Great Barrier Reef, coral reefs are dying from the warmer ocean temperatures—these are the rainforests of the ocean, where 65% of the world's fish species dwell. In the North Pacific, salmon are starving as their food disappears, and migrating north to escape waters that are warmer than 7° C.[9] If the salmon go, so will the orca whales, eagles, and bears that depend on them for food. Alpine plants are retreating up the mountainsides in Austria. Butterfly ranges are shifting north in Europe and California. Adelie penguin populations in the Antarctic have fallen by 33% since 1975 as the winter sea ice melts. The World Wide Fund for Nature has warned that a third of the world's habitat could disappear or change beyond recognition by 2100, including Newfoundland, Ontario, British Columbia, Quebec, Alberta, Manitoba, and the Yukon where more than half the area is at risk.[10]

Prediction: Tropical diseases will spread.

Reality: Malaria has been transmitted by mosquitoes in the northeastern US states and in Toronto; the West Nile virus has arrived in New York; in Mexico and Columbia, dengue fever has spread to higher elevations—4,000 feet above its normal range.

Prediction: Increase in weather-related disasters.

Reality: From Mozambique to Honduras, and from Canada to China, weather disasters have been proliferating. In 1998, violent weather caused $89 billion worth of damage, killing 32,000 people and displacing 300 million. Insurance companies paid out $91.8 billion in losses from weather-related natural disasters from 1990–1998, four times more than weather-related claims in the 1980s.[11] In China, the 1999 flooding of the Yangtze River region killed 3,500 people, destroyed 5 million homes, and dislocated 200 million lives. In 2000, natural disasters rose by 100 to a record 850; storms accounted for 73% of the insured losses, floods for 23%.[12]

And this is only the tip of the melting iceberg.

Reading Notes

The Greenhouse Effect

1. "Atmospheric carbon dioxide concentrations over the past 60 million years" by Paul N. Pearson & Martin R. Palmer, *Nature*, Aug. 17, 2000.

2. "Oceanography: Stirring times in the southern ocean" by Sallie Chisholm (MIT), *Nature*, Oct. 12, 2000.

3. Effects on carbon storage of conversion of old-growth forests to younger forests, by M.E. Harmon, W.K. Ferrell and J.F. Franklin, *Science* 247(1990): 699–702.

4. "A note on summer CO_2 flux, soil organic matter, and microbial biomass from different high Arctic ecosystem types in northwestern Greenland," by M. H. Jones, J. T. Fahnestock, P. D. Stahl, and J. M. Walker, *Arctic, Antarctic, and Alpine Research*, Feb. 2000. www.colorado.edu/INSTAAR/arcticalpine.

5. "Acceleration of global warming due to carbon-cycle feedbacks in a couple climate model," by Peter M. Cox et al., *Nature*, Nov. 9, 2000.

The Greenhouse Gases

1. In 2000, it was listed on Roschem Pacific Group's chemical inventory (www.roschem.com/pravail.html) in Australia, but it has since been removed.

2. *Global warming in the 21st Century. An alternative scenario*, by James Hansen et al. (NASA Goddard Institute for Space Studies), 200. (www.giss.nasa.gov/gpol/abstracts/2000.HansenSatoR.html)

The Enhanced Greenhouse Effect

1. "Climate and atmospheric history of the past 420,000 years from the Vostok ice core, Antarctica," by J.R. Petit et al., *Nature*, June 3, 1999.

2. "Atmospheric carbon dioxide concentrations over the past 60 million years," by Paul Pearson and Martin Palmer, *Nature*, August 17, 2000.

3. "How warm was the medieval warm period?" by Thomas Magnuson et al., *Ambio*, Feb. 1, 2000; also "Historical trends in lake and river ice cover in the Northern Hemisphere," by John J. Magnuson et al., *Science*, Sept. 8, 2000.

4. "A doubling of the sun's coronal magnetic field during the past 100 years," by M. Lockwood et al., *Nature*, Vol. 399(1999), p. 437.

5. "The record breaking global temperatures of 1997 and 1998: Evidence for an increase in the rate of global warming?" by Thomas Karl et al., *Geophysical Research Letters*, March 1, 2000.

6. See "Forests and soils may speed up global warming," Hadley Centre for Climate Research, UK, Nov. 8, 1998.

The Climate Impacts

1. "Warming of the world ocean," by Sydney Levitus et al., *Science*, March 24, 2000.

2. Alan Strong, National Oceanic and Atmospheric Administration, July 2000.

3. "Growing season extended in Europe," by Annette Menzel and Peter Fabian, *Nature*, Vol. 397, No. 6721 (1999).

4. Barnaby Briggs, Birdlife International.

5. World Wide Fund for Nature (Climate): "An early spring."

6. For references see www.climatehotmap.org.

7. National Oceanic and Atmospheric Administration news release, *Washington Post*, April 19, 2000.

8. Story by David Roberts, *Globe and Mail*, April 3, 2000.

9. David Welch, Fisheries Canada, paper in *Journal of Fisheries and Aquatic Science*, 1999.

10. "Global warming and terrestrial biodiversity decline," WWF 2000.

11. "Destructive storms drive insurance losses up: Will taxpayers have to bail out insurance industry?" by Seth Dunn & Christopher Flavin, Worldwatch Institute, 1999.

12. Munich Re, Dec. 29th 2000.

Eating Tasty Clones: Is Cloned Steak Good for You?

RONALD BAILEY

Ronald Bailey is a science journalist for *Reason* magazine, a monthly libertarian publication that promotes itself as the magazine of "free minds and free markets." Bailey is the editor of *The True State of the Planet* and *Earth*

Report 2000: Revisiting the True State of the Planet, as well as author of *ECOSCAM: The False Prophets of the Ecological Apocalypse.* In these works, Bailey argues that the claims of environmentalists are often unscientific and hysterical.

Second Chance was cloned from a 21-year-old steer named Chance who obviously could not pass on his genes any other way. Second Chance or his descendants could end up on your dinner plate one day. Since the birth of the sheep Dolly, the first mammal cloned in 1996, researchers have succeeded in cloning a host of farm animals including goats, pigs, mules, and cows. Since producing animal clones is very expensive, it's unlikely that many clones will soon end up as Salisbury steak or a rack of lamb. Instead cloning is being used to preserve and pass along genes from superior or rare animals. Still, one day, as cloning becomes more efficient, meat and milk from clones will be sold to consumers. Is that a problem?

First, people already regularly eat lots of clones, that is, cloned fruits and vegetables. This includes most wine grapes, and all seedless grapes. Granny Smith, Red Delicious, and Gala apples are all clones, as are garlic and most blueberries. One might think that being genetically identical might actually enhance food safety since people have already eaten the clones' forebears without ill effects.

Similarly, the forebears of many animal clones will already have been served as hamburgers or barbecue with no apparent ill effects on consumers. So it seems reasonable to think that if the forebear was tasty and harmless that its genetically identical twin will also be equally tasty and harmless. The notoriously cautious National Academy of Sciences found last year that "There is no current evidence that food products derived from adult somatic cell clones or their progeny present a food safety concern." The NAS added, "The products of offspring of cloned animals were regarded as posing no food safety concern because they are the result of natural matings." Despite the lack of evidence that eating cloned animals or products derived from them is somehow unsafe, the NAS panel recommended "that an evaluation of the composition of food products derived from cloned animals using available procedures would be prudent to minimize any remaining food safety concerns." And that is being done.

Last week, the US Food and Drug Administration (FDA) after reviewing the available scientific evidence issued a preliminary report that concluded, "Edible products from normal, healthy clones or their progeny do not appear to pose increased food consumption risks relative to comparable products from conventional animals."

But in modern America, no new technology goes unchallenged. So-called consumer activists like Carol Tucker Foreman from Consumers Federation of America caution against animal cloning. However, Foreman offers no scientific evidence that there may be any safety problems with animal cloning, just pandering to vague fears about new technologies.

Earlier this week, an FDA scientific panel essentially backed the safety findings of the agency's preliminary report, but split down the middle on approving the use of cloned animals for food on the basis of animal welfare concerns. Cloning technology is still so crude that it often takes hundreds of attempts to produce one healthy clone.

The FDA panelists pointed out that many cloned animal fetuses never come to term and many die of defects shortly after being born. (Food safety note: The FDA already forbids putting diseased and defective animals into our food supply and these rules would clearly apply to defective clones.) Given the panoply of animal welfare issues that could be raised with regard to using animals as food, it seems a bit peculiar to worry overmuch about cloning. And cloning can improve animal welfare too. For example, much animal pain and suffering could be eliminated by cloning disease-resistant animals.

So relax—thanks to cloning, you may soon safely enjoy a nice medium rare New York strip from Third Chance, Fourth Chance, Fifth Chance, or even 10,000th Chance.

Danger Lurks in a Biotech World

DAVID STEELE

With a Ph.D. in genetics and molecular biology, David Steele is a molecular biologist at the University of British Columbia. He designed and constructed the world's first artificial mitochondrial gene, but chose to keep it in the common domain rather than patent it. In addition to professional research into genetics, he is also an author and activist, writing on a variety of environmental, health, and social justice issues. Although genetic research holds much potential, Steele is deeply concerned about his profession's ability to create a disaster.

I'm a molecular biologist. I've used molecular techniques to study heredity, evolution, gene expression and even components of heart function (strangely enough using yeast as the model organism). I know how powerful molecular biology can be and how vast its contribution has been to our understanding of life's basic processes and to our medical well-being.

But I'm worried. Very worried.

Molecular biology, like most sciences, arose from intellectual curiosity. Academic scientists wondered how life works; what kind of information we could cull from manipulating its basic building blocks, what we could learn from shuffling these building blocks around.

The approach proved wildly productive. We've gained unprecedented insights. We've learned what underlies countless diseases, how the basic machinery of our cells operates, and, to varying extents, how to manipulate those operations for our own purposes. We've learned so much that we think we know what we're doing. But all that knowledge cannot compare to what we do not know. And it is in our unrecognized ignorance that the greatest danger lies.

A few years ago, researchers at the Australian National University demonstrated just how appallingly dangerous our ignorance is.

These scientists were trying to make a contraceptive vaccine for mice—a vaccine that would make the animals sterile. To that end, they constructed an artificial virus genetically coded to express (produce) a normal mouse protein. Ordinarily, the protein increases antibody production. Since the Australian group was trying to get the mice to make antibodies to their own eggs, the approach seemed reasonable enough. But the experiment went terribly wrong.

Instead of making sterile mice, the technique made dead mice. And the deaths were not by a mechanism that the scientists would have predicted. They thought they knew what they were doing. But they couldn't have been more wrong. Instead of boosting the effectiveness of the mouse immune system, the virus effectively shut that system down and killed the animals.

The virus was contained in the lab and it apparently poses no danger to humans, but that's not the point. The fact is that every day, in labs around the world, scientists are constructing artificial viruses that can infect humans. Many are designed to do precisely that. Some are made for pure research purposes, others to be used, potentially, for "gene therapy"—a hoped-for means to cure genetic diseases in living humans. Should one of these viruses go hopelessly wrong like the Australian mouse virus did, watch out!

What the Australian researchers have very clearly demonstrated is that viral experiments are dangerous. Very dangerous. Even when we truly believe that we understand what we're doing, even when our goals are very laudable—like curing disease and ameliorating suffering—the results of our experiments can be disastrous. Fortunately, the Australian virus was (very likely) limited to the confines of their lab. A very great deal of biotech research has no such limitations.

Genetically-engineered food organisms, for example, are cropping up all around us. Successive Canadian governments have bent over backwards to help the biotech giants bring these "products" to market. In the United States, as the New York Times has reported, Monsanto essentially wrote its own regulations. Not surprisingly, they're extremely lax. In both the U.S. and Canada, there is very little government oversight.

As the Royal Society of Canada stated in their stinging 2001 report on genetically engineered (GE) or modified (GM—these terms are interchangeable) foods in Canada, regulators go out of their way to accommodate the biotech giants. In their government-commissioned study, the Society's distinguished panel pointed out that Ottawa is in conflict of interest. It both promotes and regulates the GE food industry. And testing is shoddy, to say the least. Field trials are almost always sloppily performed; their results can be virtually uninterpretable. From studies like these, we can't even tell whether the crops perform as advertised, let alone whether they pose any dangers.

Yes, the occasional GE food might have some benefits for some of us. But many GE crops have the potential—over periods of even just a few years—to create new superweeds and new superpests. (In fact, they already have. Triply herbicide-resistant canola has appeared in the wild—the product of successive cross-pollination of genetically-engineered varieties.) Loss of genetic diversity as specific GE crops become popular with farmers could leave us vulnerable to widespread crop failure and famine.

Occasionally, GE foods might even present unforeseen direct health hazards to humans. Based solely on crude chemical comparisons and unproven biological assumptions, North American regulators declare GE crops to be "substantially equivalent" to their conventional brethren. These crops—such as GE soy and canola—can then be commercially cultivated and sold to consumers. Yet, to quote the Royal Society of Canada's report, "this approach [substantial equivalence] is fatally flawed for genetically modified, or GM, crops and exposes Canadians to several potential health risks, including toxicity and allergic reactions." Still, virtually none of these possibilities are even rudimentally tested, and GE crops are planted despite the unknown dangers.

But if you think GE crops are bad, there's more.

Biotech has an even more pernicious side. Animals are being brought into the act. New cloning technologies have yielded goats who secrete drugs or spider silk in their milk. Pigs are "engineered" for human organ transplants; salmon modified to grow two or three times faster than their wild relatives. They are among a plethora of animals engineered to serve human purposes.

Putting aside the important ethical considerations involved in exploiting individual animals in these ways, all of these technologies have obvious potential dangers. "Super salmon," for example, could potentially decimate wild populations. Viruses lying latent in animal organs might give rise to new diseases if transplanted into humans. As Doctors and Lawyers for Responsible Medicine warn, animal-to-human transplants are "a transplant surgeon's dream, but a virologist's nightmare."

And that's not all. Whole animals are now being cloned. Dolly the sheep was first. Pigs, cows and others have followed. None has been born without the cost of innumerable "defective" sibs—animals who may live only hours, who may be born with deformed limbs or lacking internal organs. Even the healthy clones may be doomed to shortened lifespans—we're not sure, but their chromosomes seem to reflect the age of the animal that was cloned, not that of a young newborn. And now, unethical scientists are racing to clone human beings. How they can live with themselves, I have no idea.

The explosion in biotechnology is occurring precisely as more and more research is being directed towards private ends. Even much of academic science is becoming commercial. It couldn't happen at a worse time. The dangers are bad enough in publicly-funded experiments. But at least they're subject to review by other scientists and by government organizations like the Canadian Institutes of Health Research. Private research frequently circumvents these protections. There are no peer-review panels to sound the alarm if an experiment seems particularly dangerous. Indeed, for proprietary reasons, much private research is kept secret. And, as demonstrated in the example of GE foods, the drive to bring a product to market can easily trump testing for even the most predictable of dangers.

Greatly increased public vigilance is needed badly—and soon! Like physics and chemistry before it, biology is proving to harbour serious dangers—dangers that, left unchecked, could easily eclipse its promise.

Yes, biotechnology may bring us new treatments and medicines for diseases we cannot now alleviate. Yes, it may do even more. But it can't be allowed to do so at any cost. Just as the victim of an atomic bomb blast or dioxin-induced cancer has little interest in General Relativity or organic chemistry, we may well find ourselves unconcerned with even major medical breakthroughs if molecular biology inadvertently (or intentionally, in the hands of unscrupulous persons) brings us plague or famine.

We're a clever bunch, we humans. But our cleverness is far outstripping our intelligence. The time for a substantial, informed public debate on these issues is definitely at hand. There is a lot of promise in science, but not in unrestrained science. Scientific disasters will be rare. But because living creatures multiply, rare events may quickly seem not so rare. Who knows when an ill-conceived GE organism might collapse a whole ecosystem? Who knows when a killer virus may be unwittingly unleashed?

In Defense of Tree-Spiking

PAUL WATSON

Paul Watson is an eco-activist, who works to end whaling, sealing, wolf culls, clear-cut logging, and nuclear testing. Author of *Seal Wars: Twenty-Five Years on the Front Lines with the Harp Seals* and *Ocean Warrior: My Battle to End the Illegal Slaughter on the High Seas*, Watson is a founding member of Greenpeace and the Sea Shepherd Conservation Society. An advocate of animal rather than human rights, Watson regularly risks his life to save endangered species. His use of direct action tactics has alienated him from moderate environmentalists, as is clear in his testimony for the controversial practice of tree-spiking.

Tree-spiking is one of the most effective tactics yet developed to protect old-growth forests. It is a controversial tactic, but the most effective tactics are always controversial. Why tree-spiking? As the originator of tree-spiking as an environmental tactic, I feel it is my responsibility to defend its legitimacy.

As a child I witnessed my father break a chain saw on a horseshoe that had been nailed to a tree a century before and became over time an internal armour protecting the heart of the elderly and noble being. I was delighted. In the mid-sixties I spiked some trees to protect them from developers in my neighborhood. It was not successful. The trees were cut down, but with the small satisfaction of two broken chain saws.

Then, in 1982, the Grouse Mountain Ski Resort in North Vancouver, British Columbia announced that they were selling the timber rights to the south slope of Grouse Mountain. The decision meant that loggers would bald face the mountain overlooking the city of Vancouver. The public was outraged. The North Vancouver City Council was unsuccessful in stopping the decision from going ahead. Despite petitions from school-children and appeals from prominent citizens, the trees were doomed. The resort would not relent.

I organized a small cadre of concerned eco-activists and we formed the group called the North Vancouver Garden and Arbor Club. We started out early on a Sunday morning, each armed with a hammer and a backpack filled with metal spikes. The six of us were able to successfully spike some two thousand trees. At the same time we pulled out every survey stake we could find. We posted over three dozen warning signs stating that the entire condemned lot had been randomly spiked. Then we drove into Vancouver and dropped off press releases to the media.

The next day the shit hit the fan. The Vancouver *Sun* and the Vancouver *Province* both ran the story on the front page with banner headlines. We followed up by interviews with television stations—all of us wearing masks and identifying ourselves as spokesperson Wally Cedarleaf.

Within a day, the sawmills stated flatly that they had no intention of buying logs from the spiked lot. The deal was off. The Grouse Mountain Resort people were furious. We were denounced as terrorists and criminals by those we thought were our allies: the North Vancouver City Council, and Greenpeace and assorted other eco-bureaucrats. We didn't give a damn—the fact was that the trees were saved, Grouse Mountain would remain intact. It was a tactic that worked.

The Royal Canadian Mounted Police (RCMP) investigated the case and their sleuthing led them to our doorsteps, where we were questioned but not charged. The logging interests were quick to realize that any publicity over such a simple tactic would do them more harm than any benefit they would derive from prosecuting us. Not only was it a tactic that worked, it was a tactic that we could get away with.

Prior to the spiking I had consulted a good friend who was an arborist. I asked him for pointers on how to spike the tree without causing it any harm. He provided me with the advice that I needed. I then made enquiries of the logging industry while pretending to be an insurance investigator. I asked if there were safety mechanisms on chain saws that would prevent the chain from breaking and striking the operator. I was assured by the industry that such an accident could not happen, for all the chain saws used had chain guards to prevent a broken chain from whipping back into the face of the logger. I was also told that the sawmills required safety shields between mill saws and their operators.

Again posing as an insurance investigator, I asked, "Is it possible for a logger or a sawmill worker to be injured if the mill saw should strike a metallic object embedded in a log?" The answer from three different industry spokespeople was a definite "No." The companies I questioned were MacMillan Bloedel, Crown Zellerbach, and Weldwood Lumber.

Therefore, I concluded that tree-spiking was a perfect tactic. It would not hurt the tree. It would not hurt the loggers or sawmill operators. It was simple and easy to do. Materials were easy to obtain. It was not illegal. It could not even be defined as damaging property, since trees—being living sentient beings—are not and never will be human property. Recognition of trees as property is a clear statement of anthropocentric thought.

A few months after the spiking of Grouse Mountain, I ran into Mike Roselle in a Greenpeace hang-out in San Francisco. Another participating member of the Garden Club and I told Mike about the incident and the tactic. He was thrilled with the idea, and because of Mike many others became involved.

Thus it was with both pride and satisfaction that I relished reports of tree-spiking from California, Oregon, Washington, and Alaska. One report came from the Bahamas and another from Sweden of spiking operations that had saved forest land. Native Indians spiked trees on Meares Island in British Columbia. Tree-spiking was becoming epidemic. For the first time, the logging industry found itself on the defensive.

The industry reacted with propaganda about the dangers of tree-spiking to humans, conveniently forgetting that only a few short years earlier they had informed me (in my insurance-investigator guise) that an injury was not possible. Industry money was channelled into lobbying politicians to pass laws making tree-spiking illegal. The industry began to spend large sums on security and investigation. But the forests are vast and detection is difficult, and all the new laws and pumped-in money have not paid off with the conviction of a single tree-spiker.

Tree-spiking is also a tactic that keeps the issues of old-growth forests and clear cutting in the news. It is itself a controversial issue, and as such is guaranteed to provide consistency to discussion in the media and among the public. With the tactic of tree-spiking the defenders of the forest have a weapon with which to keep the logging industry and their lackey workers on the defensive.

Tree-spiking has continually stimulated the imaginations of many eco-defenders. The original tactic has benefitted from the addition of ceramic spikes, the use of augers, and the employment of twist nails, and thus the trees have benefitted. When the industry threatened to log spiked trees to spite our efforts I suggested that ecologists escalate our campaign by spiking cut logs both on the floating booms and in the industry yards. Escalate if you like, you bastards, and we'll go for the heart of your operations—your machinery. Thus we have found that tree-spiking can be both a defensive and an offensive tactic.

In a biocentric context, tree-spiking is simply a form of preventative medicine. It is the inoculation of a tree against the disease of logging. But in the context of our society, money talks, and industry money has successfully swayed anthropocentric opinions against tree-spiking.

Unfortunately, there was a weak link in our movement. The anthropocentric socialist types, whose hearts bleed for the antiquated rights of the workers were won over. Concerned that the logger was a "victim," these so-called defenders of the forests have proceeded to weaken our one totally effective tactic by denouncing it.

I was in attendance at the Environmental Law Conference in Eugene, Oregon in the spring of 1990. Judi Bari and Daryl Cherney said that there was unanimous consensus at the tree-spiking work-shop that the tactic should be retired. There was not! Judi Bari even told me at the conference that she considered me to be the enemy, but many Earth Firsters were in opposition. It was a tragedy that Judi and Daryl were hurt when their car was bombed.[1] We will probably never know what really happened, but it will be a greater tragedy if the bombing continues to give martyr status to two people who have seriously compromised the established principles of Earth First!

Redwood Summer was not an Earth First! type of operation. Civil disobedience is costly to its participants, both financially and physically. It is a tactic that springs from the deep Judeo-Christian ethics of self-sacrifice and voluntary self-inflicted persecution. It was not a tactic that was ever practiced by North American native peoples. The establishment loves CD. The authorities are trained to deal with it, there are no surprises.

The Redwood Summer people would have us believe that the loggers are not our enemies. Judi Bari considers them her allies, while at the same time accusing me of being her enemy. The reality of her views is plain. She is acting from an anthropocentric ethical foundation, while I come from a biocentric base.

The hands of the individual who would destroy a tree are the hands of a person prepared to murder a sacred and respected cit-izen of this planet. Livelihood, material well-being, these are not sufficient justification for this crime against nature. Loggers are just pathetic foot-soldiers for the corporate generals of the logging industry. Certainly they are being exploited by the companies, but they have made the decision to be exploited. The trees have not.

Yes, I realize that humans use wood and believe themselves dependent upon the cutting of trees. I also realize, however, that to a vastly reduced population wood could be made available without killing trees. Dead wood; weather preserved wood; living planks cut from living trees (a practice that provided Northwest coastal Indians with planks without depriving the world of a tree); cotton and papyrus for paper; these sources are all alternatives to the wholesale destruction currently practiced by the logging industry. There are alternatives, the most important being disciplined conservation. Yes, this is extreme, but so is massive clear-cutting to provide cheap logs for Japanese mills and bags of redwood charcoal for California cook-outs. I could occasionally even condone the cutting of a living tree: if it was diseased, and done with the proper respect, and used for a noble purpose. Unfortunately, 99.9% of all trees killed are in good health and are used for ignoble purposes.

A few years ago, a Santa Cruz reporter told me that she did not believe that all the redwoods in California were worth the life of a single human being. What incredible arrogance. This opinion is the extreme view of anthropocentric Judeo-Christian thinking. I am of the extreme opposite view. To me, all of the human beings in California are not worth the extinction of one of the mighty and revered ancient forest dwellers we have chosen to call redwoods.

The debate really comes down to this: Is Earth First! a movement of anthropocentrics, a movement of biocentrics, or is it a little of both? Can the anthropocentric mind-set work harmoniously, or even work at all, with the biocentric mind-set? One thing is certain, that there is a vast chasm between the two modes of thought. Perhaps there is a need for two Earth First! groups, one for anthropocentrics and the other for biocentrics.

As for myself, I do not believe in loggers, I believe in trees. I do not believe in fishermen, I believe in fish. I do not believe in miners, I believe in the rocks beneath my feet. I do not believe in pie-in-the-sky spirituality, I believe in rainbows, rivers, mountains, daffodils, and moss. I do not believe in environmentalists, I believe in the environment. I am a proud traitor to my species, in alliance with my mother the Earth in opposition to those who would destroy her; those who would tear down the sun to make a buck; those insignificant parasites who believe that the Earth is here to serve human interests.

The Earth abides. We overly glorified primate apes will pass, for we are a stupid species, incapable of relating intelligently to nature, with harmony and respect. We have chosen not to consider ourselves to be interdependent, and have bestowed divinity upon ourselves to justify our separateness from the divine beauty of the living Earth. We must either change or pass, and in our passing the rocks will scream joyously at the Earth's liberation, which will be their reward for our disappearance. Or, if we survive, it will be as equal citizens, who have finally realized that the path to bliss lies in surrendering to nature, not dominating her. But to survive we will have to endure the humiliation of voluntarily giving up our anthropocentric throne of domination.

If we are removed from the Earth, the loggers will slowly fade from her consciousness like unpleasant and distant memories. If we survive, the loggers will also fade from the consciousness of humanity, as perverse and embarrassing aspects of our once primitive selves. Either way, the logger is a nothing, an insignificance, a virus, a rot, a disease and an aberration against nature, and I for one will not weep a single tear at his demise.

To sum up, I would like to repeat that tree-spiking is a tactic that works. It does not hurt trees. It does not injure people. It is simple. It is not costly. The logging barons have little defense against it. They moan and they groan and they gnash their teeth, but they can do little—except of course to employ the old tactic of divide and conquer. They can manipulate members of our movement and spread division and hatred among them by exploiting their anthropocentric Judeo-Christian morality. In this way they can spread their rot among us and destroy us.

But whatever political stance that the Earth First! rank-and-file takes—the reality is that tree-spiking will continue. It continues in northern California, even more covertly, because it is now plain that advocates may fall victim to former brothers and sisters. Continue it shall, despite the laws of society, despite the so-called "rights" of the loggers and their ilk. Tree-spiking is an idea, and an idea is impossible to kill. It will continue, and I will continue to advocate it until the day I die. No compromise, not now or ever.

Reading Note

1. Jordan, I have no idea who bombed the car. Our group has never been suspect, and we are not concerned if people think we are or not. I do stand by my concern that the bombing gave martyr status to two people who have compromised a very effective tactic.

Is Globalization Good for Canada? Yes

MICHAEL TAUBE

Michael Taube is a journalist and conservative commentator who contributes columns and editorials to the *Toronto Sun*, *Toronto Star*, *Globe and Mail*, *National Post*, *Windsor Star*, *Hamilton Spectator*, *Moncton Times*, as well as other major journals and newspapers in Canada and the United States. In contrast to activists such as Naomi Klein or Kalle Lasn, Taube argues that globalization is a social, moral, and economic good.

I don't think there is any question that globalization is of great benefit not only for Canada, but also for the entire world.

The process of globalization creates an enviable playing field for economic growth by limiting the amount of trade barriers and opening up the free market. It allows for greater foreign investment, creates more choice for consumers, and increases the stature of capitalism in society.

Of course, not everyone agrees. In Canada, protectionists like Maude Barlow and Buzz Hargrove fear the possibility of the loss of both Canadian industry and thousands of jobs. In the United States, an unusual merger between right-wing columnist Pat Buchanan and Democratic Representative Richard Gephardt has been initiated due to NAFTA and the Mexican economy woes. Even popular U.S. conservative author William Bennett has warned about the problems of laissez-faire capitalism.

Many have written negative articles and books about globalization. Barlow and Tony Clarke recently came out with a book attacking the Multilateral Agreement on Investment. Business magnate George Soros has written twice in the *Atlantic Monthly* about his fears. William Greider of *Rolling Stone* threw everything and the kitchen sink against globalization.

The primarily left-wing rants of these protectionists have done little to stir my interests. As a self-described libertarian conservative, I can think of no better option to follow other than globalization for three reasons.

First, globalization will provide an equal opportunity, on a level playing field, for potential success. As the eminent economist Milton Friedman once said, society has tried to create a "free private enterprise exchange economy," or competitive capitalism. Competition breeds a drive for people to succeed within the confines of the free market. There is always a risk factor involved, but the risk reward is a strong motivator for most.

Second, globalization will open up the lines of international trade. No longer will a government be a babysitter to a weak business industry. If a product in Canada is inferior to a product from Korea, the smart consumer will buy the latter. Only the strong will survive, and only the inventive will live to fight another day.

Third, globalization will enhance the technological market. Global products like the Internet and E-mail have opened up the lines of communication in a quick, efficient manner. Information has become readily available at the push of a button. While not perfect, the technological boom has enhanced the future prospects of globalization.

A typical attack on globalization by the left is that it looks out for the individual rather than the interests of the community. Ergo, the free market will not be able to benefit everyone, and can be seen as unsympathetic to the needs of others.

Keep in mind that nobody ever said life was fair, and that also goes for the free market. Globalization produces winners and losers, not a socialist communal fantasy of free money and protecting a country's economy. Individuals will succeed in the global economy on the basis of merit, hard work and creativity. There won't be generous handouts in the new world markets for economic and political failures.

Yet, one could argue that Canadians are actually compassionate capitalists. You will find few voices on the left or the right opposed to basic social services, the implementation of basic health care, or even basic human rights. Getting from A to B might be different, but the general feeling of compassion exists.

Globalization opens up a whole new range of trading possibilities and free market activity. The world is becoming smaller, but the availability of monetary gain and new industry possibilities are staggering. To be honest, I wouldn't have it any other way.

The Global Economic Pyramid Scheme

KALLE LASN

Kalle Lasn is the founding editor of *Adbusters*, a magazine that exposes the abuses of capitalism and consumerism. "The Global Economic Pyramid Scheme" is a selection from Lasn's first book *Culture Jam*. In it, Lasn argues that our blind commitment to economic growth is akin to cancer, an ever-expanding disease threatening to consume our planet itself.

Seven men with genial smiles stand shoulder to shoulder on a broad lawn inside a matrix of cordoned-off boulevards. A hundred photographers snap their picture. The seven call each other by their first names, but just about everyone else calls them "Mister." The police are on high alert. The G-7 economic summit is one of the very few occasions where the leaders of the most affluent nations are together in one place. If aliens were planning an effective tactical strike on Earth, here and now would be the best time and place.

These seven men, here to coordinate their economic, financial and trade policies, stand at the helm of the global economy. Between them they control more than two thirds of the world's wealth. They carry the clout within the World Bank and the International Monetary Fund. They wield the power at the World Trade Organization. When their finance ministers say "Go" by lowering taxes and interest rates, people around the world open their wallets. When they say "Stop" by pulling the macroeconomic levers the other way, people grow nervous. They cut back. Jobs are lost. Lives are put on hold.

Of course, the global economy is like the gorilla that sits where it wants; the G-7 leaders don't have a firm rein on it. However, through their power to direct global economic policies, and through reassuring spectacles like the G-7 summit, the leaders create the *perception* of mastery. And in politics, perception is everything. The leaders maintain their authority because *we believe*.

At every summit the focal point of discussion is how to maintain economic growth. Growth is the sine qua non of consumer capitalism. Without growth the global economy as it is currently structured makes no sense. There seem to be no alternatives. But there *is* an alternative—one that has never been discussed at any summit.

TWO SCHOOLS OF THOUGHT

The view that in good times or bad, growth will set us free is a classic argument coming from economics' so-called expansionist camp. Expansionism remains the dominant economic paradigm because expansionists (sometimes called neoclassical economists) are the dominant economic policymakers of our time. They are the professors at our universities, the policy advisers to our governments, the brains in most of the think tanks. Their confident logic shapes the economic strategies by which we live.

The competing view of global economic reality—the ecological worldview—is the new kid on the block. Its vision is not quite fully formed, its logic is a little less confident. Its proponents probably make up fewer than one in fifty of all the practicing economists and economics professors in the world today. Though rapidly growing in acceptance, ecological economics has so far been little more than a minor irritant to its dominant expansionist rival.

The two worldviews are chalk and cheese. Or, if you like, heaven and hell.

Ecological economists (also known as bioeconomists) foresee an apocalypse. They warn that we have reached a unique juncture in human history—that, ecologically speaking, the world is already "full" and further expansion will lead us into an ecological nightmare, a prolonged and possibly permanent "age of despair."

The expansionists, by contrast, see growth not as a problem but as the solution to our economic woes. There is no reason why growth cannot continue indefinitely, they claim. "There are no . . . limits to the carrying capacity of the Earth that are likely to bind at any time in the foreseeable future," pronounced Lawrence Summers, former chief economist of the World Bank. "There isn't a risk of an apocalypse due to global warming or anything else. The idea that the world is headed over an abyss is profoundly wrong. The idea that we should put limits on growth because of some natural limit is a profound error."

This almost unbelievably arrogant view is shared by other expansionists who put their faith in technology. "If it is easy to substitute other factors for natural resources," says Nobel laureate Robert Solow, "then . . . the world can, in effect, get along without natural resources, so exhaustion is just an event, not a catastrophe." The late Julian Simon, author of *Scarcity or Abundance? A Debate on the Environment*, once boasted: "We have in our hands—in our libraries really—the technology to feed, clothe, and supply energy to an ever-growing population for the next seven billion years."

Within the ecological camp, of course, these are fighting words. Worse, they're grievously irresponsible and just plain false. William Rees, coauthor of *Our Ecological Footprint* and a leading spokesman of the new economics, warns that the fivefold expansion in world economic activity since World War II (and a twentyfold increase this century) "has produced an unprecedented level of material and energy exchange between the ecosphere and the human economic subsystem." He points out that 40 percent of terrestrial and 25 percent of marine photosynthesis have now been diverted to human use. He sees ozone depletion, climate change, deforestation, soil degradation and the loss of biodiversity as unambiguous warning signals telling us to stop stressing our ecosphere or die. In 1994, fifty-eight World Academy of Science directors released a document declaring, essentially, that humankind is proceeding down an unprecedented and catastrophic path which will destroy the support systems upon which life depends. Overpopulation, overconsumption, inappropriate technological applications and economic expansion are changing the biophysical features of the Earth.

Ecological economists accuse expansionists of pawning the family silverware—of "liquidating" the planet's irreplaceable natural capital for short-term gain. Robert Ayres, in the *Journal of the International Society for Ecological Economics,* writes: ". . . there is every indication that human economic activity, supported by perverse trade and 'growth' policies, is well on the way to perturbing our natural environment more, and faster, than any known event in planetary history, save perhaps the large asteroid collision that may have killed off the dinosaurs. We humans may well be on the way to our own extinction."

ECOLOGICAL ECONOMICS

Assume for a moment that our survival is indeed threatened. What do we do? How can we address that threat? An obvious answer is to pursue sustainability. To design a new economic system that gives us what we need without sacrificing the well-being of future generations. For ecological economists (or bioeconomists), leveling the playing field between generations is *the* big challenge of our time. Nothing else comes close. And the solution is nothing short of a cultural revolution—an about-face in our values, lifestyles and institutional agendas. A reinvention of the American dream.

Expansionists see the pursuit of sustainability as a much simpler proposition: Create as much wealth as possible by freeing up markets, privatizing government services and eliminating barriers to trade. This will, according to their theories, produce a new round of economic expansion that will create the wealth we need to tackle environmental degradation, poverty and other economic woes.

But there's a flaw in the expansionists' argument. They have no accurate way of measuring the economic progress they keep talking about. Their only measure of growth is the Gross Domestic Product (GDP), and it is seriously flawed.

Consider: When the *Exxon Valdez* spilled its load of oil onto the Alaskan coast, $2 billion was spent trying to clean up and minimize the ecological damage. That money then circulated throughout the American economy, resulting in a significant increase in the GDP. When the Gulf War broke out, America's GDP rose again. Money changed hands. The country became "healthier." Indeed, every time there's a car accident or a newly diagnosed cancer patient, whenever personal or societal catastrophes occur, the GDP goes up and the economy "gains."

Consider: Walking, biking and using mass transit contribute less to the GDP than using a car. Trains contribute less than airplanes; an extra blanket or sweater contributes less than raising the thermostat; one-child families contribute less than six-child families; eating potatoes contributes less than eating beef; starting a vegetable garden contributes less than buying produce at the supermarket; staying home to raise your daughter contributes less than getting a part-time job at Wendy's. Indeed, the GDP fails to assign any value at all to unpaid or volunteer work. Work done by tens of millions of North Americans simply does not show up on the expansionists' radar. Similarly, the GDP fails to assign any value to declining fish stocks or disappearing forests. It's as if these negatives simply don't exist.

The GDP measures "goods" but not "bads." It cannot distinguish economic benefit for social gain from economic benefit for social loss. Conducting economic policy based solely on the GDP, says Canadian political scientist Ronald Coleman, is like driving your car without a gas gauge. The engine seems to be running fine, but for how long? There's no way to know.

That's why ecological economists have spurned the GDP and developed their own measures of economic progress. The three graphs on the next page show the GDPs of the U.S., U.K. and Germany all soaring merrily upward from 1955 through the 1980s. However, a more accurate measure of economic progress, the ISEW (Index of Sustainable Economic Welfare), developed by Herman Daly and John Cobb in 1990, tells another story. When some of the "bads," such as pollution, depletion of nonrenewable resources and car exhaust–related health costs, are factored in, a very different picture of the economy emerges. The U.S., German and U.K. economies all show no improvement in economic welfare since the 1970s. In fact, economic welfare levels off and starts falling quite dramatically in each country.

The ISEW (as well as the GPI, or Genuine Progress Indicator, pioneered by the San Francisco think tank Redefining Progress) exposes the expansionists as a bunch of eager beavers without a well-considered business plan, pseudoscientists urging the world to follow their lead before they themselves have clear bearings. Neoclassical economists cling to their mathematical models like children to their teddy bears. They operate in a kind of academic isolation that does not acknowledge the effects of their policies on the real world. Their world is the world of "revealed preferences" and "rational expectations," of "perfectly voluntary exchange" and "negative externalities" that can be dismissed. Their world is not our world. Their world does not exist.

"The difference between science and economics," says Ferdinand Banks in *Truth and Economics,* "is that science aims at an understanding of the behavior of nature, while economics is involved with an understanding of models—and many of these models have no relation to any state of nature that has ever existed on this planet, or any that is likely to exist between now and doomsday. The word that comes to mind when confronted by these fantasies is fraud."

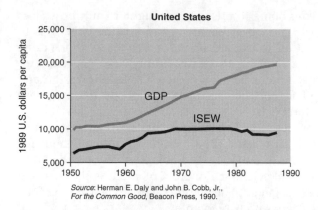

United States

Source: Herman E. Daly and John B. Cobb, Jr.,
For the Common Good, Beacon Press, 1990.

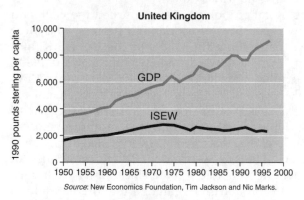

United Kingdom

Source: New Economics Foundation, Tim Jackson and Nic Marks.

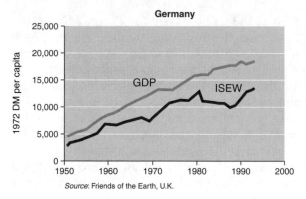

Germany

Source: Friends of the Earth, U.K.

Two different ways of measuring economic progress: Gross Domestic Product (GDP) and the Index of Sustainable Economic Welfare (ISEW). When pollution, depletion of nonrenewable resources, car exhaust–related health costs and other social and ecological costs are subtracted from the GDP, then economic "progress" levels off around 1975 and starts falling thereafter.

THE DOOMSDAY MACHINE

In 1996, news stories of a bizarre and tragic wholesale fraud began filtering out of Eastern Europe. In Bulgaria, Romania, Russia, Serbia and Albania, citizens who had sunk their savings into investment schemes that promised money for nothing got a glimpse of the dark side of the free market. In Albania close to 90 percent of the dirt-poor population had put some or all of its money in "foundations," which were actually simple pyramid schemes. No one knew what they were investing in, exactly, but the pitches were electrifying, the promised returns too enticing to resist: cars, tropical vacations, triple your money in three months, a new and better life for everyone. The people believed. And why not? "Albanian money is the cleanest in the world," reassured President Sali Berisha. If the government endorsed these schemes, surely they were legitimate. Many Albanians took the plunge. They bet the family fruit stands, sold their homes and their livestock. In Albania, as elsewhere in post-Communist Europe, new investors eventually dried up and the funds began failing. Finally, the house of cards came down. People rioted. They had nothing left. Albanians collectively lost a billion dollars—three times the national budget deficit. They had trusted their government and they had been betrayed.

The response in the West was predictable. Bemused pity might best sum it up. We shook our heads at those poor benighted bastards who had been persuaded to "bet on miracles."

But how different is *our* economic fable? Don't we trust our financial advisers, our expansionist economists, our political leaders as blindly as Albanians trusted theirs? Most of us have no idea where our money is. It's not in the bank where we left it. The bank injected it into the bloodstream of the global money market. Vast sums move through this market every day and collect at certain hot spots. After a Canadian company announced it had found the world's biggest gold deposit in the Indonesian rain forest, everyone wanted in. The penny stock soared to nearly $300 a share—until allegations of fraud surfaced and the house of cards came tumbling down, and with it billions of investor dollars, including hundreds of millions invested through pension funds. We sink billions into mutual funds and retirement plans, assuming these to be secure, broad-based, blue-chip investments. But what's in these funds? Just as with hot dogs, you don't really want to know. Some of your money may be bolstering the economies of dubious, often atrocious, even genocidal regimes.

About half a million people around the world wake up every day, leave the world of people, work and nature, and play money games in cyberspace. They invent new instruments (futures, bonds, derivatives, arbitrage, etc.), each with its own risks and rewards, creating $50 in play money for every $1 worth of real products and services actually circulating in the world. They further inflate the amount of "money" in the system by borrowing from each other and bidding up prices. Trillions of dollars slosh around this system every day making billions of dollars of virtual profits for the nimble and the quick. Even as these people sleep, their computers continue searching for margins of profit, automatically triggering buys and sell-offs when the conditions are right.

At the U.S. investment house Kidder Peabody, a single trader reports $1.7 trillion in phony trades over two years before he is caught. At Barings Bank in Britain a young broker, praised for having an "almost unique capacity" to produce big profits without taking significant risks, loses $1.3 billion in one month. He bankrupts the 233-year-old bank with his enthusiasm for Japanese futures.

Those famed, highly speculative "derivatives" aren't just the special currency of young sharks. The accounting firm of Ernst and Young revealed in 1997 that nearly a third of the investment funds it had been tracking included derivatives. Overall, 97 percent of the world's monetary transactions are now speculative. In 1970, the figure hovered around 30 percent.

Blind trust is a scary thing. We give up control of our money. We assume the markets will hold and our nest eggs will grow, when in truth our investment portfolio is often held together with baling wire and blind faith.

And what about the global economy? Is it viable? Is there enough real "estate," real factories, real jobs, real gold mines? Is there enough good topsoil? Are there enough fish left in the sea? Is there enough real economic progress to keep the whole thing growing? And if so, for how long?

On October 27, 1987—Black Monday—the Dow Jones Industrial Average fell 554 points, the biggest single-day plunge in ten years. Circuit breakers on the NYSE kicked in and shut down trading. Just days earlier, Hong Kong's Hang Seng Index had suffered a similar crash, joining a half dozen Asian economies that had fallen or would soon fall in a domino effect of pessimism. Americans—a plucky lot—rebounded quickly. Analysts here called the dive a "correction." Investors jumped back in and the Dow was soon soaring toward 10,000 again, as if nothing had happened. But something *had* happened. The synchronized crashes showed the awesome degree to which world markets are now codependent; how the global economy is now one entity. Everything we do has global implications. Crisis is never far away. The Japanese, Chinese and Asian "tiger" economies have proven much more precarious than we thought. Our own economy depends, to a great extent, on managed public moods and panic held at bay by carefully scripted reassurances from the G-7 leaders and Alan Greenspan at the U.S. Federal Reserve. What would happen if, on top of our current insecurities, the fear of escalating climate change (planetary ecology and economy caught in a deadly downward spiral) suddenly became real to us? Here's a good guess: a crash to dwarf Black Friday and Black Monday. You've got to wonder how long we can continue playing the neoclassical expansionist game, living off our natural capital and calling it income, before the pyramid collapses and the G-7 leaders head for the hills.

The Albanians may have been naive, but their actions were understandable. They had to do *something* with their money because it was rapidly losing its worth. The Japanese, Koreans, Malaysians, Indonesians, and to some degree the rest of us are now caught in a similar vise. We're worried about the future. We don't want to suffer in our old age. We want a secure sum to retire on. We're nervous and impatient. We want our money to grow quickly. So we try stocks, bonds and futures, and hope our nest egg is growing. "Invest my money wisely," we tell our brokers and we place our future in their hands.

Pyramid schemes depend on a continuous supply of dupes (early contributors being paid from the pockets of later ones). When no new contributors can be found, these schemes fail. In the expansionist model of the global economy, future generations—our children and our children's children—are the dupes. As supplies of clean water and air grow scarce, as forests, cod, salmon and wildlife vanish, as climatic instability escalates, we will eventually reach a point where one generation suddenly balks, unable to buy into the scheme. How close we are to that moment of truth is anybody's guess.

Recently I saw a TV news item about a town in Nebraska where the accumulating smoke from wood-burning stoves was making the residents sick. Asthma sufferers had to be hospitalized. Children couldn't play outside after school. A local bylaw was finally enacted to restrict wood burning to Monday, Wednesday and Friday afternoons. Many townspeople were outraged. How dare someone tell me what to do in my own home! they howled. What's next? You're going to tell me I can't drive my car? Can't own a gun? Can't have a second child, like in China?

I'm well acquainted with this type of response. Every year the Media Foundation tries to purchase airtime for its "Buy Nothing Day" TV campaign, which asks Americans to put away their wallets on the last Friday of November. Every year every major network turns our ad down, but one program—CNN *Headline News*—takes our money and runs our spot. Every year after the ad airs, dozens of irate viewers jam our 1-800 line. "Get out of this country, you pinko tree-huggers," one concerned citizen explained last year. "Go back to where you came from."

For an enormous number of people, the idea that they should set limits on themselves is unthinkable: "Why should I cut back? This is *my* paycheck, this is *my* life." Any restriction on this unfettered freedom to consume just does not square with the American dream. Our current economic system cannot tolerate any reduction in consumption. We simply cannot deal with that idea. *That is our rigidity.* And that is the kind of rigidity that brings civilizations down.

Meanwhile, back at the G-7 summit, the world leaders are putting on a good show for the thousands of journalists, reporters and TV crews. There are daily news releases, communiqués, background papers, joint declarations and photo ops. The PR people do their thing. A protest erupts as a few thousand people link hands and try to circle one of the leaders' meetings, but on TV this demonstration comes off as merely another part of the spectacle, somehow lending even more credibility to the event and reinforcing its importance and legitimacy.

The U.S. president reads some words prepared for him by his policy advisers. Millions around the world watch the proceedings on the evening news. We feel mildly reassured. These guys must know what they're doing. Despite the recent worrisome rumblings, the global economic vessel is on course. The unsinkable ship of dreams proceeds into the night. Inured, we grab the remote, switch away from the news and settle on *The X-Files*, where agent Fox Mulder is once again sniffing out some wild conspiracy.

Girls Will Be Girls

PATRICIA PEARSON

Patricia Pearson is an author and columnist who has won national awards for her crime journalism. She is also author of *Playing House—How Hard Can Motherhood Really Be?* and *Area Woman Blows Gasket and Other Tales from the Domestic Frontier.* Her first book, *When She Was Bad*, looks at the way the media tends to rationalize and downplay violent crimes by women.

"Everyone starts out totally dependent on a woman. The idea that she could turn out to be your enemy is terribly frightening."

—Lord Astor, British philanthropist, 1993

This story of violence begins with a war. It was America's war, the razzle-dazzle one in the Persian Gulf, where the desert was a proving ground for a new generation of heroes. Stormin' Norman Schwarzkopf came out of that war, and General Colin Powell, and CNN, and high-tech missiles. And the soldiers who died on the sand, who were injured, taken prisoner, whose names we never caught—for them, yellow ribbons bedecked the nation's trees. They were the heroes to whom one little girl, ten-year-old Tina Killie, of Wrightstown, Wisconsin, carefully penned a letter, at the instruction of her teacher, to support the troops of Operation Desert Storm. Tina addressed her envelope to "any soldier," and her teacher mailed it to the United States Army.

Months went by, the war wound down, and Tina Killie was dreaming up what to wear for Halloween when all of a sudden she received a reply. All the talk in her school and on television about the courageous men of war had distilled into a living human being, a hero with a heartbeat, with the desert in his boots and the sun in his eyes, crouched over a canteen table writing personally, to her. "Don't be misled by my handwriting," the letter began. "I am a guy—I just have fairly decent penmanship because I once took up calligraphy as an art." The soldier seemed to know that he had to explain away, at once, the stereotypes of manhood and apologize for being nothing more or less than a person. "I shall [begin] what I hope will be a continued pen pal between us," he wrote in his lovely script, "by giving a quick description of myself. I have been in the army ever since graduation [from high school in Las Vegas]. I am 6'1" and 165 pounds. I love to run . . . I used to run track in high school."

Army Specialist Anthony Riggs, one rank shy of sergeant, nicknamed "Slowpoke" by his buddies because he was gentle and hard to rile, had gone into the army because he couldn't afford to go to college. He was stationed with the Forty-third Air Defense Artillery, D Battery, a unit that operated Patriot missiles in Saudi Arabia. Over the next four months, as America's precision war gave way to a jagged peace, Riggs sent Tina more than a dozen letters. He included tokens of his adventure abroad, like a Pepsi bottle with Arabic script, and she sent him reminders of comfort, like carefully packaged boxes of chocolate chip cookies. "I hope you don't mind me calling you Angel," he wrote in one of his last notes. "It's because you're so nice to me and yet we've never met. It's nice to know there are people like you still growing up in America."

Riggs's surprise at her kindness was curious. It measured, perhaps, the distance American soldiers had traveled since World War II, when Yankees were so famous for their optimism. Now it was the end of the century, and Riggs was an African American who lived in the bleak heart of downtown Detroit, where optimism had been subsumed by a stalwart determination to simply survive. "I have no intentions of becoming one of this war's casualties," he wrote to his mother in Las Vegas. "With the Lord's grace and his guidance, I'll walk American soil once again."

On March 16, 1991, Specialist Riggs strode jubilantly across the airport tarmac in Fort Bliss, Texas, and gave his twenty-two-year-old wife, Toni Cato Riggs, a tentative "D'ya still love me?" hug. Toni had driven across the country to welcome him home with her three-year-old daughter, Ambere. For that, and for being home, he was immensely relieved. After spending several months equal parts scared and bored senseless, he'd made it to safe ground. He craved what was heartening: some french fries, a little romance, and when he got back to Detroit, a move *out* of there, to a small house being offered by the army on a base in Warren, Michigan.

While Riggs was away, Toni had returned to the childhood home where her grandmother, Joan Cato, had raised her—a small wooden house on once-genteel Conley Avenue in Detroit. The yellow ribbon she had tied to the porch slumped in the cold March rain as the couple slogged back and forth between the house and Riggs's Nissan Sentra, filling it up with their belongings, on their first day back in the city. By two in the morning, the car was crammed with old furniture, Ambere's toys, Toni's school books, Anthony's army stuff, just one more haul to do, then a weary stretch of the shoulders and a fitful sleep. Anthony was still outside when Joan Cato noticed that the porch light had gone out. Toni went to the doorway to switch it back on. She stopped in mid-stride, jerked into stillness by gunfire. In Detroit, this was dismal and predictable terror, not shocking so much as depressing. When it stopped, Joan and Toni peered through the screen. They saw the Nissan pulling away. Oh, Lord, this was violence coming right on home. Anthony was on the ground. He was hit. Just like the war. That impersonal. Within moments, he was dead.

It didn't take long for the dispiriting irony of this veteran's urban murder to be grasped by every politician and columnist in the nation. Within twenty-four hours, Detroit City Council's president Maryann Mahaffey had pegged it "the great American tragedy." In

Washington, at the Senate subcommittee hearing on the Brady Bill, mandating a seven-day waiting period for handguns, Specialist Riggs arose repeatedly as the day's bitterest case in point. Never mind Saddam Hussein. American men were dying at *one another's* hands, in their own home-grown "combat zones." The statistics spoke plainly. "During every 100 hours on our streets, we lose three times more young men than were killed in 100 hours of ground war in the Persian Gulf," Health and Human Services secretary Louis Sullivan had testified. "Where are the yellow ribbons of hope and remembrance?" he wanted to know. A spokesman for Detroit's mayor Coleman Young gave a statement. "A new war needs to be fought on the home front," he said, ". . . so this gallant young man would not have died in vain."

Seven hundred citizens filed into Detroit's Little Rock Baptist Church to honor the life of Anthony Riggs. Congresspersons Barbara Rose-Collins and John Conyers flew in from Washington to attend. The Reverend Jesse Jackson's voice resounded from the pulpit, memorializing a man he did not know, who had been "any soldier" and was a different sort of hero now. "What is the redeeming value in this tragic loss of life?" Jackson asked. "Somehow Anthony has brought us together. By his blood a nation could be saved. Not Kuwait, but America. He illuminates and illustrates, by living and dying, the crisis and challenge of a generation of young African-American men. There's a need to cry out: 'Stop the violence.'"

Detroit's greatest soul singer, Aretha Franklin, her voice as eloquent as the preacher's, led the congregation in a hymn, and Jackson escorted Toni to the coffin to pray. A bugler played taps while an American flag was lifted from the casket, ceremoniously folded, and handed to the solemn young widow. Toni wasn't as articulate as the pundits and scribes who'd swept her husband up into their symbolic world, but she managed to echo their point: "I can't believe I've waited all this time for him to come back and he does, and then I lose him again," she lamented.

The community rallied swiftly and emphatically around Riggs's family. Tina Killie sent Anthony's mother, Lessie, a sweatshirt that said, "Somebody in Wrightstown loves you." A local Honda/Jeep Eagle dealership offered Toni a car. The NAACP posted a ten-thousand-dollar reward for information leading to the killer's arrest. On March 23 homicide detectives found Anthony's stolen car parked on a residential street about a mile from where he died. Strangely, the family's packed belongings were still inside. It wasn't a robbery. So what was it? Something gang-related? Riggs gunned down as a message? Mistaken for somebody else? Detectives also found a .38-caliber pistol in a Dumpster near the car,

matching the bullets in the fallen soldier. They put through a regis-
tration trace. The ownership came back to someone named Antonio
Shelby, who proved to be a local street tough and a crack dealer,
currently on probation. Hauled in and grilled, Shelby told a story
that turned this senseless urban murder on its head. He had lent his
gun, he said, to nineteen-year-old Michael Cato, who was his
friend. Cato was also, as it happens, the son of his godmother,
Paula, and the brother-in-law of Anthony Riggs. Cato was the
shooter, Shelby said. But it wasn't his idea. The idea belonged
to Toni.

Michael Cato was arrested on March 25, on the strength of
Shelby's confession. Swiftly giving in to his predicament, having no
talent for lies, he explained what had happened. Toni Cato Riggs,
older sister, the smarter and tougher-minded of the two, who had
protected Michael since they had been neglected as children by their
drug-addicted mother, had asked him to murder her husband. She
would split with Michael, she said, her two-hundred-thousand-dollar
payoff in life insurance. Then they could get out of the neighborhood,
do something better. So Michael borrowed Antonio's gun, and the
plan went into motion.

Detroit was stunned. The pundits were speechless. What eulogies were there to fashion about this little twist? The killer was
family. The violence had nothing to do with men at all, it had been
arranged by a woman. Instantly, the voices of anguish fell silent. In
place of a nation's impassioned pleas for reconciliation came a
couple of news stories reporting the gossip of neighbors. Toni Cato
Riggs was promiscuous. She had been "runnin' around with a lot of
men." It was whispered that she had herpes. Another rumor was
that she was pregnant. "That's a fact," a Conley Avenue neighbor
named Ollie Hicks told *USA Today*, though it wasn't. "I always knew
she was selfish and self-centered," said Anthony's mother, Lessie.

Army Sergeant Gary Welliver told a reporter that, come to
think of it, when Toni met Anthony in Fort Bliss she'd told him she
wanted a divorce. "An interesting way to get greeted," Welliver
said sarcastically. Reporters unearthed the unsavory fact that Toni
was already married to another man when she married her soldier.
She still hadn't divorced Marcus Butler, Ambere's father. They also
found out by interviewing her cousins and girlfriends that Toni was
a restless, disconsolate woman who didn't love Anthony and didn't
want to be an army wife in the suburbs. Anthony himself had
described Toni's unhappiness in a letter to his mother from the war.
"Toni has wrecked my car again," he wrote Lessie; "I don't know
what's on her mind. . . . Mom, I would put my head through the
neck of a hot sauce bottle to please her."

A reader sifting through the details from the papers, now offered up as unimportant true crime fluff, might begin to glimpse the discord in Toni and Anthony's marriage, how one man was being hurt, one woman stifled, and both were trying to assemble new lives from what shreds of opportunity the inner city provides. Anthony took the legitimate route and joined the army. Toni went the illicit route and arranged a shooting, like the ones she saw around her every day.

But the fact that Riggs was embroiled in familial rancor and fell victim to it held no meaning for the citizenry of Detroit. "What I did, I did for a soldier," the Reverend James Holley of Little Rock Baptist Church said, referring to his arrangement of the funeral. "What bothers me is that those of us who live here felt one hundred percent the way the media did, that this was the kind of . . . violence we've grown used to." Reverend Holley did not mean the violence in his community in which women are principal players, as mothers and lovers and sisters and daughters. He wasn't referring to child abuse, infanticide, spousal assault, or school yard and girl gang aggression. He did not take, for his reference point, the eighty thousand women arrested for violent crime in America the year that Riggs died or the thousands of others whose violence was invisible and went unremarked upon. He meant masculine violence, permissible or illicit, heroic or profane, but publicly engaged in and displayed. "It makes me think I need to take a long look at myself," he concluded, of his initial assumption about Riggs's fate. "Have we come to the point that we just automatically perceive ourselves this way?"

What a society perceives about violence has less to do with a fixed reality than the lenses we are given through which to see. Before the twentieth century, the man who beat his mule or his child was not a violent man. Nor was the woman who lashed her dog or, in some eras, abandoned her newborn to die of exposure. Rape is violent, but only in the last twenty years have we perceived that a husband might be his wife's rapist. The violence that words inflict is newly perceived, and so is the violence of "harassment" and "hazing." Our perception of violence is selective, and changeable. What the citizens of Detroit had "grown used to," as Reverend Holley put it, was one dimension of destructive human behavior. Boys were gunning down boys, to be sure. But girls and women were contributing their share to the cycle of rage, and injury, and pain.

Women commit the majority of child homicides in the United States, a greater share of physical child abuse, an equal rate of sibling violence and assaults on the elderly, about a quarter of child sexual abuse, an overwhelming share of the killings of newborns, and a fair preponderance of spousal assaults. The question is how do we come to *perceive* what girls and women do? Violence is still universally considered to be the province of the male. Violence is masculine. Men are the cause of it, and women and children the ones who suffer. The sole explanation offered up by criminologists for violence committed by a woman is that it is involuntary, the rare result of provocation or mental illness, as if half the population of the globe consisted of saintly stoics who never succumbed to fury, frustration, or greed. Though the evidence may contradict the statement, the consensus runs deep. Women from all walks of life, at all levels of power—corporate, political, or familial, women in combat and on police forces—have no part in violence.

It is one of the most abiding myths of our time.

The notion that women are a homogeneous species of nurturant souls has myriad wellsprings, but the deepest, perhaps, has to do with our basic conception of the body.

Violence, we believe, is implicit in the construction of the male: the chest-beating ape evolved into the soldier, the rapist. Men are propeled into conquest by a surge of testosterone, and build their blocks of power on the strength of their physique. Research may show that women are tougher, longer-living, more tolerant of pain, but research is dry and pedantic. Literature rejoices in the docility of female flesh, its yielding form, its penetrability. The female body fosters life itself. Women do not physically thrust and strut and dominate. To picture women's aggression, men would have to picture women's bodies bereft of the erotic, the maternal, the divine. No such sacrifice is required in conjuring male aggression. Muscle and hormone are the twin pillars upon which all our darkest human urges stand: lust, rage, jealousy, revenge, the craving for power, the quest for control. Dark urges, and yet the capacity to express them is also held up as a matter of masculine strength and of valor. "It is highly probable," wrote Anthony Storr, one of this century's most famous theorists on violence, "that the undoubted superiority of the male sex in intellectual and creative achievement is related to their greater endowment of aggression." Masculinity, according to sociologist James Messerschmidt, "emphasizes practices toward authority, control, competitive individualism, independence, aggressiveness, and the capacity for violence."

A 1996 book about the primate origins of human aggression, *Demonic Males*, made it clear in the title that, whether we began as creatures of earth or as creatures of God, it is men who wreak the havoc. Men destroy, women create. Men are from Mars, women are from Venus. The gender dichotomy is remarkably enduring, and surprisingly crude.

So what is its basis in fact?

Over the last twenty years, a host of scientific research projects have zeroed in on the physical underpinnings of human behavior, with results that pose a sharp challenge to the biological maleness of aggression. Testosterone, the oldest chestnut, has fallen into disrepute of late, as laboratory experiments call the causative effect of the hormone into question. One comprehensive literature review pronounced research to date to be utterly inconclusive on the influence of male hormones on violence. A major flaw in the research has been that testosterone, like adrenaline, increases in people exposed to conflict. The populations most often tested for it are prison inmates, who already have higher levels because of where they are—in an edgy, tense, combative cage. "The outcome of aggressive or competitive encounters," noted the reviewer, "can increase or decrease testosterone levels." Elevated levels have been measured in *female* prisoners, as well as in winners of "a cash prize" in a tennis tournament, recipients of medical degrees, and the triumphant competitor in a wrestling match. "Does the hormone modulate the behavior," asks psychologist David Benton, "or does fighting and winning increase the release of the hormone?" For all its celebrity, testosterone is an elusive player in this game. It explains nothing, after all, of Toni Cato, or the mother who pummels her child, or the girl in a gang with a switchblade.

In fact, a more compelling culprit than hormones in violent behavior may be the wiring of the human brain, in a way that does not discriminate one sex from the other. There is fascinating work being done on the effect of head injury on the human propensity for aggression. Frontal lobe damage, for example, can cause perfectly calm people to lose their impulse control, which is usually governed by the cerebral cortex. They revert to the most primal emotions, zooming from annoyance to homicidal fury in a matter of seconds, with no mood in between. We know this in its less extreme form as "hair-trigger temper." Its more voluble expression is called "episodic aggression" or "rage attacks." But why would it affect only men? It doesn't. Pauline Mason of Toronto was driving on a highway in 1992 when a spring flew off a transport truck, smashed through her window, and struck her head. She went amnesiac for some months, was permanently blinded, and grew wildly and erratically violent, to the point where her scared spouse initiated divorce proceedings.

How many other women undergo this Jekyll and Hyde transformation? Thousands? The scientific literature is mum. Men are the standard bearers of violence, and masculine violence the measure.

A study released in early 1996 evaluated the impact of lead ingestion on delinquency in children. According to the study's authors at the University of Pittsburgh, "bullying, vandalism, setting fires and shoplifting" all increased in children exposed to lead-based paints on pipes and plumbing in their homes. The authors cautioned that lead should be considered a serious hazard to children for this reason. But they only studied boys. What about girls? If they're exposed to lead, what happens to them?

Researchers at Johns Hopkins University in Baltimore have discovered that if you breed male mice without the gene that produces nitric oxide—a molecule that allows nerve cells to communicate—they grow up to be the rodent version of soccer hooligans, beating the hell out of each other without provocation. But what do female mice do? The author of the experiment, Dr. Solomon H. Snyder, concedes that the focus of the research has been on males. As he told Natalie Angier of *The New York Times*, "Not much could be concluded about behavioral changes in females."

In 1995, research by the psychologist Adrian Raine and his colleagues at the University of Southern California revealed that juvenile delinquents with low heartbeat and sweat rates, signaling sluggish nervous systems, proved more likely to become adult criminals than fellow juveniles with swift nervous system responses. "If you have chronically low levels of arousal," Raine said, "the theory is that you seek out stimulation to increase arousal levels back to normal." Raine and his colleagues took the pulse rates of adolescent boys. Who knows what happens to girls?

Biological research has gone down several other trails. Serotonin, a neurotransmitter in the brain, may be related to violent behavior. So might the body's electrical impulses, since some violent criminals show markedly erratic electroencephalogram readings. Certain irregularities in brain function show up in the magnetic resonance imaging scans of psychopaths, suggesting a severance in the links between emotion and language. Prozac has recently taken some blame for heightening impulses to suicide. And blood sugar levels have been connected to impulsive aggression, most famously in the so-called Twinkie defense, in which the man who assassinated San Francisco supervisor Harvey Milk and mayor George Mosconi pled not guilty on the basis of temporary insanity because his depression was deepened by eating too much junk food. Biocriminologists will continue to tinker with the physical mechanisms of horrid behavior and haul their findings into court. But at what point will the exclusive application of this research to men cease to hold?

In primate research, all it took was one scholar, the primatologist Sarah Hrdy, to pose the right questions and challenge the myth of exclusively male aggression. Conducting field research in Africa in the 1970s, Hrdy observed that, in monogamous primates, loyalty was imposed by the females, not the males. "Any prospect of polygyny," she wrote, referring to the practice of having multiple mates, "would be precluded by fierce antagonism among females of breeding age. In most monogamous species, rival females are physically excluded from the territory by the aggressiveness of its mistress." Hrdy dubbed this the Hagar phenomenon, a reference to the biblical Sarah, wife of Abraham, who drove her husband's mistress into the desert. "The basic dynamics of the mating system depend not so much on male predilections"—the mythic hairy ape dragging his female away by her scruff—but "on the degree to which one female tolerates another." According to subsequent research by Reijo Holmström, female primates also kill one another's offspring and freeze one another out of feeding groups so that rivals become vulnerable to starvation.

The lesson revealed in this research, as well as in the findings of biocriminology, is that aggression is not innately masculine, but that evidence lies within the eye of the beholder. As long as patriarchs and feminists alike covet the notion that women are gentle, they will not look for the facts that dispute it. Hrdy has suggested that one reason other primatologists continue to assume males are the sole aggressors is that what females do doesn't look like violence. In other words, one reason women dwell outside the discourse on aggression is because of the tendency of scholars to define aggression in a specifically masculine way.

Regardless whether we assign it a positive or negative value, we tend to conceive of violence as a collection of assertive, public acts: fistfights, bar brawls, gun duels, the collision of soldiers on a field. Violence is the spectacle of teenaged boys beating one another up and mobsters blowing rivals away. It is physical; it is direct. The violent person targets his victim head-on. Pow. Boom. Crack. Defined this way, as in-your-face physical aggression, what we are really talking about is a gendered style. Visible physical aggression is a masculine display, which, many parents insist, shows up early in boys. Scholars who study preschool children, however, find that injurious physical aggression is committed equally by boys and girls. A little girl who has been displaced by a new baby is just as likely to thwack the baby over the head with her juice cup as a boy is. The psychologists Anne Colby and William Danon note that "there is very little support in the psychological literature for the notion that girls are more aware of others' feelings or are more altruistic than boys." We all begin our lives as selfish creatures with poor impulse control, out to defend our vital interests as we see them. But what happens to boys at the preschool level is that they begin to engage in much higher levels of "playful aggression" than girls do. What parents are noticing is that their boys have begun to dress-rehearse for gender, engaging in varieties of masculine gesture and display. This sort of aggression, playful in preschool and combative by high school, has nothing to do with the preconditions of criminal *motive*. It has to do with posturing. James Messerschmidt calls it "doing gender." Boys play rough because we expect them to play rough. Seventy percent of respondents to a 1968 survey conducted for the National Commission on the Causes and Prevention of Violence said that "they believed it was important for a boy to have a few fist fights while he was growing up." Evidently, most boys do. Every year since 1976, about half of all men in the United States have answered "yes" to the question "Have you ever been punched or beaten by someone?"

"Where I grew up, in Mississippi and Arkansas," wrote the novelist Richard Ford in 1996, "to be willing to hit another person in the face with your fist meant something." What did it mean? That you were brutish, power-mad, in love with someone else's pain? "It meant you were—well, brave . . .," wrote Ford. "As a frank, willed act, hitting in the face was a move toward adulthood, the place we were all headed—a step in the right direction."

Aggressive display is a cultural practice, and even within the United States there are cultural variations in the degree to which men deploy it. Researchers at the University of Michigan recently explored the link between elevated violence rates in the southern United States, for example, and "the culture of honor." This southern belief, which endures long past the outlaw of duels, is that insults must be met with an aggressive defense. Theorizing that the culture of honor obliges southern men to behave more violently than northern men, the researchers divided a group of students according to where they'd been raised. The students—unaware of the experiment—were bumped in a corridor and called "asshole." Northerners reacted mainly with amusement, whereas southerners more often got angry. In a second experiment, the students were put on a collision course with the experimenters in the hallway, setting up a game of chicken, to see whether they, or the experimenter, would step out of the way first. Again, northerners were quicker to give way, less inclined to feel that losing the game "damaged their reputation for masculinity."

British men follow a different model for masculinity. Their ideal is more likely to be "a stolid, pipe-sucking manhood, unmoved by panic or excitement," admirable for showing reason and self-restraint. In a review of violence rates in Western countries, anthropologist Elliott

Leyton speculated that the British rates are much lower because of these cultural ideals. As Leyton points out, certain factors that contribute to the commission of serious violence—individual pathologies, life stresses, childhood maltreatment, and social upheaval—are constant in every society. But levels of displayed aggression fluctuate, according to cultural norms.

What would happen, then, if women felt entitled or compelled to express themselves physically in a public arena, if standing up to fight were not just a manly ideal but a womanly one as well? Would they resist the opportunity because they are not *inherently* aggressive—neither quick to anger, nor desirous of power, nor keen to brandish their own strength? In fact, the capacity of women to use masculine violence emerges very clearly in those societies that sanction its expression. Anthropologist Victoria Burbank has found that women engage publicly in physical aggression in more than eighty contemporary societies around the world, with other women—their rivals for status, dominance, and resources—the most frequent targets. Like men's, women's aggression differs in severity and purpose from place to place. On Margarita Island, off the coast of Venezuela, the anthropologist H. B. Kimberly Cook "found that women are *more* violent than men in the expression of aggression." They engage publicly in fistfights and verbal assaults, with "the most common theme underlying fights between women [being] paternity issues" and status. Against men, they use various techniques of "social control," or what they call *"parar el macho,"* to quell male machismo. "When I first got married," one twenty-two-year-old fisherman told Cook, "I used to talk disrespectfully to my wife. . . . One day my mother took a board and hit me across the mouth. Blood came out of my lip. I cried and said, 'Mama, why did you hit me?' She answered, 'So that you learn respect for your wife.'" Men are slapped, kicked, hit, and berated, and they don't see such behavior as trivial or unfeminine. It is a point of pride that, "Yes, my wife knows how to *parar el macho*." It is also a point of pride for the women. "A woman's physical strength and ability to defend herself is . . . central in the self-concept of women."

The same is true of Aboriginal women in Australia. Victoria Burbank observed 174 fights in one community and found that women started nearly half. When women were physically injured in fights, their aggressors were women about half the time. Noting that "Western theories, metaphors and stereotypes of female aggression and victimization frame our understanding" but do not speak universal truth, Burbank asked the women how they saw their behavior. They viewed it as natural. Aggression was "the expected, if not inevitable, outcome of anger," for both men and women, and wasn't seen as socially deviant.

Anthropologist Maria Lepowsky studied aggressive strategies on the island of Vanatinai, near New Guinea, where men and women are held to be equal in economic, political, marital, and sexual relations. "Males and females experience equally strong emotions of envy, jealousy, frustrated desire and rage," she observed. "There is no perception that a man's feelings of anger are stronger than a woman's." But equality in itself doesn't make women physically violent. In that particular culture, both sexes are expected to curtail verbal and physical aggression. Instead, they may use sorcery or witchcraft, and indeed that is the most prevalent form of violence on the island. Lepowsky only witnessed five incidents of physical violence in ten years of field research. Four of the fights were instigated by women; two of their victims were sexual rivals.

APPENDIX

Common Grammatical Mistakes

"Me fail English? That's unpossible!"

—Ralph Wiggum, *The Simpsons*

1. SENTENCE FRAGMENTS

A complete sentence is one that expresses a finished thought, and stands on its own. In contrast, a fragment is an incomplete sentence, one missing a vital ingredient such as an active subject or verb.

Fragment: In order to understand the concept of infinity, a person should imagine only one thing. *Human stupidity*. (Voltaire)

OK: In order to understand the concept of infinity, a person should imagine only one thing: human stupidity.

The phrase "Human stupidity" forms a fragment because it can't stand as an independent sentence, for it has no verb and performs no action.

Fragment: Peter Parker walked away from Mary-Jane. *Leaving her to wonder about his true identity*.

OK: Peter Parker walked away from Mary-Jane, leaving her to wonder about his true identity.

"Leaving her to wonder about his true identity" is also a fragment because it can't stand on its own; it has no subject to carry out its action. These errors sometimes slip under our radar because a line can have both a noun and a verb, yet still be a fragment.

> **Fragment**: Love, the only disease you cannot cure, the only disease you don't want cured, the only disease you willingly catch.
> **Fragment**: The English gentleman galloping after a fox. The unspeakable in full pursuit of the uneatable. (Oscar Wilde)

Both these sentences have verbs, but they're not active. Any words that follow a preposition or subordinating clause cannot stand as a complete sentence, and must connect to an independent clause. Many sentence fragments arise because people begin a sentence with a subordinating conjunction such as "but" or "because."

> **Fragment**: I never forget a face. *But in your case, I'll make an exception*. (Groucho Marx)
> **OK**: I never forget a face, but in your case, I will make an exception.

2. FUSED SENTENCES AND COMMA SPLICES

A fused or spliced sentence describes two sentences presented as one. A fused sentence joins two separate ideas without any distinguishing features; a comma splice joins two complete thoughts with a comma, when they need to be separated by a period or semicolon.

> **Comma splice**: Don't knock *masturbation, it's* sex with someone I love. (Woody Allen)
> **Fused Sentence**: Those are my *principles if* you don't like them, I have others. (Groucho Marx)
> **Comma Splice**: Behind every successful man is a *woman, behind* her is his wife. (Groucho Marx)
> **Fused Sentence**: A single death is a *tragedy a million* is a statistic. (Joseph Stalin)

These statements contain distinct subjects, different actions, and separate ideas. The individual sentences need to be separated with either a semicolon or a period.

> **OK**: Don't knock masturbation; it's sex with someone I love.
> **OK**: Those are my principles. If you don't like them, I have others.
> **OK**: Behind every successful man is a woman. Behind her is his wife.
> **OK**: A single death is a tragedy; a million is a statistic.

The two independent sentences can also be joined together using a subordinating clause or a conjunction.

OK: Those are my principles, but if you don't like them, I have others.

3. ACTIVE AND PASSIVE VOICES

The English language has two voices: active and passive. In the active voice, a subject carries out a direct action that is received by an object.

Active: Mike Tyson bit Evander Holyfield's ear.
             (subject) (verb)   (object)

The passive voice inverts this pattern, so that the receiver of the action becomes the main focus of the sentence, while at the same time, the true performer of the action shunts to the end of the sentence. In other words, the subject becomes the object, and vice versa. The verb also changes from its active to its passive state: the verb "to be" plus the past participle.

Passive: Evander Holyfield's ear *was bitten* by Mike Tyson.

In the passive voice, the performer of the action becomes unnecessary, and can disappear entirely.

Passive: Evander Holyfield's ear *was bitten*.

The passive voice has some legitimate uses. For example, writers use it when they do not know who carried out an action.

Passive: Stonehenge *was built* several centuries before the Druids arrived in Great Britain.
Passive: My Austin Mini *was scratched* in the parking lot last night.

However, the passive voice tends to weaken writing, making it wordy and unclear. As a general rule, writers should use the active voice for improved clarity and verve.

Passive: An embargo on all Canadian goods *was threatened* by the American government.
Active: The American government threatened an embargo on all Canadian goods.

Some writers use the passive voice to deliberately conceal the person who carried out an action, and so diminish or hide responsibility. The active voice is more fair, accountable and honest.

Passive: Mistakes were made in the days leading up to the September 11 crisis.

Active: President Bush made mistakes in the days leading up to the September 11 crisis.

Use the active voice for increased accuracy.

4. SUBJECT/VERB AGREEMENT

A subject/verb agreement error occurs when the subject of a sentence differs in *number* with its verb.

Subject/Verb Error: Only *one* in a million writers *use* hyperbole correctly.

This is an error because the actual subject of the sentence is "one," which should take a singular verb form, "uses." To fix this problem, identify the real subject of a sentence, and make it agree in number with the verb.

OK: Only *one* in a million writers *uses* hyperbole correctly.

OK: The *tigers* of wrath *are* wiser than the horses of instruction. (William Blake)

Subject/Verb Error: The *need* of the many *outweigh* the need of the few. (Spock)

Subject/Verb Error: Just like the turtles, *every one* of us *make* progress by sticking our necks out.

The subject and its number can be tricky in the following cases.

A. NOUNS THAT FOLLOW PREPOSITIONS

A noun that follows a preposition can never be the subject of a sentence.

Subject/Verb Error: *Plato*, as well as all the other Greek philosophers, *were* not influenced by the Greek philosophers.

Subject/Verb Error: In Canada, the *number* of PR flaks *are* more than double that of journalists.

B. INVERTED WORD ORDER

When a sentence is written back to front, we can easily mistake the subject and the object of a sentence.

Subject/Verb Error: Without contraries are no progression.

OK: Without contraries *is* no *progression*. (William Blake)

Subject/Verb Error: Against stupidity *contends* in vain the *gods* themselves.

C. COMPOUND SUBJECTS

Some subjects appear plural, but really refer to one thing in the physical world.

>**OK**: *Macaroni and cheese is* my favourite dish. (It's one kind of food)
>**Subject/Verb Error**: *Smith & Wesson design* a fine handgun. (Smith & Wesson is one company)
>**Subject/Verb Error**: *Harry Potter and the Chamber of Secrets make* for an entertaining read. (*Harry Potter and the Chamber of Secrets* is a single book)

D. EITHER . . ./OR . . . , NEITHER . . . NOR . . . , NOT ONLY . . . BUT ALSO . . .

When using *either/or, neither/nor, not only/but also*, the verb agrees with the noun closest to it.

>**OK**: Neither famine nor *wars destroy* a nation.
>**Subject/Verb Error**: Not only the Liberals, but *Paul Martin have* to be held accountable.
>**Subject/Verb Error**: Either the coach or the *players is* not earning their pay.

E. NONE/NOT ONE

"None" and "Not One" are singular nouns that take singular verbs.

>**Subject/Verb Error**: *None* of the Toronto Maple Leafs *have* any talent.
>**OK**: *Not one* of the Calgary Flames *is* over 28 years old.

5. SHIFTS IN NUMBER, PERSON, AND GENDER

A shift occurs when a pronoun does not agree in number, person, or gender with the word or thing to which it refers.

>**Shift in Number**: *Anyone* who wants to own a cat should get *their* heads examined.

"Anyone" is a single subject, while the phrase "their heads" is plural. To fix this problem, make the numbers agree.

>**OK**: *People* who want to own a cat should get *their* heads examined.

Shifts can also occur when a sentence starts in one person, and then shifts to another.

>**Shift in Person**: When *one* is lost, *you* should consult your Bible.

This sentence begins in the third person, and shifts to the second. Fix the problem by making the voices agree.

OK: When *one* is lost, *one* should consult the Bible.

Some shifts occur because the writer has not included both genders.

Shift in Gender: *Every CEO* must bring *his* day-planner.

A CEO can be either male or female, and so the pronoun should be gender-neutral.

OK: *Every CEO* should bring *his or her* day-planner.
OK: *All CEOs* should bring *their* day-planners.

This shift problem leads to the impression CEOs are exclusively male. Professional language avoids such sexist language and uses gender-neutral terms.

6. PARALLELISM

A sentence that lists a series of items or actions should try to keep them in the same grammatical form. A parallel structure makes things easy to read. Its absence makes sentences confusing and illogical.

Faulty Parallelism: Kent tried *pleading, threats, and shouting*, but Roger would not return his Céline Dion album.

The problem arises here because two words have the "ing" ending, but one does not. To fix the problem, put all three words in the same form.

Parallel: Kent tried *pleading, threatening, and shouting*, but Roger would not return his Céline Dion album.

Some examples of parallelism can involve entire phrases.

Faulty Parallelism: The students *observed* the teacher's clothing, *debated* her fashion sense, and *their feelings* were she dresses like a sack of turnips.

This problem can be fixed by putting the parallel clauses in the same grammatical form.

OK: The students *observed* the teacher's clothing, *debated* her fashion sense, and *decided* that she dresses like a sack of turnips.

7. MISPLACED, DANGLING, AND SQUINTING MODIFIERS

A modifier is a word or word group that gives information about another word in a sentence. When a modifier is placed far from the word it modifies, the sentence can create confusing, unintended meanings, a mistake called a misplaced modifier.

Misplaced Modifier: The bureau was given to me by my aunt *with stumpy legs and wide drawers*.
Misplaced Modifier: *Slobbering and drooling*, Karla gave a sausage to the bulldog.
Misplaced Modifier: Serina gave a gift to Leif, *wrapped in a thin white bow*.

In each of these cases, the reader gets confused because the modifier is adjacent to a word that it is not actually modifying. The error disappears when the modifier appears next to the noun or verb it truly modifies, so that no confusion can possibly arise.

OK: The bureau *with the stumpy legs and wide drawers* was given to me by my aunt.
OK: Karla gave a sausage to the *slobbering and drooling* bulldog.
OK: Serina gave Lief a gift *wrapped in a thin white bow*.

A dangling modifier is one that has no word to modify. It "dangles" because it is describing something absent from the sentence.

Dangling Modifier: *As a member of the Chess Club*, the fame, fortune and easy sex are sometimes too much to bear.

The italicized words describe a person, but the sentence has no human being for the words to modify. Correct this problem by introducing a noun to which the modifier can connect.

OK: *As a member of the Chess Club, I* sometimes find the fame, fortune, and easy sex too much to bear.

A squinting modifier is one that can apply to more than one word in the sentence.

Squinting modifier: Christine muttered *after the class* she planned to kill Dr. Lewis.
Squinting modifier: I have for sale one dog, *neutered*, just like family.

The problem here is that the italicized words may mean more than one thing. What happened after the class? Christine's muttering or her murder plan? Who is neutered? The dog or the family? Correct this problem by moving the modifier, and adjusting the sentence so that it can only modify one word.

> **OK**: *After the class*, Christine muttered that she planned to kill Dr. Lewis.
>
> **OK**: Christine muttered that she planned to kill Dr. Lewis *after the class*.
>
> **OK**: I have for sale one *neutered* dog that acts just like family.

8. MIXED CONSTRUCTS

A mixed construction occurs when a sentence mixes two grammatical patterns that do not logically fit together.

> **Mixed Construct**: The reason why Grunge music disappeared *is because* Kurt Cobain committed suicide.

This sentence fuses two different patterns to express cause and effect. To fix the problem, separate the two different grammatical forms.

> **OK**: Kurt Cobain's suicide *is the reason why* Grunge music disappeared.
>
> **OK**: Grunge music disappeared *because* Kurt Cobain committed suicide.

9. FAULTY PREDICATION

Faulty predication occurs when the subject of a sentence performs an action that it can't logically carry out. The subject doesn't fit sensibly with its predicate.

> **Faulty Predication**: *An effect* of extended marijuana use *can cause* low ambition and lethargy.

"Low ambition" and "lethargy" can't be caused by an "effect," because they both are effects themselves. The sentence must be rewritten so that it has a subject that logically fits with its verb.

> **OK:** Extended marijuana use can cause low ambition and lethargy.

Some faulty predication occurs when the verb "to be" joins two nouns that are not equal, as Charles Schulz did in a famous line from his *Peanuts* comic strip.

> **Faulty Predication**: Happiness is a warm puppy.

When two words are joined by an "is," the subject and object must be of a similar class.

> **OK**: Happiness is a feeling one gets from a warm puppy.

Many instances of faulty predication occur when people use "is when," "is where," "is how," and the like.

Faulty Predication: MS *is when* the cells in the nervous
   system lose their myelin coating.
Faulty Predication: Democracy *is where* the mob rules.

The verb "to be" equates the subject with the object, yet MS is not a time (a "when"), nor democracy a place (a "where"). Rewrite the sentence to avoid these patterns.

OK: *MS is a disease* in which the cells in the nervous system
   lose their myelin sheaths.
OK: *Democracy is a form of government* wherein the mob rules.

10. SEMICOLON AND COLON ERRORS

A colon is a punctuation mark that introduces an object or a series of items. Normally, a complete sentence comes before a colon.

OK: The Colonel used my favourite oxymoron: military intelligence.
OK: Disraeli identifies three kinds of deception: lies, damned
   lies, and statistics.

Problems with the colon arise when the lead-in sentence is not complete.

Colon error: Canada has many mediocre rock stars, such as:
   Bryan Adams, Shania Twain, and Glass Tiger.

The words "such as" connect the following names to the main sentence, and so a colon is not needed.

OK: Canada has many mediocre rock stars, such as Bryan
   Adams, Shania Twain, and Glass Tiger.
OK: Canada has many mediocre rock stars: Bryan Adams,
   Shania Twain, and Glass Tiger.

Other errors occur when the listed items grammatically link to the independent clause.

Colon error: I can resist *anything*: *except* temptation.

The colon intrudes between the main and subordinate clauses, and so is unnecessary.

OK: I can resist anything, except temptation. (Oscar Wilde)
OK: I can resist any enticement, except one: temptation.

The semicolon is a punctuation mark that functions much like a period, separating two independent clauses that can stand on their own as complete thoughts. The semicolon differs from the period in that it suggests that the two ideas are very closely related, that is, two sides of one coin.

> **OK**: To lose one parent may be regarded as a misfortune; to lose both looks like carelessness. (Oscar Wilde)
>
> **OK**: She got her good looks from her father; he's a plastic surgeon. (Groucho Marx)

Problems with the semicolon occur when the words on either side of it do not form a complete thought.

> **Semicolon error**: Sex is *dirty*; *only* if it is done right.

The second half of this line is a subordinate, not an independent, clause that can't stand on its own. Therefore it can't use a semicolon.

> **OK**: Sex is dirty, only if it is done right. (Woody Allen)

Exercises

Identify and correct the grammatical errors in the following sentences
1. You don't appreciate a lot of stuff in school until you get older. Stuff like being spanked every day by a middle aged woman. Stuff you pay good money for later in life. (Emo Philips)
2. I got some new underwear the other day. Well, new to me. (Emo Philips)
3. Many people wonder why Canadians club those cute little baby seals on the head. Because sending them into space is too expensive.
4. Every woman becomes like her mother, that is her tragedy. No man does, that is his. (Oscar Wilde)
5. It's not that I am afraid to die I just don't want to be there when it happens. (Woody Allen)
6. If you steal from one author, it's plagiarism, if you steal from many, it's research.
7. My classmates would copulate with anything that moved. But I never saw any reason to limit myself. (Emo Philips)
8. Statistics can prove anything 98% of all people know that.
9. Because I have too much to do is why I am going to bed.
10. Sex is like pizza; even when it is bad, it is still pretty good. (Woody Allen)
11. My Brain: it's my second favourite organ. (Woody Allen)
12. When choosing a movie, there are many factors that cross my mind.
13. High sticking is two minutes in the penalty box.

APPENDIX

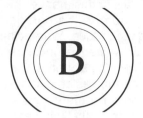

B

Paragraphs

A paragraph is a chunk of writing that develops a single idea. Although a paragraph may be composed of many sentences, all of them work cooperatively towards a single goal: proving the main idea. Each sentence may look at a different aspect or feature of the principal idea, restating or refining it, but they're all unified in the exploration of one topic. Like the many instruments of a symphony, a paragraph brings together a variety of sentences to express and explore a single, melodic theme.

Usually the paragraph declares its own idea in a general, broad statement known as the *topic sentence*. The topic sentence states the working principle around which the paragraph builds itself.

> *Vancouver is the best city in Canada*. First of all, it has unmatched physical beauty. Surrounded by mountains and old-growth forest, edged by the sea and the Gulf islands, Vancouver offers beachcombing, sailing, skiing, and hiking, all within its city limits. Other cities may have a multicultural character, but few in Canada have the range of ethnic diversity that Vancouver offers. The best of China, Japan, Greece, Italy, France, Spain, Thailand, Iran, and India, not to mention the vibrant First Nations communities, help make Vancouver a vivacious mélange of cultures. Home of the largest entertainment industry north of Hollywood, this city boasts fantastic theatres and art galleries, all with a west coast flair. No wonder the UN has placed Vancouver at the top of its list of most livable cities for three straight years.

The italicized topic sentence establishes the general frame of the paragraph (the claim that Vancouver is the top city in Canada), and each sentence develops a specific feature of the claim (natural

412 APPENDIX B • PARAGRAPHS

beauty, multiculturalism, the arts, the UN report). Any paragraph grows by weaving the general and the specific in this manner.

The topic sentence can appear anywhere in the paragraph, depending on what effect the writer wants to produce. When placed at the beginning of a paragraph, the topic sentence declares the paragraph's subject in a clear, unequivocal manner, orienting readers quickly. The drawback to this method is that the style quickly becomes obvious or preachy, and for variety's sake, an author might wish to place the topic sentence in the middle of the paragraph. After first reading through some supportive facts, a reader might be more inclined to accept a topic sentence as true. For a similar reason, a writer might place a topic sentence at the end of a paragraph, as a kind of punch line to the paragraph.

No firm rule dictates the position of a topic sentence. A good writer chooses a position that delivers the desired effect. Indeed, in some cases, a paragraph may have no topic sentence, allowing the facts to speak for themselves.

When writing a paragraph, try to keep in mind three virtues: unity, development, and coherence.

UNITY

A good paragraph looks at one and only one idea. It stays focused on the single proposition it wishes to establish, and never veers off into new territories and fresh subjects, no matter how interesting. A well-written paragraph is unified, with all parts working harmoniously to achieve one purpose.

In contrast, a paragraph that lacks unity makes for a confusing read.

> Unions have done more harm to Canadian society than good, despite the claims of organized labour cheerleaders such as Bob White. Unions began as a way for workers to demand fair wages, and to protect themselves from abuse or exploitation. Tommy Douglas helped set up some of the first Canadian unions in the province of Saskatchewan, as well as inaugurating socialized medicine in this country, another debacle. Today, people have lost the vital sense of self-reliance and pride in their own efforts, and expect someone to look after them from cradle to the grave.

This paragraph begins with a viable idea about the dangerous effects of unionization, but the second line subtly shifts the argument from one of complaint to affirmation. The third line changes focus again, and introduces new ideas about socialized medicine. The final line expresses a sympathetic philosophy, but does not clearly connect the idea to the topic of unions. The whole paragraph comes across as a rambling mess of ideas without purpose.

Here's the same opening idea, but kept on a single track.

> Unions have done more harm to Canadian society than good, despite the claims of organized labour cheerleaders such as Bob White. Unions may have begun as a way of protecting the worker from exploitation and abuse, but labour rights have swollen to such an obscene extent that a company now can't fire union members even if they're incompetent, lazy, or grossly negligent. By providing lifetime security without any connection to productivity, union contracts create a workplace environment that ignores performance and encourages sloth. And perhaps most importantly, union contracts have artificially raised wages so high that they're completely disproportionate to their services. A janitor lucky enough to be in a union receives a yearly salary twice as high as the independent janitor competing in the free market.

Each sentence of this paragraph looks at a specific harm created by unionization, and so every line works to achieve the same goal. The sentences differ slightly in focus, but each offers a facet of the same subject. The unity of the sentences produces a clear, focused discussion.

DEVELOPMENT

A paragraph should do more than merely present an idea; it should provide enough information so that its idea is presented in a complete, thorough, and balanced manner. Just as the public distrusts a reporter who omits vital information, so too does a professor criticize a student's paper if it neglects facts, details, or important considerations. Such omissions reflect an incomplete understanding of the issues, as well as sloppy research. If an idea is debatable, the writer must provide sufficient or compelling proof to persuade the reader that the idea is right. Without adequate proof, the claim made in the topic sentence comes across as weak and unconvincing.

The key word here is sufficient. In the ideal world, a writer can offer exhaustive proof and authoritative explanations. In the real world, however, people—especially students—seldom have the luxury of such time, space, and energy. The trick then is to provide enough proof to persuade your readers, without seeming scant or hasty. Claims that lack evidence come across as unfounded.

> Political correctness is a moral tyranny that flies in the face of common sense and fair play.

> The Apple Company makes a superior computer to any PC on the market.

> The European and American witch-hunts were a direct consequence of men's hatred and fear of women's power.

> Fish farms spread disease and produce unhealthy salmon. They create more social costs than they earn in profits.

None of these examples persuades the audience because their ideas remain unproven. Although each holds potential, they fail to establish the truth of their propositions, and so risk being dismissed as empty promises. Some paragraphs run into development problems by offering partial explanations, undefined terms, and oversimplifications. The third paragraph here, for example, offers one perspective on the witch craze, but neglects other legitimate explanations (such as religious intolerance, personal gain, or hysteria). The fourth paragraph offers tantalizing ideas, but does not flesh out the nature of "disease," "unhealthy salmon," and "social costs" in a way the reader can meaningfully understand. Such vagueness leaves the main idea in an embryonic state, at best.

One way to develop a point is through examples, illustrations, and case studies. Such instances provide real-life evidence that supports and corroborates the claims made in the topic sentence.

> In 1997, the Supreme Court of Canada forced the Boy Scouts organization not only to admit girls to their ranks, but equal numbers of boys and girls. No such requirement was imposed on the Girl Guides. In 2002, school boards banned the teaching of Mark Twain's classic *Huck Finn*, Shakespeare's *Merchant of Venice*, and James Fenimore Cooper's *Last of the Mohicans* because these works contained racist characters, despite their overall anti-racist message. In 2003, a Toronto bus driver was punished for playing Christmas carols over the PA system of his bus. Political correctness is a moral tyranny that flies in the face of common sense and fair play.

By no means the final word on the debate, this paragraph has at least given readers enough substance to make a case against the perils of political correctness.

COHERENCE

The average paragraph presents a large variety of sentences and facts to support its claim. A coherent paragraph is one that connects these sentences to each other so that they flow in a smooth, natural, and ordered stream.

A skilled writer will use many different strategies for designing coherent paragraphs. A simple tool for connecting points is the transition, a linking phrase that hooks up one sentence to another in a logical manner. If you wish to build upon a previous idea, you may use transitions that signal addition, such as *In addition, Moreover, And, Also, Furthermore, Likewise, Similarly,* or *What is more.* If you wish to reject or criticize a previous notion, you can use transitions that signal a contrasting relationship, such as *However, Nonetheless, Yet, Nevertheless,* or *On the other hand.* Transitions provide simple, but effective links in the chain of a paragraph.

Some information can be more effectively arranged in a chronological pattern that follows the points as they unfold naturally in time. Transitions of time (*In the beginning, Then, Next, Finally*) help make the stages clearer to the reader. Perhaps a subject may be better served by arranging points in order of importance. If so, the writer uses transitions of rank, such as *First, Second, Third,* and so on. A journalist describing an anti-war demonstration may organize a paragraph by imitating the movement's of the eye as it scans from the left to the right across the crowd, or from the edges of the street to the centre of the stage. From top to bottom, from surface to underground, from close to far, spatial strategies work well in paragraphs, lending order to information, the way a camera makes a narrative out of disconnected images.

Coherence can also be achieved through repetition of key words from the topic sentence, so that each part of the paragraph clearly echoes the main idea. If a topic sentence addresses the perils of genetically modified foods, the rest of the paragraph may make connections by using words like DNA manipulation, bioengineering, gene-splicing, GMOs, and frankenfoods.

Whatever method employed, paragraphs must have some sort of structure. Without a coherent pattern, readers are confronted with a jumble of disconnected facts that confuse and overwhelm.

Animal testing is a barbaric practice that should be banned in any civilized nation. The average shopper doesn't realize the amount of suffering that goes into a product before it reaches the marketplace. Rabbits are suffocated, poisoned, burnt, and disfigured. Women shouldn't soak their hands in blood just to look pretty. Scientists have lots of alternatives to testing their products on living organisms. A rat's bio-chemistry has important differences to a human's. A monkey may be able to handle a chemical that turns out to be poisonous to a human.

These points all have potential, but they don't connect to each other in a sustained, cumulative way.

Animal testing is a **barbaric** practice that should be banned in any civilized nation. **First of all, such experimentation** produces an enormous amount of **suffering** for the animal subject, a fact hidden from the average shopper. **For example**, the rabbits used to test makeup suffer horrors such as suffocation, poisoning, chemical burns, and lacerations, enduring **enormous pain** for the rather shallow goal of women's beauty. **More importantly**, the results from **animal testing** may not be applicable to a human population, for a simple reason: our biochemistries differ from test **animals**. The most common **lab animal**, the rat, has a capacity to handle poison that people lack, and **consequently** some **rat-based research** declared medicines safe that were actually lethal to humans. **Finally**, reliable alternatives to animal testing exist, making **the cruel practice** not only unreliable, but also unnecessary.

Thanks to a few transitions ("First of all," "More importantly," and "Finally"), some repeated key words ("animal testing," "experimentation," "test," "lab animal," "rat-based research"), this paragraph flows in a more natural, understandable manner.

APPENDIX

Summary

A summary is a genre of writing that presents the ideas of another writer in a more concise form. The summary reduces the original text by leaving out unnecessary details, while emphasizing the author's main points. Although a summary records the ideas of another writer, it must be expressed in the student's own words.

Students and scholars use summaries throughout their academic careers to

- Make complex texts manageable and clear
- Provide an alternative form of citation to direct quotation
- Demonstrate an understanding of a source text
- Emphasize certain aspects of a source text.

HOW TO BEGIN A SUMMARY

Before you can effectively summarize a text, make sure you understand it.

1. Read through the entire article without making a single mark on the text.
2. After reading the article, write one sentence that expresses the general idea of the text. This is its thesis.
3. Reread the article, and underline the key points that develop the thesis.

This strategy helps you identify the central ideas of a text.

WHERE TO LOCATE KEY IDEAS

Writers usually place main ideas in very traditional, obvious spots.

1. Check the essay's title. It often identifies the focus of the essay.

2. Look for a thesis or statement of purpose in the first paragraph, or near the beginning of an article.
3. Look for the topic sentence of each paragraph, the organizing principle upon which a paragraph constructs itself.

HOW TO RECOGNIZE KEY IDEAS

One of the functions of a summary is to condense a text. Thus, the basic skill of summarizing relies on the knowledge of what to keep, and what to remove.

1. Identify and keep statements that express large ideas, refer to big groups, or have significant consequences for society.

   After much research, scientists have finally determined that women are unequivocally smarter than men.

   We know this sentence probably identifies a main idea because it makes an absolute claim about large classes of people.
2. Omit examples, illustrations, anecdotes, detailed descriptions, and specific details.

   At Argyle Secondary, instructor Susan Dunbar notices that female students tend to score 10 percent higher than male students.

This sentence expresses a single fact that confirms and corroborates the main idea and so should be cut from a summary.

3. Remove word games, rhetorical flourishes, metaphors, and analogies. Writers frequently develop their ideas by using poetic and narrative devices that add zest and interest. Cut these.

   No: Rampton and Stauber say that the PR industry is to truth as prostitution is to sex.
   Yes: Rampton and Stauber argue that the PR industry can't be entirely trusted to tell the truth because it accepts money.
4. Remove repetitious material.

THE STYLE OF A SUMMARY

A summary tends to follow the conventions of academic writing (see Chapter 6). However, the summary has further stylistic requirements that demand the student treat the source material in a neutral, fair, and complete manner. When you write a summary, make sure that it satisfies the following style guidelines.

1. Restate the writer's ideas in your own words.

   A summary not only records an author's ideas, but also demonstrates that the student has understood the original essay. In order to display this understanding, students must accurately restate the main idea, but *in language that is almost entirely different from the source text.* Sometimes it may be impossible to avoid repeating a few key words or highly specific terms, but otherwise a summary should say the same idea in wholly fresh language.

The ability to restate an idea in different language is a sign that students have understood the material.

If the summary borrows too closely from the source text, the student may be penalized for plagiarism. Some universities have very strict rules that limit the number of words that can be copied from the original text, setting the bar as low as two or three similar terms.

2. Signal your summary to the readers.

When you begin to paraphrase a source text, make sure that you declare this shift to your readers. You can do this very easily by identifying the paraphrased author and the text at the very beginning of your summary.

In *Culture Jam*, Kalle Lasn declares that our desire for economic growth is a form of cancer.

With an obvious declaration of author and text, readers know that you have shifted from your own commentary to someone else's ideas.

3. Remain neutral. Don't comment upon the author's ideas.

In a summary, a student should be a neutral and passive conduit of the other person's ideas. An essay may later shift to a critique of a text, as long as the student indicates this shift in attitude. However, every author deserves a fair and impartial representation of his or her ideas, before they're criticized. This is one function of summary: to represent ideas accurately and without bias.

4. Avoid jargon in favour of clear, simple language.

One of the functions of a summary is to make essays clearer and simpler. Don't try to impress people with fancy language.

No: Religious doctrine and dogma is paramount to a kind of psychological necrophilia; it focuses the worshipper's psychic energies not on empirical reality, but on the phantasm of an afterlife.
Yes: Religion may place an unhealthy emphasis on the afterlife, which may not exist.

5. Don't quote, if you can help it.

One function of summary is to indicate to professors that you have understood the text. If you rely on quotations from the original essay, you come across as a parrot who mindlessly repeats words and phrases, rather than as an independent thinker who can restate general ideas in new language.

6. Try to keep the original order of ideas, if possible.

Most essays have an internal logic to the presentation of their ideas that should be mirrored in a summary.

7. Provide in-text citation and a "Works Cited" page.

Because a summary is a form of research, source information must be cited and documented. This should include two different pieces of information.

- The author's last name and the page number of the book where the information originates, in parentheses, after the summarized material
- A separate MLA-style "Works Cited" page attached to the end of any summary or essay that summarizes another author's work

A SUMMARY CHECKLIST

After you are finished writing your summary, ask yourself the following questions:

- Size: Does my summary meet the required word limit?
- Accuracy: Have I represented the author's ideas fairly?
- Complete: Have I covered all of the writer's ideas?
- Is my summary free of critique?
- Have I cut out all unnecessary examples and illustrations?
- Is my language sufficiently different from the author's words?
- Have I provided MLA or APA documentation?

APPENDIX

Documentation

All college or university writing needs documentation of its sources. This documentation appears in two different places in a student essay: short parenthetical references within the body of the essay itself, and a longer bibliographic description of all sources on a separate page at the end of the essay.

The two most common styles of documentation are those of the Modern Language Association (MLA), used primarily in the humanities, and the American Psychological Association (APA), used mostly in social sciences.

MLA

IN-TEXT CITATION

The purpose of the in-text citation is to provide enough information for the reader to find the full entry on the "Works Cited" page at the end of the essay. This normally requires two bits of information: the author's name and the page number of the quote. The usual method places these bits of information in parentheses after a quote or paraphrased material.

> At the beach, Leopold Bloom wonders about "that fellow at the graveside in the brown macintosh" (Joyce 19).

From this bit of information, the reader looks up the entry under James Joyce on the "Works Cited" page, and finds the quote on page 19 of Joyce's text.

The author's name does not have to be listed in the parentheses if it has already been mentioned in the lead-in sentence or is clear from the context.

> Joyce describes the sound of the ocean as "a fourworded wavespeech: seesoo, hrss, rsseeiss, ooos" (41).

Sometimes students quote from many works by the same author. In these instances, the in-text citation must distinguish between the various novels, stories, or articles that appear on the "Works Cited" page. The in-text citation thus expands to include the author's name, a short title of the work, and the page reference.

> The final story of the collection opens with an image of the caretaker's daughter, who "was literally run off her feet" (Joyce, *Dubliners* 175).

When a quote needs to be edited or shortened, writers use an ellipse (three periods separated by spaces) to indicate the removed material.

> Stephen laments, "I fear those big words . . . which make us so unhappy" (Joyce, *Ulysses* 26).

Small editorial changes, such as alterations to capital letters, pronouns, or tense, can be made to the text, as long as they don't seriously alter the quote's meaning. Show these changes by placing them in square brackets.

> According to J. Paul Getty, "[His] formula for success is rise early, work late, and strike oil" (235).

The original quote in this case begins with a first-person "my," changed to "His" to fit the third-person style of the paper.

THE "WORKS CITED" PAGE

The "Works Cited" page is a list of all the quoted or consulted texts, arranged in alphabetical order by last name of the author. The purpose of the "Works Cited" page is to provide detailed bibliographic description of source material, so readers can track down and verify the original materials.

Include on the "Works Cited" list only texts that you have quoted or paraphrased. Do not include texts you have only read or found interesting. Professors will tend to question the role of these materials in your essay.

The MLA has developed a formal method for listing the information that must be followed on any entry. Many different kinds of materials may go into an essay, but students tend to rely on books and anthologies, periodicals, and electronic sources.

1. BOOKS AND ANTHOLOGIES

Although not all of this information may be available or relevant, the "Works Cited" entry for a book usually appears in this order.

1. Author's name
2. Title of short work
3. Title of book or anthology
4. Name of editor or translator
5. Edition number
6. Volume number
7. Name of series
8. Place of publication
9. Publisher
10. Date of publication
11. Page number(s)

The listing for the author's name begins with the surname, followed by a comma, and then the first name. The basic entry for a book looks like this.

Marcuse, Herbert. *One Dimensional Man*. Boston: Beacon Press, 1968.

The second and subsequent lines of a "Works Cited" entry are indented. If a book has more than one author, the "Works Cited" entry inverts the name of the first, but not the subsequent authors.

Stauber, John, and Sheldon Rampton. *Toxic Sludge Is Good for You!* Monroe
    (ME): Common Courage Press, 1995.

If you cite more than one work by the same author(s), describe the first source in full, then abbreviate the second and subsequent entries by replacing the name of author(s) with three dashes.

Stauber, John, and Sheldon Rampton. *Toxic Sludge Is Good for You!* Monroe
    (ME): Common Courage Press, 1995.
———. *Trust Us, We're Experts*. New York: Penguin, 2002.

The three dashes indicate that the same authors wrote both works.

Students often find themselves quoting from anthologies, collections of works by many writers. These require more information on the "Works Cited" entry, including the short title of the work, and the individual page numbers of the piece.

Pell, Derek. "The Elements of Style." *Avant-Pop: Fiction for a Daydream Nation*.
    Ed. Larry McCaffery. Boulder: Black Ice Books, 1993. 49–82.

Note that the titles of large items such as books and anthologies appear in italics, while the titles of short items such as poems and articles appear in quotation marks.

2. PERIODICALS

Journals and magazines are printed regularly, and so have slightly different citation requirements than books and anthologies. Usually an entry requires the following basic information.

1. Name of author(s)
2. Title of short work
3. Title of periodical
4. Volume number
5. Issue number
6. Date of publication
7. Page number(s)

Here's what a typical journal entry looks like. Note that no period appears after the journal title.

Jackson, William B. "Rats—Friends or Foes?" *Journal of Popular Culture* 14.1
    (Summer 1980): 27–32.

The entry for a newspaper follows the same pattern, but has no volume or issue number, and includes the section with its page number.

Suzuki, David. "The Case for Kyoto." *Globe and Mail* 22 Sept. 2001: A5.

3. THE WEB AND ELECTRONIC SOURCES

The Web contains a glut of information, in various forms and shapes, including books, journals, blogs, and homepages. Documentation of Web materials follows the same basic pattern as a print source, but adds information specific to the Web, such as the electronic address and date accessed. Web pages don't always list all the information needed, but generally a scholar should provide the following information, in the following order.

A. Author's Name

As with any MLA citation, begin with the author's name, if available. If anonymous, list the entry according to title.

B. Title of Work

Use the title as provided by the material. If a title is missing, you may provide a short description of the material.

C. Print Information

A lot of Web postings arise as electronic versions of materials published previously in print (called "print analogues" in MLA lingo). For example, newspapers often post columns on the Web, after they have had their run in newsprint. As a rule, you should provide all available information regarding the print version at the start of any Internet citation, followed by the relevant electronic information.

D. Electronic Publication Information

Web and electronic materials have unique features that should be listed after the print information has been recorded. This may include such facts as the title of the Web site, the database name, the date of a posting, the name of a spon-soring body, or the kind of medium (such as a CD-ROM).

E. Access Information

Because the Web is in a state of constant flux and change, it's important to list two key bits of information about any source you cite from this medium.

• The date you accessed it
• The Web address enclosed in angle brackets

A typical Internet citation looks like this:

Filmer, John. "Martin Versus Harper: The Fake Debate." *Znet* 25 May 2004.
    <http://www.canadaforum.com/content/showarticle/martinharper.html>.

APA

Like the MLA, the APA system of documentation requires a short in-text citation that cross-references with a full list of all sources at the essay's end, entitled "References." Although the systems are very similar, they have a few key differences.

IN-TEXT CITATION

APA documentation requires the author's last name and year of publication placed in parentheses after any quoted or paraphrased material in the body of the essay itself. Page numbers are not always required in APA, but may be added for clarity.

> The Potlatch ceremony of the West Coast Native Indians may actually be a ritualistic way of redistributing wealth (Harris, 1974).

> Marvin Harris (1974, p. 112) suggests that competitive feasting helps Native populations expand and prosper.

Note that a comma appears between the author's name and the year, and that all page numbers have a "p." before them.

If the work has two authors, the last names of the authors are joined with an ampersand "&."

> (Francis & Smith, 1994)

For works with three to five authors, list all the authors for the first entry, followed by the year. For the subsequent entries, list the first author followed by "et al." (Latin for "and others").

(Van de ven, McKendry, & Hansen, 1998)   [First reference]
(Van de ven et al., 1998)   [Subsequent references]

For works with six or more authors, list the first author, followed by "et al." and the year.

(Crandall et al., 1996)

THE "REFERENCES" PAGE

The "References" page is a list of all quoted, paraphrased, or consulted texts, arranged in alphabetical order by last name of the author. The APA system of reference follows many of the same rules as the MLA system, but has some vital distinctions. For example, APA documentation places the year of publication in parentheses directly after the author's name. A book by one author looks like this.

Shlaim, A. (1995). *War and peace in the Middle East.* New York: Penguin Books.

Note that the author's surname is listed in full, but only initials are given for the first name. Also, only the first word of the title and subtitle, as well as proper nouns, are capitalized.

The listing for a book with two or more authors records all the authors' names, in inverted order.

Morrow, F.G., & Wade, J.M. (2003). *The perception of gender.* Toronto: Harcourt Brace & Company, Canada.

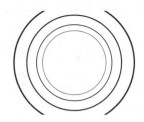

Copyright Acknowledgements

Bureaucrat's Indian," from *The Imaginary Indian*. Arsenal Pulp Press, 1992. Reprinted with permission. **Pages 108–12:** Drew Hayden Taylor, "Pretty Like a White Boy." Reprinted with permission of the author. **Pages 112–16:** M. NourbeSe Philip, "Why Multiculturalism Can't End Racism," from *Frontiers*. Mercury Press, Stratford, Ontario, 1992. Reprinted with permission of the author. **Page 117:** "How Do I Know If I Have Shopping-Related ICD?" from *Adbusters* July/August 2001. Reprinted with permission.

Chapter 3, Metaphors, page 131: Margaret Atwood, "you fit into me" from *Power Politics*. © 1971, 1996 by Margaret Atwood. Reprinted by permission of House of Anansi Press. **Pages 131–32:** Lynne Crosbie, "all my seasick sailors" from *Queen Rat* © 1998 by Lynne Crosbie. Reprinted by permission of House of Anansi Press. **Pages 132–33:** Earle Birney, "Canada: Case History." Reprinted with permission of the Estate of Earle Birney. **Page 133:** Marilyn Dumont, "Leather and Naughahyde" from *A Really Good Brown Girl*. Brick Books, 1996. Reprinted with permission. **Pages 133–34:** George Elliot Clarke, "Primitivism," from *Saltwater Spirituals and Deeper Blues*. Pottersfield Press, 1983. Reprinted with permission of the author. **Pages 134–35:** Pei Hsien Lim, "untitled three" from *Swallowing Clouds*, ed. Andy Quan and Jim Wong-Chu. Vancouver: Arsenal Pulp Press, 1999. Reprinted with permission. **Pages 135–39:** George Lakoff, "Metaphors That Kill," from www.guerrillanews.com, 2003. Reprinted with permission from the author. **Pages 139–44:** Linda McQuaig, "Tax Haven in the Snow," from *Behind Closed Doors* by Linda McQuaig. © Linda McQuaig, 1987. Reprinted by permission of Penguin Group (Canada), a Division of Pearson Penguin Canada Inc. **Pages 144–50:** Naomi Klein, "Don't Fence Us In." Originally published in *The Guardian*, October 6, 2002. Reprinted with permission of the author.

Chapter 4, Simple Words, pages 162–67: Robert Anton Wilson "On Sodomizing Camels" and "What Is Against Nature" from *Natural Law*. Loompanics Unlimited, 1986. Reprinted with permission. **Pages 167–74:** Thomas Szasz, "Disease." Reprinted by permission of Open Court Publishing Company, a division of Carus Publishing Company, Peru, IL, from *The Untamed Tongue: A Dissenting Dictionary* by Thomas Szasz, © 1990 by Thomas Szasz. **Pages 174–78:** John Ralston Saul, from *The Doubter's Companion*. © John Ralston Saul, 1994. Reprinted by permission of Penguin Group (Canada), a Division of Pearson Penguin Canada, Inc. **Pages 178–86:** L. Susan Brown, "Does Work Really Work?" from *Kick It Over* 35, Summer 1995. Reprinted with permission of the author.

Chapter 5, Questions, pages 199–207: Harold Bloom, "Preface and Prelude" from *The Western Canon: The Books and School of the Ages,* © 1994 by Harold Bloom, reprinted by permission of Harcourt, Inc. **Pages 207–12:** Ellen Fein and Sherrie Schneider, "Don't Talk to a Man First (and Don't Ask Him to Dance)" and "Don't Discuss *The Rules* with Your Therapist," from *The Rules* by Ellen Fein and Sherrie Schneider. © 1995 by Ellen Fein and Sherrie Schneider. By permission of Warner Books Inc. **Pages 212–15:** REAL Women of Canada, "Marriage Between a Man and A Woman," www. realwomen.ca/com/pamphlets/01_marriage.htm. Reprinted with permission. **Pages 215–19:** NARTH, "Our Purpose" from www.narth.com/menus/statement.html. Reprinted with permission. **Pages 219–21:** Ward Churchill, "Declaration of War Against Exploiters of Lakota Spirituality," from *Indians Are Us?* by Ward Churchill. Toronto, Between the Lines, 1994. Reprinted with permission.

Chapter 6, Genres, pages 235–43: Alison Hearn, "Image Slaves" from *Bad Subjects: Political Education for Everyday Life,* Issue #69, June 2004. Reprinted with permission. **Pages 246–47:** Spencer Holst, "The Zebra Storyteller," from *The Zebra Storyteller* by Spencer Holst. Station Hill Press, New York. Reprinted with permission. **Page 248:** Jon Scieszka, "The Really Ugly Duckling," from *The Stinky Cheese Man and Other Fairly Stupid Tales* by Jon Scieszka, illustrated by Lane Smith, © 1992 by Jon Scieszka, text. Used by permission of Viking Penguin, a Division of Penguin Young Readers Group, a Member of Penguin Group (USA) Inc., 345 Hudson Street, New York, NY 10014. All rights reserved. **Pages 248–51:** Ellie Tesher, advice columns. Reprinted with permission—Torstar Syndication Services. **Pages 251–54:** Dan Savage, excerpts from "Savage Love." Reprinted with permission. **Pages 261–63:** Taras Grescoe, "White Peril" from *The Georgia Straight,* June 1995. Reprinted with permission from the author.

Chapter 7, Media, pages 279–99: David Model, "Deception" from *Corporate Rule.* Black Rose Books, 2003. Reprinted with permission of the author. **Pages 299–311:** James Winter, "Preface to *MediaThink.*" Black Rose Books, 2002. Reprinted with permission. **Pages 311–15:** Mark Kingwell, "Ten Steps to the Creation of a Modern Media Icon," from *Marginalia: A Cultural Reader* by Mark Kingwell. © Mark Kingwell, 1999. Reprinted by permission of Penguin Group (Canada), a Division of Pearson Penguin Canada Inc. **Pages 315–21:** Elayne Rapping, "Watching the Eyewitless News," from *The Progressive* Vol. 59, No. 3, 1995 pp. 38–40.

I N D E X